Psychology of Emotion

Interpersonal, Experiential, and Cognitive Approaches

Paula M. NIEDENTHAL
Silvia KRAUTH-GRUBER,
and François RIC

Psychology Press
Taylor & Francis Group

NEW YORK AND HOVE

Published in 2006
by Psychology Press
711 Third Avenue, 8th Floor
New York, NY 10017
www.psypress.com

Published in Great Britain
by Psychology Press
27 Church Road, Hove, East Sussex BN3 2FA
www.psypress.com

Psychology Press is an imprint of the Taylor & Francis Group, an informa business

Typeset by Macmillan India, Bangalore, India
Printed and bound in the USA by Edwards Brothers, Inc. on acid-free paper
Paperback cover by Anú Design
Paperback cover artist: Corrine Niedenthal
Paperback cover illustrations: "Jazz Singer" (1961); "First Born" (1961); "Red Nude" (1962)

10 9 8 7 6

Library of Congress Cataloging in Publication Data
    Niedenthal, Paula M.
    Psychology of emotion : interpersonal, experiential & cognitive approaches / Paula M. Niedenthal,
    Silvia Krauth-Gruber, and François Ric.
            p. cm. – (Principles of social psychology)
    Includes bibliographical references and index.
    ISBN-13: 978-1-84169-401-6 (hardback : alk. paper)
    ISBN-10: 1-84169-401-0 (hardback : alk. paper)
    ISBN-13: 978-1-84169-402-3 (pbk. : alk. paper)
    ISBN-10: 1-84169-402-9 (pbk. : alk. paper)   1. Emotions. I. Krauth-Gruber, Silvia.
    II. Ric, François. III. Title. IV. Series.

    BF531.N54 2006
    152.4–dc22   2006005419

ISBN13: 978-1-84169-401-6 (hbk)
ISBN13: 978-1-84169-402-3 (pbk)

ISBN10: 1-84169-401-0 (hbk)
ISBN10: 1-84169-402-9 (pbk)

Contents

About the Authors

Paula M. NIEDENTHAL received her Ph.D. from the University of Michigan and was on the faculty of the departments of Psychology at Johns Hopkins University and Indiana University (USA). She is currently Director of Research in the National Centre for Scientific Research and member of the Laboratory in Social and Cognitive Psychology at Blaise Pascal University in Clermont-Ferrand, France. Her areas of research include emotion–cognition interaction and representational models of emotion. Author of more than 70 articles and chapters, and several books, Dr. Niedenthal is a fellow of the Society for Personality and Social Psychology.

Silvia KRAUTH-GRUBER is Assistant Professor at the University Paris Descartes where she teaches social psychology. Her research interests include the expression and regulation of emotions and the embodiment of emotional knowledge.

François RIC received his Ph.D. at the University Paris 10 – Nanterre and he is currently Assistant Professor at the University Paris Descartes, France. His current main areas of research interest are related to the interaction between emotion and cognition, and especially to the role of affect in information processiong and in social judgment.

Preface

Psychology of Emotion: Interpersonal, experiential, and cognitive approaches is intended to introduce students to the scientific study of emotion. General theories of emotion are discussed and compared, but the primary goal of the book is to summarize and draw conclusions from the now enormous body of experimental research. To this end, we also consider in some detail the ways in which researchers measure and manipulate emotions in the laboratory and even in the field.

As we are social psychologists by training, much of the reviewed research emanates from the field of social psychology. However, because emotion processes are evidenced at all levels of psychological analysis as the name of the book implies, we also draw on the psychology of personality, developmental psychology, and cognitive psychology. The chapters therefore address the structure of emotional experience, the function of emotions, the distinction between so-called primary and secondary emotions, the perception and recognition of facial expression of emotion, emotion regulation, the relations between emotion and cognition, the experience of emotions in a group, and the important roles of gender and culture in emotional expression and experience.

Two recent books, the *Handbook of Affective Sciences* (Davidson, Scherer, & Goldsmith, 2003) and the *Cognitive Neuroscience of Emotion* (Lane & Nadel, 2000) are very good resources for instructors interested in the biology of emotion, which is not addressed in the book. Students can find an excellent review of the biology of emotion in the annex of *The Science of Emotion: Research and tradition in the psychology of emotion* (Cornelius, 1996).

One of the exciting facts of the psychology of emotion is that researchers active in this field are not over-represented in one or two countries of the world. The psychology of emotion is actively researched in all countries of Europe, the United States, and Asia, in particular. We try to illustrate this international nature of emotion research in two ways. First, we cite and describe work from researchers from many different countries.

Second, we try to use everyday examples to convey the international flavor of the research. The examples also serve to depict similarities and differences in emotional life worldwide.

In addition to using many examples, we try to bring students and instructors closer to the actual research by reprinting the stimuli and findings of representative studies, as well as illustrative photographs and cartoons. We find that this empowers the reader and allows him or her to evaluate, in a more informed way, the conclusions that can be drawn from the work.

The chapters of this book vary in complexity and difficulty in reasonably close approximation to the complexity and difficulty of the current literature in the area. Thus, the concepts in some chapters may seem more difficult to grasp, and less intuitive, than those in others. Because this variability reflects reality, we are comfortable with it, and hope the reader is too. Emotions are interesting and we all speculate about them and even are convinced of our own theories. In the end, good data, however, allow us to evaluate both the folk theories and the academic theories.

Acknowledgments

The authors could not have written and produced this textbook without the help of a large number of people. For reading and providing lengthy and invaluable feedback on entire chapters (and sometimes revisions of those chapters), we thank Theodore Alexopoulos, Lisa Feldman Barrett, Markus Brauer, Julie Collange, Genevieve Coudin, Daniel Effron, Phoebe Ellsworth, Cynthia Haddad, Ursula Hess, Bob Kleck, Batja Mesquita, Jerry Parrott, Peter Salovey, and Bo Santioso. For reading parts of chapters for accuracy, and answering innumerable follow-up questions, we thank Andy Calder, Jon Haidt, David Matsumoto, Kelly Mix, Randy Nelson, and June Tangney. Kelly Mix, Peter Salovey, and June Tangney also bought and sent us books that we had trouble finding in our local libraries.

For graciously sharing their figures and photos, we thank Mary Lokken, Curtis Padgett, Jim Russell, Klaus Scherer, and Jessica Tracy. And for providing information on biblical references to some of the self-conscious emotions, we thank Morris Niedenthal (Homiletics) and Ralph Klein (Old Testament) of the Lutheran School of Theology at Chicago, as well as Corrine Niedenthal for organizing, editing, and sending it.

The book would never have been produced without the competent help of Armelle Nugier, who made many of the figures and worked tirelessly on the long bibliographies. Paul Dukes and Julia Moore at Psychology Press were enthusiastic and Helen Baxter was our excellent editor.

Finally, the authors thank, respectively, Markus, Alexandre, Théo, Sebastian, and Benjamin; Werner, Alban, and Felix for their unfailing support, assistance, patience, and love throughout the writing process.

What are Emotions and How are They Studied?

Imagine what your life would be like if you could not experience emotion. What if you felt no joy at seeing a newborn baby, and you felt no pride on receiving a long worked-for diploma? What if you felt no anger and no fear when you heard that a country was going to war with another? What if you felt no jealousy at seeing a boyfriend or girlfriend flirt with someone else at a party and you felt no awe when standing in the nave of an 11th century cathedral? What would your life be like then? Would we even call it human life? And could human life indeed exist if we felt no emotion?

Perhaps life would seem human without emotion if you believed that emotions were undesirable states, reflecting animalistic vestiges of our evolutionary past. This idea emphasizes the "human" qualification of the expression "human life." A dominant theme in philosophy for many hundreds of years was that emotions, or passions as they were sometimes called, actively opposed – or interfered with – the more desirable and lofty processes of Reason (Solomon, 1976, 1993). The specific idea, which was espoused by philosophers from Plato to Descartes, and was a central idea in the thinking of the Stoics such as Zeno de Citium, Epictetus, and Marcus Aurelius, was that reasoning and having emotions were antithetical to each other and that, in fact, the passions disrupted reason entirely. If only we could control our animalistic emotions we would reach higher levels of being and thinking, that is, of being human! Since reason was seen as a human virtue, emotions were thus basically undesirable, at least to men and scholars. Sometimes, in addition to being relegated to the experience of animals, emotions were also relegated to the (somewhat lower existence of) women and children. Even in today's world, people in some cultures view displays of emotion, particularly in public places or generally in front of strangers, as undesirable and as casting doubt on the psychological health of the person expressing his emotions. In other cultures, public expression of emotion is so commonplace as to not draw any attention at all. Certainly the authors of this book, all living in France, are indeed accustomed to seeing emotion expressed, and expressing their own emotions, when driving on the streets or walking in Paris and other French cities.

You could also dispense with emotions as fundamental for human life if you believed that emotions were simply epiphenomenal, meaning that you thought that they had no particular purpose or function. A dominant theme in experimental psychology for almost 75 years, up to the 1970s, was that behavior could be understood as motivated and shaped by simple principles of reward and punishment. If we really pushed these principles of learning to their strongest conclusion, the thinking fashionable at that time went, then there was no reason to believe that emotions (other than diffuse positive and negative reactions to the punishments and rewards) were functional, vital, or necessary. One consequence of behaviorism, advanced by B. F. Skinner, was that it became popular, in the laboratory and in the home, to believe that "mother's love" was not special or useful. Mother's love was, in fact, something to *overcome* because frequent and overt expressions of love, such as kissing infants, was sure to lead to trouble in the child's development. In fact, many learning theorists intepreted everything from breastfeeding to infants' smiling behavior in terms of simple positive reactions to rewards and negative reactions to punishments. So, for almost 75 years a mother's expressed love for her children was intellectually and ultimately practically "out of style" among most scientists in parts of Europe and in the United States. In summarizing this perspective, B. F. Skinner once wrote that: "We all know that emotions are useless and bad for our peace of mind and our blood pressure" (Skinner, 1948, p. 92).

In part due to changes in the very definition of emotion, since the 1960s, experimental psychologists have thought differently about emotions. First of all, they have actually thought rigorously about emotion per se, which distinguishes them not from the philosophers, but from the previous generation of experimental psychologists (with only a very few notable exceptions such as Bull (1945) and Duffy (1941)). Importantly, psychologists who study emotion have recognized that emotions are fundamental to human social behavior. As we will discuss throughout this book, emotions hold people together in social groups, help to determine priorities within relationships, signal to the person experiencing the emotion the state of her relation to the environment, and also signal to other people the motivational and emotional state of the person experiencing the emotion. Emotions can motivate adaptive action in the individual experiencing the emotion. And, the communication of emotion can elicit adaptive behavior on the part of a perceiver. Furthermore, psychologists have noted that emotions and their expressive components (that is, their expression in posture, facial gestures, and verbal and nonverbal aspects of language) are elicited largely by social stimuli – particularly other people or features of other people – in social situations; emotions are controlled and shaped by these social situations; and they, in turn, serve to shape social situations.

In the present book, we evaluate what we know about emotion by insisting on the nature of the scientific research that supports those ideas (Davidson et al., 2003). Our hope is that readers will think critically about these examples of scientific research and decide for themselves if they agree with us that the research provides a good test of the ideas.

Furthermore, since we reference the work, we hope that readers will be inspired to go back to the original research in order to develop a deeper understanding of what the research involved and what it actually demonstrated. When we know that an idea was never really tested with scientific research, we will certainly say that. In addition, when we know that research that had an important impact on thinking about emotion in psychology was not very good research, or actually produced poor and misunderstood results, we will mention that as well.

The Scope of the Phenomenon

One of the most vexing problems for students of emotion (and so-called experts as well) is that researchers who study "emotion" often are actually studying different things. And sometimes, perhaps even more frustrating, they say they are studying different things – at least they use different words – when they are actually studying the same things! What exactly constitutes the category "emotion"? You might offer up several examples of different emotional states in order to define the category. But saying that emotions are, for example, states of joy, fear, and sadness, is just passing the problem to the next level of analysis. Then we have to ask what are joy, fear, and sadness, and what is it about them that makes them all an emotion? You might say that they are all states in which you feel highly . . . well, emotional. But, of course, that is circular reasoning.

When you try to define the category, you can see that it is very difficult to agree on all the states or experiences that we would call emotions in the first place. Do stress, optimism, depression, joy, phobic reactions, surprise, and psychological wellbeing all belong in the category of things that are emotions? It is hard to say. As we shall see, emotions theorists have published lists of terms that try to exhaustively enumerate the emotions. But the problem is that those lists are not the same length and even when they are, they often contain different states. One of the ways we can curb the frustration of our readers for the time being is to limit the scope of the book. We focus here on the understanding and implications of transient subjective states and reactions that are "normal" or "everyday" in the sense that they have not taken on incapacitating, long-term proportions. We will discuss emotions that most people have experienced, such as guilt, pride, disgust, anger, and joy. And the point is to see how emotions are elicited, how they unfold, by which behaviors they are expressed and controlled, and to see how they *affect* other behaviors of interest to psychologists, such as stereotyping, group interaction, self-regulation, persuasion, social perception, as well as how they are *influenced* by phenomena of interest to psychologists, such as personal and group identities, social norms, and culture.

In contrast, we will not discuss the nature of stress and stress responses. Stress is not the topic of this book largely because it is a very broad term that refers to an individual's reaction to his own assessment of his mental and physical adjustment in the face of environmental and psychological challenges. Furthermore, even though people may say "I feel stressed," this does not mean that stress is best defined as an emotion or even as a feeling. In addition, we will not discuss temperament (but see Goldsmith, 1993, for a review of the topic). That is, we will not be talking about how people vary in their typical emotional tone, or their tendency to be happy or grumpy or anxious much of the time. This is because temperament seems to be a largely genetically encoded, cross-situational

affective tendency, and may be best to study as one component of personality by researchers who study personality development.

Neither will we discuss emotional disorders or pathologies, such as
depression or clinical anxiety, because these are defined not only in terms
of emotional states, but also many other cognitive and behavioral manifestations that are not possible to explore in this book (but see Oltmanns &
Emery, 1995, for a thorough treatment). And finally, except where
specifically noted, we will not talk in detail about moods, which are relatively objectless (that is, they do not have a clear event or object that
elicited them) and long term when compared to specific emotions (see
Parkinson, Totterdell, Briner, & Reynolds, 1996, for a comprehensive discussion). When we talk about mood, we do so because the term was used
by the researcher, or because the particular phenomenon we are talking
about seems to function similarly for moods and for emotions.

Definitions of Emotion

Even with all this limiting of the phenomenon down to non-pathological,
transient states, definitions of emotion are still vague and highly variable.
Emotions have been defined and studied as internal phenomena that can,
but do not always, make themselves observable through expression and
behavior. So, to make the study of emotion tractable, researchers often iso-
late parts of what could be called an emotional state or reaction and use it
as *the* indicator of emotion. Then they use a single measure of that indicator of emotion. For example, some researchers define emotions as feeling
states and measure those states with self-report questionnaires. These
researchers tend to ask: "how much sadness, joy, fear, anger, and so forth,
are you feeling (on a scale from 1 to 7) right now?" (e.g., Brandstätter, 1981,
1983; Scherer, 1984a). Using self-reports of emotion makes the assumption
that emotions are at least potentially conscious and that individuals can
reflect on those conscious states and quantify them (see Barrett, 2004, for a
discussion of this point).

Other researchers define emotions in terms of physiological reactions
and feedback from the peripheral nervous system (e.g., James, 1890; Lange,
1885/1922), and then measure those types of reaction by assessing heart rate
or electrodermal responses (e.g., Ax, 1953; Ekman, Levenson, & Friesen,
1983). Still other researchers define emotions in terms of facial expression
and its feedback and have developed methods to measure such expressions
(e.g., Ekman, Friesen, & Ancoli, 1980; Izard & Malatesta, 1987; Zajonc, 1985).
Note that neither the physiological nor the expression indicators require

that emotions be conscious. And finally, a large number of researchers define emotions in terms of a collection of cognitive evaluation and labeling processes, and measure those processes through self-report of evaluation, attribution, and judgment (e.g., Frijda, 1986; Roseman, 1991; Scherer, 1988; Smith & Ellsworth, 1985).

Another complexity in the definition of emotion is that researchers differ in what they believe causes an emotion to occur in the first place. As we shall see later in this chapter, some researchers, who take an evolutionary approach to emotion, believe that human beings are biologically prepared to respond to specific objects and events with specific emotional responses (e.g., Darwin, 1872/1998; Izard, 1977; Öhman, 1986). Other researchers believe that emotions are elicited by processes of evaluation that link events in the environment to the ongoing goals and needs of the appraising individual (e.g., Frijda, 1986; Scherer, 1988). And still other researchers see emotions as produced by a combination of these (e.g., Campos & Barrett, 1984; Campos & Stenberg, 1981; Johnson-Laird & Oatley, 1992). Note that if you make these different assumptions, then you tend to induce emotions very differently in the laboratory and those different ways of eliciting emotions are likely to make certain emotional behaviors more or less observable and more or less central to the state.

These diverse views all have some validity to them. And their complexity can be seen as more manageable if we view emotions not as single "things" that are elicited and sometimes expressed, but rather, along with Keltner and Gross (1999), as "episodic, relatively short-term, biologically-based patterns of perception, experience, physiology, action, and communication that occur in response to specific physical and social challenges and opportunities" (Keltner & Gross, 1999, p. 468). This definition is broad, but it does force us to approach emotion as something that has many psychological and behavioral manifestations. In addition, it acknowledges that emotions are at least potentially functional. Thus, using this definition, scientists can proceed to ask questions about what the component processes of emotions are, and what the functions of emotions are. And much of this chapter and the next will deal with those questions.

Emotions as Component Processes

If we acknowledge that emotions are composed of a number of distinct processes, then we have to ask what those component processes are. An inclusive list would contain at least the following: subjective feelings, expressive motor behavior, cognitive appraisals and styles, physiological arousal, and the readiness to take particular action as to the component process (e.g., Frijda, 1986; Leventhal & Scherer, 1987; Scherer, 1984a). For example, during a state of anger, one might feel tense and hot; produce a frown, furrowed eyebrows and narrowed eyes; interpret the current situation as unfair, negative, and controllable; experience high arousal; and clench the fists in a readiness to strike. Table 1.1 presents a summary of how happiness, anger, sadness, and fear might be conceptualized from a component process approach (Scherer, 2000).

An advantage of a component process approach to defining emotion is that it has the potential to characterize the richness of the subjective and behavioral aspects of emotion that we experience in everyday life. It thus encourages researchers to measure several, rather than just one, aspects (components) of emotion in experimental studies of emotion. However, a component process approach is not completely clear about whether the components should act as a concerted whole to produce a single state called an emotion. Some specific interpretations of the component process approach seem to imply that component processes should cohere most of the time (e.g., Lazarus, 1991; Roseman, 1984, 1991; Scherer, 1984a). By this interpretation it seems clear that during a state called an emotion, for example during fear, all components mentioned above point to the experience of that *same* emotion, fear. If you see a bear in the forest, a favorite example of William James, you might experience strong physiological arousal, have an urge to run, open your eyes and mouth wide, and feel something that you label as fear.

But some research shows that the different components of emotion do not always point to the experience of a unitary emotion (Bradley & Lang, 2000). Why they do not always cohere is a matter of some debate. For example, social norms within a culture can influence the outward expression of an emotion. Thus, an individual in an industrialized western country might feel like laughing at a funeral because she suddenly remembers a funny joke about a priest and a rabbi. However, especially after a particular age, she would probably control her laughter, suppress a smile or tendency to giggle, and display sadness at least on her face, if not also in bodily gestures. Social norms are one force that can decouple components processes, such as its feeling and its expression on the face or body. And even if a person is not actively trying to suppress parts of an emotion, its components may not always cohere. For example, some research has shown that individuals who are more expressive facially, and who report stronger feelings of emotion, may actually show *less* physiological evidence of an experience of emotion (e.g., Buck, 1979; Field, 1982).

TABLE 1.1

Examples of Appraisals and Differentiated Responses for the Emotions of Happiness, Anger, Sadness, and Fear

Verbal label	Appraisal profile	Facial expression	Vocal expression	Physiological symptoms
Happiness/ joy	Event seen as highly conducive to reaching an important goal or satisfying a need		Increases in pitch level, range and variability as well as vocal intensity	Heart beating faster, warm skin temperature
Anger/ rage	Unexpected event, intentionally caused by another person, seen as obstructing goal attainment or need satisfaction; person judges own coping ability as high, considers action as violating norms		Increase in pitch level and intensity level Increase in high-frequency energy in the spectrum	Heart beating faster, muscles tensing, changes in breathing, hot skin temperature
Sadness/ dejection	Event that permanently prevents need satisfaction, seen as uncontrollable by human agency; subject feels totally powerless with respect to consequences		Decrease in pitch level and range as well as intensity level Decrease in speech rate	Lump in throat, crying/sobbing, muscles tensing
Fear/ terror	Suddenly occurring event, potential but not certain consequences threatening fundamental goal of survival or bodily integrity, urgent reaction required, subject uncertain about ability to master the situation		Strong increase in pitch level and range Increase in high-frequency energy in the spectrum Increased speech rate	Heart beating faster, muscles tensing, change in breathing, perspiring, cold skin temperature, lump in throat

From Scherer, K. R. (2000). Emotion. In M. Hewstone, & W. Stroebe (Eds.), *Introduction to social psychology: A European perspective* (3rd ed.) (pp. 151–191). Oxford: Blackwell.

If the component processes do not cohere, then what is an emotion? In fact, a different interpretation of the component process account holds that indeed there is no one thing that is an emotion (Barrett, 2006) and that the various components can be elicited by different objects or events and proceed independently, or else combine in innumerable ways to produce highly nuanced emotional experiences (Clore & Ortony, 2000; Ellsworth & Scherer, 2003). By this interpretation, the situation in which recalling a joke makes one feel like laughing and in which knowledge of social norms keeps one from laughing is one in which two different emotion processes (an action readiness and an emotional regulation process) were engaged. There is really no need to try to fit them together into one emotional reaction or even one category of experience (Barrett, 2006). And the same can be said of the situation in which an individual shows a so-called discrepancy between his facial expression and his underlying physiology.

Evaluating the component process account by reference to the tendency of the components to cohere is premature in any event, because even the research demonstrating that components of emotions can be uncoupled or uncorrelated can be criticized on at least two counts. First, it could be that in real-life, naturally occurring emotions, the components are usually highly coherent. The apparent decoupling could be based on observations from a handful of laboratory demonstrations in which experimental participants were induced to experience emotions but were not given any opportunity to *act* on those emotions. If individuals do not have to act, then a certain part of the emotion physiology may not change accordingly.

There is also the problem of *time course*, or of how emotions unfold over time. It could be that for a while all of the component processes usually cohere and all point to the same emotional experience, but then later processes come into play to decouple them. For example, it could be that after all components of emotions come together to define the state of amusement, other processes intervene to control or change that state, perhaps because the state is considered unacceptable in the current social situation. The fact that emotion components can be decoupled over time does not necessarily mean that they do not initially occur in a coherent way, particularly when the opportunity to do so is present. Because of the lack of opportunity to act, and because of the absence of time course analyses of emotion (with regard to the question of the coherence of components) at this point in time we cannot even say with certainly if the components of emotion do or do not typically cohere.

An overall evaluation of the component process account leads us to believe that it is a useful way to approach the scientific study of emotion. This approach acknowledges that emotions are not one single thing (like a facial expression, or the report of a feeling state), not a rigid program, and it also acknowledges that there is interaction among the components. Such an approach might also imply certain things about emotions – that their different processes cohere to produce a discrete or unitary state, for example – that are a matter of debate and the likely subject of future research.

Theories of Emotion

In order to have the intellectual tools to evaluate some of the inconsistency in the scientific study of emotion, and in order to understand why researchers have conducted research as they have, we must introduce the major theories of emotion. These have already been referred to, and will be referred to again, many times, throughout the book. Our goal is not to provide complete accounts of the major theories of emotion. Integrative accounts can be found in Cornelius (1996) and Strongman (1996). Instead, we try to provide enough of an overview of each theory to allow us to rely on the theories throughout the book as they motivate certain research questions and conclusions that we consider in more detail.

First, let us be clear about what we are talking about when we say "theory." Theories of emotion are testable statements about the causes of an emotion, the processes by which the states are differentiated into definable experience, the order in which the components of the emotion occur, and how the different components of emotion interact. It may appear to you at first pass that some of these are obvious. For example, the third concern, the order in which emotional processes unfold, could seem to you so obvious that it does not need to be specified, studied in research, or debated. But this might actually be the most debatable part of emotion theory. When she was writing her doctoral thesis, one of the authors of this book attended a seminar for graduate students on theories of emotion. At the beginning of the course, the professor (R. B. Zajonc) handed out a piece of paper that listed a number of components of an emotional episode such as eliciting event, subjective state, expressive behavior, cognitive appraisals, autonomic nervous system (ANS) activity, and so forth. The students in the course had to cut out these labels, paste them onto a piece of paper in a particular order that represented how they thought an emotion unfolds, and then defend that ordering in front of the professor and the other students. Practically all possible orders could be defended! The labels that were chosen – because all did not have to be used – and the order in which they were pasted down, constituted each student's theory of emotion. Figure 1.1 shows some possible orderings. Interestingly, each of these orders is associated with a major theory of emotion.

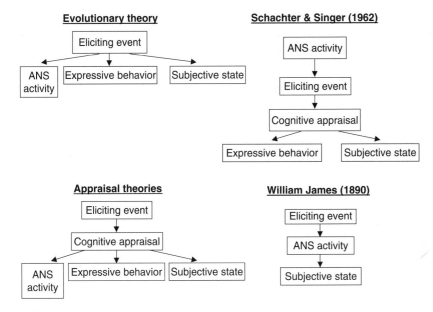

FIGURE 1.1. Examples of different theoretical orderings of the components of emotion.

Despite variability within them, the most important, broad theoretical approaches to the psychology of emotion are *evolutionary theories*, *cognitive appraisal theories*, and *social constructionist theories*. Depending on which theoretical approach is adopted by a scientist, the specific methods employed for producing and measuring an emotion in the laboratory, the types of emotions under scrutiny, the way in emotions are thought to be elicited and regulated, and the intended application of the research findings, the results may be quite different.

Evolutionary Theories

The evolutionary approach to emotion is based in part on the thinking of Charles Darwin and begins with the assumption that emotions are biologically based and provided adaptive advantages for the organism experiencing them over evolution (Darwin, 1872/1998). According to Darwin, emotions increased the chances of individual survival because they were appropriate problem-solving responses to challenges posed by the environment. Despite the obvious complexity of emotions and their inherent scientific interest, Darwin was most interested in using emotional *expression* to support his theory of evolution. To this end, he traced the continuity of emotional expression from "lower" animals to humans. In addition, he noted that many animals and humans manifest an apparent increase in body size during displays of rage. The apparent increase is due in part to the erection of body hair or feathers, and also a more expanded posture.

In theorizing about the continuity of facial expressions of emotions across various species, Darwin suggested that expressions originally served functions that he called "serviceable habits," and thus have evolved as hardwired expressions of discrete subjective states, even if they no longer serve the same function. For example, disgust, Darwin suggested, is associated with a gesture that represents the expulsion of food from the mouth and avoidance of the intake of an odor through the nose, precisely because the function of disgust in the past was to prevent individuals from ingesting dangerous substances. These days individuals do not have to worry too much that they are about to ingest a food or drink that is dangerous. Nevertheless, because in our evolutionary past the facial gesture associated with expulsion was serviceable, we still make this grimace when we encounter things, such as dog feces, for example, that produce the feelings of disgust.

Darwin also argued for a communicative or signaling function of facial expression. Specifically, he suggested that facial expressions allow members of the same species to know the subjective experience of the expresser, and therefore the emotional significance of the situation in which the expresser finds himself, as well as the expresser's likely actions. This particular function of facial expression was not well developed by Darwin, but it has inspired much research over the last several decades. The idea will be discussed in greater detail in Chapters 2 and 4.

The evolutionary biology approach in psychology, and the psychology of emotion in particular, is now a much more developed science; it goes well beyond Darwin, but shares some of the basic assumptions of evolved function through natural selection (Cosmides & Tooby, 2000; Nesse, 1990). According to current evolutionary thinking, all of human nature, meaning the developing, species-specific computational architecture of the human mind and neural architecture of the human brain, evolved through natural selection to successfully solve adaptive problems that were posed millions of times over the course of evolution (e.g., see Cosmides & Tooby, 1987). In this view, emotions are viewed as genetically coded programs that are triggered by objects or events that are evolutionarily recognizable (as related to biologically relevant or adaptive problems), and that when triggered serve to coordinate a number of the body's functions, including motor systems, perception, conceptual frameworks, energy level, effort allocation, and physiological reactions, in the service of solving the problem (Cosmides & Tooby, 2000).

One of the most thorny concepts here, at least for students of emotion, is the notion of an adaptive problem. The adaptive problem is, after all, what presumably elicits the emotion (now) and designed the emotion (in the past). What constitutes an adaptive problem to be resolved – at least in part – by an emotion and how do we know one when we see one? It is actually a mistake to classify adaptive problems in terms of short-term survival of the individual. The concern of evolution, in most current views, is the survival of the gene. In this view, a particular feature of the neural architecture will spread over generations because it enhances the possibility of dealing successfully with recurring *reproductive opportunities* (such as the appearance of a potential mate) or, alternatively, *threats to reproduction* (such as the appearance of a sexual rival).

Drawing on Scott's (1958) analysis of animal behavior, a modern emotion theorist who takes an evolutionary perspective, tried to list the behaviors that represent problem-solving behaviors that are associated with a small set of emotions (Plutchik, 1980, 1984). Plutchik (1984) enumerates eight adaptive behaviors – withdrawing, attacking, mating, crying for help, pair bonding, vomiting, examining, and stopping/freezing – and argues that they are associated with fear, anger, joy, sadness, acceptance, disgust, expectancy, and surprise. Similarly, MacLean (1993) proposes six behaviors – searching, aggressive, protective, dejected, gratulant (triumphant), and caressive – that have been linked to six corresponding basic emotional responses – desire, anger, fear, dejection (sadness), joy, and affection, respectively.

As can be seen, all these behaviors are related to opportunities and threats to reproduction. And if they seem vague or abstract, this is because adaptive problems are not limited to a small number of domains of behavior such as sex, violence, and eating. Rather, because objects and events in the environment are intricately causally related, the principle of enhancement of reproduction touches on every domain of human life, including the nature of attribution and counterfactual reasoning, and subtleties of facial expression and helping. Thus, an evolutionary approach to emotion involves a meticulous give-and-take mapping of the environment to the structure and function of the emotions.

Cognitive-appraisal Theories

If the evolutionary approach links emotions to biological adaptation in the distant past, appraisal theories of emotion link them to more immediate cognitive processes of evaluation of meaning, causal attribution, and assessment of coping capabilities. More generally, appraisals are "psychological representations of emotional significance" for the person experiencing the emotion (Clore & Ortony, 2000, p. 32). One of the primary inspirations for the development of cognitive appraisal theories was the observation that different individuals can experience different emotions in response to the same event or stimulus. For example, the experience of failing an exam may cause one individual to experience anger, another to experience sadness, and a third to experience shame. Thus, some theorists strongly doubt the existence of biologically relevant stimuli, or at least claim that the set of signal stimuli for emotion is a very small set of emotional antecedents. Another problem is that evolutionary and other biological theories cannot really explain what causes an emotion to occur in the first place, except to argue that some stimuli systematically produce a fear response and others produce a disgust response. The evolutionary approach could be criticized as being an ad hoc dictionary of stimuli that are presumed to systematically elicit certain emotions. The question is, what is it that leads a person to experience a specific, differentiated, emotion (e.g., Roseman, 1984)?

A concern with the role of cognition in the differentiation of emotion was stimulated in part by an early study by Schachter and Singer (1962), which showed that cognition could differentiate emotion. These psychologists proposed that individuals sometimes experience physiological arousal that does not have a known cause. The arousal motivates individuals to explain the cause and nature of the arousal, which as consequence gives rise to a discrete emotional state. In their classic study, Schachter and Singer injected participants with epinephrine, which enhances arousal, or with saline solution, a placebo that causes no physiological change. They then informed some of the participants injected with epinephrine to expect an increase in arousal; other participants were left uninformed about these effects. Later, when the epinephrine had taken effect for those who had received it, all participants were placed in a situation in which they interacted with a confederate of the researcher who either acted in a euphoric or an angry manner. Subsequent assessment of participants' emotions showed that those who had received epinephrine and were uninformed about the accompanying arousal, but *not* those participants who received placebo or who had an expectation of arousal, reported feeling the same emotions as those expressed by the confederate. That is, participants who experienced unexplained arousal sought an explanation in their environment, and this appraisal determined their precise emotional state.

Actually, the reported data in support of the above conclusions were extremely weak, and often lacked statistical significance. However, the idea that cognition could differentiate emotional experience had enormous theoretical influence. Modern cognitive appraisal theories, beginning with Arnold (1960) do not focus on unexplained arousal, but do hold that discrete emotions arise from processes of evaluation of significant events and of attributions of the causes of those events (e.g., Frijda, 1986;

Lazarus, Averill, & Option, 1970; Parkinson & Manstead, 1992; Roseman, 1984; Scherer, 1999; Smith & Ellsworth, 1985). In particular, whether it be unconsciously or consciously, individuals assess the degree to which events are positive or negative, whether they impede or facilitate their goals, whether they are controllable or not, whether they are novel or familiar, and whether reactions to the event will be completely over-whelming or manageable. Depending on the result of the pattern of eval-uations that characterize the resulting appraisal, a discrete emotion is evoked. A summary of the patterns of appraisals predicted to be associated with four discrete emotions, based on Scherer's (1997) model, is pre-sented in Table 1.2, while Table 1.3 lists the critical appraisal dimensions proposed by four appraisal theories.

You will notice in these tables that there are different numbers of crit-ical dimension of appraisals in the different theories that are summarized. However, there are important core similarities. For instance, pleasantness, novelty, and goal relevance are present in some way in all lists. In addition,

TABLE 1.2
Examples of Theoretical Postulated Appraisal Profiles for Different Emotions Based on Scherer's (1997) Appraisal Model

Stimulus evaluation checks	Anger/rage	Fear/panic	Sadness
Novelty			
• Suddenness	High	High	Low
• Familiarity	Low	Open	Low
• Predictability	Low	Low	Open
Intrinsic pleasantness	Open	Open	Open
Goal significance			
• Concern relevance	Order	Body	Open
• Outcome probability	Very high	High	Very high
• Expectation	Dissonant	Dissonant	Open
• Conduciveness	Obstruct	Obstruct	Obstruct
• Urgency	High	Very high	Low
Coping potential			
• Cause: agent	Other	Other/nature	Open
• Cause: motive	Intent	Open	Chance/neg
• Control	High	Open	Very low
• Power	High	Very low	Very low
• Adjustment	High	Low	Medium
Compatibility standards			
• External	Low	Open	Open
• Internal	Low	Open	Open

Note. Open indicates that different appraisal results are compatible with the respective emotion.
From Scherer, K. R. (1999). Appraisal theories. In T. Dalgleish, & M. Power (Eds.), *Handbook of cognition and emotion* (pp. 637–663). Chichester: John Wiley & Sons.

TABLE 1.3
Comparison of the Appraisal Criteria Postulated by Different Appraisal Theorists

Scherer	Frijda	Roseman	Smith/Ellsworth
Novelty	Change		Attentional activity
• Suddenness			
• Familiarity	Familiarity		
• Predictability			
Intrinsic pleasantness	Valence		Pleasantness
Goal significance		Appetitive/aversive	
• Concern relevance	Focality	Motives	Importance
• Outcome probability	Certainty	Certainty	Certainty
• Expectation	Presence		
• Conduciveness	Open/closed	Motive consistency	Perceived obstacle/ anticipated effort
• Urgency	Urgency		
Coping potential			
• Cause: agent	Intent/self–other	Agency	Human agency
• Cause: motive			
• Control	Modifiability		
• Power	Controllability	Control potential	Situational control
• Adjustment			
Compatibility standards			
• External	Value relevance		Legitimacy
• Internal			

From Scherer, K. R. (1999). Appraisal theories. In T. Dalgleish, & M. Power (Eds.), *Handbook of cognition and emotion* (pp. 637–663). Chichester: John Wiley & Sons.

there is general agreement that some of the appraisals, such as the appraisal of unexpectedness, are quite primitive whereas others, such as the appraisal of compatibility with one's or society's standards, require more complex cognitive processing. One question to ask about appraisal theory, then, is how theorists have decided how many dimensions are needed to describe basic emotional experience. Scherer (1997) has proposed three approaches to defining appraisal dimensions that seem to characterize how dimensions have been identified and endorsed in appraisal theories. One is a minimalist approach, in which the theorist tries to reduce appraisal constellations down a set of basic "motive constellations" or prototypic themes (Lazarus, 1991; Oatley & Johnson-Laird, 1987). Another approach is an "eclectic" approach, where the idea, in contrast, is to find as many possible appraisal dimensions as are needed to maximize the differentiation of the emotional states in all their subtlety (e.g., Frijda, 1986, 1987). And finally, Scherer (1997) has identified a "principled" approach, whereby theorists propose a restricted number of dimensions that can be demonstrated to be necessary and sufficient to predict the occurrence of the primary emotional states. In any event, the idea for all such theories is to try to be able to predict which emotion results based on the obtained values on the number of dimensions of interest. Although the predictive power does increase with the number of dimensions, research tends to show that researchers can correctly classify 40% to 50% of 15–30 emotional states, when one averages across the emotional states (the ability to predict some emotional states is actually much higher, and others much lower); quite a respectable outcome.

Support for appraisal theories comes largely from studies in which experimental participants are asked to recall an emotional event from their past, and then to evaluate it on the appraisal dimensions of interest to the researcher (e.g., Frijda, Kuipers, & ter Schure, 1989; Manstead & Tetlock, 1989), and from studies in which participants read descriptions of events that are conducive to specific patterns of appraisal, and then rate their expected emotional reactions (e.g. Ellsworth & Smith, 1988; Reisenzein & Hofmann, 1990). Perhaps most compelling are the supportive findings of studies in which emotions are manipulated or are measured in real-life emotional situations, and appraisal processes are assessed concurrently (e.g., Folkman & Lazarus, 1985; Smith & Ellsworth, 1987). In a delightful study conducted in the field, Scherer and Ceschi (1997) videotaped travelers as they reported that their luggage was lost to an agent at the baggage claim office of a large European airport. The investigators then interviewed the travelers about their appraisals of the situation and about their subjective feelings. As expected by appraisal theory, individuals varied in their emotional reactions to the same experience of losing luggage. Moreover, and consistently with most appraisal theories , the more that the event was perceived as obstructing one's current goals, the more the individual experienced anger, and to some degree worry, in the event.

The implications of appraisal theories are that emotions do not unfold in a hardwired way in response to certain situations or objects, but that the emotional significance of the events and objects depends on the goals and the perceived coping capacities of each individual, in a given situation. Thus, appraisal theories can comfortably predict that one person will respond to a stimulus with fear while a second will respond to the same stimulus with anger. Emotions are differentiated and can be associated with different physiological processes and facial expressions in this view, but the antecedent of the emotion – the specific profile of appraisal – determines which discrete emotion is experienced.

Social Constructionist Theories

Have you ever seen the tee shirt, sold in many countries, that asks you how you are feeling today? One of the authors bought this tee shirt in Italy where the question is "Come ti senti oggi?" On the tee shirt, the possible

FIGURE 1.2. A tee shirt asking how you are feeling today and listing 30 options.

answers to that question are represented both by facial expressions and by verbal labels (see Figure 1.2). Whether you buy this tee shirt in France, Italy, or England, the shirt looks pretty much the same, and even proposes the same emotion labels and the same cartoon faces. But it would not be possible to create this tee shirt in some countries. In the English language, there are between 500 and 2000 words that refer more or less to emotions (*shame*), affective or valenced states (*tranquility*), and cognitive-affective states (*vengeance*). These can be translated with more or less success into most European languages. However, in Malay (a language spoken in Indonesia) there are about 230 emotion words, and in Ifaluk (a language spoken on an atoll in the Western Pacific), there are only about 50. Clearly, then, there is enormous cultural variation in the number of words individuals use to talk about emotions. Furthermore, direct translations are often impossible or misleading.

The analysis of cultural differences in language for emotion, and in emotional practices, is one inspiration for a social constructionist theory of emotion (e.g., Lutz, 1988). The social constructionist approach is a general theoretical orientation within the social sciences that is most strongly associated with anthropology, sociology, philosophy, and psychology, and used to understand human states, artifacts and conditions, such as the mind, gender, the self, and indeed, emotion. As a general rule, this approach rejects the idea that there are biological realities, or *nativism*, and suggests that most human states, artifacts, and conditions are societal constructions that serve certain overarching goals of the society (e.g., Gergen, 1985; Gergen & Davis, 1985; Harré, 1986). Thus, from this point of view, emotions are considered to be products of a given culture that are constructed *by* the culture, *for* the culture.

James Averill (1980a) is one major representative of the social constructionist position in the psychology of emotion. His definition of emotion is as "a transitory social role (a socially constituted syndrome) that includes an individual's appraisal of the situation and that is interpreted as a passion rather than an action." This definition contains elements of the other views of emotion we have already discussed, but with the twist that the way in which the emotion gets played out is a prescribed social role, like a dance, whose precise expression and the situations in which it occurs are developed and defined – constructed – by society.

Specifically, the notion of a syndrome contains some of the notion of component processes. The component processes emphasized by this approach are subjective experience, expressive reactions, psychological reactions, and coping responses. Although we already suggested that it is unclear whether the possible component processes of a given emotion should or do occur together, for every experience of emotion, and for every type of emotion, the social constructionist position explicitly states that the decoupling of the components of emotion is a fact of emotional experience. From this view, there is no need to think of each emotional episode or each emotion as having all these components or as having specific patterns of each that are always the same. According to Averill, "there is no single response or subset of responses, which is essential to an emotional syndrome" (Averill, 1980b, p. 146).

Importantly, these emotional syndromes are learned; they are based in attitudes that reflect the practices, norms, and values of the culture in which the individual was raised. Indeed, in the strongest constructionist view, an individual cannot experience any given emotion until he has learned to interpret situations in terms of the standards and moral imperatives endorsed by the culture that are relevant to that emotion (Armon-Jones, 1986a). In order to identify the emotions to be studied from this perspective, Harré and his colleagues (1986; Harré & Parrott, 1996) have argued that one must start with an analysis of emotional language because "looking at the uses of words not only sensitizes the investigator to his or

*"Okay, Okay, I understand now. When you want to say
'I'm sooo excited' you shouldn't translate literally."*

her own ethnocentric presuppositions, but also allows for the possibility
that other cultures may use closely related concepts in very different
ways" (Harré, 1986, p. 5).

Harré calls attention to at least five types of cultural variation in emotional phenomena that motivate a social constructionist view of the emotions
(a detailed discussion of culture will be provided in Chapter 9). First, he suggests, there are observable inversions in standards of valuations across culture. For example, in some cultures situations that have elements of danger
call not for fear but for a sense of bravery, and the expression of fear in some
cultures would be inappropriate and undesirable. It would thus be wrong to
talk about "fear" as occurring in danger situations across culture. Second,
there are tendencies in one culture to suppress emotions altogether that are
actively encouraged in other cultures. The Japanese, for example, encourage
and value a type of emotional baby-like dependence on others that is
specifically not valued and discouraged in most western cultures. Third,
there are observations of extreme emotions in some cultures that exist in
only milder forms in other cultures. For example, some feelings of shame,
especially on behalf of another person, are debilitating and painful in
Spanish culture, and much more fleeting and less aversive in other cultures.

Fourth, particular emotions seem to have changed or dropped out of common language, across the history of the same culture. In the Middle Ages and Renaissance, for example, religious men were known to suffer from the feeling *accidie*, which entailed a gloominess over a failure to maintain one's devotion to God (see Spackman & Parrott, 2001, for example research). And finally, Harré proposes cultural variation in "quasi-feelings" or feelings states, such as that referred to by the word *cozy* that show important cultural variation in the values and social contexts that they imply.

As can be seen, the social constructionist view thus agrees with the cognitive appraisal approach that emotions result from an assessment of the situation and one's capacity to deal with it, and rejects the idea that there are biologically relevant antecedents that completely determine the emotion. However, the emphasis here is on the nature of the moral values of the culture that provide the specific content to the appraisal and meaning to the situation. The ways in which constructionist approaches to emotion try to respond to challenges from nativist approaches (such as evolutionary theory), while still incorporating the obvious importance of biology in the experience of emotion, can be found in the compelling writings of Armon-Jones (1986b).

Can We Study Emotions? Or, How Can We Study Emotions?

When one of the authors was a student at the University of Wisconsin, a public university in the United States, the governing senator of that state, Senator Proxmire, gave out what he called annual "Golden Fleece" Awards. These were actually institutionalized criticisms presented to people or institutions that Proxmire believed were wasting taxpayers' money. The first Golden Fleece Award was given, in 1980, to Elaine (Hatfield) Walster for her research on romantic love. The research was funded by the National Science Foundation of the United States, an agency that receives money from the government, which is then allocated to programs of research on the basis of scientific merit. Proxmire claimed that since romantic love should not be the topic of scientific inquiry, using taxpayers' US dollars to pay for such a research program was a terrible waste of money. Many people do believe that romantic love is the exclusive domain of philosophy. Certainly, from Aristotle to Sartre romantic love finds an important place. However, subsequently researchers other than Walster have investigated aspects of romantic love, and an evaluation of that research would probably produce a judgment quite different than that of Proxmire: romantic love does have a place in science, particularly the sciences of psychology and neuroscience. Since you may well hold Proxmire's general bias as regards all emotions, however, in the next section, we will discuss how emotions can be and are studied in the laboratory.

Manipulating Emotions in the Laboratory

Many researchers who study emotion try to make experimental participants feel emotions or experience parts of emotion in the laboratory. Because in most western countries scientific research must conform to a set of ethical guidelines, scientists cannot just do anything they please to produce an emotion in experimental participants. For example, they must try to induce emotions whose intensity does not surpass that typically experienced in daily life by individuals who do not suffer from affective disorders (such as clinical depression or anxiety) or other psychopathologies. In addition, experimentally induced emotions, to meet ethical guidelines, should be induced by stimuli that are, and are likely to be, encountered in everyday life rather than by strange or extreme interventions. The induction of very painful emotions, such as grief, is often limited as well. And finally, the emotions should be *extinguishable* – particularly if they are negative or painful – and indeed *extinguished* before the participant leaves the laboratory.

One reason that a researcher would induce an emotion in the laboratory is, of course, to test predictions of a specific theory of emotion. For example, a researcher might want to know what facial expressions or physiological changes co-occur with a particular subjective state. The researcher would first find a method of inducing the state of interest, and several other states to compare to that state. Then she would induce those states in a number of experimental participants and measure the expressive or physiological changes that occur.

Another reason that researchers might induce an emotional state in experimental participants is in order to study how that state is related to behavior or to some type of other mental function such as perception or attention. For instance, before instructing the participant to perform a task that measures perception, memory, or even the tendency to engage in helping behavior, the researcher might induce an emotional state in some of them, and a neutral state in others. If the participants in whom an emotion has been induced behave differently on the cognitive task, or tend to help more (or less), for instance, then conclusions about the relation between emotion and some cognitive processes or behavior can be drawn with reasonable certainty.

Ethical guidelines were not in place in the 1950s, and so an example of a well-known experiment conducted in 1953 demonstrates the type of experimental manipulation of emotion that could not be conducted today. The problem under investigation was the possibility that specific patterns of autonomic nervous system activity characterize discrete emotions, such as joy and fear and anger. The researcher, Ax, wanted to find out whether anger and fear were characterized by specific patterns of autonomic nervous system activity. He measured 14 different indicators of autonomic nervous system activity such as heart rate, respiration, blood pressure, and muscle tension. So, under the cover story of testing the validity of polygraphs, or lie detectors, Ax (1953) hooked participants up to a number of devices, such as an electric shock generator. Then, as their autonomic nervous system indicators were being recorded, for some of the participants Ax staged a malfunction of the shock generator; the generator spewed sparks and the experimenter became overtly distressed. Predictably, the participants experienced high levels of fear. Participants in the anger condition, by the same token, were subjected to five minutes of abuse by an impolite polygraph operator, and this elicited high levels of anger. In fact, Ax (1953) found relative specificity in the patterns of participants' autonomic nervous system activity. Despite their high levels of arousal and negative valence, the two states of fear and anger differed on seven of the 14 measures. These types of difference will be discussed in the next chapter. For now, the point is that, at least until the 1970s, emotions could be induced in the laboratory by recreations or enactments of extremely provocative situations. This is no longer the case; it is no longer possible to conduct a study with such extreme dishonesty and unusual levels of provocation. Furthermore, as we shall see in discussing research throughout this book, such extreme provocation is not necessary. Here we describe three of the methods for inducing emotion in the laboratory that are the most often used and most often mentioned in this book, and we then discuss the study of naturally occurring emotions.

Films

One way to induce emotional states or reactions in the laboratory is to present participants with short films or film segments – even from well-known movies that have appeared in the cinema – that have been demonstrated in pilot testing to produce a particular emotion or reaction in *most* individuals. You might wonder how do we know which films produce which emotions? Researchers must always study the emotional effects of the method before using it in a major experiment.

For example, Philippot (1993) conducted a study of the emotional effects of a number of film segments. He showed the segments, each of which lasted between three and six minutes, to 60 research participants, all of whom were francophone (the films were all shown in the French language, although some were originally in English). He had pilot tested the set of film segments in order to choose a final pool of 12 including two segments that induced each of five different emotions (anger, disgust, sadness, happiness, and fear) and a neutral state. In the main experiment, the 60 participants watched each film segment and reported on how it made them feel in two different ways. First, they rated their feelings on a French-language version of a questionnaire that had been developed by Izard, Dougherty, Bloxom, and Kotsch (1974) called the Differential Emotions Scale. This scale provides words that belong to 10 broad emotions categories: interest, joy, sadness, anger, fear, anxiety, disgust, scorn, surprise, and happiness. There are three items from each category, so, for example, to measure joy the questionnaire lists the words *amused*, *joyful*, and *merry*. Participants rate each word according to how much they feel that way at any given time (from "not at all" to "very strongly"). Later the experimenter can average the ratings of the three words for each category in order to know how much joy, anger, interest, and so forth, the participant felt. After completing the DES, Philippot's participants also freely listed their own words for the feelings they had experienced during the movie segments.

A number of different statistical analyses of both the questionnaire responses and the freely generated responses demonstrated that Philippot had indeed found movies that provoked very specific emotions in most individuals. For example, the segments he had preselected to induce joy did induce joy quite specifically, and joy more than any other emotion. You can see the list of the films that he studied in Table 1.4. One caveat to this is that the films chosen to induce anger tended also to induce disgust, and those that were chosen to induce disgust also induced some anger. Subsequently, Gross and Levenson (1995) developed a set of 16 movie segments, presented in English to American experimental participants, that successfully induced specific emotions of amusement, anger, contentment, disgust, sadness, surprise, a neutral state and fear, although their manipulation of fear was somewhat weak.

Since the work of Philippot and Gross, many researchers have used the film segments developed by these researchers to conduct research both on emotion and on the effects of emotion on other psychological processes. Researchers who have preferred to use segments that they themselves select are, of course, required to demonstrate empirically that their movies have the desired emotional effect (see for example, Dalle & Niedenthal, 2001). It should be noted, in completing this section, that most of the films

TABLE 1.4
Film Excerpts Used to Induce Discrete Emotions

Source film	Expected emotion	Segment description
		Film series I
The Old Gun (1985)	Anger	A man discovers his wife and daughter massacred by the SS during WW2. In a flashback the massacre is depicted
Faces of Death (1986)	Disgust	A slaughterhouse is presented in a graphic way. Animals are shown as their throats are slit and skin removed
Kramer vs. Kramer (1979)	Sadness	A father is alone in a park with a young boy. The parents of the little boy have just split up. The child is crying; the father looks lonely and desperate
Le Magnifique (1973)	Happiness	A series of gags about the hero escaping from a KGB-like agent, from a French comedy parodying James Bond movies
Psycho (1953)	Fear	A woman, the only customer of an isolated motel, goes to her room and takes a shower. A shadow appears in the background, approaches and stabs her with a knife
Documentary	Neutral	Excerpts from a Belgian national television documentary, which consists of the introduction by a speaker of a program on town policy
		Film series II
Sophie's Choice (1982)	Anger	In Dachau concentration camp, a German officer humiliates a young woman and forces her to choose which of her two children should be sent to the gas chamber
Faces of Death (1986)	Disgust	In an exotic restaurant, a little monkey is trapped on a table. Using a hammer, the people at the table hit the monkey's head until it screams and faints. Its skull is opened and served to the guests, who eat it
Kramer vs. Kramer (1979)	Sadness	A father is with his little boy at bedtime. The boy is crying because his mother has left. The father looks lonely and overwhelmed
Le Magnifique (1973)	Happiness	Second excerpt from the French comedy parodying James Bond movies that consists of gags in which the hero tries to seduce a beautiful woman on the beach
Halloween (1981)	Fear	At night while the children are sleeping, a babysitter hears noises and goes upstairs to explore. She discovers a bloody corpse, and a shadow holding a knife appears in the back room
Documentary	Neutral	An excerpt from a Belgian national television documentary, consisting of an interview of a police candidate

From Philippot, P. (1993). Inducing and assessing differentiated emotion-feeling states in the laboratory. *Cognition and Emotion, 7*, 171–193.

used to induce emotion in laboratory research are more benign than many currently popular television shows!

Music

Another way to manipulate emotional state in the laboratory is to expose experimental participants to music that has been previously demonstrated to evoke the same emotion in most individuals. At first pass you might object that music is very personal and that the reason a particular song or piece of classical music can produce an emotional state is that for a given individual that music was paired with an emotional event (or events) in the past. For instance, you might have been in love when a particular song was popular on the radio. You now associate the song with that time of being in love, and so the song always produces a particular feeling (either joy, or perhaps sadness) in you. If the effects of music were this idiosyncratic and open to experiential influence, then it would be very labor intensive to manipulate emotion with music. The researcher would have to find out which music makes each experimental participant feel which emotion and then go out and find those pieces of music and record them before bringing those participants into the laboratory!

While it is true that music is probably often conditioned to produce particular emotions, including positive feelings due to mere repetition, songwriters can choose words that produce systematic emotional effects, of course, and even more interesting, composers can use different musical intervals to produce emotional effects that they have in mind. And these effects seem to be quite basic, at least in western countries (Costa, Fine, and Ricci Bitti, 2004). For example, Costa, Ricci Bitti, and Bonfiglioli (2000) found that dissonant (compared to consonant) bichords were perceived as unstable, furious, and tense (see also Bozzi, 1985; Chailley, 1985). So a piece of music with many dissonant chords will likely make the listener feel somewhat anxious. In addition, people tend to perceive minor chords as sadder and gloomier than major chords, and high-pitched tones are associated with positive emotions, whereas low-pitched tones tend to express negative emotions. Tempo is another powerful way of expressing emotions in music. Slow tempi tend to express low arousal emotions whereas fast tempi are associated with high arousal emotional states (Gagnon & Peretz, 2003). These different qualities of music can also be combined to produce an endless palette of emotional expressions in music: in a given piece of classical music the adagio typically sounds much sadder than the allegro, which sounds more joyful.

As an example of the use of music to induce emotions, Niedenthal and Setterlund (1994) exposed participants to the allegro portion of three pieces by Mozart (*Eine kleine Nachtmusik, Divertimento No. 136*, and *Ein musikalischer Spass*) as well as some portions of the *Concerto in C Major* and the *Concerto in G Major* by Vivaldi. Other participants listened to the *Adagio for Strings* by Barber, *Adagietto* by Mahler, and the adagio from the *Piano Concerto No. 2 in C Minor* by Rachmaninov. Participants then rated their emotional states on a questionnaire called the Brief Mood Introspection Scale (BMIS; Mayer & Gaschke, 1988), which lists 16 different high and low arousal positive and negative emotions. These ratings were later subjected to a *discriminant function analysis*, a statistical procedure that asked which of the emotions significantly discriminated between the two conditions. The results of that analysis are presented in Table 1.5. The list of structure coefficients reveals that, consistent with the research on music cited above, individuals who listened to the allegros felt *happy, content, lively, peppy,* and *active* and that those who listened to the adagios reported feeling *sad, gloomy, tired,* and *drowsy* (and a little *fed up*). Thus it appears that the allegros induced a high energy joy and the adagios induced a lethargic sadness. Importantly, these were the only feelings that discriminated the two conditions. The conditions could

TABLE 1.5

Mean Ratings of Items on the Brief Mood Introspection Scale (BMIS) by Participants Who Listened to Happy and Sad Music, and Correlations of Items with the Discriminant Function

Adjective	Happy ($n = 148$)	Sad ($n = 143$)	Structure coefficient[a]
Sad	1.48	2.39	.77**
Gloomy	1.46	2.20	.61**
Tired	2.75	3.31	.43**
Drowsy	2.59	3.16	.40**
Active	2.35	1.73	−.59**
Lively	2.59	1.80	−.56**
Peppy	2.35	1.66	−.55**
Happy	3.20	2.61	−.54**
Content	3.43	3.08	−.31**
Fed up	1.34	1.52	.19*
Caring	2.85	3.0	.14
Calm	3.36	3.49	.13
Loving	2.84	2.96	.10
Nervous	1.45	1.53	.07
Grouchy	1.40	1.45	.06
Jittery	1.61	1.55	−.04

Note. Ratings could range from 1 to 4; higher numbers indicate greater self-report of the particular state.
[a] Conditions were coded such that happy condition = −1 and sad condition = 1.
*$p < .05$; **$p < .001$.
From Niedenthal, P. M., & Setterlund, M. B. (1994). Emotional congruence in perception. *Personality and Social Psychology Bulletin, 20*, 401–411.

not be differentiated by the other positive (e.g., *loving*, *caring*) or negative (*nervous*, *grouchy*) feeling states. Or put differently, the two types of music did not differentially induce those other feelings not related to joy or sadness; such feelings were induced equally in both conditions. In using music to manipulate emotions in the laboratory, this kind of empirical demonstration that the manipulation was effective is always necessary.

Recalling Emotional Experiences

A third way that experimenters induce emotional states in the laboratory involves asking participants to get active in the process of experiencing emotion, and to retrieve memories of events that they experienced personally and in which they felt certain emotions.

You might not realize it at first pass, but the idea that the retrieval of a memory of an emotional event will cause an individual to experience the same emotional state that they experienced during that event requires that the researcher accept a model of memory according to which memories preserve emotional state information that can also be retrieved. A number of different models of memory make this type of claim. For example, Bower's (1981) associative network model of emotion proposes that emotions – perhaps specific emotions such as anger, fear, joy and so forth – are represented in memory as central units of information ("nodes") that are linked to other units that represent other ideas that are associated with the emotion. Such ideas might involve past events that have evoked the emotion, verbal labels for the emotion, descriptions of the emotion, and the behaviors, expressive activity, and physiological events that constitute the emotion. According to the model, the experience of an emotion activates its unit in memory. Activation then spreads from the central unit to related information, thereby potentiating the use of that information in ongoing processing. Thus, in this view, if a person retrieves an emotional memory, they will experience at least some of the original emotion. The idea that the retrieval of specific memories will induce an emotional state is also consistent with Lang's (1979, 1984) bio-informational network theory, although Lang's theory accounts for the effect in a slightly different way.

Schwarz and Clore (1983) and Strack, Schwarz and Geschneidinger (1985) used the retrieval of emotional memories to instantiate emotional states in the laboratory. They showed, further, that the way in which the memory is retrieved determines whether an emotion is felt. Specifically they demonstrated that the retrieval of emotional memories in a pallid way – a way that does not focus on the emotional parts of the experience, but still accurately describes the situation – does not reactivate the original emotion. By the same token, a retrieval that involves attention to the vivid emotional aspects of the situation tends to reactivate the original emotion. This is an important demonstration because it shows that we are not obliged to re-experience an entire emotional event each time we think back about the eliciting event. The way that we think about it influences the impact that that memory has on our present emotional state.

Once an emotion is induced through the retrieval of personal memories, then, again, its influence and its concomitants can be measured. For instance, Krauth-Gruber & Ric (2000) studied how emotions induced in this way relate to the use of stereotypes, extending similar work by Bodenhausen and his colleagues (e.g., Bodenhausen, Kramer, & Süsser, 1994a).

Naturally Occurring Emotions

A second important way to examine the questions of what occurs during an emotion, and how emotions are related to cognitive processes and behavior, is to examine the behaviors of individuals who are experiencing a state naturally. There are three broad ways of using naturally occurring emotion in research on emotion:

1. measuring the state when the participant comes to the laboratory and relating that state to measures of another behavior
2. measuring emotions outside the laboratory with the use of diaries or small computers
3. the use of quasi-experimental methods, in which the experimenter seeks out groups of people likely to be naturally experiencing specific emotions and another group likely to be in a neutral state, and then compares the behavior of the groups.

It should be noted right away that if an experimenter measures participants' emotions either in the laboratory or as they go about their daily life, and then measures another behavior in order to see how the emotions and that behavior are related, he is conducting *correlational* research. This means that the experimenter is not randomly assigning participants to emotion manipulations and then observing the influence of the manipulation on something else, but, rather, relating two existing conditions of the participants. These two conditions may even be two different emotional states of the participants. The major problems with correlation research are two. First, one cannot draw strong causal conclusions from the results. If there is a relation between two emotions or between an emotion and a behavior, such as helping, one does not necessarily know which caused which (though some methodological and statistical techniques are available for drawing stronger causal conclusions even from correlational designs).

The second, related, problem is that naturally occurring emotions may be associated with many psychological states, any one or several of which might be responsible for an observed relationship with the other variable measured in the study. For example, people who report at the moment that they are sad might also tend to be people who are chronically depressed (and sad much of the time). People who are depressed have a whole constellation of biological and cognitive features other than being sad which may be associated with the behavior of interest to the researcher. Thus, a particular effect observed in a particular study on "sadness and behavior" might be due not to sadness, in fact, but to one of these other features of depression. The problem of third variables is normally dealt with in experimental research by the procedure of random assignment to condition.

Contrariwise, it is also very useful to conduct research on naturally occurring emotions because these are, after all, the psychological states that the researcher assumes she is creating in the laboratory. In order to demonstrate the validity and generalizability of laboratory research, studying both emotions induced in the laboratory and emotions that occur naturally may be the best research strategy.

Relating a Naturally Occurring State to Behavior in the Laboratory

In relating an emotional state to a behavior in the laboratory, the researcher conducts a study that seems very similar to the kinds of studies we have already described in illustrating methods for manipulating emotions (for instance, with film or with music). The most important aspect of this work, however, is to be sure that the measure of emotion is an established, psychometrically sound assessment instrument, and that it measures emotions in a way that is consistent with the guiding theory of emotion.

A very general distinction is that between emotion and affect. Some instruments are designed to measure general affective states, such as the Positive and Negative Affect Scale (Watson, Clark, & Tellegen, 1988), the Multiple Affect Adjective Checklist – Revised (MAAC-R) by Zuckerman and Lubin (1985), and the Current Mood Questionnaire (Feldman Barrett & Russell, 1998). The BMIS, discussed earlier, can also be used to measure general positive and negative affect and high and low aroused states. Other instruments can measure specific emotional states, such as Izard's (1977) Differential Emotions Scale (see Boyle, 1984).

In an example of correlational research using naturally occurring emotions, Mayer and colleagues (Mayer, McCormick, & Strong, 1995) were interested in studying mood-congruent memory. The mood congruence effect, discussed in greater detail in Chapter 6, is the tendency for individuals in a particular emotional state, or a mood, to retrieve information from memory that has the same emotional or affective tone (in the case of a mood). This effect is predicted by the Bower (1981) associative network model of emotion, described earlier. In three studies, Mayer and colleagues had participants complete a category-retrieval task and an association retrieval task. In the category-retrieval task participants were given a category, such as *attitude*, and they had to provide one member of the category whose name started with a certain letter. For example, participants might have been provided with the letter *p* for the category *attitude*. Pretesting had demonstrated that the most likely responses to the category prime had different affective tones. For *attitude*, likely responses were *positive*, *pessimistic*, or *poor*.

In the association-retrieval task, participants were given a word to associate to, such as *marriage*, and they were provided with two letters, one of which they were supposed to use to produce an association. Again, pretesting had shown that the different likely associations to *marriage* using the *d* or *l*, also had different affective tones. For example, the likely responses to *marriage*: *d/l* were *divorce*, a negative response, and *love*, a positive response. After participants had completed these two tasks, their moods were measured using the BMIS (and calculating positive and negative affect scores; see Mayer & Gaschke, 1988 for details).

A mood-congruence hypothesis states that the generation of pleasant members of categories on the category-retrieval task and the generation of positive associates on the association-retrieval task will be positively correlated with mood, if higher scores indicate more positive mood. Stated differently, the expectation is that the more positively one feels, the more positive category members and associations one will generate during these tasks. In three studies, in which the retrieval tasks were varied slightly in their format, strong support for mood-congruent memory was observed.

Studying Naturally Occurring Emotions with Diaries and Experience Sampling

There are some techniques for studying emotions and their concomitants as they occur, "online," or almost so, in real life. We have already noted that real life emotions may have some different characteristics than those experienced in the laboratory. If we are interested specifically in real-life emotions, then there is another advantage to assessing them online. The advantage is that it avoids the problem of asking people to remember emotions. People's memory for emotional experience and emotional events is not always very good; people tend to recall certain emotions and emotional events better than others. For instance, many individuals would prefer to forget angry emotions and the surrounding events, and/or think that such emotions are undesirable, and so tend to under-report them or report them inaccurately.

Using diaries, which people fill out every night, for instance, or every time a particular emotion occurs, we may get a better idea of the emotions that people feel and some of the situations that cause them. Oatley and his colleagues (Oatley & Duncan, 1992, 1994), building on other emotion research that relied on a diary methodology (e.g., Averill, 1982; Gates, 1926), have conducted extensive diary studies of the emotions happiness/joy, sadness/grief, anger/irritation, fear/anxiety, and disgust/hatred. For example, in Oatley and Duncan (1994), the authors were interested in their ability to predict the occurrence of these five emotions from the goal-relevant elicitor, based on the theory of Oatley and Johnson-Laird (1987). Oatley and Johnson-Laird's (1987) theory, which is, in fact, a mixture of cognitive and evolutionary theories of emotion, predicts that experiences of achievement cause happiness, loss causes sadness, frustration causes anger, a conflict of goals causes anxiety, and that interactions with toxic things cause disgust.

Participants in their study were asked to complete a page of a diary any time that they experienced one of the five emotions listed above, and it was strong enough to cause bodily sensations, thoughts that they could not stop, or if they found themselves acting or feeling like acting in an emotional way (or, obviously, any combination of those conditions). Participants were further asked to provide complete accounts of four emotion episodes in all. For each of the four emotion episodes, the participants rated the intesity and the duration of the emotion on separate scales. They then wrote about where they were when the emotion occurred, who they were with, what had happened and what they were doing. These accounts of the emotion episodes could later be coded for the antecedents of the emotions (see Oatley & Duncan, 1994, for details of the coding procedure).

Results showed, first, that anger and happiness were the most frequently experienced emotions, and that sadness and disgust were the least frequent, although this result should be interpreted carefully as participants were, of course, in control of which emotion episodes they were willing to report. More importantly for the theoretical concerns of the research, Oatley and Johnson-Laird's theory of emotional antecedents was strongly supported. Based on theoretical expectations, that is, the researchers could predict which emotion was felt based on the categorization of the elicitor,

69% of the time on average. Thus, if they had classified an event as reflecting a loss, then most of the time their participants reported feeling sadness, and if the event were classified as indicating an achievement, then most of the time the participants reported feeling happiness.

Recently, the availability of the internet and palmtop computer technology has allowed some researchers to conduct rigorous *experience-sampling* studies of emotion. In experience sampling, participants access the internet or carry palmtop computers (or in the past, a beeper along with some booklets containing questionnaires; e.g., Feldman Barrett, 1995a) and are given precise instructions about when to fill out computer-based questionnaires. The questionnaires might measure features of states of emotion and the situations for them, for instance, or any other aspect of emotion or other behavior of interest to the emotion researcher.

There are three basic schedules for the collection of experience-sampling data. First, researchers may request that participants fill out the computer-based questionnaires at regular times throughout the day, such as morning, noon, and in the evening. This is called *interval-contingent* responding. Second, the researcher may ask participants to fill out the questionnaires in response to specific types of event, for instance, whenever they have an emotion that lasts a certain amount of time. This is called *event-contingent* responding. And finally, the researcher may ask the participant to complete the questionnaires whenever the palmtop computer signals them to do so. This is called *signal-contingent* responding. Much more detail about the use of experience-sampling techniques can be found in Christensen, Feldman Barrett, Bliss-Moreau, Lebo, and Kashub (2003) and Feldman Barrett and Barrett (2001).

In an example of the use of experience sampling, Barrett (2004) wanted to know if people's self-reports of momentary emotional experience were determined most, and most simply, by their understanding of emotion words. To appreciate this problem, imagine a person, let us call him Thomas, who when you ask him to talk about emotions, just uses the words "good" and "bad." Further, if you asked him to provide you with information about the meaning of more emotion words he uses *happy*, *excited*, and *interested* as more or less equivalent (essentially "good") and he uses *scared*, *angry*, and *bored* as more or less equivalent (essentially "bad"). The question of interest about Thomas is whether, when he is asked to report on his feelings in every day life, he reports all feelings as good or bad, because this is how he thinks about emotion, or if he is actually able to detect more qualities of his subjective experience, even if they do not conform to his "good" versus "bad" belief system. If everyone's reports of their feelings match exactly their language-based beliefs about emotional life, this casts some doubt on the usefulness of self-report measures of emotion. The alternative, and what the researcher hopes, is that individuals' self-reports of emotion are more like descriptions of the phenomenological qualities of their subjective experience.

In a first study, Barrett (2004) measured participants' ratings of the similarity of 16 emotion words in the laboratory, and then had them complete questionnaire measures of their own emotional experience, three times a day for 60 consecutive days. On the measures, participants rated the extent to which they were feeling 88 different states. In a second study, Barrett again assessed perceived similarity between 16 emotion terms, and then collected ratings on 29 emotion-related states, on palmtop computers, at random times, 10 times a day for 28 consecutive days. A third study largely replicated the second.

With these data, Barrett could assess the degree to which people base their self-reports of emotion entirely or partially on their representation of language about emotion. Specifically, the initial ratings of similarity allowed Barrett to create a map of the understanding of emotional language for each of her participants. Then, she could compare that map with the experience-sampling data. Findings suggested that for most individuals the language map could not completely explain the structure of their subjective experience of emotion. This suggests, then, that when individuals report on their emotions, they are doing something other than, or in addition to, accessing natural language for emotions; presumably they are doing something closer to describing a subjective state. This does not mean that we can do away with the study of emotional language. Rather, it means that we need to study language and reports of subjective state in tandem.

Naturally Occurring Emotion and Quasi-experimental Designs

In a quasi-experimental study, the experimenter examines two groups of participants, but does not randomly assign participants to experimental conditions in the laboratory. Instead, the researcher might examine a behavior among people who, because of something about their current situation, are thought a priori to be likely to be in a particular state, and compare the behavior to people who are thought to be in a more neutral state, or a different state altogether. For example, you could imagine, based on our discussion of the emotional impact of some films, that individuals leaving a cinema after having seen a film known to be very uplifting will be, on average, in a very happy state. And you could imagine that people reading in a library at the same time might be in a rather neutral state.

In an example of a quasi-experimental field study, Niedenthal and Dalle (2001) wanted to see how happiness affected categorization. The research was motivated by a particular theory, emotional response categorization theory (Niedenthal, Halberstadt, & Innes-Ker, 1999), according to which individuals, when in emotional states, tend to group objects and events in the world into categories that correspond to the emotions that those objects and events typically elicit, instead of other bases of categorization. That is, most of the time individuals use categories in which the members are presumed to be the "same kind of thing" because they look more or less alike. For instance, in our daily life we often use categories such as "tables," "birds," and "women." Those categories are based on the perceived similarities between tables, birds, and women, respectively. According to the theory of emotional response categorization, however, when people are feeling emotional, they often categorize differently. They focus more on the emotional connotation of objects rather than the perceptual similarity of objects. For instance, when in an emotional state, individuals might tend to group together Dostoyevsky's novel *Crime and Punishment*, a rainy day, the old man who lives alone down the street, and a dinner in a particular restaurant in East Berlin in 1982 (Niedenthal et al., 1999). One might say that this is a category of "things that produced a sad state." Much laboratory research has provided evidence for this idea (e.g., Dalle & Niedenthal, 2003; Innes-Ker & Niedenthal, 2002; Niedenthal et al., 1999).

To test the idea that individuals naturally experiencing happiness (versus neutral mood) also tend to categorize on the basis of emotional equivalencies, Niedenthal and Dalle went to two weddings that they knew to be taking place in different locations in central France. The expectation was that the invitees at those weddings, if recruited for the study before drinking, but after the ceremony, would be in a very happy (and still sober) state. At the same time, another experimenter recruited individuals walking down the street in a city in central France at more or less the same time. The expectation was that those people would be, on average, in a more neutral state.

Individuals at the weddings and on the street were approached and asked to participate in a brief psychological experiment, which involved completing two short questionnaires. The first questionnaire measured categorization, and the second measured emotional state. Results of the first questionnaire showed that individuals at the weddings tended to form categories based on emotional equivalences between objects significantly more than did individuals who were recruited while walking down the street (see Niedenthal & Dalle, 2001, for details about the measure of categorization). Results of the emotion measure showed that, as expected, invitees at the weddings were much happier than individuals walking down the street, who were in a generally neutral state.

Notice therefore that Niedenthal and Dalle (2001) could study groups of participants who were in naturally occurring emotional states, and draw conclusions about how the emotions are related to other cognitive processes, without needing to bring individuals into the laboratory to receive a treatment that evokes an emotion. This type of study thus enhances the ecological validity of the idea of emotional response categorization, as it shows that the phenomenon occurs in daily life and not just in the laboratory.

Summary

The primary purpose of this chapter was to hook you: to present a definition, with all its confusion and complexity, of *emotion*, and to present the way that major theories approach this topic and prepare it, so to speak, for experimental study. We saw that the evolutionary theory of emotion holds that emotions are biologically evolved, functional responses to certain opportunities and challenges posed by the environment. One of the key predictions of the evolutionary theory of emotion, which we will revisit several times in this book, is that there is a set of universally recognized facial expressions of emotion. The major contribution of cognitive appraisal theories of emotion is that emotions are elicited and differentiated by evaluations (appraisals) of the environment with respect to the current goals and interests of the individual experiencing the emotion. Thus, although some appraisal theories might agree that in the end there are a set of emotions that turn out to be universal, this is not due to biologically based affect programs, but rather due to the fact that humans have similar fundamental goals and consensual ways of assessing the possibility for those goals to be facilitated or hindered. Finally, we introduced you to the social constructionist theory of emotion, which states that emotions are phenomena that are constructed by societies, not natural kinds, and elaborated within linguistic and cultural contexts. Social constructionist theories were the first to argue that the different components of emotion can be quite separate and have separate time courses, and that an inevitable set of components does not accompany all emotional episodes.

In the second part of the chapter, we introduced a number of ways in which emotions can be studied in the laboratory and in the field. We described how emotional states can be induced in the laboratory, including with the use of film, music, and guided recall of past emotional events. Techniques for assessing individuals' ongoing emotional states, notably with the use of experiential sampling methods, were also discussed. In the end, we may have confused you about something you thought was so basic and straightforward – your emotional life – we hope that we also showed you that questions about emotions can be addressed in experimental research. By using many methods and assessing many parts of the whole elephant that we call an emotion, we can start to get closer to some truths about the components of emotion and their harmony or disharmony; about the involvement of all of "human nature" – the processes of the mind and the body – that make up an emotional experience; and about the role that emotions play in social life, the topic of the remainder of the book.

Structure and Function of Emotion 2

> *Contents at a Glance*

Suppose that you held the belief that positive emotions are good and negative emotions are bad. What would this belief presuppose? The belief would presuppose at least two things. One is that you accepted that there are two categories of emotion, good ones and bad ones, a little like Thomas, whom we encountered in the last chapter. Furthermore, you would be endorsing a hedonistic approach to emotions if, by positive being good and negative being bad, you meant that positive emotions were pleasant states to be experienced and sought out, and negative ones were unpleasant states, experiences to be avoided at all costs. But suppose you were not actually saying that positive emotions involved feeling good (and that is good) and negative emotions involve feeling bad (and that is bad). Suppose, rather, that you meant that positive emotions cause people to think right, and do good things, and negative emotions cause people to think poorly, and to do bad things. Here too you would be clumping all positive emotions together and all negative emotions together. And you would be endorsing the idea that there are beneficial motivations that, in part, constitute the experience of positive emotions, and destructive or harmful ones that, in part, constitute the experience of negative emotion.

Any of these assumptions on your part would be well within the bounds of ordinary, even consensual, belief in most western countries. Indeed, institutions all over Europe, the US, and elsewhere in the world, teach such beliefs. However, the beliefs do not completely reflect the theoretical or empirical state of the art in the psychology of emotion. In this chapter, we discuss the nature of the basic issues, which we refer to as problems of the *structure* and *function* of emotion, and provide an overview of the differences of opinion and the nature of the data on which they are based. Theory and research on the structure and the function of emotion is necessary for further refining the definition of emotion that we work with in the study of emotion in psychology.

Structural Accounts of Emotion

What do we mean when we talk about the structure of emotion, what data do we examine when trying to address this question, and what do analyses of those data mean? When we ask about structure, we are asking quite simply about the number of irreducible experiences that count as emotions, and what they should be called. The notion of irreducibility is sometimes difficult to understand, but it is made easier by comparing it to the search for basic elements in chemistry. The basic elements are the building blocks of all matter. As you know, quarks are even smaller than the atoms of an element, but it is only when they combine with other quarks that they form atoms that have recognizable traits. As far as we know there are only so many basic elements, over 100 of them at the last count. While there may be more out there to discover, the basic elements remain the same. Iron atoms found on earth are the same as the iron atoms found on the moon.

How do the elements relate to the structure of emotion? In many ways, the search for irreducible emotional states has the same status as the search for elements. What we want to know is, what are the basic elements of emotional life? As is true in all there is to know about emotion, this inquiry involves the study of both behavior (defined very broadly to include self-reports, expressive behavior, somatomotor and autonomic nervous system phenomena, complex action, and cognition) as well as the brain. In what follows, we focus largely on behavioral data, rather than relevant data on neural structures. (The reader interested in learning more about data that speak to the structure of emotion from the neurosciences is referred to Cacioppo, Gardner, & Berntson, 1999; Davidson 1992; Heller, 1990, 1993; Lane and colleagues, 1997; Ochsner & Barrett, 2001; and Panksepp, 1998.) What should be noted is that while a model of the structure of emotion sometimes also corresponds to a particular overarching theory of emotion, one cannot equate a theory with a model of emotion structure in a one-to-one fashion.

The types of data that researchers collect and evaluate in order to ask questions about the structure of emotions are as varied as the data that address all problems in the psychology of emotion per se. We will refer often to two of the major types of data in the following sections, which we will call experiential/linguistic data and component process data.

Experiential and Linguistic Data

Probably the type of information most heavily used in the investigation of the structure of emotion is self-report of the subjective experience of emotion. Self-reports are usually expressed by ratings of the extent to which words denoting emotional states characterize one's subjective experience at the present time (or at a time in the past, or averaged over a given period of time). Some researchers also investigate people's knowledge about emotion words, with the expectation, consistent with the social constructionist assumption discussed in the last chapter, that words that are used to talk about and label emotion reflect something real about emotional experience.

A number of statistical techniques permit one to use experiential and linguistic data in the analysis of structure. One of the most frequently used is *factor analysis*. Factor analysis is a technique that uses the correlations between observed variables (e.g., people's ratings of different emotion terms) to estimate common underlying themes or meanings; the factors. In the case of the study of emotion, the factors are interpreted as something like irreducible states. Factor analysis also reveals structural relationships linking factors to the observed variables. For example, it tells us whether a rating of a particular emotion term is strongly or weakly associated with the factor, and whether it is negatively or positively correlated with the factor. As will be seen, this technique can be applied to almost any scaled data related to emotion. For example, one can factor analyze ratings of other people's expressed emotions, not just ratings of one's emotional experience.

A second major statistical technique used to understand the basic structure of emotion is *multidimensional scaling* (MDS). MDS is used to detect meaningful underlying dimensions (which, in this case, are again interpreted as irreducible emotional states) that allow the researcher to explain similarities or dissimilarities (distances) between the objects or experiences under study. For example, in the study of emotion structure, MDS can be used to analyze perceived similarities between a number of different emotional states or, subtly different, the perceived similarities between the meanings of a number of different emotion words. In factor analysis, the similarities between objects – in this case, the emotional states – are expressed in the correlation matrix. Using MDS, any kind of similarity or dissimilarity matrix can be analyzed, in addition to correlation matrices.

Component Process Data

While the subjective experience of emotion is part of the total emotional experience, by component process data we mean the other facets that make up an emotion, such as its manifestations in expression, posture, voice and physiological responding. When we study such behaviors, one question we can ask involves the number of different fundamental manifestations that are observed. Again, as with the elements, we can ask how many distinguishable emotional tones of voice there are, or how many facial expressions there are. Do people perceive systematic differences between each of the negative facial expressions of emotions (e.g., fear, anger, and sadness), or do they actually just distinguish between negative and positive facial expressions?

Many different types of statistical procedure and analysis can be used to analyze data collected from the state of the component processes during different emotions. However, it is not as simple as it seems. Natural categories, categories of things that exist in the world, are fuzzy in nature. This means that their boundaries are not clear, and therefore that membership in the categories is a matter of degree rather than an all-or-none affair. How do we decide on the boundaries of irreducible states when there are no absolutes? By what criteria do we say that a certain number of facial expressions belong to their own category? As we shall see, some analyses of this question are more satisfying than others.

Basic (and Discrete) Emotions

In addition to the people like Thomas, who speak of "good" and "bad" emotions, and apparently feel either good or bad, there are also people, like, say, Dominique, who appear to experience states that possess greater subtlety (Barrett, 2004, calls this greater subtlety "high granularity"). People such as Dominique say that they are feeling *angry, sad, joyful, proud, interested*, and *loving*. This way of speaking seems to suggest that individuals, or perhaps just a subset of individuals, experience discrete, highly differentiated, emotional states. Perhaps, therefore, there exist a finite number of irreducible emotional states that correspond to the labels *angry, sad, joyful*, and so forth.

One account of this possibility posits a set of basic emotions. There are at least two specific ways that the idea of basic emotions has been used in the literature (e.g., Barrett, 2006; Ortony & Turner, 1990). One is that a small set of emotions, the basic emotions, are the fundamental elements of emotional life that can be combined to produce other, more complex emotions, in a way similar to colors. The second meaning of basic emotions insists on the idea that there are a small number of emotions that have a biological basis and that are encoded in the genes (e.g., Ekman, 1984; Izard, 1977; Johnson-Laird & Oatley, 1992; MacLean, 1993; Plutchik, 1984; Tooby & Cosmides, 1990). This latter meaning is the more widely used, and is strongly associated with the evolutionary theory of emotion. Of course, biological bases and genetic coding are not easily observable facts. Thus, different theorists have proposed different numbers of basic emotions, emphasizing to greater and lesser extent the different types of data relevant to this point that we discuss below. Still, as Oatley and Johnson-Laird (1996, p. 365) have aptly noted: "The precise number of basic emotions is less important than the hypothesis that each kind of emotion has specific functions and that mechanisms that evolved to serve these functions map diverse events into a small set of emotional modes." Furthermore, despite disagreement over the precise number of basic emotions, most basic emotion theorists do consistently include the five emotions of *joy, sadness, anger, disgust*, and *fear* among the basic emotions, and they sometimes add *surprise* (e.g., Ekman, 1984; Izard, 1977; Johnson-Laird & Oatley, 1992; Plutchik, 1980; Tomkins, 1962, 1963).

Although the notion of discrete emotions is appealing to some theorists, the notion of biologically basic emotions is not appealing to others (e.g., Ortony & Turner, 1990). Still, one can posit the existence of discrete, irreducible emotional states, without assuming that the states have an innate biological basis, with all that comes along with that claim. In this less nativist discrete emotions approach, emotional states are differentiated, defined, and labeled through experience, represented as schemas or organized units of information in memory, and bound by culture (e.g., Averill, 1980b; Harris, 1993; Lewis, 1993; Oatley & Johnson-Laird, 1996; Saarni, 1993). The states that result from these processes are discrete and irreducible. Many of the findings that are summarized below are consistent with both approaches to characterizing the structure of emotion in terms of discrete irreducible states, although we will try to distinguish between the data associated specifically with the basic emotions view, and those that support a discrete emotions view.

Experiential and Linguistic Data

Some support for the theory of irreducible discrete emotions comes from early factor analytic studies of self-report ratings of emotional experience (e.g., Borgatta, 1961; Izard, 1972; Nowlis, 1965). Such studies suggested that the structure of emotion could be characterized by between six and 12 (depending on the theorist) *independent monopolar factors* that were labeled as specific emotional states such as *anger*, *anxiety*, *sadness*, and *elation*. The fact that the revealed factors were *monopolar* means that emotional experience was apparently structured in terms of dimensions running from "no feeling" to "strong feelings" of the six to 12 discrete emotions. That is, the factors were not defined by so-called polar opposite emotions, such as *happy* and *sad* at either end, for instance (but see Plutchik, 1980). The *independence* of the factors means that there were no systematic relations between the discrete emotions. For example, it was not found that when someone was *sad*, they were most definitely or most definitely not *anxious*.

Some analyses of word meaning also provide support for the idea that there is a finite set of discrete, irreducible, emotional states. We have mentioned that social constructionists believe that language provides much information about actual emotional experience. Some theories of categorization and category structure would also make such a claim, although from a more nativist viewpoint. In an important paper on the structure of categories, Rosch and Mervis (1975) made the often cited claim that categories "cut nature at its joints." What that statement means is that people's categorical knowledge is not made up in their heads, but represents perception and experience that is grounded in the external world. Such a perspective suggests that studying the categorical structure of knowledge about emotion could provide important insights into the structure of experienced emotion in that it assumes that people represent emotions in a way that preserves a given (perhaps biological) reality.

Rosch primarily studied natural categories such as "birds," and artifactual categories such as "furniture." To summarize very simply, what she showed was that most categories, natural and artifactual alike, are organized *hierarchically*. Specifically, she proposed and found support for the idea that such hierarchies are composed of abstract *superordinate* categories, such as "furniture" at the top of the hierarchy, *basic*-level categories, such as "chairs" in the middle, and *subordinate* categories, such as "chaise longue" representing the most specific categories at the bottom of the hierarchy. Most important for the present treatment, Rosch and others viewed the basic-level categories as having a special status. Indeed, basic-level categories have been demonstrated to be labeled by single, short words that are learned early in language acquisition; they are the most abstract category associated with a single perceptual image; they are spontaneously used for naming a given object; and they provide the best tradeoff in terms of distinctiveness of features from closely related categories while still being rich in information (Mervis & Crisafi, 1982; Niedenthal & Cantor, 1984; Rosch, Mervis, Gray, Johnson, & Boyes-Braem, 1976). Basic-level categories might therefore be said to be representations of fundamental categories in the world, and that making finer distinctions, as represented in subordinate categories, is adding detail, but not new fundamental categories, to one's knowledge repertoire.

Several researchers have since tested the applicability of aspects of Rosch's theory of category structure in the domain of emotion knowledge in order to learn more about the structure of emotion categories (e.g., Fehr & Russell, 1984, Shaver, Schwartz, Kirson, & O'Connor, 1987, for studies of English words; Niedenthal, Auxiette, Nugier, Dalle, Bonin, & Fayol, 2004, for a study of French words; and Zammuner, 1998, for a study of Italian words). For instance, in Shaver and colleagues' (1987) work, experimental participants were supplied with 135 cards, each containing the English name of one emotion or affective state. The participants sorted the cards into piles that represented, for them, groups of words whose meanings went together, or were similar. The card sorts were analyzed with another statistical technique, termed *hierarchical cluster analysis*, that identifies clusters of variables (emotion words, in this case) and provides information about their hierarchical relations.

Figure 2.1 presents the findings of that study. The important point to take away is that there are three levels in the structure. The most abstract contains the categories of *negative* and *positive* emotions. Then there are what appear to be five or six basic categories. Shaver and colleagues label these *love, joy, anger, sadness*, and *fear*. Although they find a possible *surprise* category, they are not in favor of allocating it the status of a basic emotion

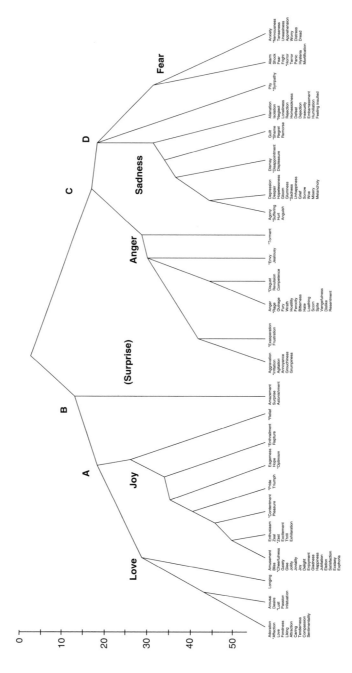

FIGURE 2.1. Results of hierarchical cluster analysis of the names of 135 emotions. From Shaver, P. et al. (1987). Emotion knowledge: Further exploration of a prototype approach. *Journal of Personality and Social Psychology, 52,* 1061–1086.

category. Finally, there are many subordinate categories that reflect fine gradations of the five or six basic categories. For example, as can be seen, the category *fear* can be further broken down into something like *horror/panic* and *nervousness/dread*. The authors note that the five basic categories revealed by the hierarchical cluster analysis are the same as those shown by Bretherton and Beeghly (1982) in their study of emotion terms learned in early childhood. In addition, these five basic categories correspond to the emotions most often proposed to be biologically basic ones in the various lists of basic emotions (e.g., Ekman, 1984). Therefore, they take their findings as support for a theory of discrete emotions. They believe, along with others, that the five or six basic-level categories have a specific status, as representing something like irreducible emotional states. Additional analyses of language also draw a similar conclusion (e.g., Conway & Bekerian, 1987; Johnson-Laird & Oatley, 1989).

Component Process Data

Emotional behaviors have also been studied in the search for evidence of irreducible emotional states. In what follows, we discuss evidence from studies of facial expression, the expression of emotion in the voice (emotional prosody), and physiological indicators of emotion, especially measures of autonomic nervous system functioning.

Facial Expression

The component of initial interest and debate in the study of emotion structure was that of facial expression of emotion. Darwin's theory, and its interpretation by other theorists since, most notably Ekman (1982), Izard, (1977) and Tomkins (1962, 1963), endorsed the idea that there exist a set of basic emotions for which there are innate neural programs that generate specific patterns of motor response. Support for this idea would be the discovery of a finite set of universally recognized and produced facial expressions of emotion (Figure 2.2). Although much such evidence exists, the conclusion of universality of facial expression based on the existing recognition studies is still widely debated. Furthermore, evidence of universality does not constitute the only data required for accepting the notion of innate motor programs.

Other research fails to provide consistent support for the idea that a full-blown, discrete motor program is automatically produced whenever one of the five facial expressions occurs (e.g., Carroll & Russell, 1997). Chapter 4 describes at length the debate concerning the universality of a small set of facial expression of emotion, so we will not do so here. The

FIGURE 2.2. Joy is one of the expressions considered to represent a basic emotion.

conclusion that will be drawn from that chapter can be revealed, however. It is that at this time the evidence falls in favor of the universality account.

Somewhat different evidence in favor of discrete emotions comes from research on the *categorical perception* of facial expression. Categorical perception is a phenomenon that was initially demonstrated in the domains of color perception and the perception of speech sounds. The experimental paradigm for demonstrating categorical perception is a psychophysical one in which *identification* (naming stimuli) and *discrimination* (distinguishing between stimuli) performance is compared for a set of objects. Evidence for categorical perception is obtained when two conditions hold. These conditions are, first, that an individual gives a set of stimuli ranging along a physical continuum, one name on one side of a category boundary and another name on the other side, and second, that the individual discriminates smaller physical differences between pairs of stimuli that straddle the boundary, and therefore come from two categories so defined, than between pairs of stimuli in which both stimuli fall within one category (i.e., one side of the boundaries or the other). Thus, in categorical perception, there is a quantitative discontinuity in discriminability at the category boundaries of a physical continuum (Harnad, 1987). The interpretation of evidence of categorical perception is that the categories revealed have a perceptual basicness.

In an initial test of categorical perception of facial expression, Etcoff and Magee (1992) constructed facial expression continua between pairs of drawings of faces that expressed different emotions (e.g., happy–sad) using

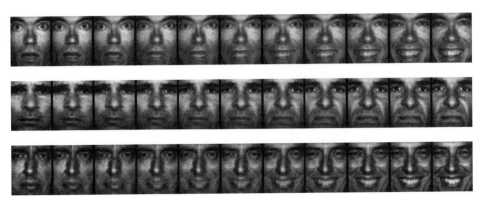

FIGURE 2.3. Face continua used to study categorical perception of facial expression. The first panel shows a surprise-to-happy continuum, the second a sad-to-disgust continuum, and the third a sad-to-happy continuum. From Padgett, C., & Cottrell, C. W. (1998). A simple neural network models categorical perception of facial expression. In *Proceedings of the Twentieth Annual Cognitive Science Conference*, Madison, WI. Mahwah, NJ: Lawrence Erlbaum Associates, Inc.

a computer technique for blending two (or more) images, called *morphing*. The procedure resulted in eight continua, each of which contained 11 faces of uniform physical difference. Identification and discrimination performance by experimental participants was obtained. Results revealed evidence for categorical perception of *happiness, sadness, fear, anger,* and *disgust*. And this effect, while still debated in terms of its existence and meaning, has been observed in other studies that used morphed photographs rather than drawings (e.g., Calder, Young, Perrett, Etcoff, & Rowland, 1996; de Gelder, Teunisse, & Benson, 1997; Young, Rowland, Calder, Etcoff, Seth, & Perrett, 1997). Using a similar technique, called *dissolving*, to produce the continua, Padgett and Cottrell (1998) reported a neural network model that produces largely the same results as humans observed in Young and colleagues' work (1997). These findings provide some evidence for the discrete categorical nature of facial expression of emotion (see Figure 2.3).

Vocal Affect

The physiological events that occur during an emotion, especially changes in the activity of the autonomic and somatic nervous systems, produce important changes in speech production. Some of these include changes in respiration, vocal fold vibration, and articulation (see Johnstone & Scherer, 2000, for a detailed discussion). One of the questions that have been asked, therefore, is whether there are patterns of vocal affect that correspond to discrete emotions.

There are two basic methodologies used to examine this question. One, very similar to the methodology used to study the recognition of facial expression of emotion, involves asking perceivers to recognize the emotion conveyed in voice samples. Such studies are often called studies of the *decoding* or perception of vocal affect. In one such study, Scherer, Banse, Wallbott, and Goldbeck (1991) recorded two male and two female actors speaking nonsense sentences that conveyed different emotions. Specifically, sentences that conveyed *joy, sadness, fear, anger,* and *disgust* were developed. The researchers then presented these vocal stimuli to naive participants, in four different judgment studies, and asked the participants to rate the extent to which the stimuli conveyed each of the five emotions. The mean recognition accuracy, averaged over the four studies, was about 56%. Note that this is much higher than would be expected by chance, that is, if the participants were just guessing. Other studies have observed similar levels of recognition accuracy for the same five emotions, averaging around 60% accuracy, in addition to other emotions such as love and surprise (e.g., Banse & Scherer, 1996; Van Bezooijen, 1984). Furthermore, there is some evidence for high cross-cultural recognition accuracy as we will discuss in Chapter 9 (e.g., Frick, 1985; Scherer et al., 1991).

A second methodology relies on statistical analysis of the physical properties of speech, or *acoustic parameters*. In analyzing vocal affect in terms of its acoustic parameters (including for example, fundamental frequency, intensity, and pitch), the researcher wants to know if there are specific patterns of parameters associated with specific emotions. Due to difficulties developing appropriate speech samples for specific emotions and the fact that researchers sometimes do not analyze multiple speech characteristics and multiple emotions in the same study, it is not yet clear whether vocal affect has physical properties unique to specific emotions. Some suggestive evidence along these lines has been reported by Scherer and colleagues (1991) and by Banse and Scherer (1996). Summary descriptions of the patterns of acoustic correlates of different emotions can be found in Johnstone and Scherer (2000).

Finally, some research supports the idea that there is evolutionary continuity of vocal emotion expression. For example, data from studies conducted by behavioral biologists suggest that there are significant similarities in the vocal expression and communication of emotional states across species: angry states are typically expressed by loud, harsh vocalizations while fear and anxiety are typically associated with high-pitched, shrill vocalizations. Scherer (1985) has suggested that some of these same similarities across species extend to human vocalizations as well.

Autonomic Nervous System Activity

William James, as well as a Danish contemporary named Lange, proposed the idea that there are distinctive patterns of autonomic arousal that correspond to discrete emotions. This *peripheralist* position was attacked for over a century, both by scientists who believed that arousal that was nonspecific and thus could not possibly differentiate discrete emotions, and by those who believed that the autonomic nervous system responds too slowly to support discrete emotional states. While still inconclusive, however, recent research suggests that some physiological parameters do differentiate some pairs of emotion (see Cacioppo, Klein, Berntson, & Hatfield, 1993 for an extensive review).

Levenson, Ekman, and Friesen (1990) conducted a study in which they induced emotions in participants with the use of a procedure that leads the individual to produce facial expressions. In the procedure, called the Directed Facial Action task, the experimenter directs the participant to contract certain muscles, without mentioning the facial expression that is formed by the full pattern of the contracted muscles. After establishing the facial expression, Levenson and colleagues measured, among other things, heart rate, finger temperature, skin conductance, and muscle activity. The results of these measures for the emotions presumably induced by the expressions of *anger, fear, sadness, disgust, happiness,* and *surprise* are depicted in Figure 2.4. As can be seen, different emotions were similar to each other and different from the remaining emotions on different indicators. For instance, *anger* showed larger finger temperature change than all the other emotions studied. By the same token, *anger, fear, sadness,* and *disgust* were all associated with greater change in skin conductance (more sweating, that is) than were *surprise* and *happiness.* One interpretation of the findings is that no single indicator of autonomic nervous system functioning distinguishes among all the emotions. Another way to see the data, however, is that they show that different emotions distinguish themselves on different indicators, and that we have not yet found the patterns that characterize each emotion. Of course, one problem with this study is that it relies on the idea that changes in facial expression are associated with emotional changes (Zajonc & McIntosh, 1997). Some of the participants in the study did indeed report subjective changes in emotional state, in the intended way, but others did not. While autonomic changes were more clear and distinctive for those participants who also said that they had experienced the intended emotion, it is not clear whether this methodology is appropriate to provide the best test of the differentiation of emotion by the autonomic nervous system. Furthermore, the effort required to contract the muscles may have had more to do with the pattern of autonomic nervous system changes than any experienced emotion (Boiten, 1996).

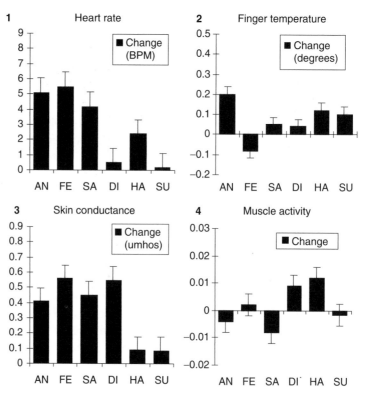

FIGURE 2.4. Heart rate (panel 1), finger temperature (panel 2), skin conductance (panel 3), and muscle activity (panel 4) and standard errors during six emotional configurations. AN = anger, FE = fear, SA = sadness, DI = disgust, HA = happiness, SU = surprise. From Levenson, R. W. et al. (1990). Voluntary facial action generates emotion-specific autonomic nervous system activity. *Psychophysiology, 27*(4), 363–384.

In a comprehensive study of anger and fear, Stemmler and colleagues (Stemmler, Heldmann, Pauls, & Scherer, 2001) induced emotion-arousing experiences in the laboratory with procedures that bear some superficial relations to the more violent study conducted by Ax (1953), which was described in Chapter 1. The results of the study showed that in addition to increases in heart rate, as noted in the Levenson study as well, fear is also characterized by contractility of the heart musculature and respiration rate, while anger is characterized by a rise in diastolic blood pressure and in peripheral resistance. Emotion-specific differences in autonomic nervous system functioning are predicted by evolutionary theories of emotion, which hold, as we have noted, that emotions serve to coordinate bodily processes for the production of adaptive action. Indeed, the pattern of autonomic nervous system functioning during fear that was shown by Stemmler and colleagues is appropriate for producing a flight response, whereas the activity that characterized anger is consistent with the mobilization of a fight response (Stemmler et al., 2001).

So are there Basic or Discrete Emotions?

If you have been worrying about the lack of consensus in the number of discrete or basic emotions identified by the theory and research in the previous sections, as well as in the inconsistencies in the actual research findings, you are not alone. The research related to the debate concerning the existence of discrete or basic emotions that we presented in the previous sections was characterized in a "glass half full" sort of way (see Johnson-Laird & Oatley, 1992, for further discussion). That is, one might go away from the summary feeling as if the structure of emotion corresponds to the discrete emotions view, and that perhaps there is even a set of biologically basic emotions. But all the findings just described could also be seen as flawed in their ability to support such a view because they are just not consistent or conclusive enough to support such a strong conclusion (see Ekman & Davidson, 1994, for different views on this issue). What is another possible answer to the question of the structure of emotional experience?

Dimensional Accounts of the Structure of Emotion

Some emotions theorists have read the lack of coherence in the literature on discrete emotions to mean that the account is indeed flawed, on both empirical and, more importantly, conceptual, grounds. They see the evidential glass as "half empty" and have therefore proposed a different answer to the question of the structure of emotion. In this alternative approach to modeling the structure of emotion, the variability that seems to be reflected by the discrete emotions is held to be reducible to a smaller number of underlying dimensions.

Researchers who take this view usually endorse a two-dimensional structure of experienced emotion (e.g., Barrett & Russell, 1999; Feldman Barrett, 1995a, 1995b; Lang, Bradley, & Cuthbert, 1990; Larsen & Diener, 1992; Mayer & Gaschke, 1988; Reisenzein, 1994; Russell, 1980, 1989; Schlosberg, 1952; Watson & Tellegen, 1985). The two dimensions, with some differences in how they are believed to be related to each other, correspond to the degree to which a state is *pleasant* versus *unpleasant* and the degree to which a state is experienced as *activated* versus *deactivated*. As Russell and Feldman Barrett (1999) have pointed out, to express the same idea as pleasant versus unpleasant, some researchers have used the labels *good–bad, pleasure–pain, approach–avoidance, rewarding–punishing,* or *positive–negative*. But all such terms more or less refer to "how well one is doing" at the level of subjective experience (Russell & Feldman Barrett, 1999). In addition, labels other than *activation* have been used, such as *arousal, tension, activity,* but such labels all refer to the level of experienced energy or mobilization of the state.

The evidence in favor of a two-dimensional structure for experienced emotion is interpreted as meaning that states we call happy and sad and angry can be reduced to the psychological, and perhaps biological, dimensions of pleasantness and activation, and that any given emotion can be described as a blend of pleasure and activation. For example, many states that we call *anger* could be characterized as highly unpleasant and moderately activated. And many states of fear could be described as moderately unpleasant and highly activated (e.g., Russell & Feldman Barrett, 1999).

Most of the data used to develop and test dimensional accounts of the structure of emotion are experiential and linguistic in nature. Specifically, many studies published in the years since the publication of the studies that reported that emotional experience could be described by six to 12 monopolar factors (and even some reported before, such as Osgood & Suci, 1955, and Schlosberg, 1952) reveal a two-dimensional structure. Both factor analytic and multidimensional scaling studies tend to demonstrate that self-reported emotional states and ratings of the meanings of emotion words conform to this structure. Russell (1980) has proposed that the initial findings of some number of monopolar dimensions was due to the response formats that were used in the research; that is, he suggested that theory-guided response formats produced theoretically expected results, namely, of a small set of factors corresponding to expected discrete emotions such as *sadness, elation,* and so forth.

Even though researchers have repeatedly found a two-dimensional structure, they do not necessarily interpret the relationships between the dimensions or even the meaning of the dimensions in precisely the same way. Figure 2.5 depicts the ways in which three different theorists have described the meaning of the two dimensions. As can be seen, although the terms used are slightly different, Larsen and Diener (1992) and Russell (1980; Russell & Feldman Barrett, 1999) both consider the two structural dimensions of emotion to be something like pleasantness and activation. The differences between them are relevant to a later discussion.

Contrariwise, although Watson and Tellegen (1985) also find a two-dimensional structure, these researchers have argued that a rotation of the

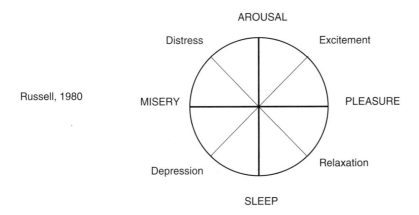

Russell, 1980

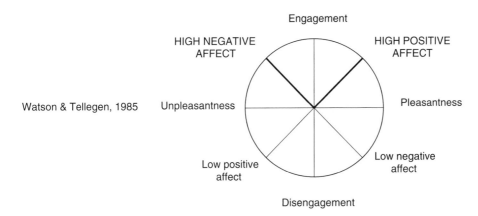

Watson & Tellegen, 1985

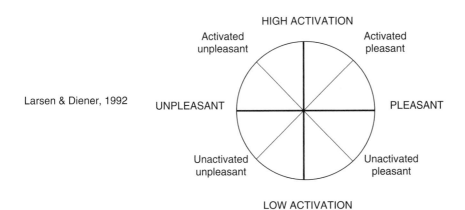

Larsen & Diener, 1992

FIGURE 2.5. Three descriptive models of experienced affect. From Russell, J. A., & Feldman Barrett, L. (1999). Core affect, prototypical emotional episodes, and other things called emotion: Dissecting the elephant. *Journal of Personality and Social Psychology, 76*(5), 805–819.

axis of the observed factors by 45° provides the most appropriate characterization of it. That is, while two dimensions, pleasantness and what they call *engagement* versus *disengagement* (which can be considered a reinterpretation of the activation dimension) emerge from their data, they hold that the dimensions of theoretical interest lie 45° between those axes, and should be labeled *negative activation* (NA; high to low) and *positive activation* (PA; high to low; formerly called positive and negative affect; see Feldman Barrett & Russell, 1998; Watson, Wiese, Vaidya, & Tellegen, 1999). The idea is that when the individual is engaged in an experience and feels quite unpleasant and highly activated, this constitutes an irreducible state called negative activation. When the individual is engaged in an experience and feels quite pleasant, this is an irreducible state called positive activation. This particular model of the dimensional structure of affect motivated the development, by Watson, Clark, and Tellegen (1988), of a widely used scale to measure affective state called the Positive and Negative Affect Scale (the PANAS), and a more recent model by Cacioppo and colleagues (e.g., Cacioppo, Gardner, & Berntson, 1999) proposes similar ideas.

In support of the model, Watson, Tellegen and colleagues make a couple of important points. First, they note that most of the terms that individuals use to actually label their emotional states cluster in these parts of the dimensional space (that is, corresponding to the 45° rotation), so that characterizing emotion structure with a focus on these parts of the space is important. Further, they are most interested in the *high* NA and *high* PA, in part because they do not believe that words such as *sleepy* that anchor the low affect ends of the dimensions necessarily refer to actual emotional states.

Bipolarity and Independence

When describing the six to 12 monopolar factors that some earlier theorists thought represented the structure of emotion, we referred to the problem of *mono* versus *bipolarity* of the factors and the issue of factor *independence*. These are concepts that refer to structural issues that continue to plague the discussion about the structure of emotional experience, and we will mention them in more detail here.

First, bipolarity refers to the conceptualization of the end points of the dimension or factor that describes part of the experience of emotion. When one determines that, for example, a set of emotion ratings can be accounted for by two dimensions or two factors, one must then decide, based on the actual data and the ways in which each word or state is related to the dimensions, how to conceptualize and then name the dimensions and their endpoints. In Figure 2.5, we saw that Russell (1980), for example, labeled the dimensions he highlights in his account of the structure of emotion in a way that reflects a belief in bipolarity (see also Russell & Feldman Barrett, 1999). Specifically, he, like Larsen and Diener (1992), labels the horizontal dimension *pleasant* on one end and *unpleasant* on the other. This decision is not random, but implies that he believes that negative and positive feelings are related such that the presence of one implies the absence of the other. In this view, one cannot truly feel negative and positive feelings at the same time (which does not mean that one cannot *vacillate* between them).

Looking now at the model associated with Watson and Tellegen (1985), in the same figure, one can see that not all people agree on this point. In the Watson and Tellegen model, the two rotated dimensions, as we have seen, are labeled NA (high to low) and PA (high to low). This means that these researchers believe that pleasantness and unpleasantness are not bipolar, but that they correspond to two monopolar factors, meaning that one can be in a more or less positive state, and one can be in a more or less negative state at any given time. Similarly, Larsen and Diener (1992) appear to see the activation dimension as monopolar, meaning that there is activation or not of the state. Russell, in contrast, clearly views that dimension as bipolar, such that activation and deactivation are opposite qualities of a given emotional state.

Related to the issue of bipolarity is the question of independence of factors or dimensions. This is a question of whether one aspect of emotion structure has an inevitable influence on or relation to the other. In the Watson and Tellegen (1985) model, for instance, negative and positive affect are represented as independent monopolar factors (for a related view, see McCrae & Costa, 1991 and a corresponding mechanistic account by Cacioppo et al., 1999). The idea is that not only are the two types of affect not polar opposites, but they also do not affect each other in a systematic way. A particular emotional state can be characterized by more or less PA *and* more or less NA. Those theorists who hold on to the idea that positive and negative feelings are bipolar opposites now point to recent findings that suggest that evidence inconsistent with bipolarity is due to problems of measurement and the statistical handling of measurement error (e.g., Green, Goldman, & Salovey, 1993).

In an attempt to reconcile the existing data and discussion, Feldman Barrett and Russell (1998) have proposed that arguments in favor of monopolar, independent factors corresponding to positive and negative affect in part lie in an inattention to the activation dimension of emotion structure. Indeed, you might have noticed that the theoretical discussion of bipolarity has focused largely on the pleasantness dimension. In their

Positive OR Negative affect   Positive AND Negative affect

analysis, Feldman Barrett and Russell (1998) argue that there are two independent bipolar dimensions that define the structure of emotion. Those dimensions are our old friends, pleasantness and activation. They propose further that both factors are bipolar, *and* are independent from each other, meaning that changes in activation do not have a systematic effect on the pleasantness of a state, and vice versa.

Simple Structure or Circumplex?

Another debate among those who promote dimensional models of emotional experience concerns whether states cluster in the regions defined by the two-dimensional space or whether they show a different relation to the dimensions. For a number of empirical reasons, some theorists argue that a simple structure best characterizes the data from self-reports of emotional experience (e.g., Morris, 1989; Zevon & Tellegen, 1982). A structure is said to be simple when every variable correlates with only one of the factors that characterize the observed structure. If there are two independent dimensions, then the structure is called simple when the emotion terms tend to cluster in groups that are about 90° apart, for instance, along the axes themselves. If we accept the idea that the two dimensions are pleasantness and activation, then one simple structure would be one in which emotions tended to cluster into groups called pleasant/activated, unpleasant/activated, pleasant/deactivated, and unpleasant/deactivated.

On another view, the structure is best described as a *circumplex* (e.g., Barrett, 2004; Larsen & Diener, 1992; Russell, 1980, 1989; Watson & Tellegen,

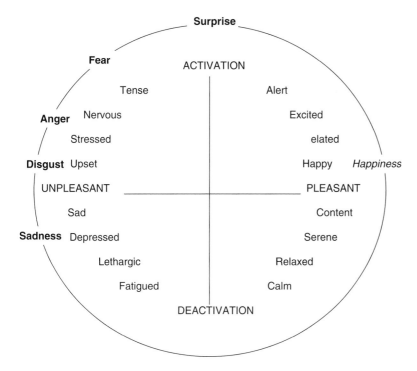

FIGURE 2.6. The inner circle shows a schematic map of core affect. The outer circle shows where several prototypical emotional episodes typically fall. Modified from Feldman Barrett, L., & Russell, J. A. (1998). Independence and bipolarity in the structure of current affect. *Journal of Personality and Social Psychology, 74,* 967–994. © 1998 by the American Psychological Association.

1985). When variables (such as ratings of emotion terms) intercorrelate such that their relations can be best represented by a circle, they are said to form a circumplex. The mathematical requirement for confirming that a set of variables form a circumplex is that the variables are equidistant from the center of the circle, but clear statistical tests of this are not always easy to interpret (although see Russell & Feldman Barrett, 1999, for some useful clarifications). Figure 2.6 shows an idealization of the circumplex and some of the emotion states that define its perimeter. Figure 2.7 shows the original circumplex reported by Russell (1980). Although both figures demonstrate the idea of a circumplex, the idea that this best characterizes the structure of affect is not always accepted, and even those who have proposed circumplex structures, indeed those just cited here, are not in agreement about the ways in which emotional states are related or where they appear on the circumplex. This is important because such decisions strongly affect the way in which emotional states are conceptualized and measured (see Watson et al., 1999).

One critic of the circumplex model, Scherer (e.g., 1984b), argues that the circle structure is strongly dependent on the emotion items that are used in

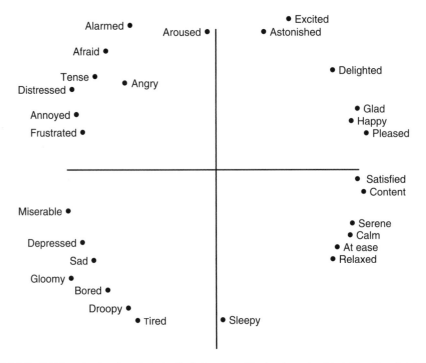

FIGURE 2.7. Multidimensional scaling solution for 28 affect words resulting in a circumplex. Adapted from Russell, J. A. (1980). A circumplex model of affect. *Journal of Personality and Social Psychology, 39,* 1161–1178.

the measurement of emotional state, and that when different or more extensive samples of states are used, a circumplex is not revealed (cf. Russell & Feldman Barrett, 1999). Furthermore, it has been objected that a circumplex is only observed when many states that are affective but arguably not emotions are used in the analysis. The terms that are most often objected to are states of low activation, such as *sleepy* and *tired.* Are those emotional states to be used in assessing the structure of emotion? Unfortunately, a clear answer is not yet forthcoming. It depends on how you define "emotion."

So does the Structure of Emotion Correspond to Two Dimensions?

As with the thinking and the data that favor a discrete or basic emotions characterization of the structure of emotional experience, the thinking and the data in favor of a dimensional account are both compelling and problematic at the same time. One criticism of this model is its very heavy reliance on self-report data. In applying consciousness and then verbal labels to their experience, individuals may inherently alter it. Another criticism is that adherents to this approach are modeling something other than the structure of emotion. Perhaps they are modeling the structure of evaluative judgment, the representation of attitudes, or perhaps the nature of something more basic than emotions, something that Russell and Feldman Barrett (1999) have called "core affect."

Core affect is defined as a neurophysiological state that is "the most elementary consciously accessible affective feelings" (Russell & Feldman Barrett, 1999). Even if dimensional models do, in fact, characterize core affect, however, this does not mean that core affect is not the basic, irreducible structure of emotional states. Russell and Feldman Barrett (1999) argue that core affect is indeed the basic stuff from which more elaborated (and perhaps more rare) "prototypic emotional episodes" are constructed. But it could also be that something like core affect has a structure that is dimensional in nature, and that there are emotions that conform to a discrete or basic emotion structure. In the final analysis, the relationship between the two characterizations of the structure of emotion – basic emotions versus dimension structures – will be the topic of continuing scientific research.

Functional Accounts of Emotion

The various accounts of the structure of emotion just discussed are concerned with what emotions are; how they should be carved up and labeled. This concern, as we have seen, leads to frustrations over the translation of emotion words from one language to another, debates over the biological basicness and universality of different emotions, and discussions of the pros and contras of self-report data. We compared the study of emotion structure to the search for basic elements in chemistry. A similar goal characterizes the activities of some neuroscientists. Neuroscientists who take a structural approach to the study of the brain often identify a behavior of interest, which may vary from the behavior of the senses such as vision or audition to more complex behaviors such as aggression, and then try to specify the brain regions or circuits that subserve the behavior. Other neuroscientists take a functional approach to the study of the brain. A function account of the brain changes the focus of research from the linking of structure and behavior to a concern with the history and environment surrounding the development of the brain systems, and with the beneficial consequences that they have for the organism. The guiding idea is that the structure of the brain is what it is because of its functional consequences. A functional approach to the study of emotion has the same grounding and set of objectives (Keltner & Gross, 1999).

As we noted in Chapter 1, it was not always the case that psychologists and philosophers considered emotions functional, in the sense of adaptive and beneficial to the organism. In fact, Keltner and Gross (1999) propose that there have been three major views on the adaptive functionality of emotions. The first, already discussed, is the view that emotions have no adaptive function at all. This view, advanced by the Stoics, and revisited in the Enlightenment period of 18th-century Europe, asserted that emotions disrupt reason and therefore should be controlled, suppressed, or otherwise done away with (Solomon, 1993).

A second perspective, probably associated most closely with Darwin (1872/1998), was that emotions once served important functions, but that these functions involved solutions to environmental challenges encountered in the distant past that are no longer encountered in the present. Darwin thus thought, for instance, that facial expressions were vestiges of the past. Once functional, but no longer so. Freud (1930/1961) advanced a similar view of emotions, not merely emotional expression, and worried that modern society made demands on human emotions that were not consistent with the demands posed in the distant past. He suggested that this inconsistency, and the stress it involved, was a fundamental cause of neuroses.

The final, functionalist perspective can be said to characterize most current thinking in the study of emotion (e.g., Barrett & Campos, 1987; Cosmides & Tooby, 2000; Johnson-Laird & Oatley, 1992; Keltner & Haidt, 1999, 2001; Plutchik, 1980). A functionalist view of emotion, similar to the view of functional neuroscientists regarding the brain in general, is that emotions serve more or less the same functions that they served in the past and that their current structure was shaped by encounters with a small number of problems posed repeatedly by the environment, broadly defined. The goal of the functionalist approach to the study of emotion, then, is to try to identify the problems of adaptation as they once were and as they present themselves in modern society, and to determine the types of response that constitute solutions to those problems. Those types of responses can then be called types of emotion. Or they can even be described as responses, such as approach and avoidance that are susceptible to description by one or two dimensions.

As we shall see, it is not necessary to take an evolutionary perspective on emotions to believe that they are functional and constitute solutions to environmentally imposed challenges. Many appraisal theorists and social constructionists also view emotions as functional problem-solving phenomena, with the latter also holding that emotions are necessary for the perpetuation of the society and its values and institutions. However, these approaches do not necessarily endorse the idea that the emotions are encoded in the genes; discrete emotions and their specific manifestations, by these accounts, are transmitted from one generation to another largely by social learning.

The various general theories do, however, focus on functionality that can be characterized at different levels of analysis, running from the benefits for the individual through benefits for society as a whole (Keltner & Haidt, 1999, 2001). Here we will discuss functional analyses at three levels: those of the individual, the dyad, and the group. We suggest that taking a look at different levels of analysis leads us to posit an *adjustment* function, a *communication* function, and a *social coordination* function at the three levels, respectively. We note at the outset, of course, that the functions that emotions serve at these levels of analysis do not extend to pathological states of emotion, such as clinical depression or phobias. In this discussion, we remain faithful to our initial definition of emotion, as "episodic, relatively short-term, biologically-based patterns of perception, experience, physiology, action, and communication that occur in response to specific physical and social challenges and opportunities" (Keltner & Gross, 1999).

Function of Emotions for the Individual

A concern with the intra-individual functions of emotion is a concern with the benefits of the organismic changes that occur during emotions for the individual him or herself. A general principle is that while a feeling may be subjectively unpleasant, or while certain attendant endocrine or autonomic responses may be costly to the body, on average there is a largely beneficial adjustment function that emotions serve, for most people, most of the time.

Researchers who represent this concern have investigated the physiological changes that occur during emotion-eliciting events, and have argued that such changes provide bodily support for taking appropriate action, such as flight in fear and attack in anger (e.g., Levenson, 1992; Stemmler et al., 2001). Others have examined the nature of cognitive processes such as attention (e.g., Mathews & MacLeod, 1994), perception (e.g., Schupp, Cuthbert, Bradley, Hillman, Hamm, & Lang, 2004), categorization (Niedenthal et al., 1999), judgment (e.g., Lerner & Keltner, 2000), reasoning (Bless, Clore, Schwarz, Golisano, Rabe, & Wölk, 1996b) and decision making (e.g., Damasio, 1994) during emotional states, and have made a case for the adaptive value of each of these for the general adjustment of the individual. For example, it appears that emotions regulate the use of attention in such a way as to maximize responding in the immediate situation (e.g., Derryberry & Tucker, 1994). Rather than characterizing the potential function of each of these organismic changes, however, here we describe two general theories of the intra-individual functions of emotion.

One such integrative theory is Tooby and Cosmides' evolutionary theory of emotion (e.g., Tooby & Cosmides, 1990). As a rule, evolutionary models depict the mind as a set of information processing programs, or *modules*, like a computer that is specialized to solve different adaptive problems, and physically instantiated in the neural circuitry of the brain. For example, by this account, there are programs that are relied on to solve the problems of face recognition, heart rate regulation, meeting sleep requirements, and the detection of predators. Each program is triggered by distinct environmental cues. A fascinating problem with this modular view of mind is that such an architecture should possess the weakness of being very dysfunctional when two or more highly incompatible programs are simultaneously activated. For instance, what would happen if one desperately needed sleep and at the same time also detected the presence of a predator? Needing to meet a sleep requirement and needing to deal with a predator at the same time would cause the organism's systems to function in completely incompatible or incoherent ways. Just like a pinball machine, the body would say "tilt" and shut down. Apparently, individuals do not shut down, so then we can ask, which specialized mental program would win out in this situation and why?

Cosmides and Tooby (2000; Tooby & Cosmides, 1990) nominate emotions as the solution to this fundamental problem of coordinating the brain's different functional programs. They define emotions as superordinate mental programs that "orchestrate" and prioritize the functioning of the entire set of mental programs when critical events arise. Thus "each emotion entrains various other adaptive programs – deactivating some, activating others, and adjusting the modifiable parameters of still others – so that the whole system operates in a particularly harmonious and efficacious way when the individual is confronting certain kinds of triggering conditions or situations" (Cosmides & Tooby, 2000). Those critical situations, of course, are situations related to the challenges to and opportunities for reproduction, such as losing one's mate or being attacked by a predator.

The first step in this functional argument is, thus, the assertion that emotions orchestrate and prioritize mental programs. Of course, this orchestration itself then has to be shown to be functional, meaning that somehow the right or most useful program wins out in directing behavior in any given situation. For instance, needing sleep has to be put aside for a while if one is about to be eaten by a predator. The second step, therefore, involves assessing the functionality of the total mental state that characterizes each emotion for adjusting to the situation that triggered it. Cosmidis and Tooby (2000) provide a careful analysis of fear, showing how that state causes changes in the whole system that support the avoidance of danger. Such an analysis will eventually have to be applied to each emotion. Thus for instance, we might now ask why, during an angry state, do individuals rely more or stereotyping (Bodenhausen, Sheppard, & Kramer, 1994b), tend to be optimistic in their judgments (Lerner & Keltner, 2000), generate blame cognitions (Quigley & Tedeschi, 1996), and experience a rise in diastolic blood pressure (Stemmler et al., 2001)? What function does this package of systemic changes serve for the individual?

Another integrative theory, Oatley and Johnson-Laird's (1987) cognitive theory of emotion, shares some ideas with the evolutionary approach just described. For example, Oatley and Johnson-Laird (1987) also believe that emotions are adaptations to environmental challenges and opportunities posed repeatedly over the course of evolution, and that the emotions serve the primary function of coordinating a modular mental architecture. However, these theorists present a different view of how this works, and try to define the function of each emotion somewhat more precisely. In their view, strongly inspired by earlier ideas of Mandler (1975) and Simon (1967), emotions come about when individuals judge, consciously or unconsciously, that progress on their current goals is threatened or otherwise requires some adjustment. That is, specific emotions occur when progress on specific types of goal – which happen to be universal and highly repetitive – is *interrupted*. In Oatley and Johnson-Laird's view, the emotion then reorganizes and redirects the individual's activity in the service of a new goal or at least in such a way as to deal with what has just occurred.

Table 2.1 presents what Oatley and Johnson-Laird propose, based on both empirical and theoretical considerations, to be the five basic emotions. Also listed are the nature of the interrupt of the current goal/activity that triggers each emotion, and the way in which the emotion causes a transition to a subsequent state. One can see that, from this view, if an individual experiences a failure of an important plan or a loss of an active goal, this will activate the experience of sadness. Sadness is then associated with the tendency to stay still or withdraw (which has the important benefit of soliciting caretaking) or else a search for a new plan (which has the benefit of alleviating the sadness). As mentioned in Chapter 1, Oatley and his colleagues (e.g., Oatley & Duncan, 1992, 1994) have found some support for these ideas using diary study methodology. Thus, these authors argue that emotions are functional in that they provide an intra-individual evaluation of ongoing goal-directed activity, and then guide behavior in a way so as to respond to the meaning of that signal. Oatley and Johnson-Laird (1987) are comfortable with describing five types of signal and adaptive response, what they consider to be the five basic emotions; however, they are open to the discovery of more such emotions.

As far as the present authors know, no researcher has yet constructed a computational model that implements the ideas of Cosmides and Tooby

TABLE 2.1
Five Basic Emotions Together with Their Elicitors, or the Junctures at which They Occur, and the Transitions They Accomplish

Emotion	Juncture of current plan	State at which transition occurs
Happiness	Subgoals being achieved	Continue with plan, modifying as necessary
Sadness	Failure of major plan or loss of active goal	Do nothing/search for new plan
Anxiety	Self-preservation goal threatened	Stop, attend vigilantly to environment and/or escape
Anger	Active plan frustrated	Try harder, and/or aggress
Disgust	Gustatory goal violated	Reject substance and/or withdraw

From Oatley, K., & Johnson-Laird, P. N. (1987). Towards a cognitive theory of emotions. *Cognition and Emotion, 1,* 29–50.

(2000) or Oatley and Johnson-Laird (1987). Recent advances in computational neuroscience have made significant progress on somewhat simpler models of emotion, however (e.g., Sander & Koenig, 2002).

Function of Emotions for the Dyad

If the function of emotion for the individual is to motivate adaptive action, and to facilitate adjustment to environmental demands, then very often we need to know what other individuals are feeling, especially other people who we care about and trust. If we know their emotions, we can understand what they are doing and why, as well as what we should be doing in the same situation (Buck, 1983, 1988). Indeed, an emotion experienced and expressed by an individual can be communicated to another, even if the other has not experienced the event that gave rise to the emotion in the first place. Emotional communication of this nature relies, in part, on the hardwired emotional response to the sight of a facial expression of emotion (among other gestures). This strong linkage was demonstrated in studies by Dimberg (1982, 1988) who showed that even very short, 8-millisecond presentations of pictures of faces of angry and happy faces elicited in perceivers facial muscular responses that corresponded to the perceived expressions. For example, *zygomaticus major* activity – which occurs when individuals smile – was higher when participants viewed a happy, compared to an angry, face. In addition, *corrugator supercilii* activity – which occurs when individuals frown – was elevated when participants viewed an angry face, and it decreased when participants viewed a happy face.

Developmentally, one of the first types of emotional communication and transmission occurs between infants and their caretakers. Although there are hardwired emotional responses to particular challenges and opportunities in the environment, such as those to facial expressions as just noted, it is also the case that caretakers can and must teach infants to have specific emotional reactions to (initially) ambiguous objects and events in order to generate in them appropriate adaptive behavior. Electric outlets are an example of an ambiguous stimulus in the sense that they are such a recent technological development in evolutionary history that there is no reason to believe that humans would be hardwired to be fearful of them. And yet, caretakers need to communicate to babies that outlets are dangerous. By expressing strong and sudden fear when a baby approaches an outlet, a caretaker can elicit similar fear in the baby, which will result in the appropriate avoidance behavior of other outlets in the future (Mineka & Cook, 1993). (Of course, this means that caretakers can also transmit inappropriate fears and phobias as well!) Because babies are not yet able to understand the complex idea that "outlets are potentially dangerous because they can deliver electrical shocks," learning through this kind of communication is thus vital and functional. Indeed, infants who cannot learn through emotional communication are at risk (Field, 1982).

Emotional communication between caretakers and infants has been termed *affective contagion* (Hoffman, 1977), *affective attunement* (Stern, 1985), and *emotional resonance* (Campos & Stenberg, 1981). The influence of emotional communication from a caretaker on infants' behavior was demonstrated in a study by Klinnert (1984). In the study, 12- and 18-month-old infants were confronted with an unfamiliar toy. When the toy was presented, the infant's mother expressed either joy or fear, or else she maintained a neutral expression. Compared to the neutral condition, when the mother expressed fear about the toy, her infant moved toward her (for comfort), and when she expressed joy, the infant felt confident enough to move away (to explore or otherwise go on with life). Subsequent research has shown that infants can learn emotional responses to objects and events from other familiar individuals as well. In a relevant study by Klinnert, Emde, Butterfield, and Campos (1986), infants were again confronted with an unfamiliar toy. This time, however, the joy or fear expression was displayed by a familiar experimenter, while the infant's mother sat nearby and conveyed no emotion. Results showed that 83% of the infants noted the experimenter's emotional communication. The infants' subsequent actions and expressive behavior toward the toy were influenced by the emotion expressed by the experimenter, as well. Those infants who had received a fear communication of the toy were wary of it, while those who had received a happy communication were more interested in it.

A second type of emotional communication involves a more complex exchange and a slightly different kind of outcome. In emotional attunement or resonance the infant experiences the same emotion as that expressed by a caretaker or the sender of the emotion. In that case, there is a one-to-one matching of the emotion in the service of teaching the infant an appropriate response to an initially ambiguous eliciting circumstance, or category of circumstances. But emotions also communicate information about the expresser's perception of current situations as well as his or her behavioral intentions (Fridlund, 1991; Hess, Banse, & Kappas, 1995). And this may have the aim of eliciting a completely different emotion in the perceiver.

For example, over emotional and cognitive development, a child learns about the meaning of an anger expression, particularly when it comes from a parent or other superior. When a parent expresses anger the child may experience fear, for instance. The fear indicates that the child knows that anger signals that she has committed a violation of certain social or familial standards, and that punishment may be delivered (Averill, 1982). Similarly, when the parent expresses disappointment or sadness, the child may experience guilt or shame, perhaps through processes of empathy with the parent (Hoffman, 1983, 1984). The generation of this different, sometimes called "complementary," emotion by the communication of a specific emotion is intended to cause behavioral changes in the child such that when he or she encounters a similar situation in the future, the initial behavior is not reproduced (Harris, 1989). This kind of communication of standard violation, or other disappointment or dissatisfaction, and the emotions it produces in the perceiver, continue throughout the lifespan, of course.

Finally, emotions communicate important information about the nature of, or the potential of, any interpersonal relationship (Frijda & Mesquita, 1994; Keltner & Haidt, 1999, 2001). Imagine that, with no emotion at all, you told another person that you found them attractive and would like to have an intimate relationship with them. This is how a robot might express love. Such a cold communication would bring about none of the hormonal and motivational effects that displays of love and desire actually cause in animals and humans in nature (Eibl-Eibesfeldt, 1989). Posture, facial expressions, and vocal patterns do a very efficient job of conveying love and sexual interest, and appear to be readily triggered by cues related to positive mate potential such as beauty, youth, and signs of physical health (Buss, 1989; Buss & Barnes, 1986). For example, smiles communicate positive emotion, and people who smile are perceived as happy and open to a relationship (e.g. Deutsch, LeBaron, & Fryer, 1987). Further, the frequency of smiling by an individual affects his or her perceived warmth and attractiveness (Mueser, Grau, Sussman, & Rosen, 1984).

Other communications of emotion define the power relationship between two individuals. Cross-culturally, humans perceive individuals with lowered, furrowed brows as dominant, and those with raised brows as submissive (Keating et al., 1981; Senior, Phillips, Barnes, & David, 1999). Since such facial signals constitute components of the facial expressions of anger and fear, respectively (Ekman & Friesen, 1978), this suggests that individuals with power or status generally seem to express more anger in interpersonal interactions, and submissive individuals seem to express more fear and surprise. The communication of these different emotions both signals and maintains the power differential in the relationship. Miller (1997) also describes the way in which the emotion of contempt was traditionally used to mark and maintain differential power relationships. Those of higher rank or prestige expressed contempt to subordinates in part in order to communicate an indifference or lack of necessity to generate the energy to express anger.

Frijda and Mesquita (1994) further discuss shyness as an emotion that, communicated through the signal of blushing, constitutes an acknowledgment of the superiority of another person. Shyness on the part of women in dyadic interaction with men has been deemed appropriate, even desirable, in western countries, because it indicates that the woman acknowledges the superiority of the man. Interestingly, shyness is viewed as a positive social emotion in societies that value status distinctions, and is viewed more negatively in those societies in which status distinctions are not valued (Shweder, 1994).

In sum, through processes of direct imitation and through processes of empathy, individuals generate in other individuals both similar and complementary emotions in the service of a number of specific interpersonal aims. Emotions communicate appropriate emotions and behavioral responses in infants, they signal information about the relationship between standards and behavior, and they communicate much about the nature of intentions and motivations within a dyad (Buck, 1988).

Function of Emotions for the Group

There has been less research devoted to the study of the function of emotions for the group, but a number of findings have been brought together to suggest that emotions are vital for social coordination at the group level. And they do so in a number of different ways (Frijda & Mesquita, 1994; Haidt, 2003; Keltner & Haidt, 1999, 2001).

One of those ways appears to be the creation of bonds that help members define the boundaries of their group and remain loyal to it (or else, choose to leave it; Haidt, 2003). When strong joy is generated at the

(a)

(b)

(c)

FIGURE 2.8. These individuals are swimming across the Strait of Messina between Italy and Sicily (a). After the swim, their joy at the accomplishment, and their cohesion after the swim is shown in their facial expressions (b) and in their common tee shirt (c).

conclusion of a sporting event, for example, the fans of the winning team as well as the team members themselves feel particularly cohesive. Furthermore, they may at least temporarily show explicit signs of their group membership, by wearing particular clothing or other insignias for a period of time after the event (Cialdini, Borden, Thorne, Walker, Freeman, & Sloan, 1976). Figure 2.8 shows just this phenomenon. The first photograph shows a group of people who all took on the challenge of swimming across the Strait of Messina, which links Italy to Sicily, and which has notoriously strong and dangerous currents. After their successful swim, the individuals, shown in the second photograph, gather together to document their mutual success and the joy that results. Later, one of the swimmers, depicted in the last photograph, wears a tee shirt that says on the front "Stretti nello Stretto 2004" ("Together in the Strait 2004"), and on the back "Traghetti? Che sono? Lo Stretto di Messina a Nuoto. 8 Agosto 2004" ("Ferries? What are ferries? Swim the Strait of Messina. 8 August 2004!").

As in the case of the swim across the Strait of Messina, group cohesion and identification function may be particularly important in the case of positive emotions, including joy, awe, and ecstasy (Heise & O'Brien, 1993). However, negative emotions may also bring people together because individuals who feel sadness or grief often prefer to be with others who have shared the common, difficult, fate and are experiencing similar emotions (Schachter, 1959). For example, during strongly emotional national elections, members of a losing candidate's party may feel very closely related and highly identified with each other; and they may draw a sharp boundary, perhaps sharper than usual, between themselves and members of the opposing party or parties.

Emotions may also be elicited in an individual by other group members in order to exclude him or her from the group, at least until a behavioral or other change has been brought about. For instance, public shaming rituals have been used to define group boundaries and to remind both the shamed person and all other group members of the accepted social norms that characterize the group (Scheff, 1988). A well-known criminal museum in Rothenburg, Germany, that documents instruments of torture and punishment from medieval times displays various "masks of shame" that societies used to regulate group members' behavior. Specifically, the violator of a law or norm had to wear the mask in order to elicit ridicule from other group members, as a punishment. One particularly interesting mask is the "flute of shame" (*die Schandflöte*), which was used to punish those who violated norms for the quality of music played in the king's court (see Figure 2.9)! Some countries even in this day and age have considered the possibility of requiring former prisoners to wear tee shirts that announce the crime for which they were incarcerated. The goal again is to generate public shame for having violated a societal norm, or, in this case, law. As Frijda and Mesquita (1994) have noted: "Shame stimulates behavior that leads to acceptance by the group, in addition to stimulating behavior that flees group rejection; agreeing with the group norm is one of these behaviors. Therefore it may be seen as stimulating group cohesion" (p. 78).

A second important social coordination function of emotions is their role in facilitating the problem of group governance (Keltner & Haidt, 1999). In order to provide group governance, social groups typically produce, either by explicit or implicit means, a hierarchy of individuals or subgroups. As with emotion communicated within dyads, certain emotions such as anger, contempt, and pride communicate superiority and power to lower status group members. Such emotions communicated to the group can elicit feelings of awe in lower status group members, which

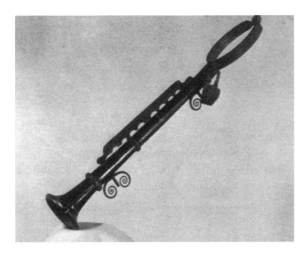

FIGURE 2.9. The flute of shame (*die Schandflöte*). Used in the Middle Ages to induce shame in individuals who played bad music, and to induce public humiliation. Photograph provided by the Kriminalmuseum, Rothenburg, Germany.

serve to preserve the higher status individual's authority (Fisk, 1991). In careful experimental work, Keltner and colleagues have also shown that embarrassment displayed by lower status group members also communicates submissiveness to higher status group members, and serves an appeasement function (e.g., Keltner, Young, Heerey, Oemig, & Monarch, 1998). In an ingenious laboratory study, for example, Keltner and colleagues arranged for two high- and two low-status members of American university social groups, called fraternities, to tease each other. Analyses of the teasing behavior showed that, when teased by higher status individuals, the lower status individuals expressed more embarrassment and smiling, apparently to appease the teasers. When teased by lower status individuals, the higher status individuals expressed more facial hostility, presumably in order to reassert their position in the social hierarchy. A careful analysis of the nonverbal expressions of embarrassment is provided by Keltner and Buswell (1997).

In sum, for the group, emotions serve to define group boundaries and maintain social structure and norms within the group. Living in groups is, of course, a very significant problem to be solved (Trivers, 1971). Without fundamental ways to make people feel that they want to facilitate the functioning of the group, adhere to group rules and norms, and recognize group leaders, this very significant problem would not be solved and societies would probably fail. Emotions seem to be at least part of the solution to living successfully in groups.

Positive Emotions

It may appear that we have spent particular attention on the functions of negative emotions. Except for fleeting mentions of love and awe, it is true that many examples in the preceding sections concentrate on the importance of sadness, fear, anger, shame, and embarrassment for the functioning of the individual, the dyad, and the group. In some ways, this focus on negative emotions is compelling. If experiences that feel negative can be useful for the individual, the dyad, and the group, maybe they are not so undesirable after all. Fredrickson (1998) has pointed out that negative emotions have indeed received the lion's share of attention in research on emotion and especially on their functions. She has attributed the lack of attention to positive emotions and their functions to a number of causes. One is that models of emotion often do a poor job of differentiating between positive states in the first place. Most typically, they focus exclusively on what they call joy or happiness, without considering the possible distinctions between other positive states. In addition, because

TABLE 2.2
Summary of the Action Tendencies and Resulting Skill or Social Outcome Associated with Four Positive Emotions

Emotion	Action tendency	Outcome
Joy	Free activation/play	Motor skill acquisition
Interest	Exploration	Knowledge acquisition
Contentment	Mindful broadening of ideas	Knowledge integration and elaboration
Love	Attachment and bonding	Social relationships

From Fredrickson, B. (1998). What good are positive emotions? *Review of General Psychology, 2*, 300–319.

negative emotions seem to be associated with problems, sadness with withdrawal and depression, for example, and anger with aggression and behavioral and physical health problems, negative emotions call out for attention. Since positive emotions at non-clinical levels do not seem to cause many problems for individuals or for society, they do not call out for research attention with the same urgency. And yet, one can discern a clear attempt to distinguish among the positive emotions, by just a few theorists, notably, Carroll Izard (1977) and Silvan Tomkins (1962). Fredrickson (1998) draws on the thinking of these two theorists, and several others, to more richly elaborate the definition and functions of the positive emotions of *joy, interest, contentment,* and *love.* The definitions of these emotions, the changes that these emotions cause in behavior, and the consequences of these behaviors, as summarized by Fredrickson, are outlined in Table 2.2.

Broaden and Build

Fredrickson has recently proposed a broaden-and-build model of the functional role of positive emotions. She argues that the different positive emotions, in different ways, *broaden* the individual's momentary thought–action repertoire. She notes, for example, that positive emotions are associated with an expansion, or widening, of the focus of attention (Derryberry & Tucker, 1994). Instead of focussing exclusively on details, individuals in positive emotional states tend to show a broadening of their scope of attention, and are able to take into the system a wider number of cues and meanings from the environment. In addition, positive emotions are associated with a broadening of the use of information that they take in. This was originally illustrated by a number of different research programs conducted by Alice Isen (e.g., Isen, Daubman, & Nowicki, 1987;

Isen, Johnson, Mertz, & Robinson, 1985; Isen, Niedenthal, & Cantor, 1992). Isen's research demonstrated that when in positive emotional states, individuals are more creative in the sense of accessing more distant and more interesting meanings and associations in memory, and in the sense of constructing more inclusive categories, than individuals in neutral or negative states. More recent research by Bless and his colleagues has extended this idea, and shown that positive emotions separate individuals from a strict reliance on details present in a given situation, and are, rather, associated with the use of broader, general knowledge structures (e.g., Bless, Clore, Schwarz, Golisano, Rabe, & Wölk, 1996b; Bless & Fiedler, 1995). Finally, positive emotions appear to broaden the scope of action as well. People's actual choices and their solutions to problems that are posed to them reflect a more expansive relationship to the environment. As an example of this, Renniger, Hidi, and Knapp (1992) showed that different play objects that elicited interest in children also elicited a wider variety of ways of playing with those objects (compared to objects that did not elicit interest), as well a wider variety of behavior within each different way of playing.

An important consequence, perhaps *the* important consequence, of broadening the attentional-cognitive-behavioral repertoire of the moment, according to Fredrickson (1998) is that positive emotions then lead to a *building* of physical and psychological resources that can be relied on in the future. The desire to play that is stimulated in juveniles of many species by the emotion of happiness results in the development of new physical skills, for example. Rough-and-tumble play, as it is called by ethologists (e.g., Boulton & Smith, 1992), serves both to generate muscular and vascular fitness, but also to rehearse a number of skills that will be important later in life, including the negotiation of danger, and social confrontations. In a more straightforward way, the emotion of interest leads to the development of a greater knowledge repertoire. And happiness also motivates learning and facilitates performance on many kinds of task as well. Finally, positive emotions serve to build social resources by establishing positive relationships with others, particularly ones in which a norm of reciprocity is developed and maintained.

Fredrickson develops two functional implications of the broaden-and-build model. One is that positive emotions may "undo the negative aftereffects of negative emotions." There are many such aftereffects. In fear and anger, for example, the autonomic nervous system is typically highly active. Positive emotions may serve to re-establish equilibrium following negative emotional arousal of this kind. In an interesting study of this hypothesis, Fredrickson and Levenson (1998) had experimental participants watch a film that uniformly induced fear and heightened cardiovascular activity. The participants were then randomly assigned to watch one of four additional films. The four films elicited either contentment, mild amusement, sadness, or neutral emotion.

Results revealed that the participants who watched the films that produced one of the two positive emotions, contentment or mild amusement, returned to their baseline levels of cardiovascular activation more quickly than those who watched the film that elicited neutral emotion, and much more quickly than those who watched the sad film. In this sense, the positive emotions repaired the physical symptoms of fear induced by the initial film; symptoms that are metabolically costly for the body. In a more extended way, therefore, Fredrickson argues that positive emotions can protect physical health. By returning the body to quiescence after an experience of a costly negative emotion such as fear and anger, positive emotions can, over time, protect the physical health of the body itself.

Social Functionalist Account

In a social functionalist analysis of positive emotions, Shiota and colleagues have outlined the importance of positive emotions in the development and success of interpersonal relationships (Shiota, Campos, Keltner, & Hertenstein, 2004). These authors point to at least two critical adaptive problems, or tasks, that individuals face and must resolve in order to have successful relationships. A first critical problem is that of *identifying relationships partners*. A good partner for a romantic relationship, for example, will have a certain amount of similarity to the individual, and possess features that suggest that he or she is healthy and likely to produce viable offspring (e.g., Buss, 1989; Langlois & Roggman, 1990). How do individuals realize or come to know that any given individual is worth pursuing? Positive emotions such as desire provide information to the very individual who is feeling the emotion, that a particular other person is a good candidate for a romantic relationship. Furthermore, if he displays those feelings of desire, the relationship candidate can respond accordingly. Thus, positive emotions both signal that a good candidate has been encountered and they motivate behaviors such as flirting that communicate that feeling to the potential partner. A second task involves the *maintenance* of an intimate relationship, once initiated. To successfully maintain a romantic relationship, individuals engage in behaviors such as expressions of affection and proximity maintenance, that are motivated by positive emotions such as love and compassion. The display of these positive emotions serves to reward the relationship partner directly by eliciting pleasure, and by signaling a strong commitment to the relationship (Gonzaga, Keltner, Londahl, & Smith, 2001).

These two tasks do not characterize the problems faced in romantic relationships exclusively. The same type of analysis can be applied to the problems of parent–child relationships as well as friendship relationships. Positive emotions, especially love, are importantly implicated in the ways in which infants and parents bond to form attachment relationships (Shiota et al., 2004).

Summary

The purpose of this chapter was to provide an overview of the ways in which theorists in the area of emotion carve up their topic of research. As we have discussed, in an approach similar to that of a chemist, a psychologist who studies emotion can seek out the basic elements, or building blocks, of emotional life. Finding and characterizing emotions and their manifestations, or even trying to advance understanding of an emotion that seems too obvious to require scientific attention, is the goal in the study of the structure of emotion. The discrete emotions account, and the biological view, which we call the basic emotions account, hold that there is a set of non-reducible states that we call discrete or basic emotions. Evidence for these discrete states comes from research on linguistic categories for emotion, the universal recognition of facial expressions of emotion, analyses of vocal properties of emotion, and some differences in autonomic nervous system activity among emotions. A completely different approach to the structure of emotional experience holds that states that may seem to be discrete, perhaps because we label them with separate words, can be reduced to at least two dimensions. Those dimensions are sometimes called pleasantness–unpleasantness and activation–deactivation. But other interpretations of the defining dimensions of emotional experience are also possible.

We came to the conclusion that there is evidence both for discrete states, possibly basic emotions, and also for underlying dimensions of experience. More recently researchers have tried to capture both in more inclusive models of emotional experience (e.g., Russell & Feldman Barrett, 1999).

We complemented our discussion of the structure of emotion with a consideration of functional approaches to emotion. It is widely accepted that emotions are functional, but there are many ways of thinking about just *how* they are functional. We considered a number of levels of analysis, running from the function of the emotion for the individuals, to the dyad, and finally to the group. Certainly an understanding of what it means to take a functional approach to the study of emotion will change the way the reader understands and interprets the following chapters on the relationship between emotion and cognition, and on self-conscious emotions.

Self-conscious Emotions   3

Here is a question that students often pose when they take a class in which the topic of the scientific study of emotion comes up: "Is it OK that I am very often jealous?" When pressed, they then admit that their boyfriend or girlfriend says that they are too jealous too frequently. Or even more worrying, they say that their relationships almost always fail because of their tendency to be jealous. In Chapter 2, we filled many pages discussing the basic structure of emotional experience. Not until we considered the functions of emotion, later in the chapter, however, did we refer, and then rather fleetingly, to the kinds of complex emotion that might be of greater concern and interest to the average individual: not only jealousy, but also shame, guilt, envy, and pride. These emotions preoccupy because they can occasionally lead to very strong, sometimes disruptive, behaviors. Perhaps more critically, they have important interpersonal implications, and social and moral functions (Barrett, 1995; Tangney, 2002b). Thus, people are not only consumed by these emotions, they are sometimes consumed by the *idea* that they are consumed by these emotions.

In contrast to the set of emotions that are referred to by some theorists as "basic" emotions, these more complex emotions have been called "cognition-dependent" emotions (Izard, Ackerman, & Schultz, 1999). The term stresses the important idea that such emotions rely on the realization of significant cognitive achievements before they emerge in full-blown fashion. They thus appear later in development than the category of emotions called basic emotions. Because of the nature and content of the processes that cognition-dependent emotions rely on, and their implications, such emotions have also been called "self-conscious emotions," and that is what the category is called here (Tangney & Fischer, 1995). The idea is that all such emotions rely on having a *sense of self* and that all such emotions in some way involve *injury to or enhancement of the sense of self* (Harter, 1999; see Figure 3.1). Importantly, the antecedent condition for a basic emotion such as sadness can also involve the self-processes that we discuss next. However, the processes are not *necessary* for the experience of the basic emotions per se. In contrast, the self-processes we discuss are considered a necessary precondition for the experience of self-conscious emotions, indeed they are defining of them (Lewis, Sullivan, Stanger, & Weiss, 1989; Tangney & Dearing, 2002; Wallbott & Scherer, 1995).

As distinguished from the so-called basic emotions, the self-conscious emotions also show greater variability across cultures in their subjective experience and associated display rules (e.g., Kitayama, Markus, & Matsumoto, 1995) that were traditionally not thought to be associated with universally recognized facial expressions (e.g., Ekman, 1992; although we shall see that recent research casts this claim into some doubt), and tend to

FIGURE 3.1. Self-conscious emotions become possible when children have developed a sense of self and a sense of self-worth.

appear as subcategories of the basic emotions in linguistic analyses (e.g., Shaver et al., 1987; see Chapter 2). Some people have argued that this variability across culture and tendency to see self-conscious emotions as secondary to basic emotions has to some extent impeded empirical study of such emotions by according them a second-class status (Tracy & Robins, 2004a).

Cognitive Achievements Underlying Self-conscious Emotions

All self-conscious emotions require that the individual is capable, first, of representing the self as an entity separate from others (e.g., as distinct from the mother). A self-concept, or a sense of self as distinct, develops in toddlerhood, beginning around the age of 2. We infer this because toddlers begin to use the pronouns "I," "me," "mine," and because they pass the *rouge test*. In the rouge test, a small dot of rouge is covertly applied to a child's nose and the child is then confronted with a mirror. If the child indicates that they recognize themselves in the mirror by touching the rouge or wiping it off their noses, they are said to have developed a representation of the self (Lewis & Brooks-Gunn, 1979). That is they "know" that something is wrong or different about *themselves*.

Toddlerhood is also when self-conscious emotions are first evident, but these undergo a great deal of elaboration during childhood and adolescence. In particular, between the ages of 2 and 3 self-conscious emotions become clearly linked to self-evaluation. To illustrate, at age 2 a child might feel sadness at failure and joy at success. However, at age 3 they will specifically feel pride when they succeed at difficult (compared to easy) tasks and feel shame when they fail on easy (compared to difficult) tasks (Lewis, Alessandri, & Sullivan, 1992). These findings suggest that pride and shame, compared to joy and sadness, rely on a sense of self-worth. The role of a sense of self in self-conscious emotions is further emphasized by research that demonstrates that primates that engage in self-representational processes, such as orangutans and chimpanzees, do reliably display self-conscious emotions such as embarrassment and pride (Hart & Karmel, 1996; Russon & Galdikas, 1993). In contrast, animals that lack a sense of self appear not to experience such emotions (despite the fact that their owners might claim that they do!).

Self-evaluation and *social comparison*, which are also important processes underlying self-conscious emotions, develop gradually throughout the primary school years. Over that period, comparisons become more complex and nuanced as children become increasingly sophisticated in their conceptual skills. For example, the self-statement "I like to run" becomes "I'm a good runner," and later becomes "I'm the best runner in my class," which then even later becomes "I'm a pretty good runner, but so are Annette and Sabine. At least I'm better at running than I am at tennis." Notice that these changes reflect development in the general ability to recognize similarities, make ordinal comparisons, and take perspectives other than one's own. Different perspectives by the self on the self can also be represented and compared, and these are importantly involved in the experience of self-conscious emotions. For example, children come to represent concepts of their "ideal" self and of the self that they or others think they ought to be. Comparisons between what the self is actually like and, for example, the ideal self, can then be made, and this process can underlie self-conscious emotions (Higgins, 1987).

A final cognitive achievement is the *internalization of standards and norms*, taught by caretakers and reinforced by society (Lewis, 2000). Early in development, children rely to some degree on external standards and norms in order to experience self-conscious emotions at all. For instance, the presence of an audience is initially necessarily for a child, with a sense of self, to experience pride. And a child may experience shame only when his or her inappropriate behavior is actually observed by someone else (Harter & Whitesell, 1989). However, when societal and familial standards for appropriate behavior have been internalized, self-conscious emotions can be experienced even in the absence of a physical audience.

Not all self-conscious emotions rely on all these achievements. In the present chapter, we group emotions into two subcategories based on the specific cognitive capacities that ground them. In the first section, we discuss what we will call the *social comparison emotions*. These emotions, envy and jealousy, involve, as the name implies, comparisons with qualities, possessions, and outcomes of other individuals. The subcategory of self-conscious emotions that we consider in the second section of the chapter is called *self-evaluation emotions*. These emotions, including guilt, shame, embarrassment, pride, and hubris, involve self-evaluation that is based on comparisons to personal standards and goals, as well as moral values taught by the social environment.

Social Comparison Emotions

We have just stated that social comparison emotions involve the ability to represent the self, or possess a self-concept, as well as – as the name implies – the ability to compare the self to others and to make a relative

evaluation of the self based on that comparison. The emotions we will consider in depth, envy and jealousy, both have these characteristics (Parrott,
1991; Salovey & Rothman, 1991; Silver & Sabini, 1978). That is, we assume
that in most instances of the two emotions one's attributions, stature, abilities, or other qualities, are compared to those of another person, and the
resulting comparison, within specific social contexts, results in discrete
feelings. The fundamental social comparison nature of envy was pointed
out by Francis Bacon (1561–1626), the English philosopher, who said:
"Envy is ever joined with the comparing of a man's self; and where there
is no comparison, no envy." In this section of the chapter, we start with a
discussion of the distinction between envy and jealousy. We then go on to
summarize the more detailed analyses of the two emotions and the supporting empirical evidence, noting at the outset that envy is a much less
studied emotion than is jealousy.

Distinguishing Envy from Jealousy

In scholarly thinking, a conceptual distinction has been made between
jealousy and envy. The distinction refers to the psychological situations
under which the two emotions arise and the qualities of the feelings themselves (e.g., Heider, 1958; Russell, 1930; Solomon, 1976). Jealousy has been
held to be the state that arises when *an individual believes that an important
real or potential relationship is threatened by another individual*. (Note, however, that people may also feel jealous because they believe that an important relationship is threatened by the other person's passion for playing
tennis, interest in taking care of their car, or going to movies alone; that is,
threatened by a rival that is not in fact another individual.) By this account,
then, jealousy occurs in situations in which there are three entities
involved: the jealous person, the person with whom the jealous person has
a relationship, and the rival who threatens that relationship (usually a person, but as noted, is sometimes a hobby or other nonhuman entity). The
subjective experience of jealousy has been characterized as involving feelings of anger, fear of loss, and suspicion. In contrast, envy has been defined
as the state that arises when *an individual believes that another individual has
something that he or she wants but does not yet, or ever will, have*. Thus, the situation in which envy is experienced involves two people: the envious person and the envied person. And the subjective experience of envy has been
characterized by longing, ill will, and feelings of inferiority (Salovey &
Rodin, 1984).

A problem for the scientific study of these emotions is that many
laypeople, perhaps even you yourself, use the word *jealousy* in situations

in which the scholarly distinction claims they should feel and use the word *envy*. Think of a time when someone treated you badly and you just could not figure out why. You say to your friend: "Frank has been distant and almost mean to me at work." Your friend might respond: "He is just jealous because you got selected to work on that interesting and important project, and he didn't." If we apply the above definitions of jealousy and envy, then what your friend "meant to say" was that Frank was envious of you. Does this mean that the scholars were wrong? Not necessarily. There are a number of ways to look at this apparent confusion in the uses of the words *jealousy* and *envy*.

Smith, Kim, and Parrott (1988), who were concerned with just this issue, conducted a study in which they asked experimental participants to describe examples of times in their lives when they were jealous and when they were envious. Two judges then coded these descriptions in terms of whether the situations conformed, or not, to the scholarly definitions of the two terms. The researchers also asked the participants to evaluate a series of feelings in terms of whether they were characteristic of either or both of the two states. The findings showed that individuals used *envy* relatively precisely and specifically as referring to situations in which they felt that someone had something (a personal quality, a possession, a role) that they did not have, but wanted (and or wished that the person did not have). In contrast, as you might suspect from the example of Frank, individuals used *jealousy* to cover both situations. When writing about jealousy, they tended to describe both classic situations of jealousy, in which they believed that a significant relationship was threatened by a rival, as well as situations in which another individual had something they wanted but did not have.

Does this mean that jealousy is not an emotion distinct from envy? In other words, do such findings mean that the states are actually the same things? Not according to other results of the same study. Analyses of the ratings of the feelings that characterize the two states suggested that jealousy and envy are quite distinct when many fine-grained feelings are considered (cf. Salovey & Rodin, 1986). Table 3.1 shows the specific, nuanced, feelings that Smith and colleagues' participants said characterize jealousy and envy, as well as both jealousy and envy to some degree. As can be seen, envy was described as a state that involves feelings of ill will and longing, in addition to feelings of being inferior, whereas jealousy was characterized by feelings of hostility and hurt, as well as feelings of being rejected. Thus, while individuals seem to use jealousy more generally (and perhaps incorrectly) than the term envy, even laypeople report that the states are phenomenally distinct (as also confirmed by the results of another study by Parrott & Smith, 1993).

TABLE 3.1
Percentage of Participants Indicating that Feeling States were More Characteristic of Envy or Jealousy

Attribute	Jealousy	Envy
Suspicion	90****	10
Rejection	86****	14
Hostility	82****	18
Anger at other(s)	82****	18
Fear of loss	76****	24
Hurt	76****	24
Cheated	72****	28
Desire to get even	72***	28
Resentment	70***	30
Spite	69***	31
Malice	68***	32
Intensity	68***	32
Motivation to improve	11	89****
Wishful	24	76****
Longing	28	72****
Inferior	31	69***
Self-aware	32	68***
Self-critical	38	62*
Dissatisfied	39	61*
Frustration	57	43

$*p < .05; **p < .01; ***p < .001; ****p < .0001$.
From Smith, R. H. et al. (1988). Envy and jealousy: Semantic problems and experiential distinctions. *Personality and Social Psychology Bulletin, 14,* 401–409.

One interpretation of the "overuse" of the word jealousy in situations in which someone means envy is that people do not like the moral connotations of the word envy (Sabini & Silver, 1982; Schoeck, 1969). That is, envy, which is derived from *invidere*, the Latin word meaning "to look upon with malice" is a state that is taught in most religious traditions to be highly undesirable. The ancient Greek term, *phthonos*, which covered both jealousy and envy, was considered a state of distress provoked by the good fortune of others, and had terrible consequences. In Judeo-Christian writings, this is the feeling that the devil had for mankind, Cain for Abel, Joseph's brothers for Joseph, and Saul for David. Mohammad, the Islamic prophet, warned his followers to "avoid envy, for envy devours good deeds just as fire devours fuel." Thus, there may be strong aversion, in many countries and cultures, to using the word *envy* to denote a feeling because it has historically been considered a sin (Sabini & Silver, 1982).

Parrott and Smith (1993) have also suggested that ambiguity in the daily use of the term jealousy may be enhanced because real-life jealousy situations often contain elements that provoke envy as well. For example, an individual might both be jealous because a rival is threatening an important relationship, and be envious of those qualities of the rival that make him or her a serious threat to the relationship (Salovey & Rodin, 1984, 1986). Parrott and Smith (1993) provided evidence for such an idea in a study in which experimental participants were asked to write autobiographical accounts of experiences of envy or jealousy. Careful examination of the descriptions of the situations in which participants said they had experienced envy revealed that "pure envy" situations were very rarely accompanied by elements of jealousy; when instructed to describe envy, individuals seem to come up with examples that conform to the traditional definition. However, descriptions of situations in which jealousy was experienced were very often accompanied by elements of envy.

This finding was supported by the results of a second study in which participants read scenarios in which a protagonist experienced a classic jealousy- or envy-producing experience. Participants rated the way they imagined the protagonist would feel in the situations, and results showed that in the jealousy situations not only jealousy but also envy was experienced whereas in envy situations much envy but very little jealousy was experienced. Note that these findings do not explain why in a typical envy situation an individual might use the word jealousy, but it does show that jealousy is a broader term that often includes features of envy, and it shows that precise conformity to the scholars' descriptions of the word jealousy is hard to come by.

With some reassurance that envy and jealousy are distinct emotions, we can now turn to a consideration of some special theoretical issues of each, as well as supporting research.

Specific Accounts of the Experience of Envy

As we shall see, there are a number of different ways to analyze the jealousy triad, and motivations that underlie the state. In contrast, there are not diverse theories of envy. There exist, however, analyses of its different components. It is to these analyses of envy that we turn here.

Malicious and Nonmalicious Envy

A number of different thinkers about envy have distinguished a more benign (sometimes called "admiring") envy from the envy of ill will and hatred (called "malicious envy") (Neu, 1980; Rawls, 1971; Taylor, 1988). This distinction highlights the fact that something like envy can involve a disappointment with the self and a strong desire to emulate the envied other person, on the one hand, and something that involves the desire to engage in destructive behaviors and wallow in bitterness, on the other. Although some thinkers do not believe that the benign "nonmalicious" type of envy is really envy at all, Parrott (1991) argues that both can be seen as envy. The way he chooses between the two feelings is by suggesting that the nonmalicious sort of envy is characterized by the desire to have what the other has, in a longing sort of way that highlights one's own shortcomings, while the malicious sort is characterized by the desire that the other not have what he or she has at all. As Parrott notes: "To the person suffering malicious envy, the marvelous car should be stolen or damaged, the virtuous person corrupted or killed, the beautiful face covered or disfigured." Malicious envy is, of course, the sin that religious writings speak of. We can assume that the two different types of envy can occur in the very same situation, and that they depend, in part, on the focus of attention of the envious individual (i.e., on the self or on the other person). Furthermore, important interpretations of the situations underlie these two experiences as we discuss next.

Hostility and Depression Components of Envy

If ill will is at the core of malicious envy, the feeling component of nonmalicious envy is that of feeling disappointment about the comparison that is being made. What is it about the envy situation that leads to the hostility, on the one hand, and the depressive feelings, the feelings of worthlessness and longing, on the other?

This very question was addressed by Smith and colleagues (Smith, Parrott, Ozer, & Moniz, 1994). Here is what they proposed: that the specific feelings of hostility are due to the belief that the envied person possesses a high status or desirable outcomes because of an *injustice*, that is, from the perception that the person had an unfair advantage in life. This idea is, in part, based on the social psychologist Heider's analysis of envy. Central to Heider's "balance theory" is the idea that similar people should have similar, or *balanced*, outcomes (Heider, 1958). If two similar people have very different outcomes, then the less well-off one might perceive the well-off one as unfairly advantaged in the world of things. Notice the word perception. It does not matter if the envied person objectively deserved their good fortune. If it is *perceived* as an unfair advantage, then the less well-off person will experience ill will and hatred.

Smith and his colleagues proposed further that the depressed feelings in envy are due to the perception of inferiority that results from the comparison. That is, when someone sees that in comparison to the self, another individual has some sort of advantage, they will feel badly about themselves, distraught and depressed.

The relations between the focus of attention in envy situations – that is, on the possible injustice of it all, versus on the fact that one is inferior – and the specific feelings of envy were tested in a study of the autobiographical accounts of envy of 427 participants (Smith et al., 1994). After writing out the accounts, participants rated their experiences in terms of the subjective perception of injustice in the situation, the objective injustice, their beliefs about their own inferiority, and then, of course, their feelings of hostility and depression. Results of the study revealed that, indeed, beliefs about the subjective and objective injustice in the situation predicted feelings of hostility while beliefs about inferiority predicted feelings of depression.

Jealousy

We often think of jealousy as a feeling that occurs largely in romantic relationships. But siblings and co-workers may also feel jealous of another sibling or co-worker who threatens their relationship with a parent or superior, respectively (Nadelman & Begun, 1982). What happens in all jealousy situations is that the attention that one gets from a relationship with a significant person, be it a relationship partner, or a parent, is perceived to be usurped by a rival. That lost of attention is then experienced as an indicator of loss of worth to the significant person and thereby causes a threat to the individual's self-evaluation (Dion & Dion, 1975; Parrott, 1991). The social comparison underpinning of jealousy is unavoidable, as George Bernard Shaw ironically noted when he said: "Never waste jealousy on a real man: it is the imaginary man that supplants us all in the long run." Still, a focus on the rival and his or her characteristics, on the one hand, versus an analysis of the meaning of a rival within the specific relationship, on the other, has led to very different approaches to understanding jealousy. We discuss three accounts here: the self-evaluation maintenance model of jealousy (DeSteno & Salovey, 1996), the evolutionary account of jealousy (Buss, 1995; Buss, Larsen, Westen, & Semmelroth, 1992), and a social exchange theory account of jealousy (Buunk, 1991).

Self-evaluation Maintenance Model of Jealousy

In one theory of jealousy, the degree to which there is a threat to self-evaluation in situations in which there is a rival for the attention of an important relationship partner is the fundamental determinant of jealousy (DeSteno & Salovey, 1995, 1996; Salovey, 1991; Salovey & Rothman, 1991). This *self-evaluation maintenance model of jealousy* relies explicitly on the general self-evaluation maintenance (SEM) model of Tesser (1988). The SEM model is motivated by the well-documented assumption that people seek and desire to maintain a positive evaluation of the self. The theory also assumes that much of the activity of maintaining a positive evaluation of the self is played out in social interaction with people who are generally similar to the self. That is, very little of the activity involved in maintaining one's positive self-evaluation occurs in interactions with individuals from entirely foreign cultures, distant generations, or unusual social status (e.g., we tend not to compare ourselves to presidents or royalty).

The two types of social interaction that are critical in SEM are those that involve *reflective processes* and those that involve *comparison processes*. In both cases, an individual is emotionally influenced by the performance of another individual. But this perception leads to very different psychological experiences. (We will discuss superior performances by another, although the effects of an inferior performance should be clear.) Situations marked by reflective processes are those in which the superior performance of another individual makes us feel great about ourselves. Specifically, we "bask in the reflected glory" of that person's achievements or qualities (Cialdini et al., 1976). As an example of such a situation, one of the authors of this book has a first cousin who is a longstanding member of the symphony orchestra in Florence, Italy, the Maggio Musicale Florentino. As that author is shamelessly doing right here in writing this sentence, she often evokes this fact in conversations with other people, and then immediately feels good about herself through the glory reflected by her cousin. There are also situations, however, in which superior performances and attributes of close others make us feel worse about ourselves. These are situations marked by comparison processes. No reflection occurs at all, only a failure to hold onto a good feeling about the self because of this unflattering comparison. For example, perhaps your older brother or sister made excellent grades in school and, because you found yourself drawn into a comparison, you felt bad about yourself because your grades were less spectacular.

The critical question is, of course, when do people bask in glory and feel good and when do people compare, find themselves wanting, and feel worse? Tesser (1988) proposes that the situations marked by reflection versus comparison depend on the *relevance* of the performance or quality to the self-definition of the individual. According to SEM, there are only a relatively small number of domains in life that really matter to any given individual. When close others do better than we do in those limited domains, we more or less automatically compare, and we feel bad. When they do better outside those domains, we do not compare; we can bask and feel good. So, to return to the previous examples, the author whose cousin is a professional musician is, of course, herself an academic psychologist,

*"Jealous that my husband was kissing Lorraine?
She has no backhand whatsoever."*

not a professional musician. Therefore, she can bask. Contrariwise, it may be important to you to do well in school. If it is, then superior school performance by a sibling may hurt more than it helps your feelings of self-evaluation.

What do people do when they feel bad due to comparison processes? Because there is a need to maintain positive self-evaluation, the negative feelings caused by unflattering comparisons motivate behaviors intended to improve self-evaluation in some way. Some of those behaviors involve creating distance in the relationship to the close other (e.g., Tesser & Campbell, 1982), distorting one's beliefs about the other in order to see that person as less good (e.g., Tesser & Campbell, 1982), or distorting one's beliefs about oneself in order to see the self as better (e.g., Salovey & Rodin, 1988; Tesser, Campbell, & Smith, 1984), or even by interfering in some way with the successful performance of the close other (e.g., Tesser & Smith, 1980). All such activities serve to restore a positive evaluation of the self.

How can this model of self-evaluation maintenance be extended to better understand jealousy?

The model, as applied to jealousy, holds, first, that jealousy is not an either/or state. That is, people feel jealous to different degrees, and the intensity is due to the degree of threat that they perceive (Bringle, 1991). An application of the SEM to jealousy suggests, moreover, that an individual will feel threatened most acutely by, and therefore be most jealous of, rivals who excel in domains that are of the utmost important to that individual's self-definition (Salovey, 1991; Salovey & Rothman, 1991). What is interesting about this idea is that the threat is determined as much or more by the nature of the comparison between the jealous individual and the rival as by the interest in the rival shown by the object of jealousy!

In order to test the hypothesis that the intensity of jealousy is determined by the characteristics of the rival, and, specifically, that the strongest jealousy is experienced when the rival excels in domains of importance to the self-definition of the jealous person, DeSteno and Salovey (1996) undertook several studies. It is important to note that DeSteno and Salovey's participants were American university students. American university students are typically concerned with the domains of intelligence, athleticism, and popularity (Cantor, Norem, Niedenthal, Langston, & Brower, 1987; Salovey & Rodin, 1988). These are therefore the domains that DeSteno and Salovey focused on in their studies, which followed largely the same procedure: participants read scenarios that described situations in which their partner flirted with another individual of the opposite sex (this study was of heterosexual jealousy). The rival was then characterized in three different ways. Specifically, in each of the descriptions the rival excelled in one of the three domains of interest. For each of the rivals, participants rated how jealous they would be if their partner had flirted with that particular person. In an ostensibly separate set of questionnaires participants also rated the importance of each of the three domains to their own self-definition.

Individuals were much more jealous if the flirting situation happened with a rival who excelled in an area of specific importance to their self-definition. Interestingly, in their second study, DeSteno and Salovey also asked about the extent to which participants would like each rival, based on the provided description, in the event that the jealousy-provoking situation had *not occurred*. A possibility was that individuals would feel jealous of the rivals even in the absence of a threat to their relationship. In that case, the relevance of the data for a SEM model of jealousy would be cast into doubt. In fact, individuals reported that without the flirting situation, they would actually like the rivals who excelled in the domain of importance to their self-definition more than the other rivals. This is probably not surprising because the rivals were not presented as close others (who could cause social comparison processes). In such cases, similarity often predicts liking (e.g., Stroebe, Insko, Thompson, & Layton, 1971).

Evolutionary Theory of Jealousy

As we saw in Chapter 1, an evolutionary approach to psychological functioning begins with the question: what are the adaptive problems faced by members of this species? The next question is: how has the species evolved to solve these problems? What is interesting to evolutionary theorists who attempt to understand jealousy is the fact that human males have faced a specific problem of adaptation, due to their biology, which is quite different than that of females. Specifically, because females experience internal fertilization and gestation, they do not ever face uncertainty in their maternity. They know who their offspring are with 100% certainty. Males do not. Because of internal fertilization and gestation in females, in the absence of DNA testing, males always experience some degree of uncertainty in their paternity. Thus, a particularly costly adaptive problem for males involves being *cuckolded*, that is, unknowingly raising children to whom they are actually not genetically related. In species that engage in parental investment after the baby is born, such as humans, a cuckolded male risks investing time, energy, and other resources, into offspring that are actually not his. This problem should lead to the evolution of anti-cuckoldry mechanisms. Such mechanisms indeed have been identified in mammals including lions (Bertram, 1975) and nonhuman primates (Hrdy, 1979), and they should be especially evolved in human males because humans make a greater investment in offspring after birth than any other mammal (Daly, Wilson, & Weghorst, 1982; Symons, 1979). Sexual jealousy would be an efficient anti-cuckoldry device.

As noted, females know who their offspring are most of the time (barring inadvertent switching of babies in the maternity ward). They do, however, face a different adaptive challenge regarding parental investment. This challenge has quite different characteristics than the problem of possible cuckoldry faced by the male. Specifically, the problem faced by females is that of maintaining the time, resources, and commitment of the male in the offspring. The two situations in which females would risk losing a male's investment would be either if he had an affair or if he left the relationship in order to settle down with another woman altogether. This is most likely to happen when a deep emotional attachment has developed, not merely when sexual desires are met. The development of jealousy of emotional attachments would be an ideal mechanism for warding off loss of investment.

The evolutionary theory of jealousy should now be clear. The theory holds that jealousy is a mechanism that has evolved to monitor and motivate behavior to maintain a relationship that involves parental investment (current or future). Furthermore, because of their implications, threats to a relationship that involve sexual promiscuity should be of particular concern to males, whereas threats to relationships that involve emotional attachment should be of particular concern to women (Daly & Wilson, 1983). In a study of this hypothesis, Buss and his colleagues asked 202 undergraduate students to imagine a situation in which their romantic relationship was threatened by a rival (Buss et al., 1992). Participants were then asked if they would be more upset if they imagined their partner forming a deep emotional relationship or imagined their partner enjoying passionate sexual intercourse with that rival.

The results are reported in Figure 3.2. Men were most upset when they imagined their partner enjoying intercourse while women were most upset when they imagined their partner forming an emotional bond. In a second study, participants who were brought singly into the experimental lab were instructed to form three different images: walking to class feeling neutral, their partner having sexual intercourse with a rival, and their partner falling in love and having a strong emotional attachment with a rival. Measures of electrodermal activity, pulse rate, as well as electromyographic activity in the brow (*corrugator supercilii*) were taken (see Chapter 2). As is clearly shown by all measures illustrated in the figure, except for the pulse rate of women, which were not different for the two jealousy images, men showed more physiological reactivity to the intercourse image whereas females showed more response to the emotional

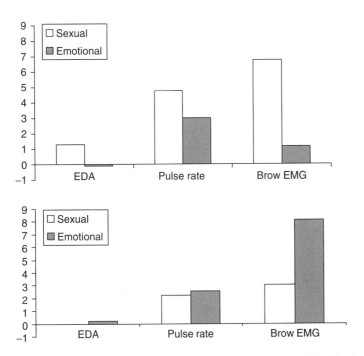

FIGURE 3.2. Means on physiological measures during two imagery conditions for males (upper graph) and females (lower graph). Based on Buss, D. M. et al. (1992). Sex differences in jealousy: Evolution, physiology, and psychology. *Psychological Science, 7,* 251–255. [Note. Measures are expressed as changes from neutral image condition. EDA is in microsiemen units, pulse rate is in beats per minute, and EMG is in microvolt units.]

attachment image. This can be taken as further evidence that males are more threatened by sexual rivals and that females are more threatened by rivals to their emotional attachment.

These quite sensational findings are not without critics, however. DeSteno and Salovey proposed a "double-shot" hypothesis to explain why the sex difference in jealousy-provoking situations is generally seen in studies using forced-choice questionnaires (i.e., what would bother you more, sexual or emotional infidelity?). They hold that the use of a forced-choice format leads individuals to consider the possible tradeoffs of the two presented options. DeSteno and Salovey (1996) demonstrated that the majority of women believe that emotional infidelity by their partner implies subsequent sexual infidelity as well, but that sexual infidelity does not necessarily portend emotional involvement. Men do not hold such a belief about women. Their research demonstrated that these differential beliefs, as opposed to something fundamental to biological sex, accounted for the sex difference in jealousy. Although women reported that both types of infidelity would cause them distress, they selected emotional infidelity as most distressing as it represented, to their minds, a double-shot of cheating (DeSteno & Salovey, 1996). Moreover, follow-up research has demonstrated that when individuals are prevented from engaging in effortful reasoning, as would be required to consider the tradeoffs of the two types of infidelity, the sex difference disappears; men and women both identify sexual infidelity as more distressing (DeSteno, Bartlett, Braverman, & Salovey, 2002). These recent findings and the account of them have led to a lively debate with some evidence for both sides (e.g., Buss et al., 1999; Harris & Christenfeld, 1996).

More recent tests of the evolutionary hypothesis examined the idea that males and females are jealous of rivals that have quite different characteristics; specifically those who have high male and female mate values, respectively. According to evolutionary theory males have high *mate value* when they can provide resources and protection to a partner and their offspring. Females, by way of contrast, have high mate value when they are very fertile and can produce a lot of healthy offspring. This suggests that males should be most jealous of rivals who possess physical strength and the ability to attain resources (as represented in status and financial prospects, for instance). In contrast, females should be most jealous of other females characterized by signs of fertility such as beauty, youth, and a low waist-to-hip ratio (Buss, 1989; Buss, Shackelford, Choe, Buunk, & Dijkstra, 2000).

This hypothesis was confirmed in a study by Dijkstra and Buunk (2002). In the study, participants rated 56 characteristics that had been previously generated as possibly inducing jealousy, in terms of how jealous they would be if their partner were to be seen flirting with an individual who possessed that characteristic. There were five main rival dimensions (or overarching categories of characteristics; see Chapter 2) that provoke jealousy. These included social dominance, physical attractiveness, seductive behaviors, physical dominance, and social status. Also, in line with the theoretical predictions, males reported being more jealous when a rival was high in social dominance, physical dominance, and social status. In contrast, females were more jealous when the rival was high in physical attractiveness. Similar findings have been obtained across a number of different cultures (Buss et al., 2000) and even for aspects of body build that are specifically related to high male versus female mate value (Dijkstra & Buunk, 2001).

Social Exchange Theory View of Jealousy

While the self-evaluation maintenance and evolutionary accounts of jealousy examine interactions between the characteristics of the jealous individual and those of the rival in understanding jealousy, another account focusses on understanding jealousy by reference to the relationship between the individual and the partner, with far less attention to the characteristics of the rival.

Buunk (1991), who takes a relational view of jealousy, has analyzed this emotion from the perspective of *exchange theory*, a theory of interpersonal relationships, especially the exchange theory perspective offered by Thibaut and Kelley (1959) and applied to interpersonal relationships by Kelley (1979, 1986). The main principle of the exchange theory of interpersonal relationships is that individuals enter into and maintain relationships to the extent that the relationship provides them with rewards. Furthermore, because rewards are usually not received in the absence of effort, individuals must also provide rewards to their partner as well as assess the extent to which the exchange of rewards is reasonable (i.e., that the cost of rewarding the other is not too high). Happy, stable relationships are, in theory then, those in which the costs and benefits of the relationships are more or less equal for the two parties. As relationships mature, the "calculation" of the costs and benefits of the relationship begins to change in at least two ways. First, the outcomes of the partners become more intertwined. Thus, individuals may come to derive vicarious pleasure (a reward) from the partner's reaction to rewards that they themselves have provided. For example, although it may be costly for one partner to always stop and buy flowers for the other, the pleasure experienced by the recipient of the flowers might provide enormous pleasure for the giver. In addition, with the onset of long-term commitment, temporary inequalities can be tolerated, and thus calculations of the rewards of a relationship begin to be made over larger periods of time.

The exchange theory perspective on relationships allows one to make a number of specific predictions for when jealousy will be most acute. For instance, it would be expected that if an individual were currently engaging in an extramarital affair of some kind, then because of the principle of reciprocity, they could be less jealous if their partner was also engaged in an affair. In a study of this question, Buunk (1983) asked men and women between the ages of 27 and 46 whether they were currently in an extramarital relationship, or had been, and how jealous they would be if they found out that their partner were having an affair. Consistent with the notion of reciprocity, both men and women indicated they would be less jealous if they were also or had been conducting an extramarital relationship. Similar findings were obtained using different samples of participants, including a student sample (Buunk, 1991). In those samples, participants completed a questionnaire called the Anticipated Sexual Jealousy Scale (Buunk, 1988). The scale measures the degree to which individuals experience negative feelings when they consider the idea of a number of different sexual behaviors occurring between their partner and a rival. The participants also completed a scale called the Extramarital Behavioral Intentions Scale (Buunk, 1988), which, just as the name implies, assesses the degree to which the respondent desires to engage in the same behaviors as those on the Anticipated Sexual Jealousy Scale outside their primary relationship. These two questionnaires were very highly correlated. That is, to the extent that an individual wanted to engage in extramarital sexual behaviors, he or she was not upset by the idea of his or her partner doing so.

Exchange theory also assumes that in order to not have to blatantly control each other's behaviors, and make their dependency on the relationship too explicit, couples tend to develop their own norms and import norms from the society regarding acceptable behavior in the relationship. The norms then provide structure to the demands for reciprocity. The extent to which individuals adopt the society standards (e.g., that extramarital relationships are wrong) should influence the situations in which they are jealous and the degree of jealousy. Consistent with this idea, Buunk (1988) found that indeed the more people endorse the norm that extramarital affairs are unacceptable, the more jealous they would be if their partner engaged in one. Furthermore, additional research showed that setting "ground rules" within the couple about what behaviors vis-à-vis members of the opposite sex (in heterosexual individuals) are acceptable, and following them, served to reduce jealousy to some degree.

A final important notion in exchange theory is that individuals are sensitive to the partner's attention to their needs, or their attention to the state of the exchange within the couple. This concern is manifest in a tendency to seek *attributions* for the partner's behavior. For instance, if the

TABLE 3.2
Correlations between Jealousy and Causes Attributed to a Partner's Extradyadic Behavior

Partner's extradyadic behavior attributed to . . .	Males	Females
Aggression	.38**	.30**
Marital deprivation	.45**	.29**
Variety	.25**	.12
Attraction	−.03	−.13
Circumstances	−.10	−.03
Pressure by third person	.21*	.34**

*p < .05; **p < .01.
From Buunk, B. P. (1991). Jealousy in close relationships: An exchange-theoretical perspective. In P. Salovey (Ed.), *The psychology of jealousy and envy* (pp. 148–177). New York: Guilford Press.

partner does not buy a gift for an individual's birthday, the individual will want to figure out why. Is it because the partner lost his or her wallet, or because they were preoccupied with something or someone else? Obviously, the latter attribution will have more meaning for the current state of the relationship than the former. Forgetting the birthday due to interest in another person suggests that the partner is not attentive to the outcomes and the needs of the individual. The tendency for partners to engage in attributional analyses should be very high in cases in which a partner has violated some rule of conduct with regard to members of the opposite sex. Indeed, in the context of one of the studies just described, Buunk found that individuals' most common reaction to an act of infidelity by their partner is to find out why it occurred. Furthermore, why it did occur was strongly related to the extent to which they would feel jealous. Table 3.2 shows correlations between the degree to which an attribution could be made to specific motives and the degree of jealousy. As can be seen, men and women responded quite similarly, although for men there was a significant relationship between the attribution that their partner needed more sexual variety and jealousy, while for women this correlation was not significant.

Functions of Envy and Jealousy

At this point we can perhaps return to the question posed at the beginning of the chapter and ask "Is it OK that I am very often jealous?" What are the functions of these emotions? Are they largely destructive? We have already hinted at the answer to this question for both emotions. Let us take envy first. If we accept Parrott's (1991) idea that nonmalicious envy is a type of envy, then we can assume that this emotion, thanks in part to the feelings of inferiority that characterize it, sometimes motivates working hard, and self-improvement. Thus, there can be positive consequences of some feelings of envy: the result of a painful social comparison process, feelings of envy, can result in self-improvement.

There also can be positive consequences of feelings of jealousy. When we realize that there is a rival for the attention of a significant other, this, of course, can be damaging to the relationship because we might act out the jealousy in destructive ways. But, by the same token, as many people have noted, a little jealousy may be good for the relationship. Why? Because it makes the partners consider the importance of the relationship, and because it may motivate reparations and improvements in the relationship. Thus, although the social comparison emotions of envy and jealousy may be painful, because they involve comparison to a greater or lesser degree, they may also motivate improvements to ourselves and our relationships by pointing out ways in which things might be made better, and by setting new, higher standards of attainment or fulfillment.

Self-evaluation Emotions

A second group of self-conscious emotions are held to be the result of processes of self-evaluation, which do not need to make recourse to the qualities of someone else. In this group of emotions, individuals examine their traits or their behaviors – through their own eyes, or the eyes of someone else – and are pleased or not pleased, delighted or devastated. An ability to judge the self in this way, as noted, depends on the capacity to view the self as an object of scrutiny, and to match characteristics of the self to the standards that have taught by the society or immediate social context, such as the family. Because such standards are often standards for moral behavior, the emotions have also been called *moral emotions* (Tangney, 1991). The group of self-evaluation emotions includes shame, guilt, embarrassment, pride, and hubris. As should be intuitively clear, the first three emotions arise when the self or something about the self is evaluated negatively; pride and hubris arise when the self or something about the self is evaluated positively (Taylor, 1985).

As we encountered with envy and jealousy, some self-evaluation emotions are not always easy to distinguish, either conceptually or empirically. In particular, the terms *guilt* and *shame* have sometimes been used interchangeably, and *embarrassment* has occasionally been viewed in the literature as a less severe or intense form of shame. We begin this section, therefore, with a discussion of the ways in which shame and guilt have been conceptualized and studied. Then we outline different accounts of embarrassment, as an emotion distinct from shame. Finally, we treat the somewhat smaller literature on pride and hubris.

Guilt and Shame: The Bad and the Ugly

There is no question that guilt and shame are punishing emotions. Although having an explicitly condemning audience can help intensify such feelings, thanks to the cognitive achievements that we have mentioned, guilt and shame are *self*-punishing acknowledgments of something gone wrong. But when is which emotion most likely to be experienced? And how do those emotions feel, or are they really the same feeing that is provoked in slight different situations? Imagine this scenario:

> Your good friend, who rarely dates, invites you to attend a party with him/her and his/her date, Chris. It is your friend's first date with Chris. You go along and discover that Chris is not only very attractive, but is also flirting with you. You flirt back. Although you are not seriously interested in him/her, at the end of the night you give Chris your phone number. The next day, your good friend raves to you about how much he/she liked Chris. (from Niedenthal, Tangney, & Gavanski, 1994a)

Let's face it. If this happened to you, the next morning you would feel some emotion. Would you feel guilty for having given Chris your phone number or would you feel ashamed of yourself? In an ultimately very influential claim, Lewis (1971) proposed that guilt is an emotion that involves identifying a self-produced *specific behavior* as bad, hurtful, or even immoral, whereas shame is an emotion that involves seeing the *entire self* as bad and worthless. Both are evaluations of the self, but the object of evaluation is either a particular behavior (that is bad) or the whole self (that is ugly), as in "I feel guilty about X, but I feel ashamed of myself." This idea suggests that if the person who flirted with Chris woke up the next morning and thought that they had engaged in one or a number of wrong and hurtful behaviors, they would feel guilt. If the person woke up and thought that they were generally a bad person, they would experience shame.

A study by Niedenthal et al. (1994a) experimentally investigated this idea of a focus on behavior versus the self in guilt and shame, respectively. They did so by examining the way in which individuals in the throes of feelings of guilt versus shame engage in *counterfactual thinking*. Counterfactual thinking is the process of mentally "undoing" a situation that has already happened (Roese & Olson, 1995). Such thinking often takes the form: "If only something had been different, then this situation would not have had occurred." For instance, if an individual's car broke down on vacation, he might think: "If only I had had the car serviced before leaving town, it would not have broken down."

Very importantly, the thing that people choose to mentally alter in reflecting on a past situation is typically the very thing that they think *caused* the situation in the first place (Wells & Gavanski, 1989). For example, in the above situation, we can infer that the person sees himself as the cause of the car trouble because his counterfactual thinking focusses on his own action (or, in this case, failure to take action). Alternatively, the car owner might have thought, "If only my wife had had the car serviced, it would not have broken down," reflecting the fact that he sees his wife as the cause, or he could even think "If only Fords were not such unreliable cars, my car would not have broken down," implicating a car company as the cause of the car trouble.

Because both guilt and shame are associated with rumination and mental undoing, Niedenthal and colleagues decided to look at the content of counterfactual thinking immediately following guilt- and shame-provoking experiences. Their reasoning was that if guilt involves a focus on immoral or hurtful behavior, then guilt should be associated with a tendency to imagine alterations of specific behaviors to undo the negative situation. In contrast, if shame involves a focus on the self, as Lewis suggested, then shame should be associated with a tendency to imagine alterations to fundamental features of the self to undo the negative situation.

In one study, the researchers examined individuals' counterfactual thoughts about past, autobiographical experiences of guilt and shame. In another study, the researchers provided participants with scenarios designed to provoke feelings of guilt, and others designed to provoke feelings of shame. For both studies, the participants were instructed to write down three counterfactual thoughts intended to undo the situations. The content of those thoughts constituted the data of interest. Analyses of the thoughts revealed that, after experiencing or imagining guilt situations, individuals most often mentally altered their behavior, thinking: "If only I had not . . . (done a bad thing), then this would not have happened." In contrast, after experiencing or imagining shame situations, individuals most often mentally altered themselves, or features of themselves, thinking: "If only I weren't . . . (a bad person), then this would not have happened." These findings support Lewis's distinction between the focus of attention on and attribution of causality to behavior in guilt and the focus of attention on and attribution of causality to the self in shame (see Sabini & Silver, 1998, for other considerations).

Of course, showing that guilt concerns behavior and shame concerns the self does not tell us anything about the phenomenal experience – the feelings – of those two emotions. Are they actually different? And what about when they occur? Can either emotion occur in any situation that involves self-evaluation? Studies on the phenomenal experiences and action tendencies associated with the two emotions, and others on the situations in which the emotions arise, provide some answers to those questions (e.g., de Rivera, 1977; Lindsay-Hartz, 1984; Tangney, 1990, 1991; Taylor, 1985; Tracy & Robins, 2004a; Wallbott & Scherer, 1988; Wicker, Payne, & Morgan, 1983).

Phenomenal Experiences of Guilt and Shame

We have seen that guilt has been characterized as a negative emotion involving the self-evaluation that results from the belief that one has engaged in a bad or immoral behavior; a behavior, often, that has in some way harmed another person. Let us look at an example of guilt in order to consider about how it feels in a more concrete way. A friend of one of the authors tells about a time when he felt guilty: he was going with his cousin by train to a Spanish town on holiday. They were both teenagers. In the same compartment with them was an unfortunate-looking, older Spanish man. Being very silly, the two cousins made fun of the man's looks, assuming that he did not speak their mother tongue (which was not Spanish). When the man eventually got off the train, he turned to them and told them to have a nice time on their holiday. And he said it in their mother tongue, with perfect fluency, in order to show them that he had understood their derogatory comments. The two cousins were racked by guilt from having made fun of the man in a language that he apparently understood. They saw that they had engaged in a very hurtful behavior.

Tangney (1991) has called the feelings of guilt "bad." They feel bad and they concern a bad action that hurt someone else (Berbdsebn, van der Plig, Doosje, & Manstead, 2004). Not surprisingly, then, the experience of guilt is one marked by a sense of remorse. Probably because guilt involves a focus on a specific behavior, the experience of guilt is characterized also by feelings of being relatively in control of the situation, and also by the feeling that it is possible to set the situation right, at least by changing one's behavior in the future (Wicker et al., 1983). Guilt is associated with distinct action tendencies (Frijda et al., 1989). Specifically, when feeling guilt people have a need to engage in behaviors that will repair the harm they have done, even if only symbolically. They also have a desire to reaffirm their beliefs about moral systems and orders, and to seek forgiveness in some way for their hurtful actions (Lindsay-Hartz, 1984).

It is no wonder that Tangney (1991) calls shame, by contrast to guilt, the "ugly" emotion. Many emotions theorists characterize shame as the more painful and distressing of these two self-evaluation emotions. The father of one of the authors recalls a personal shame experience that he recounts in such a vivid way that his listeners show bodily signs of distress. According to the story, when the father was a little boy growing up in a vast, rural area, he loved to play basketball. And, until most other boys outgrew him, he was quite good. In this rather poor rural area, schools did not have gymnasia where basketball was played on indoor courts; the children always played outside, even in the dead of winter. One season, the little boy's school basketball team was doing very well, and got to play an important game in a far-off town where the players had never been before. The mother of the little boy dressed her son in heavy woolen long underwear, as the winter was particularly cold, and drove him to the game. In fact, the school in the far-off town had its own indoor gymnasium. But when the little boy arrived, he had only his long woolen underwear to wear in the game. When he ran out on the basketball court for the very important game, the entire audience erupted in ridiculing laughter.

This is not actually very funny, is it? You can probably put yourself in the little boy's position without too much trouble, and see that for him the situation produced very painful feelings of negative self-evaluation. Lindsay-Hartz (1984), in interview studies of guilt and shame, showed that when ashamed people feel that their entire self is worthless, powerless, and small. They also feel exposed to an audience (real or imagined) that exists purely for the purpose of confirming that the self is worthless. Shame has been also shown to be associated with specific action tendencies. Not surprisingly, the action tendencies include the desire to run and hide, or to become smaller and disappear from the situation (Tangney, 1991). You can be sure that the little boy in woolen underwear on the basketball court wanted to run and hide, to disappear from public scrutiny.

Situations in which Guilt and Shame Occur

The situational determinants of guilt and shame have received somewhat less research attention than the phenomenological experiences of those emotions. In general theoretical terms, guilt has been linked to situations in which a moral transgression has occurred, while shame has been linked to situations involving public failure or defeat, social rejection (including sexual rebuffs and contempt from others), and exposure or invasion of personal privacy (e.g., Ausubel, 1955; de Rivera, 1977; Lewis, 1971; Taylor, 1985). Another important feature of the situations linked to guilt versus shame is the extent to which they occur in public. In theoretical considerations of guilt and shame, shame is said to be elicited by public exposure and dis-approval, while guilt occurs in private, where the individual is racked by pangs of conscience (Ausubel, 1955; Gehm & Scherer, 1988).

In an in-depth study of the situational determinants of guilt and shame in which Tangney (1992) asked individuals to describe autobio-graphical accounts of situations in which the two emotions were pro-voked, she found some support for the theoretical ideas presented above. Specifically, the study showed that, indeed, specific moral transgressions were more often listed as situations that provoked guilt. These included lying, cheating, stealing, infidelity, and breaking a diet (remember that gluttony is one of the seven deadly sins!). Furthermore, shame was more often elicited by situations involving failure, socially inappropriate behav-ior or dress, and sex. However, it should be noted that it was the case that no situation was exclusively associated with one or the other emotion. Moral transgressions also provoked shame, and failure also provoked guilt in some individuals.

Another study further examined situational determinants of shame and guilt among children and adults (Tangney, Marschall, Rosenberg, Barlow, & Wagner, 1994). In addition to conducting a situational content analysis of autobiographical accounts of shame and guilt, similar to the one by Tangney (1992), the research was designed to analyze the "audiences" present during the elicitation of guilt and shame in order to empirically examine the pro-posed public/private distinction. In fact, not much support was found for this distinction. For both children and adults, guilt and shame were equally likely to be evoked in the presence of others, with shame situations involv-ing audiences with slightly more people. Furthermore, guilt and shame were equally often experienced alone, with no audience at all (i.e., in about 17% of the situations for both guilt and shame, with no difference due to age). Of course, it is possible that guilt situations distinguish themselves from shame situations not by the number of people present in the situation, but by the number of people who are *aware* of the person's behavior. The data did not, however, support this alternative way of thinking about the importance of an audience. The number of people aware of the behavior that brought about guilt and shame did not differ significantly.

Guilt- and Shame-prone Dispositions

We can conclude from the analyses of situational determinants of guilt and shame that there are some situations in which one of the emotions is more likely to be experienced than the other (e.g., those identified by Tangney, 1992; see also Tangney, Miller, Flicker, & Barlow, 1996), but that many self-evaluative situations can produce either emotion. What, then determines whether guilt or shame will be experienced? Or, put differently, what will lead one individual to the conclusion that the situation means that he is bad, and another individual to the conclusion that he performed a hurtful or bad behavior (Gehm & Scherer, 1988; Wallbott & Scherer, 1988)? Recall the opening example involving Chris and your best friend. What would lead one person to think that he was a worthless friend, and another to think that it was hurtful of him to give out his phone number to a friend's love interest?

One answer to this is to suggest that some individuals have a bias to make one versus the other interpretation of ambiguous situations, or, more generally, a *dispositional tendency* to experience to guilt versus shame. Indeed, there appear to be dispositional "pronenesses" to guilt and shame, which are well established by middle childhood (Harder, 1995; Harder & Lewis, 1987). And these dispositions have stable relations to other aspects of interpersonal functioning. For example a proneness to experience guilt seems to be related to a proclivity to engage in moral behaviors and an ability to be empathic with others (Tangney, 1994). A proneness to experience shame, in contrast, is related to more maladaptive behaviors such as the inability to manage anger (Tangney, 1995), and a surplus of experiences of what Lewis (1971) has called "humiliated fury" and Scheff (1987, 1995) has called the "shame–rage spiral."

Function of Guilt and Shame in Moral Behavior

When it comes to evaluating the function of guilt and shame, theorists tend to agree that these emotions play a fundamental role in regulating moral behavior (Harré, 1980; Miller, 1992; Sabini & Silver, 1997; Scheff, 1988, 1990; Tangney, 1999). Both guilt and shame have been linked to the breaking of social norms and the receipt of formal and informal social sanctions (Dienstbier, 1984; Eisenberg, 1986, 2000; Harris, 1989; Lewis, 1993; Shulman & Meckler, 1985; Tangney, 1999). From childhood to adulthood, a standard socialization technique consists of inducing feelings of guilt or shame in an individual who has transgressed a norm or behaved inappropriately (Scheff, 1988, 1990; Scherer, 2001).

Phenomenological studies of guilt and shame, some of which have already been cited, indicate that these emotions do indeed heighten an individual's feelings of responsibility for his or her actions (e.g., Ferguson, Stegge, & Damhuis, 1991; Lindsay-Hartz, de Rivera, & Mascolo, 1995). As a consequence, individuals should be less likely repeat the same behavior in the future. So, the positive outcome of these punishing self-evaluation emotions is the development of self-control and the ability to refrain from committing immoral and self-incriminating acts. As one might glean from our treatment of guilt and shame, guilt is considered by some theorists to be the *more* moral of these two moral emotions (e.g., Tangney, 2002b). The reasons for this are that making amends (the action tendency associated with guilt) is considered more valuable than hiding (the action tendency associated with shame), that the experience of guilt reflects an ability to experience empathy and taking the perspective of another person, and that guilt does not have the same relationship to other destructive emotions, such as rage, that shame may have.

Embarrassment

Whether embarrassment should count as a *distinct* self-evaluation emotion is not obvious to everyone. Although it seems clear that embarrassment does not involve the agonizing sense of remorse about a transgression that characterizes guilt, its distinction from shame is less intuitive. Did the little boy who ran out on the basketball court in long woolen underwear, described in the previous section, feel shame or embarrassment? Is embarrassment part of the feelings of shame (Izard, 1977)? Or is embarrassment just a less intense form of shame? Most recently emotions theorists have argued for a distinction between the phenomenal experience of embarrassment, as well as the overarching situational determinants of embarrassment, and those of shame on a number of counts.

First, it appears that the phenomenal experience of embarrassment is characterized more by a sense of foolishness and fluster than a sense of being small and worthless (e.g., Buss, 1980; Plutchik, 1980). Think of a time when you felt embarrassed. What happened? Maybe you belched or farted in a crowded elevator. Perhaps you used the wrong word, which happened to have an untoward meaning, in a foreign language. Or, you might have felt embarrassed simply because you walked into a large amphitheater when a university course was already in full swing, and the professor, who was in the middle of a sentence, stopped talking as you entered. Such experiences do not really involve feelings that the self is worthless, they involve, rather, a sense of fluster, self-focus, and perhaps slight mortification. The self is negatively evaluated in these examples, but it has been suggested that it is not the *core* self, but the *presented* self, that is negatively evaluated (Klass, 1990; Modigliani, 1968).

Embarrassment also has an important and specific phenomenological and physiological feature that seems unrelated to shame: the blush. Blushing, or the visible reddening of the cheeks and neck, accompanies embarrassment *exclusively* (Miller, 2004). And the blush of embarrassment is even distinguishable from the blush that is the result of exercise, sexual arousal or intoxication (Leary, Britt, Cutlip, & Templeton, 1992). Individuals cannot control the extent to which they blush when embarrassed (Drummond, 2001). But what they *do* most often do when they are embarrassed is to apologize for their mistake, and then to repair things. Unlike in guilt where the repair involves undoing the harm done to others, in embarrassment the repair involves redressing harm done to the presented self. And such redressing can even involve giggling or laughing, behavior that is never or seldom seen in shame.

Finally, embarrassment has been distinguished from shame, in theory, in terms of the general types of situations in which it arises. A number of theorists have argued that embarrassment arises in situations in which, compared to shame, much more trivial transgressions and failures have occurred (Buss, 1980; Lewis, 1992). Furthermore, while we have seen that shame can, albeit infrequently, occur in private, most theorists agree that embarrassment can never be experienced in private. Embarrassment is usually held to be an entirely public emotion (Edelmann, 1981). Another characteristic of the situations that give rise to embarrassment is their surprise value. Embarrassment-provoking situations are considered to be ones that are usually more sudden and surprising in their onset than are shame-provoking situations (Gross & Stone, 1964).

These distinctions in the phenomenology and general situational determinants of embarrassment, versus shame, have undergone careful empirical evaluation, and findings largely support these distinctions (e.g., Manstead & Tetlock, 1989; Miller, 1996; Miller & Tangney, 1994). Thus, we will assume that embarrassment is distinct from shame, and explore more specific theories of this emotion per se, including an analysis of its functions.

Theories of Embarrassment

We have characterized embarrassment as a sudden-onset sense of fluster and mortification that results when the self is evaluated negatively because one has committed, or anticipates committing, a gaffe or awkward performance before an audience (Miller, 2004). However, there are several theories of the psychological meaning of the situation for the individual, that is, of the nature of the negative evaluation that gives rise to the feeling of embarrassment (Miller, 1995). We will first report an experience of embarrassment that was posted on the internet. Then we will describe the two main theories and explain how they account for the example. Finally, we will describe research that tests the two accounts. Here is a real-life example of a time that embarrassment was experienced:

It was the day before my 18th birthday. I was living at home, but my parents had gone out for the evening, so I invited my girlfriend over for a romantic night alone. As we lay in bed after making love, we heard the telephone ringing downstairs. I suggested to my girlfriend that I give her a piggy-back ride to the phone. Since we didn't want to miss the call, we didn't have time to get dressed. When we got to the bottom of the stairs, the lights suddenly came on and a whole crowd of people yelled "surprise." My entire family, . . . aunts, uncles, grandparents, cousins and all of my friends were standing there! My girlfriend and I were frozen to the spot in a state of shock and embarrassment for what seemed like an eternity. Since then, no-one in my family has planned a surprise party again.

Loss of Esteem (or Social Evaluation) Account

In one view, when people feel that their behavior or appearance has undermined the esteem that other people, the members of the observing "audience," accord them, they then experience a temporary loss of self-esteem, and this produces embarrassment. Some theorists focus more on the fact that the embarrassed person has lost esteem from the audience (Miller, 1996; Miller & Leary, 1992), and others focus more on the fact that the individual has not lived up to his or her own personal standards (Modigliani, 1968, 1971). Although it would certainly appear that being judged negatively by the audience is the most critical feature of the potentially embarrassing situation (Manstead & Semin, 1981; Schlenker & Leary, 1982), it is usually the case that social evaluation has an impact on self-esteem as well (Modigliani, 1971). In any event, Sabini and colleagues (2000) have noted that available data suggest that the loss of esteem in the eyes of others is at least sufficient to produce embarrassment, even if loss of self-esteem also usually occurs (Sabini, Siepmann, Stein, & Meyerowitz, 2000).

The loss of esteem theory can easily account for the frankly embarrassing situation of being found by aunts, uncles and other family members, with one's naked girlfriend straddling one's own naked back on the way to answer the telephone. Here the idea is that the act of piggy-backing naked through one's parents' house is outside of the limits of acceptable behavior. So, when aunts and uncles and parents are suddenly exposed to such behavior, particularly if they do not like to be exposed to such behavior and have no choice in the matter, one can be sure that a temporary loss of esteem for the offending parties will ensue. This will not escape notice by the galloping nudes, who will become flustered, mortified, and will surely blush.

Dramaturgic (or Social Interation) Account

Goffman (1967) held that nearly all individuals have a need to perform socially prescribed scripts and socially defined roles smoothly and competently, and are motivated to avoid failures to do so because such failures are detrimental to coherent social interaction. Based in part on Goffman's ideas, Parrott, Sabini, and Silver (1988) have proposed that embarrassment results from *disruptions* in the performance of socially prescribed roles or scripts. In such a view, then, possessing a sense of self and even a positive sense of self is a necessary cognitive precondition for the experience of embarrassment, but a loss of esteem in the embarrassing situation is not. All that matters is the individual's perception that he or she cannot competently perform a given role or script for a given context, which can count as a negative self-evaluation (Silver, Sabini, & Parrott, 1987).

There are two ways in which the galloping nudes fail to competently perform social roles and scripts. One has to do with their relationship roles. Nephews act in certain ways with their aunts and uncles, and sons act in certain ways with their parents; including aunts, uncles and parents in sexual play is not one of those ways. Thus by unwittingly involving the entire family in their cavorting, the couple can no longer perform their roles in the family (as son and nephew, and as girlfriend of said son and nephew). Furthermore, there is a social script for surprise parties. The script does not include a moment when the birthday boy (or girl) appears nude with their nude partner on their back, piggy-back style. Thus, both social roles and social scripts are violated in the example provided above. The dramaturgic account of embarrassment thus also predicts that the couple will become flustered, mortified, and will surely blush.

Comparison of the Two Theories

Initial empirical support for the loss of esteem theory of embarrassment was reported in a study by Modigliani (1971). In that study, participants failed a task that they had to perform in the context of group work, and their task performance influenced their teammates' outcomes. The teammates – actually confederates of the experimenter – then criticized their performance, in either a public or private way. Self-esteem and embarrassment were both assessed. Consistent with the loss of esteem theory, the participants' self-esteem was lower, and embarrassment was higher, in the public compared to the private conditions. However, this study did not explicitly address the way that the individuals' social interaction was affected by the experimental manipulations. Thus, while a self-esteem loss seems important, it is not clear whether it is a sufficient condition for producing embarrassment. A disruption in the performance of social scripts might also have been experienced, because the task was presented as a group exercise. So disruption in social interaction as an important determinant of embarrassment cannot be ruled out on the basis of these findings.

Parrott et al. (1988) thus conducted a study in order to vary both esteem loss and disruption in the performance of social roles in order to assess the relative contributions of each in producing embarrassment. This was done by having participants read scenarios in which the different factors were manipulated. For example, in one scenario the participants had to imagine themselves asking a co-worker out for a date and being turned down. But there were three versions of the scenario. In the *blunt no* version of the scenario, the co-worker turned down the date by simply, brutally, saying no. This should lower self-esteem and cause a disruption in social interaction. In the *transparent excuse* version of the scenario, the co-worker said that they would like to go on a date, but then said no, offering the excuse that they have a policy of not dating the people they work with. The excuse was transparent, however, because the scenario also provided information indicating that the co-worker actually *did* date other co-workers. Transparent excuse scenarios should lead an individual to suffer a loss of self-esteem but not a disruption in social interaction because the co-worker does not know that the individual has the additional information about the fact that they actually do date their co-workers. In the *credible excuse* version of the scenario, the co-worker said no, offering the excuse that they did not date other co-workers. There was no information to question the validity of this excuse. In this case, the individual should experience neither a loss of self-esteem nor a disruption in social interaction.

Results showed that the effect of the scenario content on self-esteem was as expected. In the credible excuse versions, the participants reported anticipating relatively high self-esteem. The lowest self-esteem was experienced in the transparent excuse versions, and levels of self-esteem in the blunt no versions fell somewhere in between. Levels of embarrassment were highest in the blunt no versions. However, embarrassment did not significantly differ between the credible and the transparent excuse versions (i.e., the two versions of the scenario in which social interaction was not disrupted). This suggests that when social interaction can continue smoothly, even if self-esteem is lowered, embarrassment is not likely to be produced. These results are graphed in Figure 3.3.

More recent work by Sabini et al. (2000) suggests that there is some truth to both loss of esteem and dramaturgic theories. Their study revealed independent classes of "triggers" of embarrassment and the

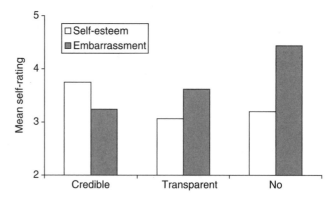

FIGURE 3.3. Mean self-esteem and embarrassment ratings as function of pretext type for co-worker story. From Parrott, W. G. et al. (1988). The roles of self-esteem and social interaction in embarrassment. *Personality and Social Psychology Bulletin, 14,* 191–202.

psychological experiences underlying the resulting feelings. Specifically, their results indicated that there is a clear category of embarrassing situations that can be called "faux pas," public gaffes, and that these situations are accompanied by a loss of self-esteem. But Sabini and colleagues also found a different trigger that involves awkward social interaction. This trigger is typified both by the situation of finding oneself the (unwanted) center of attention, which should be accompanied by the anticipation of a disrupted performance, and also by being put in a social situation that is inherently "sticky," that is, that involves the explicit criticism or lowering of another person's self-esteem. This category of embarrassment triggers was not strongly associated with a lowering of self-esteem, but was clearly defined by an unbidden and unwanted social awkwardness. Consistent with this latter category of embarrassment trigger, Lewis (2000) has also noted that merely selecting an individual at random from an audience and having the rest of the audience look at him or her will reliably produce embarrassment. And Miller (1992) has shown that singling an individual out to receive public praise will also produce embarrassment. These seem to be good examples of awkward situations that trigger embarrassment without necessarily being accompanied by a loss of esteem or self-esteem.

Functions of Embarrassment

The communication and social coordination functions of embarrassment, mentioned more briefly in Chapter 2, have recently enjoyed careful empirical scrutiny. In one such program of research, Keltner (1995) documented a universal gesture (not merely facial expression) of embarrassment. According to his analysis, embarrassment is expressed by a sequence of behaviors that involves, first, *gaze aversion*, then lower face action designed to *inhibit smiling*, followed by a *non-Duchenne smile* involving only the upturning of the lips and resembling a sheepish grin, then another attempted to *inhibit smiling*, then a downturn of the head, completed by a tendency to engage in *face touching* usually used to hide the mouth or eyes. Keltner and Buswell (1996), moreover, have demonstrated that this sequence does not accompany experiences of shame or amusement. The function of the gesture, as for the universal facial expressions that accompany basic emotions, is to communicate something to another person. Specifically, as we discussed in Chapter 2, the communication is one of appeasement; the expressed desire is for forgiveness and, thus, the reparation of a relationship. Consistent with this idea, individuals show a strong need to communicate their embarrassment explicitly, and continue to feel quite flustered and mortified if the communication is in any way hindered (Leary, Landel, & Patton, 1996).

Ample support for the idea that embarrassment gestures are recognized accurately by observers is reported in a program of research by Miller and colleagues. In one study of the accuracy of recognition of another's embarrassment, Marcus, Wilson, and Miller (1996) invited female participants into the laboratory and had them either dance along to recorded music in front of an audience (a very embarrassing task) or simply sit and listen to music (an innocuous task). The question was how accurate the audience was at detecting levels of embarrassment from the nonverbal cues of the dancing university women. They were very accurate. That is, levels of experienced embarrassment were highly correlated with levels of detected embarrassment. And this same level of accuracy was also demonstrated in a field study (Marcus & Miller, 1999).

Furthermore, the expression of embarrassment seems to have the prosocial effects that the embarrassed person desires. For example, questionnaire studies of responses to others' embarrassment show that observers try to help those who express their embarrassment, most often by communicating continued esteem for and acceptance of the embarrassed person, in spite of the gaffe or public exposure. When confronted by a display of embarrassment, observers also tend to insist on the consensual nature of the situation, offering examples of the times that they were similarly embarrassed. These prosocial reactions to expressions of embarrassment seem to be related to the fact that people tend to like more those who do embarrassing things and then actually express their embarrassment. In one laboratory demonstration of this effect, Semin and Manstead (1982) showed experimental participants videotapes of a man who accidentally toppled over a tall pile of toilet paper rolls in a grocery store. In different versions of the video, participants then saw one of four different endings to the story. In two endings, the man expressed his embarrassment. In two other endings, he did not. Fully crossed with the manipulation of the expression of embarrassment was a manipulation of reparative behavior. In one version of each of the embarrassment expression conditions (i.e., no expression versus expression), the man restacked the toppled rolls of toilet paper, and in the other he walked away. Participants rated their liking of the man, and those who saw the version of the video in which the man expressed his embarrassment, and repaired the damage that he had done, liked the protagonist most. Even the man who expressed embarrassment but then just walked away in apparent mortification was liked more than the man in the versions in which no embarrassment was expressed at all.

In a related study, de Jong (1999) had young adults read scenarios in which a shopper caused damage in a grocery store and then either blushed or did not blush. Experimental participants rated the shopper who blushed more favorably than the one who did not blush. Semin and Papadopoulou (1990) also showed that parents punish children who behave poorly in public and then clearly communicate embarrassment less severely than they punish children who engage in misbehavior, but communicate no embarrassment. Thus it seems that expressions of embarrassment indeed restore social harmony.

Pride and Hubris

Pride is a pleasant, sometimes exhilarating emotion that results from a positive self-evaluation (Lewis, 2000). Although the self-evaluation may occasionally involve reference to other people's performances (i.e., social comparison), the standard view of pride is that it results from satisfaction with meeting one's own personal standards and goals, including internalized beliefs about what is right and wrong (Tangney, 2002a; Tracy & Robins, 2004b). Pride is therefore also called a *moral emotion* in that it is assumed to reinforce the production of positive, moral acts. Of course, if pride is all so well and good, one might ask, why do Judeo-Christian and other religious writings teach that "pride goeth before a fall?" Why does pride also have a negative connotation, as in something bad, a sin, a feeling to be avoided and the expression of which is to be inhibited? In fact, most of the existent theory and research on pride attempts in some way to distinguish the positive sense of pride (i.e., as in an accomplishment) and its functions, with the more arrogant, narcissistic, pride, which in English is called *hubris*. This distinction can be found in other languages too, as in the French *fierté* (pride) versus *orgueil* (hubris). In a study of the

French emotion lexicon, Niedenthal and her colleagues indeed found that French university students rated *fierté* as a positively valenced emotion whereas *orgueil* was rated as a highly negatively valenced emotion (Niedenthal, Auxiette, Nugier, Dalle, Bonin, & Fayol, 2004).

Selves and Attributions Underlying Pride and Hubris

According to one recent theory, pride and hubris can be distinguished in a manner similar the distinction between guilt and shame made earlier in the chapter. Specifically, Tracy and Robins (2004b) suggest that pride involves exhilarated pleasure in a job well done (a behavior), whereas hubris involves an arrogant satisfaction in the self in general (see also Fischer & Tangney, 1995; Lewis, 2000). Furthermore, in this account, both emotions require that the person take credit, that is, make an *internal attribution*, for the good thing (behavior or self). An internal attribution is also an appraisal and, in different appraisal theories of emotion, has been variously called "self blame or self credit" (Lazarus, 1991), "responsibility" (Frijda, 1987), or "a causal attribution check" (Scherer, 2001).

However, the nature of the internal attributions made in pride and hubris are somewhat different. In pride, the attribution for a good behavior is made to an *unstable* and *specific* cause, of the variety "I worked hard in this particular course and as result I received a high grade." In contrast, hubris requires that the individual make a *stable* and *global* attribution for his or her goodness, of the variety "Our family is too good to accept charity." This latter type of attribution seems to typify the self-satisfied arrogance that we associate with hubris.

Behavioral Correlates of Pride and Hubris

The theoretical distinctions between pride and hubris just presented are supported in part by research that indicates that the two emotions are related to quite different behaviors and, by consequence, to quite different social outcomes. For instance, pride has been related to positive behaviors and outcomes in the area in which the individual is proud (Weiner, 1985), and to the development of a positive sense of self-esteem (Herrald & Tomaka, 2002). In a study specifically directed at a deeper understanding of the benefits of pride, Verbeke, Beschak, and Bagozzi (2004) examined the role of this emotion in the behavior of salespersons. Feelings of pride were associated with a heightened motivation to apply effective selling strategies, to work hard, and to experience feelings of self-efficacy. Pride was also associated with more positive social or citizenship behaviors, such as helping others and promoting the company in general. It thus appears that pride can have the positive benefits of enhancing creativity, productivity, and altruism (Bagozzi, Gopinath, & Nyer, 1999a; Fredrickson, 2001).

Contrariwise, hubris seems to be associated with more negative intra-individual and interpersonal outcomes (Tangney, 1999). Hubris is related to a tendency toward aggression and hostility. These reactions are likely to be due to the righteous indignation that results from narcissistic injuries, which are so frequently encountered when one thinks of himself or herself as especially worthy and deserving (Bushman & Baumeister, 1998; Morf & Rhodewalt, 2001). Consistent with this idea, hubris is not necessarily associated with high self-esteem, as one might expect, but with highly *fluctuating* or variable self-esteem (e.g. Rhodewalt, Madrian, & Cheney, 1997). Furthermore, Baumeister, Smart, and Boden (1996) propose that the arrogance and egoism communicated by feelings of hubris can be socially destructive. Specifically, when subject to displays of hubris, other individuals may try to avoid, shun, or otherwise reject the hubristic person. Consequently, excessive feelings of pride in the self (hubris) can cause conflict in and even terminate close relationships.

Hiding Expressions of Pride

It turns out that, like embarrassment, there is a gesture that communicates pride that involves a smile, a backward tilt of the head and lifting of the chin, and arms on hips or otherwise raised in some fashion to show confidence or victory (see Figure 3.4 for an example). Literate individuals in Italy and the United States can recognize the gesture of pride with greater than chance accuracy (Tracy & Robins, 2004b), distinguishing it clearly from happiness or surprise, and so can illiterate African tribe members who have had little to no exposure to western culture (Tracy & Robins, 2004a). If this is true, then there is a potential problem for pride. That is, if one feels and expresses it, but the observers of that expression do not know what attribution the proud person is assigning to their accomplishments, then how does the observer know in any given instance whether the individual is expressing pride or hubris? The distinction, as we have seen, has great social consequences. One possibility is that, because observers cannot always know the individual's attribution for his or her own accomplishments or qualities, social convention has led to a widespread inhibition of expressions of pride in many social interactions, at least in western cultures (Fischer & Tangney, 1995; see Chapter 9).

A study by Zammuner (1996) suggests that this is, indeed, the case. In her study, participants imagined themselves in two situations that typically produce pride, one professional-achievement situation and one social-achievement situation. The participants then rated the extent to

FIGURE 3.4. A gesture reliably recognized as conveying pride. From Tracy, J. L., & Robins, R. W. (2004b). Show your pride: Evidence for a discrete emotion expression. *Psychological Science, 15*, 194–197.

which they would feel a number of emotions as well as the extent to which they would communicate those feelings to another person. Pride was indeed elicited in both types of situations, but it was always felt to a much greater degree than it was communicated to others. The communication of pride was, at least, partially inhibited. Of course, expressions of pride might also be used in communicating power differences and status, and so situational differences in when pride is inhibited and when it is not should also be expected (Verbeke et al., 2004). Consistent with this idea, it has been noted that the expression of pride may have evolved as a mechanism of communicating success, thereby ensuring the person's status within a group, as well as his or her access to resources managed by the group (Keltner & Haidt, 1999; Tracy & Robbins, 2004a).

Summary

In this chapter, we examined two sets of emotions that have been called self-conscious emotions. As noted, all such emotions rely on the cognitive abilities involved in having a sense of self, and of self-reflection and evaluation. Furthermore, the first set of emotions that we examined also relies on an ability to compare the attributes of the self to those of another person. The resulting emotions, depending on other features of the situation, are envy or jealousy.

In addition to having a sense of self, and reflecting on and evaluating that self, another group of emotions requires an ability to make comparisons between standards, morals and ideals, and actual behaviors and experiences in which the self is involved. Negative self-evaluations resulting from a discrepancy between standards of moral or acceptable behavior are experienced as guilt, whereas negative self-evaluations resulting from a sense of the self as bad and unworthy are experienced as shame. Another self-evaluation emotion, as we called this group of emotions, is embarrassment. We saw that this emotion is distinct from shame in that it involves a focus on the self presented to an audience rather than the entire self, and that it is experienced as a sense of fluster and slight mortification resulting from a social awkwardness that leads to a loss of esteem in the eyes of others. Finally, pride and hubris result from a positive self-evaluation, with pride involving an experience of having done something well, whereas hubris results from an overall self-satisfaction that can be seen as narcissistic arrogance.

With the exception of hubris, we saw that these emotions all have some positive functions, particularly with regard to social relationships. Jealousy may signal that work on a significant relationship is needed, for example, and guilt may lead people not only to make amends in a particular situation, but also to try harder to avoid moral failures in the future. Thus, while many self-conscious emotions may be painful, they may be seen as necessary for the smooth functioning of complex social systems.

Facial Expression of Emotion

4

▶ *Contents at a Glance*

Imagine the following simple exercise. Frank is instructed to tell Anna that he loves her as if he means it. He smiles and purrs out the words, "I love you." It is very convincing. Then Frank is told to tell Anna he loves her again, but with an expression of anger. He furrows his brow and barks out the statement. Now he is instructed to be sarcastic. This time, Frank rolls his eyes, barely makes eye contact with Anna, and tosses off the fact that he loves her. In each communication, the expression on Frank's face, and the tone of his voice, is very different. Although each time he says "I love you," there is only one case, that in which he expresses strong positive emotion on his face and in his voice, that we as the audience are convinced that Frank might love Anna. Expressed emotions are stronger than words. We know this because different expressed emotions can change the meaning of the very same words. As discussed in Chapter 2, on the function of emotion, emotional expression is thus fundamental to human relations and social life. Successful interaction and communication with others requires not only the ability to express one's own emotions but also to correctly identify others' emotions in order to react in an appropriate way. Everyone has experienced feelings of frustration and irritation when interacting with a person who is inscrutable. How does this person really feel towards us? Is it sympathy, aversion, anger, or fear? How is the person going to act towards us? With cooperation, affiliation, or rejection? And how should we treat this person in return? With approach or avoidance?

Emotional expression refers to any verbal or nonverbal behavior by which emotions are revealed, displayed, or communicated to others. Much research has been devoted to the study of nonverbal communication of emotions including facial expression, gesture, bodily posture, and vocalization. Of these different types of nonverbal emotional behavior, however, facial expression has received the most and the most continuous attention from psychologists. Everyone is fascinated by faces, and research psychologists are no different in this regard. Facial expression is thus the focus of this chapter.

The present chapter is organized around three major topics. The first concerns the origin of facial expressions, and, in particular, the question whether facial expressions are universal or culture specific. A second topic concerns the exact nature of the information conveyed by the face, and, in particular, the question of whether facial display conveys information about the expresser's emotional state or about the expresser's social motives and intentions. This query has also led to research on the relative influence of facial expression versus the situation in which the expression is displayed on emotion attributions. Finally, facial expressions can also feed back on emotional states, potentially influencing the intensity and quality of emotional feelings. The roles of facial feedback in emotional experience and the recognition of facial expressions will therefore be discussed in the last section.

What are Facial Expressions of Emotion?

There exists a wide range of facial expressions, and not all of these are related to emotions. We as observers witness not only smiles of happiness, grimaces of disgust, and frowns of anger, but also movements of the lips during speech, movements of the mouth and cheeks during chewing, blinking of the eyes from irritation or squinting in bright sunlight, and facial movements during sneezing. Facial movements are produced through the contraction of a large number of single facial muscles and muscle groups, which create numerous folds and wrinkles on the facial skin. An understanding of how these muscles are controlled facilitates an understanding of the ways in which psychologists go about measuring and quantifying facial expression.

Facial muscles are activated by motor nerves that carry impulses from the motor cortex to the muscles themselves (Rinn, 1984, 1991). Most of the facial muscles, such as the forehead muscles and the muscles that move the eyebrows and the lips, are innervated by the seventh cranial nerve, aptly called the *facial nerve*. Some of the facial muscles are controlled by the third cranial nerve, the *occulomotor nerve*, which innervates the muscle implicated in the lifting of the eyelids, as in surprise, and which also governs pupil dilation and the movements of the eyeball. The fifth cranial nerve, the *trigeminal nerve*, innervates the muscles implicated in chewing and in clenching the jaw.

The facial nerves are innervated through two motor systems. The *subcortical motor system*, or the extrapyramidal circuit, mediates nonvoluntary, facial behavior that occurs in response to eliciting stimuli. Subcortically activated facial behavior consists of stable, fixed patterns of muscle contractions that are innate and universal, often occur outside the awareness of the expresser, and that are difficult to produce or inhibit at will. The *cortical motor system*, or the pyramidal circuit, mediates learned, voluntarily induced facial behavior that is under the control of the expected consequences of behavior. The cortical facial actions are learned responses that may vary across cultures and that can be produced and inhibited on command. The cortical motor system plays a central role in the social regulation and control of facial behavior through socially learned display rules, and influences heavily the degree and form of actual facial movements.

The finding of differential consequences of neurological lesions in the cortical and subcortical motor system on facial behavior indicates that the motor circuits function independently of one another. Lesions in the motor cortex lead to impairment of voluntary facial expressions while spontaneous, nonvoluntary expressions persist. The inverse effect can be observed in patients with subcortical lesions, who lack spontaneous facial behavior, but who are able to contract facial muscles on command. In general, however, the two motor systems interact and contribute each to various degrees to the final facial expression. This explains why facial expressions of emotion can be modulated and inhibited, but this control is not absolute and not always perfect.

Measurement of Facial Expression

The study of the facial muscles can be traced to the French physiologist Guillaume-Benjamin Duchenne de Boulogne (1862/1990) who studied the role of the different facial muscles involved in facial expressions. Duchenne induced the contraction of various facial muscles with the help of electric currents and took photographs of the resulting facial expressions (see Figure 4.1). A hundred years later, the Swedish psychologist Carl-Herman Hjörtsjö (1969) proposed a first coding system in which he described in detail the facial muscles that are associated with different expressions. His work contributed to a better understanding of the anatomy of facial muscles actions and to a resurgence of interest in the measurement of facial expression. The detailed anatomic knowledge of the facial muscles and of the facial movements they produce was essential for the development of objective methods for the measurement of facial expressions (Ekman & O'Sullivan, 1991, and Wagner, 1997, for reviews).

There are now two major approaches to quantifying facial expression; one is called the *component approach* and the other the *judgment approach*. The component approach (Ekman, Friesen, & Ellsworth, 1982a), also called the measurement approach (Wagner, 1997), involves the objective description and measurement of observable or measurable changes in facial behavior. Component studies investigate the emotion-specific facial muscle

FIGURE 4.1. Expression of surprise: Voluntary lowering of the lower jaw, and electric contraction of the forehead. From Duchenne de Boulogne, G.-B. (1862/1990). *Mécanisme de la physionomie humaine* [The mechanism of human facial expression]. Cambridge/New York: Cambridge University Press.

actions that are associated with the expresser's emotional state. Component methods include *electromyography* (EMG) and objective coding systems such as the *Facial Affect Scoring Technique* (FAST), the *Maximal Descriptive Facial Movement Coding System* (MAX), and the *Facial Action Coding System* (FACS), which is the objective measure most commonly used in facial expression research.

EMG measures the electrical discharge of contracted facial muscles with small surface electrodes that are placed on the face (for an overview see Cacioppo, Tassinary, & Fridlund, 1990). EMG recording thus can provide an accurate assessment of both visible and nonvisible, spontaneous and voluntary facial behavior. EMG activity differentiates the pleasantness and intensity of affective reactions in response to emotion-eliciting stimuli that produce no apparent facial expressions (Cacioppo, Petty, Losch, & Kim, 1986). EMG recording has also been used to distinguish between the true smile of happiness, often called an *enjoyment smile*, or the *Duchenne smile*, which implicates both the *zygomaticus major* and *orbicularis oculi* muscles, from voluntary, *strategic smiles*, also called *social smiles*, that implicate the *zygomaticus major* muscle alone (Ekman, Davidson, & Friesen, 1990).

In objective coding systems, observers describe *visible* facial muscle movements without interpreting them in terms of emotions. FAST, developed by Ekman, Friesen, and Tomkins (1971) defines and provides 77 descriptors, which consist of photographed examples of facial movements for the six basic emotions that can be observed in three parts of the face (i.e., the forehead, eyes, and lower face). Observers compare a facial expression with the examples provided in the FAST atlas, separately for each of the three parts of the face, and attribute corresponding scores. The global score indicates the emotion that is most likely expressed. Similar coding systems, developed for use with infants, are MAX, that specifies 27 descriptors (Izard, 1979), and AFFEX that allows the identification of emotional expressions by wholistic judgments (Izard & Dougherty, 1980). These systems classify facial expressions into categories, such as sadness, anger, and joy, but do not also code for the intensity of the expression or its dynamic properties.

Inspired by Hjörtsjö's coding system (shown in Figure 4.2), Ekman and Friesen (1978) developed a purely anatomically based coding system, FACS, which relies on the minimal facial muscle actions that produce facial expressions and that includes the coding of their intensity and their time course. FACS consists of 44 facial action units (AUs), that singly, or in combination, account for all visible and distinguishable facial muscle movements. FACS makes predictions concerning the AUs that are associated with specific emotional states. Some evidence for the validity of the FACS comes from studies that used self-reports of expressers' feelings or that relied on observers'

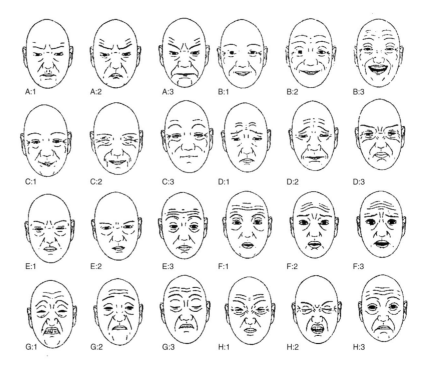

A1: resolute, firm, severe; **A2: angry (2, 4, 6);** A3: furious
B1: friendly, smiling; **B2: happy (1, 5);** B3: hearty laughter
C1: ingratiating smile; C2: crafty, slyly smiling; C3: self-satisfied smile
D1: sad (2, 3, 7), worried, grieved; D2: mournful; D3: physical hurt, tormented
E1: suspicious; E2: enquiring, examining; E3: perplexed
F1: surprised (3, 4, 6); F2: frightened (2, 3, 4, 6); F3: panic-stricken, anguished
G1: ironic; G2: contemptuous, condescending; G3: arrogant, self-sufficient
H1: disgusted (3, 4, 5, 6); H2: nauseated; H3: disappointed

(1) Zygomaticus major: pulls the lip corners up and back; (2) *corrugator supercilii/
depressor supercilii*: draws the brows together and down; (3) *frontalis pars medialis/
lateralis*: raises inner/outer brows and produces horizontal furrows on the forehead;
(4) *frontalis pars lateralis*: raises outer brows and produces horizontal furrows on the
forehead; (5) *orbicularis oculi*: tightens skin around eyes causing crow's feet
wrinkles, and raises lower eyelid; (6) *orbicularis oris*: tightens, compresses and
inverts lips; (7) *depressor anguli oris*: pulls the lip corners downwards

FIGURE 4.2. Schematic representation of facial expressions with a selection of facial muscles and the description of their visible effects on the face. Facial expressions of basic emotions in bold with the major muscles involved in parentheses. After Hjortsjö, C. (1969). *Man's face and mimic language*. Lund, Sweden: Student Literature.

judgment of emotion to identify the AUs implicated in the spontaneous facial expressions of basic emotions (Ekman & Friesen, 1982).

Unlike the component approach, the *judgment approach* is not concerned with facial muscle movements themselves, but with the information that an observer can infer from a facial expression. The approach was introduced by Darwin (1872/1998) and has become the most commonly used method for studying facial expressions, in particular in studies that test the hypothesis of the universality and innateness of facial expression. Judgment studies are based on the assumption that an observer can accurately recognize emotions from the face alone, in the absence of any information about the emotion-eliciting situation. In the standard judgment study, observers (judges) are presented with still photographs of posed facial expressions and are asked to identify the emotion expressed by the person by selecting a single emotional word from a short list of emotional words (i.e., the forced-choice response format). Accuracy is inferred from the proportion of observers that select the predicted emotion for a given facial expression and is referred to as a recognition score or an agreement score. Facial recognition is said to be accurate when the agreement between observers is significantly higher than expected by chance (Ekman, Friesen, & Ellsworth, 1982b; for a review of accuracy measurement, see Wagner, 1993, 1997).

Origin of Facial Expressions: Nature vs. Culture

In his famous book *The Expression of the Emotions in Man and Animals*, Charles Darwin (1872/1998) explained the origin of emotional expressions within his evolutionary theory and claimed that facial expressions have evolved from animal expressions, and have been preserved through natural selection because of their adaptive value. We have already encountered Darwin's idea in this book, but we expand on it here, as the chapter is devoted to facial expression.

As we have seen, according to what Darwin termed his first principle, most facial expressions are serviceable associated habits; they are rudiments of former adaptive behavior that once allowed the organism to avoid danger or to gratify desires. The bared-teeth grimace of anger, he claimed, evolved from biting another animal during a fight, and has been preserved to threaten an enemy, and to signal the readiness to attack. In his second principle of antithesis, Darwin explained some expressions by their morphological opposite nature induced by an opposite emotional state of mind. Antithetic expressions have been evolved for their "power of intercommunication" (Darwin, 1872/1998, p. 63), for their utility for communication because they can be recognized easily by others. Finally, according to his third principle, some expressions are caused by the direct action of the excited nervous system (e.g., trembling, transpiration, blushing, pallor).

Thus, as we suggested in Chapter 2, according to the evolutionary perspective, facial expressions of emotions are hardwired, innate expressions of specific emotional states and should therefore be universal, that is, the same in all humans independent of age, gender, race and culture. Darwin attempted to provide evidence of his assumption of the phylogenetic continuity of animal and human expression of emotion by observing and comparing human expressions (of infants and children, the blind, the insane, and of normal adults) with animal expressions. Darwin illustrated his universality thesis with reports of emotional expressions of members of different cultures, which he obtained from English missionaries in different parts of the world. From his observations of cross-species and cross-cultural similarities Darwin (1872/1998) concluded that: "The same state of mind is expressed throughout the world with remarkable uniformity; and this fact is in itself interesting, as evidence of the close similarity in bodily structure and mental disposition of all races of mankind" (p. 24).

Darwin's universality thesis was strongly rejected by 20th-century psychologists and anthropologists who claimed that facial expressions are determined by culture and not by nature (Mead, 1975). The cultural relativity view of facial expression is well summarized in the saying that "what is shown on the face is written there by culture." The idea that emotional expressions are the result of social and cultural learning was in line with the then dominant view of behaviorism according to which human behavior is malleable and determined by the specific environment. Proponents of cultural relativism argued that members of different cultures are exposed to different environments, which are characterized by different emotional experiences and result in different rules for emotional expression. The same expressions might therefore have different meanings in different cultures.

So, for example, Klineberg (1938), who studied descriptions of emotional expressions in Chinese literature, reported that joy and happiness is not always expressed with a smile, and conversely, that a smile does not always signal happiness, but may serve to maintain the appearance of joy and to mask feelings that are not allowed to show. LaBarre (1947) argued that a smile does not always express joy but also surprise, amusement, or embarrassment. And Birdwhistell (1970) advanced a linguistic model in which facial expressions are treated as sort of body language, called *kinesics*, that are pure products of culture. From the absence of a universal language he inferred the absence of universal facial expressions. Evidence for culture-specific expressions relied heavily on anecdotal descriptions and observations or on personal convictions rather than on systematic empirical data. Although the extreme position of cultural relativism is not endorsed today by most scientists, it has in part survived in the social constructionist view, discussed in Chapter 1, that claims that emotions are socially constructed, and in the work of some cultural psychologists discussed in Chapter 9.

Empirical Evidence in Favor of Universality

Empirical evidence for the universality thesis comes mostly from a series of cross-cultural judgment studies that were spearheaded in the late 1960s and early 1970s by two independent research groups (Ekman, 1972; Ekman, Sorenson, & Friesen, 1969; Izard, 1971). These studies showed high agreement between observers of different western (Europe, North and South America) and nonwestern (Asia, Africa) cultures who had to match photographs of posed facial expressions of six basic emotions – anger, happiness, sadness, fear, disgust, and surprise – with a single emotional label selected from a short list of emotion words (i.e., a forced-choice format). In studies that allowed observers to describe the expressed emotion with their own words (i.e., a free-response format), the agreement score was a little lower, but still higher than expected by chance (Izard, 1971).

A modified judgment method was used for members of isolated, preliterate cultures, who had to match different emotion-eliciting situations with one single photograph of a posed facial expressions selected out of three (Ekman, 1973; Ekman & Friesen, 1971; see Figure 4.3). Again, the proportion of observers who chose the predicted facial expression that fit the situation was higher than chance level. The finding that posed facial expressions of emotions are interpreted in a similar way across western, nonwestern and even preliterate, isolated cultures indicates that facial expressions are not arbitrary, socially and culturally learned expressions but that they are based on spontaneous, innate facial behavior. Further evidence for the innateness of facial expressions of emotion comes from the observation that congenitally blind children display emotional expressions very similar to the expressions shown by normally sighted children in typical emotion-eliciting situations such as smiling when engaged in social

Fear   Happiness   Anger

FIGURE 4.3. Photographs of facial expressions from which participants have to select the one that fits the story ("Her friends have come and she is happy"). From Ekman, P. (1973). Cross-cultural studies of facial expression. In P. Ekman (Ed.), *Darwin and facial expression.* New York: Academic Press.

play, pouting during punishment, and crying when left in an unfamiliar environment (Darwin 1872/1998; Eibl-Eibesfeldt, 1973; Thompson, 1941).

Criticism of Studies Favoring Universality

The interpretation of the consensual recognition of facial expressions across cultures as strong evidence for the universality thesis has been severely criticized on technical and methodological grounds. The high agreement scores obtained in judgment studies have been called methodological artifacts due to stimulus presentation, to the use of posed instead of spontaneous facial expressions, to the forced-choice response format, and to the use of the standard chance level (for a critical review of judgment studies see Russell, 1994, and a reply from Ekman, 1994, and from Izard, 1994). We describe each of these issues in turn.

First, in most judgment studies observers were presented with the entire set of facial stimuli, which may have emphasized similarities and differences and inflated the agreement score. Furthermore, the response to one facial stimulus may be influenced by the responses given to the other facial stimuli. We will discuss the effects of the immediate stimulus context on facial recognition below.

Second, the use of preselected, posed facial expressions that are generally more conventional, prototypical expressions may also produce higher agreement scores compared to spontaneously occurring expressions. Third, the standard forced-choice format used in most recognition studies was criticized for constraining observers to choose one single emotion label from a short list indicating that the options in the list were considered as mutually exclusive. Furthermore, the list was judged as too restrictive because it contained only basic emotions including the predicted "correct" emotion, but lacked plausible alternative terms (more general emotional states, situational interpretations) and a "none of these terms is correct" option. The few studies that had participants freely describe the expressions with their own words (Boucher & Carlson, 1980; Izard, 1971) generally found slightly lower recognition accuracy compared to forced-choice format. However, the free-response format is also problematic because the agreement score depends on the categorization of responses as synonyms. Broader, more inclusive categories yield higher recognition scores compared to restrictive categories (Russell, 1994). Fourth, the use of the standard chance level against which the agreement score is compared may also inflate the recognition accuracy. For example, the probability with which a given emotion word is selected by chance out of a list of six emotion words is 16.6%. However, in most judgment studies the list of response options contained only one positive emotion (happiness) and four negative emotions (anger, sadness, disgust and fear) and surprise. Russell (1994) proposed to correct the chance level for happiness to 50% (reflecting the choice between a positive and negative response options) and to 25% for the four negative emotions, and to 33% for surprise (reflecting the choice between emotions of surprise, fear and happiness with which the surprise expression is most often identified).

Further Empirical Evidence in Favor of Universality

Russell's methodological criticism and suggestions have been implemented in more recent empirical studies that nevertheless find further support for universality of facial expressions. They show that recognition scores within and across cultures are above chance level even when pitted against a corrected chance level (Ekman, 1994), when measured with an improved forced-choice response format (Frank & Stennett, 2001), and when measured with multiple methods (Haidt & Keltner, 1999). Frank and Stennett (2001), for example, used a modified forced-choice format which provided Australian observers with an extended option list of six emotion words (happiness, sadness, anger, disgust, fear, surprise), and a "none of these terms is correct" option, and they also conducted a second study in which a similar list of emotions was used but the emotion label that was correct for a given trial was removed from the list altogether. When the correct emotion label was included in the option list, most of the participants selected that label independent of the availability of a none option; very few participants used the none option. However, when the correct option was removed from the list, the majority of the participants chose the none option. Furthermore, in a third study in which the options included the six basic emotion labels and four additional plausible and related labels (i.e., alarmed, bored, contempt, excited), recognition scores remained more or less the same. In summary, when the predicted, correct emotion label was provided, it was indeed the modal choice of observers, regardless of the presence of a none option or of the presence of additional emotional labels. And, when the correct response option was removed from the list, the modal choice was the none option.

These findings are clearly inconsistent with the criticism that the universal recognition of facial expressions is due to the use of the standard forced-choice method that artificially forced agreement between observers. And they are further corroborated by a study by Haidt and Keltner (1999) that expanded the investigation of cross-cultural facial recognition of emotion beyond the usual six basic emotions to facial expression of shame, embarrassment, amusement, compassion, and contempt and to three expressions associated with self-conscious emotions (tongue biting, gaping, and

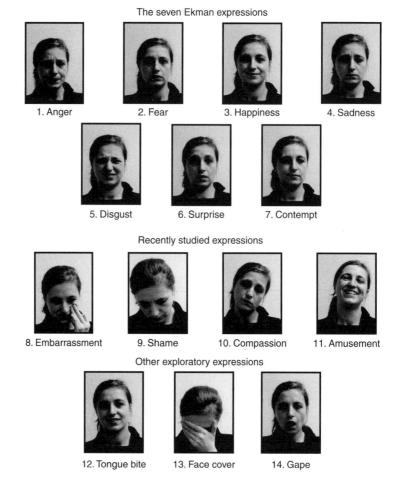

FIGURE 4.4. Photographs of facial expressions of basic emotion expressions, self-conscious emotions and other exploratory expressions. Adapted from Haidt, J., & Keltner, D. (1999). Culture and facial expression: Open-ended methods find more expressions and a gradient of recognition. *Cognition and Emotion, 13*, 225–266.

covering the face with the hand) (see Figure 4.4). First, American and Indian participants identified the facial expressions with their own words, and in a second run they used the standard forced-choice response format including 15 response options (14 options for the Indian sample). Overall recognition was clearly above chance level, yet varied in magnitude with regard to type of emotion and culture (see Figure 4.5).

Importance of Culture

Should we conclude from the studies of the universal recognition of facial expression that all facial expressions are innate? Of course not. Despite

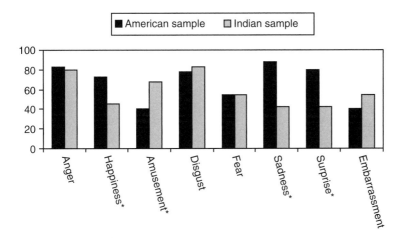

FIGURE 4.5. Recognition scores (%) for eight facial expressions of emotion for which the predicted emotion word was the modal response in both cultures; * indicates significant differences in the magnitude of recognition between the two cultures. From Haidt, J., & Keltner, D. (1999). Culture and facial expression: Open-ended methods find more expressions and a gradient of recognition. *Cognition and Emotion, 13,* 225–266.

the fact that most cross-cultural studies yield recognition scores significantly higher than expected by chance, the fact remains that the magnitude of recognition accuracy does vary with culture (Elfenbein & Ambady, 2002a; Haidt & Keltner, 1999). The highest recognition accuracy, for example, is observed in western cultures (78–95%). Recognition accuracy is lower in nonwestern cultures (63–90%), and lowest but still above chance level in isolated cultures (30–95%) (see Table 4.1). Furthermore, recognition of facial expression of emotion is more accurate when observers judge expressions of members of the same culture, a bias called the *ingroup advantage* (which is discussed in detail in Chapter 9), and when members of minority groups judge expressions of members of majority groups. Interestingly, the ingroup advantage decreases with increased exposure to members of other cultures (Elfenbein & Ambady, 2002a).

Culture-specific interpretations of the facial expressions of contempt and the tongue-bite gesture were found in the study by Haidt and Keltner (1999). Specifically, the contempt expression was interpreted as disgust by the American sample while it was interpreted as contempt by the Indian sample. The tongue-bite gesture was associated with self-conscious feelings of shame and guilt by the Indian sample, but was interpreted as sign of amusement by the American sample (see Table 4.2). Finally, the same study revealed cultural variations in the situational elicitors of the expressions of happiness and anger, despite the cross-cultural similarity in recognition accuracy and in the general emotion-eliciting domain. In American

TABLE 4.1
Median Percentage Recognition Scores in Western, Nonwestern, and Illiterate Cultures with Forced-choice and Story Method

Expressed emotion	Forced-choice method					Story method	
	Western	Nonwestern	Illiterate	Chance level		Illiterate	
Happiness	96.4	89.2	92	16.6[a]	50[b]	95	33.3[e]
Surprise	87.5	79.2	36	16.6	33.3[c]	78.5	33.3
Sadness	80.5	76	52	16.6	25[d]	78	33.3
Fear	77.5	65	46	16.6	25	80	33.3
Disgust	82.6	65	29	16.6	25	86	33.3
Anger	81.2	63	56	16.6	25	76	33.3

[a] standard chance level 16.6% – for six response options (emotion labels)
[b] new chance level for happiness 50% – choice between positive and negative emotion
[c] new chance level for surprise 33.3% – choice between three response options
[d] new chance level for negative emotions 25% – choice between four response options
[e] standard chance level 33.3% – choice between three response options (photographs)

Data from Ekman, P. (1973). Cross-cultural studies of facial expression. In P. Ekman (Ed.), *Darwin and facial expression*. New York: Academic Press; and from Russell, J. A. (1994). Is there universal recognition of emotion from facial expression? A review of cross-cultural studies. *Psychological Bulletin, 115,* 102–141

participants, the happy expression elicited situational descriptions of personal success and material gain, while the anger expression was associated with situations in which others harmed the self. For Indian participants, the happy expression was reported to be elicited by the experience of a pleasant social relationship with friends or family members, and the anger expression by the experience of unpleasant social contact.

TABLE 4.2
Culture-specific Emotion Recognition: Facial Expressions and Chosen Emotion Words, with Percentage of the American and the Indian Sample that Chose the Word as Modal Response

Expression	American sample	Indian sample
contempt	disgust (55%)	contempt (62.5%)
shame	shame (57.5%)	sadness (45%)
compassion	sadness (37.5%)	awe (30%)
tongue bite	amusement (37.5%)	guilt (27.5%)
gape	disgust (42.5%)	surprise (22.5%)

From Haidt, J., & Keltner, D. (1999). Culture and facial expression: Open-ended methods find more expressions and a gradient of recognition. *Cognition and Emotion, 13,* 225–266

Another source of cultural variations in facial display is socially and culturally learned norms, so-called *display rules*, that specify when and how emotions can be expressed depending on the social situation and cultural demands (Ekman, 1972). Ekman and Friesen (1975) distinguished several ways in which display rules can affect facial behavior. Facial expressions may display an emotion without a corresponding feeling, mask the presence of another inappropriate emotion, attenuate or enhance the apparent intensity of a felt emotion, or even entirely mask or inhibit a felt emotion.

The two opposing views of universality versus cultural relativism that once provoked a lively debate have been integrated by many scientists in an "interactionist perspective" (Elfenbein & Ambady, 2002a) in which both biological and social/cultural determinants of facial expressions are taken into account, as for example in Ekman's (1972, 1994) neurocultural theory of emotion. It seems clear that there is a strong innate component for several facial expressions of emotion. At the same time, subcultural and cultural rules for interpretation and display clearly exert a strong influence on facial displays of emotion.

What Information is Provided by Facial Expressions? Emotions vs. Social Motives

An underlying theme in the nativist position on facial expression of emotion is that the reason that facial expressions are universal is because a subset of emotions are themselves innate, and these emotions show themselves on the face. But it is not so simple. The cultural perspective points out that display rules and other cultural beliefs can influence emotional expression. If that is the case, what do facial expressions of emotion actually express? This is at issue in another hot debate in the area of facial expression of emotion. According to one current in this debate, facial displays are "expressions" of internal states of emotion. According to another current, facial expressions are means of communicating social motives and intentions.

Expressions as Emotions: The Emotion-expression View

A number of psychologists including Ekman, (1972), Izard, (1971), and Tomkins (1962, 1963) have advanced the first view, namely that facial expressions reflect the expresser's internal emotional state. This view has been called the "emotion-expression view" (Manstead, Fischer & Jakobs, 1999), the "readout view" (Buck, 1984, 1994), and the "efference hypothesis"

(Camras, Holland, & Patterson, 1993). This approach holds that the close relationship between emotion and expression is due to the existence of an innate affect program for each basic emotion that produces neural efference to the facial muscles generating distinct, emotion-specific facial expressions.

Evidence for the emotion-expression view comes from studies that show that facial expressions, as measured by observer judgments, EMG, and by objective coding systems, are associated with the expresser's felt emotions, as measured by self-reported emotional experience or physiological reactions. In the slide-viewing paradigm, also called the "sender–receiver" paradigm (Buck, 1978; Buck, Miller & Caul, 1974), participants who serve as "senders" view emotionally evocative colored slides while their facial expressions are recorded with a hidden camera. The slides fall in the categories *pleasant*, *unpleasant*, *sexual*, and *unusual*. The senders are instructed to evaluate the pleasantness of each slide. Other participants, the "receivers," who watch the sender's videotaped facial expressions have to identify the type of slide the sender was viewing and evaluate the pleasantness of the sender's emotional reaction. Consistent with the emotion-expression view, studies using this procedure have revealed that receivers accurately identify the slide category viewed by senders at better than chance levels. Furthermore, the receivers' pleasantness ratings are positively correlated with senders' self-reported pleasantness responses to the slide. Such findings suggest that observers are able to correctly "read" the pleasantness of emotional reactions from expressers' faces alone.

Similar findings of facial efference have been reported in EMG studies (Cacioppo, Bush, & Tassinary, 1992; McHugo, Lanzetta, & Bush, 1991). In those studies, pleasant stimuli produced increased *zygomaticus major* activity (smiles) while unpleasant (i.e., sad, angry, and fearful) stimuli led to increased *corrugator supercilii* muscle activity, that is, frowns.

Studies that rely on objective coding of visible facial expressions have also found a positive relationship between facial expressions and self-reported emotional experience in support of the emotion-expression view. Ekman, Friesen, and Ancoli (1980), for example, had participants view pleasant films (e.g., featuring gorilla babies playing) or unpleasant films (e.g., of accidents in the workplace) that were intended to induce positive or negative emotions. Participants' self-reports of the intensity of elicited emotions were measured after each filmclip, and their filmed facial reactions were coded with FACS. Results of the study showed that participants who displayed the critical facial action units (*zygomaticus major* activity) in response to positive films reported feeling happier, and those who displayed negative facial action units in response to negative films reported feeling more fear, surprise, pain, arousal, and disgust than those who did not express the emotion-specific facial expressions. Furthermore and in line with the emotion-expression view, the number of the critical facial action units displayed was positively correlated with self-reported intensity of positive and negative feelings.

Ekman et al. (1990) analyzed in greater detail the type of smile that occurs in response to pleasant and unpleasant films. They found a positive relationship between the enjoyment, or Duchenne smiles that involve the activation of the *zygomaticus major* and the *orbicularis oculi* muscles and self-reported happiness in response to pleasant films. Similarly, Rosenberg and Ekman (1994) showed that participants' self-reported emotions induced by disgust- and fear-eliciting films, and measured several times during the film (moment-to-moment feelings), matched their facial expressions (as measured by FACS) especially in the most intense emotional moments.

In the emotion-expression view, social factors can alter the spontaneous facial expressions of emotions, and so such factors are typically minimized in relevant studies. For example, participants in the studies just described were typically alone while watching emotion-eliciting slides or films. In these minimal social situations the facial expressions reflect above all the participants' emotional reactions induced by the emotion-eliciting stimuli. However, facial expressions can, in part, be controlled by social demands specific to the current context or by an expresser's intentions. For example, an expresser may intend to lie with his or her face. Facial display thus does not always convey reliable information about a person's feelings. But even when facial expressions are controlled, a person's emotion may still be betrayed by body movements and gestures (DePaulo, 1992; Ekman & Friesen, 1974). The impact of the social context on facial displays, neglected although not denied in the emotion-expression view, is the main interest of those who emphasize the communicative and social function of facial expressions.

Expressions as Motives: The Behavioral Ecology View

According to the "behavioral ecology" view, also called the "social communication" view, facial expressions are social signals that evolved to communicate the expresser's social motives in a particular social situation (Fridlund, 1992, 1994, 1997). Facial expressions signal what the expresser intends to do and what the expresser wants others to do. For example, a smile signals the expresser's intention to affiliate, while a sad face signals request for assistance and comfort. A person is, above all, expressing what is beneficial for him, and what serves his social motives and intentions independent of his feelings. Thus, an individual displays a sad face when he needs help or support, and not necessarily when he feels sad. Studies in support of the behavioral ecology view focus on the communicative function of facial display. They try to show that facial expressions are most often displayed in interactive situations and that they vary with the sociality of the situation (defined as the degree to which the social situation implies the – real or imagined – presence of others).

Interactive Situations

Kraut and Johnston (1979) observed the spontaneous facial expressions of bowlers, ice hockey fans, and pedestrians during interactive and non-interactive episodes. These researchers found that bowlers smiled more when facing their co-players than when facing the bowling pins, independent of their performance. They also found that ice hockey fans who were interacting with friends smiled more when their team made a goal or the opposing team made a penalty than when they were not interacting with friends. Finally, pedestrians who were conversing with another person smiled more than non-interacting pedestrians, independent of the weather (see Figure 4.6).

Ruiz-Belda, Fernandez-Dols, Carrera, and Barchard (2003) replicated the findings of Kraut and Johnston with Spanish bowlers who were filmed in a bowling alley, and Spanish soccer fans who were filmed at home while watching important matches on television. In addition, they assessed participants' feelings and analyzed the smiles during both interactive and

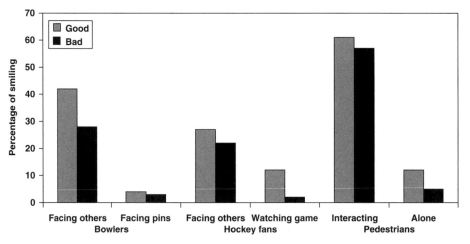

FIGURE 4.6. Percentage of bowlers, hockey fans, and pedestrians smiling as a function of the valence of the score/game/weather, and the sociality of the situation. From Kraut, R. E., & Johnston, R. (1979). Social and emotional messages of smiling: An ethological approach. *Journal of Personality and Social Psychology, 37*, 1539–1553.

non-interactive episodes using FACS. Again, bowlers and soccer fans smiled significantly more when they were in social interactions than when they were not interacting, even though they reported actually feeling equally happy in both interactive and non-interactive situations. In a related study, Fernandez-Dols and Ruiz-Belda (1995) analyzed the facial expressions of 22 gold medalists at the 1992 Olympic Games award ceremony using FACS. Gold medalists smiled more frequently when interacting with the officials and members of the audience than when they waited behind the podium to receive the medal, or after receiving the medal when they were turned to the flag to listen to their country's national anthem. These findings suggest that smiling is less related to individuals' happy feelings and depends more on the social aspect of the situation.

Sociality of the Situation

Of course, situations in which facial displays occur cannot be categorized simply as nonsocial or social (Fridlund, 1991). Rather, they vary in the degree of sociality, that is, in the extent to which they imply the physical or imagined presence of others. It could be, therefore, that the degree of sociality of a situation is related to the degree to which emotions are expressed on the face. This is exactly what was demonstrated in a study by Chovil (1991). Participants in the study were filmed while they listened to stories about close calls – dramatic consequences that almost happened, but did not – in one of four conditions that varied in sociality (rated by independent judges). In the least social condition, the participant was alone and heard about the close calls on an audiotape. In the next social condition, the participant heard the descriptions of the close calls from a person who was present in the room, but sitting behind a screen. In a more social condition, the participant heard the descriptions over the telephone. And in the most social condition, the person who described the close calls was face to face with the participant. Naturally, participants made lots of grimaces and gasps. Of interest was that facial behavior of wincing and grimacing increased systematically with the increasing sociality of the situation (see Figure 4.7). Consistent with Fridlund's behavioral ecology view, the presence of others facilitated facial display.

However, the specific impact of the social context (i.e. the presence of others) on facial display has been shown to be modulated by several factors including the familiarity between the expresser and the audience, the valence of the emotional situation, and the intensity of the emotion elicitors (Buck, Loslow, Murphy, & Costanzo, 1992; Hess et al., 1995; Jakobs, Manstead, & Fischer, 1999, 2001; Lee & Wagner, 2002). In particular, the presence of strangers tends to inhibit facial display while the presence of a

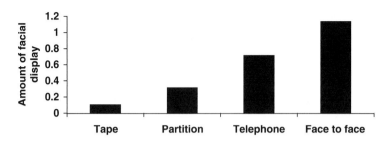

FIGURE 4.7. Amount of listeners' facial expressions as a function of the sociality of the situation. From Chovil, N. (1991). Social determinants of facial display. *Journal of Nonverbal Behavior, 15*, 141–154.

friend tends to facilitate facial display (Buck et al 1992; Wagner & Smith, 1991). In a study by Wagner and Smith (1991), for example, pairs of participants, who were either friends or strangers, watched emotion eliciting slides while their facial expressions were filmed. Facial expressions displayed in interaction with friends were later better recognized by observers than those displayed in pairs of strangers.

A differential impact of the presence of others also depends on the valence of the emotion-eliciting situation. The presence of others normally facilitates the facial display of positive emotions (i.e., enjoyment smiles) in a positive emotional situation. However, in a negative emotional situation, the presence of others tends to inhibit the facial display of negative emotions (i.e., sadness), and to facilitate the expression of social smiles (Jakobs et al., 2001; Lee & Wagner, 2002).

Finally, the impact of the social context on facial expressions varies also with the intensity of the emotion elicitor, indicating that facial expressions are determined by both social and emotional factors. Hess and her colleagues (1995) found increased emotional smiles and more intense self-reported positive emotions for highly amusing films compared to moderately amusing films, supporting the emotion-expression view. At the same time, and consistent with the social communication view, facial expressions were affected by the social context. In particular, participants displayed more enjoyment smiles in the presence of friends and marginally more social smiles in the presence of strangers than when alone. These findings suggest that both social context and emotional intensity of the film determine facial display, while the friend–stranger relationship modulates the weight of each.

Jakobs et al. (1999) replicated and extended the findings of Hess and colleagues by introducing an explicit measure of expressers' social motives. Pairs of friends watched two amusing filmclips that varied in intensity, either in the same room or in a different room, or one of them watched the filmclips while the other performed a different task, either in the same or in a different room. Participants in the control group came alone and watched the filmclips alone. Again, both emotional intensity (moderate and strong amusing film clip) and social context (sociality of the film-viewing situation) were found to influence facial expressions, as measured by FACS. On the one hand, and consistent with the emotion-expression view, funnier filmclips produced more intense positive feelings and more enjoyment smiles. On the other hand, and in line with the social communication view, the sociality of the situation enhanced social motives and increased the expression of social smiles, but did not influence the intensity of positive emotional feelings. Furthermore, this context effect on facial display was shown to be mediated by expressers' social motives including social awareness (i.e., the extent to which the participant was aware of and thought about the other person), and social motivation (i.e., the degree to which the participant imagined the evaluation of the filmclip by the other person, and their motivation to communicate about the filmclip with the other person).

The idea that facial expressions not only communicate information about the expresser's feelings but also information about the expresser's social motives and behavioral intentions is consistent with the finding that observers can correctly infer action readiness from facial expressions (Frijda & Tscherkassof, 1997). The concept of action readiness is similar to Fridlund's concept of behavioral intentions, but differs insofar as it consti- tutes a core component of emotion. Frijda (1995) suggested that the emo- tion labels that can be attributed to facial expressions imply action readiness. In this view, identifying a face as expressing anger not only implies that the person feels angry but also that the person is ready to attack. Frijda's account is consistent with the component process approach to emotion (see Chapter 1) according to which emotions include compo- nents of subjective feelings, of physiological arousal, of expressive behav- ior, and their precursors such as behavioral intentions and action readiness, and of cognitive appraisal, components that interact with each other. In this view, facial expressions can convey information about all components and they do so to different degrees, depending on their salience. In minimal social situations in which facial expressions are pre- sented alone, without information about the situation in which they occur, the expresser's feelings may be more salient. However, the expresser's social motives should become more salient when his/her facial expres- sions are embedded in a social context. The question of how context infor- mation affects the emotional message that can be inferred from the face will be discussed in the next section.

In summary, research on the meaning of facial expression suggests that facial expressions have social as well as emotional causes, and can serve both emotion-expressive and social-communicative functions, which are not mutually exclusive. Depending on the particular social context – such as whether one is alone or with others, and whether those others are strangers or friends – and depending on whether or not the emotion-eliciting event is positive or negative, facial display will be more or less spontaneous and emotional or instrumental and social.

What Information Determines the Recognition of Emotion? Face vs. Context

As we saw in the review of research on the universality of facial expressions of emotion, observers across cultures are able to infer the emotional state of a person from a photograph depicting nothing other than their facial expression. This appears to mean that facial expression has meaning outside the context in which it occurs. However, in natural settings, facial expressions do occur in context. The situation in which the expression occurs thus constitutes another potential source of information about the expresser's feelings. Furthermore, the perception of facial expressions always involves an observer whose personal characteristics, feelings, and immediate context may also influence the recognition process. In the following, we will discuss how the expresser's context and the observer's context can influence the perception and recognition of facial expressions.

Expresser Context Effects

Suppose you were watching a little boy being given some candy. His face reveals a big smile. When asked what the boy is feeling you would without hesitation answer "happiness." Why? You would probably refer to the child's "happy face," and the fact that getting candy is a situation that makes a child feel happy. In everyday life, we dispose of different cues to infer a person's emotional state. The most important such cues are the person's facial expression and the emotion-eliciting situation in which the expression occurs. Are both sources of information equally important or does one prevail, and if so, which one? The question of the relative weight of facial and situational information in emotional judgments becomes especially important when face and context convey different emotional meaning.

Imagine the above mentioned candy situation with the boy's face expressing anger or disgust. What is he feeling? Those who claim that facial expressions convey specific emotional meaning independent of the context would give facial cues more weight. They would probably infer

that the boy feels angry or disgusted, ignoring or reinterpreting the situational information. For example, perhaps he received candy he does not
like. But what would you think if you saw a big smile on the face of a
schoolboy getting a bad grade from his seemingly concerned teacher? Is
the boy really feeling happy? In this situation, the context would probably
make you doubt that the boy's smile expresses happiness.

Research on the role of facial expressions and context in emotional judgments has tried to specify the relative contribution of each source of information. In numerous studies, participants have been instructed to judge the
emotion expressed by facial expressions in isolation, or of emotion-eliciting
situations in isolation, or of consistent or discrepant combinations of both
expression and context. Every possible set of findings has been observed,
conferring the greatest weight on the expression, on the situation, or on the
combination, depending on the study. These inconsistent findings have
been attributed to methodological problems related to the experimental
material and procedure (for a review see Ekman, Friesen, & Ellsworth,
1982c; Fernandez-Dols & Carroll, 1997). Here, we discuss the three commonly used experimental paradigms, the problems they pose, and some
variables that have been found to determine the relative importance of
face and context.

The most often used and also most influential paradigm for investigating the importance of facial expression versus context on judgments of
emotional experience was developed by Goodenough and Tinker (1931).
In their "person scenario" approach, person information provided by
photographs of posed facial expressions of discrete, basic emotions is combined with context information presented through short verbal descriptions of emotion-eliciting situations (for example, "she found a dead rat in
the kitchen"). Studies using the person scenario approach have most typically found that facial cues are more influential even when situational cues
suggested an intense specific emotion (Fernandez-Dols, Wallbott, &
Sanchez, 1991; Frijda, 1969; Knudsen & Muzekari, 1983; Wallbott, 1988a;
Watson, 1972). However, a more recent study using this paradigm, by
Carroll and Russell (1996), found *limited context dominance*. When facial
cues were discrepant in terms of specific emotions but congruent in degree
of arousal and pleasantness, then the situational information determined
the specific emotion believed to be experienced by the expresser.

A second paradigm involves judgments of "candid pictures" of real-
life situations that can be found in magazines and newspapers (Munn,
1940). The photographs depict individuals' facial expressions in the naturally occurring emotion-eliciting situations. Observers judge either the
entire photograph, the face without the situational information, or the
situation information without the face. The few studies using the candid

picture paradigm found that context was as influential as facial expressions, that is, neither source of information was clearly dominant (Spignesi & Shor, 1981; Wallbott, 1988a).

A third research paradigm was introduced by Goldberg (1951), who used filmclips to provide both context and facial information. Participants were presented one of two filmclips, each consisting of four scenes, with an identical first scene (i.e., a child riding a tricycle) and an identical last scene conveying the facial information (i.e., a screaming woman). The two in-between scenes suggested either a fear-evoking situation, that is an accident, or a joyful experience, that is, a play context. Goldberg found relative influence of context on emotion judgments. In this study, the fear judgment dropped from nearly 100% in the fear context to 70% in the play context. The only other study that employed motion pictures found similar results (Wallbott, 1988b). Wallbott improved the filmclip paradigm by using realistic film material taken from existing television films and movies. A total of 60 filmclips was selected, each consisting of two scenes that followed each other in the original film. The first scenes presented the situational information (e.g., a person falling down a staircase), and the second depicted a person's facial reaction to this situation (e.g., a witness of the event with an apparently fearful expression). Observers who saw either the entire filmclip or the second take only (expression) were asked to judge the emotion expressed by the person in the last scene. Those who saw the first take only (situation) were asked to judge the emotion a person would express in this situation. Overall, context information contributed at least as much to the emotion judgments as the facial expressions. For discrepant cue combinations, context information tended to dominate over facial cues, but only when the expresser was a male actor.

The inconsistent results concerning the relative weight of facial and situational cues may be due to the particular mode of stimulus presentation employed in the different experimental paradigms (Wallbott, 1988a). For example, the dominance of facial expression found in the person scenario approach may be due to the visual presentation of facial information that allows a more direct, vivid, and less ambiguous representation of a person's actual feeling than the short verbal description of the context that says more how a person will feel in general in this situation (Carroll & Russell, 1996). When both sources of information are presented visually, as in the candid picture approach, then both face and context seem to be equally important. The slight context dominance found in the filmclip paradigm may be due to the greater salience of the filmed context that contains information about the relations between persons and their environment. Facial expressions are probably more salient when captured in a still photograph than when filmed (Elfenbein and Ambady, 2002a).

Source Clarity

One way to try to make sense out of the panoply of findings on the relative contributions of expression and situation in emotion judgments is to apply the notion of source clarity. Source clarity is defined as the amount of emotional information provided by each of the two types of information (i.e., expression and situation), and it is comprised of three components. The first of these is *source ambiguity*, which is the degree to which judges agree that a given source communicates one specific emotion. The second component is *source complexity*, which refers to the number of different emotions that different judges attribute to the same source. And a final component is *source intensity*, which is the perceived intensity of the emotional message. Judgments of the meaning of an emotional expression in its context should be determined by the clearest source.

Studies that have controlled for source clarity by using the same medium for both sources or by pairing facial expressions and situational description that received similar agreement scores have found equal weight of facial and situational cues in emotion judgments (Knudsen & Muzekari, 1983). Furthermore, contextual influence increases when facial expressions are ambiguous or neutral and less intense (Carrera-Levillain & Fernandez-Dols, 1994; Wallbott, 1988a, Watson, 1972), and when the salience of context information is heightened by the use of highly prototypical, but also rare, emotion-arousing situations, such as winning the lottery (Carrera-Levillain & Fernandez-Dols, 1994; Fernandez-Dols, Sierra, & Ruiz-Belda, 1993). But naturally, even if source clarity is manipulated or controlled in the confines of the laboratory, the clarity of expression and context information encountered in everyday life may actually differ systematically, and this may bias their relative weight in emotional judgments.

Accessibility of Emotion Categories

Facial expression judgments have been typically assessed by asking observers to choose a response from a set of emotion labels. It is possible, of course, that contexts are not naturally categorized or judged in terms of specific emotions, in the same way that facial expressions are. Facial expressions are easier and faster to categorize in terms of discrete emotions than descriptions of situations because people lack the experience of categorizing situations in terms of emotion categories. If this is true, then the facial dominance found in the Goodenough–Tinker paradigm may in part be due to the employed response format. In a study that followed this reasoning, Fernandez-Dols et al. (1991) predicted that if participants were trained to categorize situations using simple emotion terms, then weight of context in the judgment of emotional experience should increase. Consistent with their prediction, they found that the emotion judgments of participants who were trained to categorize situations with a single emotion word were equally influenced by facial and situational cues.

Source clarity and category accessibility are based on the assumption that face and context are independent and competing sources of information, each conveying its own emotional message. Therefore, when confronted with discrepant cue combinations, observers will evaluate both sources separately and choose the emotional meaning of the source that is the clearer and easier to access (Wallbott, 1988b). Another possibility is that both sources of information are related to each other and are integrated before the final decision. As we shall see, this integration process makes them susceptible to reinterpretation, in particular when they contain conflicting information.

Vulnerability to Reinterpretation

Vulnerability to reinterpretation is defined as the extent to which the interpretation of one source influences the interpretation of the other (Fernandez-Dols & Carroll, 1997). In the presence of conflicting cues, observers may reduce or solve the conflict by reinterpreting either the context or the facial expression. Studies that have allowed participants to respond in their own words and to justify their response have found several conflict-solving strategies, the most important being rationalization (Frijda, 1969; Knudsen & Muzekari, 1983).

Consider, for example, a photograph of a happy face combined with the following contextual description, intended to convey fear: "This person is trapped in a fire" (Knudsen & Muzekari, 1983). The happy face can be made plausible by adding that the person planned the fire in order to receive the insurance money, or by adding that the person can hear the fire engine approaching, and is anticipating rescue. However, the happy face can also be interpreted as a social smile that masks the true feeling of fear in order to avoid panic. This example illustrates two types of interpretational effort observers make to integrate the conflicting cues in one plausible emotional judgment. First, reinterpretation of the context consists of adding new situational information in order to make it consistent with the facial expression. Context reinterpretation is most likely when the original situational information is vague and general in tone, and when it lacks concrete, specific information (as in the person scenario paradigm in which context is presented through a short stereotypical one-sentence make-believe description of an event). Second, conflicting cues can be integrated by reinterpreting the facial cues. This consists of introducing the influence of display rules, which dissociate the person's apparent facial expression from his/her inner feelings. The facial expression is no longer perceived as reflecting the person's true emotion but is interpreted as being controlled by situational and social demands, such as not to cry in public.

Nakamura, Buck, and Kenny (1990) studied the impact of situational demands for display rules on the relative weight given to facial and contextual information using a modified version of Buck's (1978) slide-viewing paradigm. They showed that female observers relied less on facial expressions of senders who were supposedly filmed in the presence of other people, with a visible camera, compared to those supposedly filmed alone and with a hidden camera. Presumably in the former condition display rules could be at work. Male observers were less affected by situational demands for control of expressive behavior; they relied on the senders' facial expressions independent of the context.

There are also differences in how emotions are attributed to men versus women. In a study by Wallbott (1988b), which was described earlier, observers relied less on facial cues when they judged a filmclip depicting a male actor compared to actresses. The higher reliance on contextual information for male actors may be due to gender-specific decoding rules. The widely held stereotype that women express their emotions more accurately and intensely than men may generate expectancies about the extent to which expressive behavior reveals the expresser's true feelings. When judging a male expresser who is believed to be a poor expresser, observers will thus rely more on the contextual information than on his facial expression.

Observer Context Effects

The recognition of facial expressions is not only determined by the emotion-eliciting situation in which the expression occurs, but also by the observer's immediate context. Studies have shown, for example, that the emotional meaning conveyed by a facial expression depends on the types of facial expression that the observer has encountered previously, which may produce contrast effects (Cline, 1956; Russell & Fehr, 1987; Thayer, 1980a, 1980b). Thayer presented successively a series of five photographs, four depicting similar facial expressions followed by a final expression with a contrasting emotional content (a happy face preceded by sad faces and vice versa) posed by the same person (Thayer, 1980a) or by different persons (Thayer, 1980b). The same facial expression that was preceded by a series of contrasting emotional faces was judged as expressing a more intense emotion than when preceded by faces with a similar emotional expression. The contrasting facial context seems to increase the salience of the target expression.

Furthermore, Russell and Fehr (1987) showed that a preceding facial expression (the *anchor expression*) produces not only changes in the perceived intensity of the target expression, but also a qualitative change in the attributed emotion category label, particularly if the judged expression is somewhat ambiguous. Specifically, they showed that the anchor expression pushed the emotional judgment of the target expression in the opposite direction. The same neutral target face was perceived by a majority of observers as sad when it was preceded by a happy anchor expression, and as happy or surprised when preceded by a sad anchor expression. The same surprise target expression preceded by a fear or an excitement anchor expression was perceived as pleasant surprise or unpleasant surprise, respectively, and the same anger target expression preceded by a low arousal anchor expression (i.e., sadness) was perceived as anger, while it was perceived as sad when preceded by a high arousal expression (i.e., fear, anger or disgust). These contrast effects may become important in person perception.

Mood Effects

As we shall discuss in Chapter 6, observers may also perceive others' facial expressions as conveying an emotion that is congruent with their own emotional state. This idea was demonstrated in an early study by Schiffbauer (1974), who induced disgust, amusement, or neutral emotion in experimental participants through the use of audiotaped messages. The participants were then instructed to judge the emotions expressed by a series of photographs depicting different facial expressions. He observed that participants in the disgust condition attributed more disgust and other negatively valenced emotion to the expressions than both control participants and participants in the amusement condition. The observers' own emotional state apparently colored their perception of facial expressions of others in a manner congruent with their own current feelings. Similar emotion congruent processing of facial cues was found in a study by Leppänen & Hietanen (2003). Participants who were exposed to pleasant odors recognized happy faces faster than those in a neutral or unpleasant odor condition. Pleasant odors facilitated, and unpleasant odors inhibited, the recognition of happy faces. However, the affective odor context had no impact on the recognition of disgust faces.

Individuals not only interpret static facial expressions, they also scrutinize changes in others' facial expressions, sometimes in order to regulate their own social behavior. When a speaker sees a listener start to frown, for example, he may change the topic of conversation or try to be clearer in order to avoid offense or misunderstanding. Niedenthal, Halberstadt, Margolin & Innes-Ker (2000) found that people's emotional state influences their ability to detect changes in facial expressions in others. In this study, participants in whom happiness and sadness had been induced, as well as control participants, saw computerized 100-frame movies of happy or sad facial expressions that gradually became neutral as the movie progressed. Participants' task was to indicate the moment when the initial emotional expression had changed to neutrality; put differently, they had to detect the offset of the emotional expression. Expression offset was perceived later for emotion-congruent expressions. That is, happy (sad) participants perceived emotion-congruent happy (sad) expressions to persist longer than emotion-incongruent sad (happy) expressions. These results may have practical implications for individuals such as teachers, psychotherapists, and salespersons, who rely on facial cues in order to assess the impact of their intervention. Their emotional state may bias the detection of changes in facial expressions of their pupils, patients, and clients, and actually impede social interaction. A happy salesperson tends not to immediately detect the client's skeptical expression, which could delay appropriate adjustment of his behavior.

In sum, in this section we have shown how the perception and recognition of facial expressions are sensitive both to factors related to the expresser context as well as to the observer context. The facial dominance found in past research and long considered a result of the special power of facial expressions to communicate emotions, even out of context, proved to be mostly an experimental artifact. The mode of stimulus presentation (visual or verbal, static or dynamic), and the way in which facial and context cues are combined (consistent versus discrepant combinations) influence the salience and accessibility of the expression, as well as its vulnerability to reinterpretation. When confronted with conflicting cues observers reinterpret either the meaning of the context (i.e., the situation does not have the usual meaning for the person) or the meaning of the facial expression (i.e., the person's face does not reveal the person's real feelings). The recognition process is also guided by individuals' knowledge of display rules and social norms, all of which influence the attribution of emotional meaning. The recognition of facial expressions also depends on the previously encountered facial stimuli and on the observer's emotional state. Facial expressions tend to be perceived as congruent with the observer's emotional state. Furthermore, these emotion-congruent expressions are recognized faster and perceived as persisting longer.

We have discussed a number of factors that influence how facial expressions are recognized and interpreted. The debate concerning whether facial expressions are a function of the expresser's feelings or a function of the expresser's behavioral intentions in a given social context presupposes either a unidirectional feeling–expression relationship, or no relation at all. But things are actually not so straightforward. Facial expressions may not only reveal, but also *influence*, what an individual is feeling. The idea that our own facial expressions influence our emotional states has a name, the *facial feedback hypothesis*, which is the topic to which we turn next.

Facial Expressions and the Experience of Emotion: Facial Feedback Hypothesis

The facial feedback hypothesis holds that facial expressions play a causal role in the experience of emotions; the face not only expresses emotions but it can also induce or change the experience of them. The idea that emotional experience of the expresser is in part determined by his or her own facial expressions was clearly articulated by Darwin, who wrote that:

> The free expression by outward signs of an emotion intensifies it. On the other hand, the repression, as far as this is possible, of all outward signs softens our emotions. He who gives way to violent gestures will increase his rage; he who does not control the sign of fear will experience fear in a greater degree; and he who remains passive when overwhelmed with grief loses his best chance of recovering elasticity of mind. These results follow partly from the intimate relation which exists between almost all the emotions and their outward manifestations; and partly from the direct influence of exertion on the heart, and consequently on the brain. Even simulation of an emotion tends to arouse it in our mind. (Darwin 1872/1998, p. 359)

Emotions theorists since Darwin, notably Izard (1971, 1990), Tomkins (1962, 1963), and Zajonc, Murphy, and Inglehart (1989), further developed the idea that facial behavior can activate or regulate emotion experience. They proposed that facial expressions provide proprioceptive, cutaneous, and vascular feedback (i.e., feedback from the facial muscles, the skin and the blood vessels) that modulates ongoing emotional experience, the *modulating hypothesis*, or that they may even initiate the corresponding emotion, the *initiating hypothesis* (for reviews see Adelmann & Zajonc, 1989; Buck, 1980; McIntosh 1996). According to the modulating version of the facial feedback hypothesis, facial expressions influence the intensity of the emotional state induced by an emotion-eliciting stimulus: the expression of congruent facial expressions enhances, and the inhibition of congruent facial expressions or the display of incongruent emotional expressions attenuates the corresponding emotional feelings. For example, if you are already sad, the more that you frown and pout, the sadder you are. Or, if you are already sad, and you "put on a happy face," then you will be less sad. The initiating version of the hypothesis postulates that emotion-specific facial expressions can generate the corresponding emotion in the absence of any emotion-eliciting stimulus. This suggests that if you are feeling no particular emotion at all, but you make a facial expression of a specific emotion, that expression will generate in you some of the corresponding feeling.

Empirical evidence in support of the facial feedback hypothesis has been found in studies using three different methods to manipulate participants' facial expressions. In the *amplification–suppression* paradigm, participants are instructed to exaggerate or to conceal their spontaneous emotional expression induced by emotional stimuli. The *muscle-to-muscle instruction* paradigm involves direct manipulation of participants' facial muscle movements. Participants are instructed to contract specific facial muscles into a fixed facial pose portraying prototypic emotional expressions without labeling the emotions. Finally, several studies have used non-emotional tasks that manipulate facial expression without drawing attention to the face. In initial tests of the modulation hypothesis, emotions were induced by a variety of emotional stimuli such as painful electric shocks, pleasant and unpleasant slides, filmclips, odors, and by emotional imagery tasks. As we discuss in detail below, the general findings of such studies is that participants' manipulated facial expressions affect the intensity of their self-reported emotional feelings as well as their autonomic responses.

Facial Expressions Modulate Ongoing Emotions

Lanzetta, Cartwright-Smith, and Kleck (1976) showed that manipulated facial expressions in response to the anticipation and the reception of electric shocks that varied in intensity produced concomitant changes in autonomic arousal and self-reported painfulness of shocks. In a baseline sequence, participants received a first set of shocks that varied in intensity, and then rated the aversiveness of each received shock. The intensity of the impending shock was announced by a shock signal slide. In the manipulation sequence, participants were instructed to simulate no-shock reception (suppression instruction) or to simulate the reception of very intense shocks (amplification instruction), independent of the actual shock intensity announced by the signal. Consistent with the modulating version of the facial feedback hypothesis, the inhibition of facial expressions decreased autonomic arousal as well as self-reported painfulness of shocks in both the shock anticipation and the shock reception period. Meanwhile, the simulation of intense shocks led to increased autonomic arousal and higher reported painfulness and discomfort as compared to the baseline sequence (see also Kopel & Arkowitz, 1974). Similar attenuating as well as facilitating effects of facial expressions, manipulated by explicit amplification–suppression instructions, have also been found with pleasant and unpleasant films (Zuckerman, Klorman, Larrance, & Spiegel, 1981), pleasant and disgusting odors (Kraut, 1982), and with an imagery task in which participants imagined several standardized happy ("winning in the lottery") and sad situations ("death of a family member") while amplifying or suppressing facial expression (McCanne & Anderson, 1987).

More indirect means of influencing facial expression have also been employed to test the facial feedback hypothesis. For example, Kleck et al. (1976) manipulated subjects' facial expressions with the presence of an observer during the delivery of no, low or medium intense shocks. The observer's presence attenuated participants' facial displays, and produced lower self-rated painfulness of shocks compared to the alone condition. Using pleasant and unpleasant slides as emotion-eliciting stimuli, Lanzetta, Biernat, and Kleck (1982) induced inhibition of facial expression by means of a mirror installed in front of the participants. The mirror had attenuating effects on both participants' expressivity and self-reported pleasantness ratings. In several studies, a contextual amplification of participants' spontaneous facial display in response to humorous stimuli was introduced through the auditory or visual presentation of a laughing audience. For example, Bush, Barr, McHugo, and Lanzetta (1989) had participants watch several comedy clips with and without inserts of full-face laughing audience members. They found that the visual presence of an audience increased the spontaneous facial expressions of smiles (as measured by EMG activity of the *zygomaticus major* and the *orbicularis oculi*), as well as autonomic arousal (heart rate changes), and enhanced participants feelings of amusement (see also Cupchik & Leventhal, 1974; Leventhal & Cupchik, 1975).

Modulating effects of facial expressions have also been found in studies that employed subject-blind, experimenter-manipulated expressive behavior, or *the muscle-to-muscle instruction paradigm*, referred to earlier. Laird (1974) instructed participants to contract specific facial muscles involved in smile or frown expressions while watching mildly positive and negative slides. In particular, participants were instructed to pull their eyebrows down and together and to contract the corner of the jaw by clenching the teeth (anger–frown expression), or to draw the corners of their mouth back and up (happy–smile expression). Expressions that were congruent with the valence of the slides enhanced self-reported feelings, that is, "smiling" participants felt happier or more amused while viewing positive slides, whereas "frowning" participants felt angrier while viewing negative slides. Incongruent expressions were shown to attenuate the emotional response to the slides and cartoons (see also Rutledge & Hupka, 1985).

Strack, Martin, and Stepper (1988) developed an ingenious procedure for inducing the contraction of facial muscles typically involved in emotional expression of happiness (smile) in a more indirect way. Participants who believed they were taking part in a study of psychomotor coordination rated the funniness of humorous cartoons while holding a pen either with their teeth only, which produced smiling, or with their lips only, which inhibited smiling, or with their nondominant hand. The latter individuals served as a control group. Findings of the study showed that cartoons were rated as more amusing in the teeth condition and least amusing in the lip condition, with control group participants falling in between. Using a slightly modified version of the pen-holding procedure (see Figure 4.8), Soussignan (2002) found a differential impact of Duchenne and non-Duchenne smiles on subjective emotional experience and autonomic activity. Participants who posed a "real, emotional smile" (the Duchenne smile), which involves the contraction of both *zygomaticus major* and *orbicularis oculi* muscles, reported more pleasant feelings when reading humorous cartoons and showed different autonomic activity than participants in the non-Duchenne smile condition. This finding suggests that facial expressions have the strongest impact when they are prototypical of the corresponding basic emotion (see also Hager & Ekman, 1981; Levenson, Ekman, & Friesen, 1990).

Larsen, Kasimatis, and Frey (1992) extended Strack and colleagues' work to negative, sad facial expressions using a comparable, non-emotional facial manipulation procedure. As part of a divided attention experiment, participants were asked to bring together, or to keep apart, two golf tees that were attached to the brow regions above the inner corners of the eye, while viewing unpleasant slides. This manipulation produced a facial expression normally involved in negative, sad emotions (see Figure 4.9). When they had to bring the golf tees together (sad expression), unpleasant photos made participants feel sadder than when they tried to keep the tees apart (inhibition of sad expression).

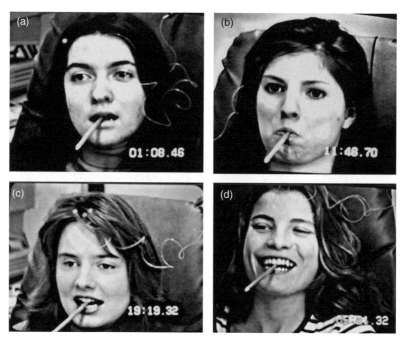

FIGURE 4.8. Illustration of the technique used to contract different facial muscles. From Soussignan, R. (2002). Duchenne smile, emotional experience, and autonomic reactivity: A test of the facial feedback hypothesis. *Emotion, 2*, 52–74.

FIGURE 4.9. Demonstration of the golf tee manipulation of *corrugator supercilii* contraction. Adapted from Larsen, R. J. et al. (1992). Facilitating the furrow brow: An unobtrusive test of the facial feedback hypothesis applied to unpleasant affect. *Cognition and Emotion, 6*, 321–338.

   The above reviewed studies demonstrate that experimentally manipulated facial expressions modulate, that is, attenuate or enhance, emotions
that are induced by stimuli other than the facial expression itself.
However, the observed effect is typically small to moderate in size and it
is usually smaller than the effect of the emotion-inducing stimulus itself
(see the meta-analysis by Matsumoto, 1987). Furthermore, the results of
these studies should be interpreted with caution, because they demonstrate quite unspecific effects of facial feedback. That is, most studies
demonstrate that facial movement produces global changes in pleasantness–unpleasantness: smiles enhance pleasant feelings, or attenuate
unpleasant feelings, whereas frowns enhance unpleasant feelings, or
attenuate pleasant feelings in response to emotional stimuli. However,
most facial feedback theorists predict emotion-specific categorical effects
of facial display on self-reported feelings. Facial expressions should
influence the corresponding discrete emotions: an anger expression
should affect only self-reported feelings of anger but no other negative
emotion. The categorical version of the facial feedback hypothesis can
only be tested when both the independent variable (face) and the dependent variable (self-reported emotions) contain at least two discrete emotions
of similar valence (Winton, 1986). There is now growing support for the
categorical version in research that demonstrates that facial feedback may
be sufficient to induce the corresponding emotional state.

Facial Expressions Initiate Emotions

Several studies have found empirical evidence to suggest that facial
expressions do not only modulate an already existing emotional state, but
can also initiate the corresponding emotional experience in the absence of
any emotion-eliciting stimulus (Duclos & Laird, 2001; Duclos, Laird,
Schneider, Sexter, Stern, & Van Lighten 1989; Duncan & Laird, 1977, 1980;
Flack, Laird, & Cavallaro, 1999, McIntosh, Zajonc, Vig, & Emerick, 1997;
Zajonc et al., 1989).
   In a well-known study, Duclos and colleagues (1989) examined the
impact of different negative facial expressions on emotional feelings using
a muscle-to-muscle instruction procedure. Participants were instructed to
contract the facial muscles involved in the facial expressions of fear, anger,
disgust, and sadness while listening to a series of neutral tones. On each
trial, they rated their feelings on several emotion scales. The finding that
participants' emotion ratings were highest for the emotion that matched the
facially expressed emotion indicates that emotion-specific facial expressions can generate the corresponding emotional feelings. Duclos & Laird
(2001) found these emotion-initiating effects of facial expressions only for

participants who were more responsive to self-produced bodily cues than to external, situational cues.

Zajonc and colleagues used a vowel pronunciation task to manipulate facial expressions (McIntosh et al., 1997; Zajonc et al., 1989). Specifically, German-speaking participants were instructed to pronounce several vowels, such as the vowel "ü" which inhibits smiling, or the sound "e" which produces an expression similar to a smile. Zajonc and colleagues (1989) found evidence for the generation of both negative and positive affect by means of this vowel pronunciation task. The "ü" sound was less liked, rated as less pleasant to pronounce, and produced worse moods in the participants than the control sound "o," and the smile sound "e" was better liked, generated better mood compared to the control sounds "o, u, i" and to the sound "ü."

Several studies have also extended the emotion-modulating and emotion-initiating effects of facial feedback to bodily postures (Duclos et al., 1989; Flack et al., 1999; Riskind, 1984; Riskind & Gotay, 1982; Stepper & Strack, 1993) and vocal affect (Hatfield, Cacioppo, & Rapson, 1994). For example, Stepper and Strack (1993) found that adopting a slumped body posture, which is associated with sadness, while receiving success feedback attenuated participants' feelings of pride as compared to those who adopted a upright position, which is associated with joy. Similarly, Duclos and colleagues (1989) found that emotion-specific body postures of sadness, fear, and anger caused the experience of the corresponding emotions, especially in participants who were more responsive to their bodily cues. Flack and colleagues (1999), who examined both separate and combined effects of facial expression and bodily posture of anger, sadness, fear, and happiness, showed that combined effects of matching facial and bodily expressions produced stronger corresponding feelings.

In addition to facial expression and bodily posture, vocal expression has also been found to affect emotional feelings (Hatfield, Hsee, Costello, Weisman, & Denney, 1995). For example, discussing an anger-provoking topic in a slow, soft voice (or a fast, loud voice) was found to attenuate (or to enhance) the speaker's self-reported anger as well as autonomic arousal (Siegman, Anderson, & Berger, 1990).

Mechanisms by which Facial Muscle Activity Influences Emotional Experience

Several mechanisms have been proposed to explain why posing a happy face can induce happiness or enhance pleasant feelings. These mechanisms may also be relevant for more general somatic feedback effects (postural and vocal feedback).

Direct Afferent Feedback Loop

One possibility is that proprioceptive and cutaneous feedback from facial muscles and skin directly affects emotional experience through afferent feedback loops to the brain (Ekman, 1973; Izard, 1977; Tomkins, 1962, 1963). From this account, facial muscle activity is part of an innate affect program that connects the motor cortex with other brain regions and facial muscles. The activation of one part of the program, for example facial activity, automatically activates the other parts of the affect program, such as the corresponding expression-specific emotional state and physiological arousal. Facial feedback is thus considered as modulating and generating discrete, basic emotions. Some authors also note that only those voluntary facial expressions that closely match naturally occurring facial display of emotions should activate the innate affect program and affect emotions (Hager & Ekman, 1981; Izard, 1990; Levenson et al., 1990).

Vascular Theory of Emotional Efference

Zajonc (1985) explained facial feedback effects within the vascular theory of emotional efference (VTEE). According to the VTEE, facial muscle activity regulates the venal blood flow to the brain and thereby affects brain temperature. Variations in brain temperature influence the release of neurotransmitter and affect the subjective emotional experience. Facial movements that increase brain temperature tend to activate unpleasant feelings whereas those that decrease brain temperature trigger pleasant feelings. Within the VTEE facial muscle activity is predicted to influence the pleasantness of emotional experience rather than inducing discrete basic emotions.

Self-perception

Laird (1974) explained facial feedback effects with Bem's (1972) self-perception theory, according to which people use the observation of their own behavior (self-produced, personal cues) and the context in which they occur (situational cues) to infer their own attitudes, preferences and feelings. In this view, facial feedback effects depend on individuals' perception of their own expressive behavior: when they perceive themselves smiling (or frowning) they infer that they are probably happy (or sad). Facial feedback effects should therefore strongly depend on people's responsiveness to self-produced cues, and some research findings indeed support this idea (see Duclos & Laird, 2001).

Conditioning

A classical conditioning account of facial feedback has also been proposed. The idea is that specific facial expressions that are frequently paired with a particular emotional state become conditioned to this emotional state (Buck, 1980). So, for instance, a smile may become a conditioned stimulus for happiness.

The different mechanisms that have been proposed to explain facial feedback effects are probably not mutually exclusive. To the contrary, the impact of the facial expressions on emotions is likely multiply determined (McIntosh, 1996). Different mechanisms may contribute differently depending on the facial manipulation procedure, and on the specific nature of the emotion displayed.

Taken together, there exists strong empirical evidence that people's expressive behavior not only modulates the intensity of ongoing emotional experience but also can generate the corresponding discrete emotion. However, these feedback effects are small to moderate (Matsumoto, 1987), and are in general smaller than the impact of emotion-eliciting stimuli. Furthermore, self-regulation of naturally occurring, event-elicited expressions produces stronger feedback effects than voluntary, experimenter-manipulated expressions (Izard, 1990). Finally, the combination of emotion-specific, congruent facial and bodily behavior seems to produce the strongest effect on subjective experience.

Importance for the Recognition of Facial Expression of Emotion

While facial feedback may prove to be a small part of the instigation and modulation of emotion, it may be very important for the recognition of facial expression of emotion. Perhaps people can recognize emotions from facial expressions because they imitate the expressions and this gives them a small summary of the feelings of the expresser. This was exactly the idea that Wallbott (1991) proposed and tested. He instructed participants in his study to identify the emotion expressed in a series of face pictures. While performing the task, participants' faces were covertly videotaped. Two weeks later, each participant was asked to watch the videotape of himself or herself while he or she performed the identification task, and to guess the category of the facial expression being judged (which was, of course, not visible). The participants identified the emotion expressed in the pictures above chance level by only seeing their own facial expressions produced while performing the task.

Niedenthal et al. (2001) also demonstrated that facial mimicry plays a causal role in the processing of emotional expression. Participants watched one facial expression morph into another, and had to detect when the expression changed. Some participants were free to imitate the expressions, whereas others were prevented from imitating by holding a pencil laterally between their lips and teeth. Consistent with the hypothesis that facial feedback influences the recognition of facial expression, participants free to imitate the expressions detected the change in emotional expression earlier (more efficiently) for any facial expression than did participants who were prevented from imitating the expressions.

Summary

Facial expressions are one of the most important stimuli in social life. They attract attention, and they do so automatically (Lundqvist & Öhman, 2005). As we have seen, facial expressions impart an enormous amount of information, about the emotional state of the expresser as well as his or her motives and needs. And some expressions do so in a universal fashion. But nothing about facial expression is quite as easy as it seems. The meaning of any given expression is open to interpretation, with important contributions from culture and from the situation in which the expression is embedded. The meaning is also open to bias from the current emotional state of the perceiver. And the term facial expression is even a misnomer. Research on the facial feedback hypothesis has shown that these gestures not only express, but also influence the subjective state of the individual who displays them. Indeed, because individuals imitate others' facial expressions, and because expressions can feedback on subjective state, they are useful pieces of information for better understanding and even empathizing with another individual, especially an individual whose emotions we really want to know (Zajonc, Adelmann, Murphy, & Niedenthal, 1987). And, as we will see in the next chapter, they are one, but not the only means to regulate one's feelings.

Regulation of Emotions

5

▷ *Contents at a Glance*

In everyday life, emotions are controlled and regulated. People fight back their tears, feign or exaggerate joy, inhibit their anger, and mask their fear. Emotion regulation refers to the processes that individuals use to influence the emotions they experience and do not experience, the situations under which they experience a given emotion, and how and whether they eventually express it (Gross, 1999).

Imagine Sophie, a university student, taking a late-night stroll with Michael, a fellow student with whom she recently became acquainted. Suddenly Sophie notices a man approaching them with a huge black dog. Sophie is afraid of dogs. She feels panic, her heartbeat accelerates, and she feels the urge to protect herself, to cross the street, to run away. But in the presence of Michael, she does not want to seem ridiculous. After all, isn't the sight of a grown-up woman running away from a dog kind of ridiculous? And she doesn't want the dog to "smell" her fear and become aggressive, either. Sophie continues walking as if nothing is bothering her. Still, she feels upset because she knows the dog is near, and she is also upset because she does not want to be so afraid of it. So, she tries to ignore the animal, distracting herself by looking up at the façades of the buildings with feigned interest. But then the dog starts barking loudly, and she cannot ignore it any more. Instead, Sophie tries to persuade herself that the dog is a friendly, well-trained dog that is under the control of his owner. But why doesn't the owner keep the dog on a leash? Now she also feels anger at the man. Still, when they pass, Sophie forces herself to walk naturally, neither slowing down nor speeding up, and she even greets the owner with a friendly smile as if trying to persuade herself and the others that everything is fine.

Why doesn't Sophie accept her feelings as they are and express them naturally? The personal and social motives that underlie emotion regulation are the topics of the first section of the present chapter. After considering these motives, we go on to consider how people go about regulating their emotions. Our above example illustrates a number of different emotion regulation strategies that can influence or change different components of the emotion process, including its cognitive, physiological, behavioral-expressive, and experiential aspects. We will also discuss the affective, cognitive and social consequences of these different emotion regulation strategies. Finally, when an emotion has been experienced, it is often described to and discussed with others, mainly with the goal of feeling better. The function and consequences of talking about one's emotion, so-called emotional disclosure or social sharing, will be the topic of the last part of this chapter.

Why do People Control their Emotions? Motivations Underlying Emotion Regulation

People have many reasons to regulate their emotions. They may do so for personal reasons, that is, because they find the emotions painful, or because they believe that the emotions might have negative implications for other people, or their relationship with others. People might also want to regulate their emotions in order to conform to social customs and social demands. But before they engage in emotion regulation individuals must be aware of their current emotional state and the possible consequences the emotion has for the self and others. People will try to influence an emotion only if they perceive a discrepancy between it and the emotions they consciously want to feel or display (Fischer, Manstead, Evers, Timmers, & Valk, 2004). Emotion regulation is thus based on individuals' emotion knowledge, which includes knowledge about the causes of emotions, about their bodily sensations and expressive behavior, and about the possible means of modifying them. Emotion knowledge facilitates emotion regulation because it provides information about the appropriateness of emotional experience, and about the possible actions that can be taken to deal with discrepant emotions. In support of this idea, Feldman Barrett, Gross, Christensen, and Benvenuto (2001) have shown that the frequency with which individuals attempt to change or suppress their negative emotions is positively related to the extent to which their knowledge of such emotions is well developed or extensive, and their ability to experience negative emotions in a discrete and differentiated manner.

So, what makes an emotion "undesirable" and thus subject to regulation? One obvious personal reason for emotion regulation is called *hedonic motivation*, that is, the motivation to avoid unpleasant, painful feelings, and to seek out pleasant feelings. For example, individuals do not want to be sad or depressed when attending a party, or to feel anxious when boarding an airplane for a long-planned and desired trip to China. Such feelings can be painful and stressful. Thus, individuals try to suppress their unpleasant feelings and to focus on thoughts or actions that produce good feelings, that make them feel joyful at the party, and that make them feel pleasure on their trip.

But emotion regulation goes beyond the simple hedonic motivation to avoid pain and seek pleasure. People may also try to enhance or inhibit emotions in order to experience and express emotions that they believe will facilitate performance in a particular situation. Erber, Wegner, and Therriault (1996) for example showed that happy participants who anticipated working with a stranger preferred to read sad, depressing stories while sad participants preferred to read humorous, uplifting stories.

Presumably participants thought that extreme emotions would not be beneficial in the situation at hand, and attempted to neutralize or balance them out to some degree. Furthermore, depending on the situation at hand, feeling good and feeling bad do not always have the corresponding positive or negative meanings. Feeling happy and relieved about the death of another person may be experienced as bad and undesirable, while feeling sad about the fact that a good friend is moving away may be experienced as good because it provides positive information about the importance of the person in one's life. Thus, feeling good and not feeling bad are not invariant emotion regulation motivations and can only be understood in the particular context in which emotions occur (Diamond & Aspinwall, 2003).

What people want to feel or to express is also determined by relational concerns involving the expected interpersonal consequences of the expressed emotions. Individuals may regulate their emotions to serve *prosocial motives*, that is, in order to protect the feelings of others. For example, concealing one's disappointment about a birthday present that does not quite live up to expectations may be motivated by the desire to not hurt or offend the person who has given it to us. Likewise, a mother hiding her fear or sadness in front of her children may be motivated by her desire not to induce fear or sadness in them.

Self-protection motives may also underlie emotion regulation. Individuals may suppress their emotions or feign an emotion in order to protect their personal safety, or to elicit helpful or salutary reactions from others. For example, a woman may suppress her own anger in order to avoid being hurt by her husband, or she may feign sadness in order to obtain assistance and help. Indirect support for the role of self-protection motives in emotion regulation comes from a study on jealousy by Zammuner and Fischer (1995). The researchers asked participants to imagine a situation intended to induce jealousy and to report their feelings and emotional reactions. As expected, most participants reported jealousy and anger as the most likely feelings, but at the same time they reported sadness and surprise as the emotions they would most likely communicate to the partner. The underlying motivation for not expressing the feeling of jealousy may be one of self-protection: expressing one's jealousy would imply blaming the partner and perhaps provoking his disapproval or anger, while expressing sadness would elicit more empathy and concern.

Finally, an *impression management motive*, or a fear of being judged negatively by others because of expressing an inappropriate emotion, often underlies emotion regulation. The motivation to avoid being evaluated unfavorably by others is based in knowledge of *emotion norms* that prescribe what emotions are appropriate in a particular context (Fischer et al.,

2004; Manstead & Fischer, 2000). Emotion norms represent thus the knowledge about *how* to respond in an emotionally appropriate way, while emotion regulation motives explain *why* people modify their emotions in view of emotion norms.

Hochschild (1983) pointed out that emotion norms not only legislate outward emotional displays but also the very feeling that can be experienced in a given situation. *Display rules* specify the emotional expressions appropriate to a specific situation, and *feeling rules* prescribe the feelings one should experience according to social and cultural conventions. Emotion norms not only specify which emotion is appropriate, but they also indicate the appropriate amount, timing and context for inner feelings and for their outward expression. Emotion norms are specific to cultures. They also vary with gender, and with people's social roles and professional occupations.

Culture-specific Emotion Norms

As we will discuss in greater detail in Chapter 9, in individualistic cultures where one's identity is defined by personal goals and achievements, emotion norms encourage emotions that signal independence, authenticity and assertiveness. The experience and expression of joy and pride are, for example, prescribed when personal goals have been achieved, and the experience and expression of anger is considered as appropriate in situations where personal goals or individual rights are threatened (Averill, 1982) and where the anger expression allows one to restore one's honor (Cohen & Nisbett, 1994).

In collectivistic cultures, the self is defined by one's relatedness to a social group. Emotion norms encourage, therefore, emotions that signal interdependence and that promote harmonious relationships, as, for example, sympathy, shame, and guilt, whereas they prescribe concealment of emotions that may impede relationships with others, as, for example, pride or anger.

Situation-specific Emotion Norms

There are also emotion norms for different situations in which individuals occupy temporary roles, as during a wedding, a funeral or graduation ceremony. For example, a bride and a bridegroom are expected to be happy on their wedding day, a mourner should feel sad, and the recipient of a long worked-for diploma should feel pride. More permanent or at least long-term social roles (i.e., spouses, parents, and children) are also associated with specific emotion conventions. Parents are, for example, expected to love their children, and spouses are expected to love each other. However, these situation- and role-specific emotion norms vary with culture. For example, in cultures where arranged marriages are common, spouses may feel freer not to love each other because they are not responsible for their choice (Hochschild, 1983).

Gender-specific Emotion Norms

Differences between women and men in the degree to which they tend to be expressive have been attributed to gender-specific display and feeling rules that are related to the different social roles women and men held in society (Fischer, 1993b; Kring & Gordon, 1998; Shields, 1987). On the one hand, the expression of relationship-enhancing "social engaging" positive emotions and the expression of powerless emotions (i.e., sadness, fear, shame, guilt) are prescribed as more appropriate for women because they are in line with the traditional feminine nurturing role. On the other hand, the expression of powerful emotions such as anger, contempt or pride is prescribed as more appropriate for men because they correspond to the traditional masculine agentic role. Furthermore, men have been found to control their emotions more for self-protection motives and for self-image concerns, while women have reported that they regulate and control their emotions more for prosocial reasons (Timmers, Fischer, & Manstead, 1998). However, gender-specific display and feeling rules tend to lose their power because of the increasing "emotionalization" of western culture. In fact, a new emotion norm is emerging that stresses the importance of expressing one's genuine feelings in social interactions. In support of this idea, Timmers, Fischer, and Manstead (2003) found that the stereotype of the emotional woman and the rational man still exists with regard to how men and women in general express their emotions (*descriptive beliefs*). However, the emotion norms with regard to what emotions should or should not be expressed by women and men (*prescriptive beliefs*) were found to be less gendered. As shown in Figure 5.1, women are still described as expressing more socially engaging and powerless emotions, and men as expressing more powerful emotions. However, no gender-specific prescriptive beliefs concerning the expression of powerless emotions of fear, sadness, and shame were found. The traditional rule that "boys don't cry" seems thus to have become less salient, at least in western cultures.

Work-related Emotion Norms

Many professions in the service sector require employees to regulate their emotional expressions and feelings. Most work-related emotion

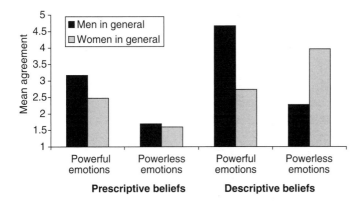

FIGURE 5.1. Participants' mean agreement with respect to prescriptive (should) and descriptive beliefs concerning the display of powerful and powerless emotions by men and women in general. From Timmers, M. et al. (2003). Ability versus vulnerability: Beliefs about men and women's emotional behavior. *Cognition and Emotion, 17,* 41–63.

norms prescribe the display of positive emotions and the suppression of negative emotions in order to increase the satisfaction of the customer and to create a warm, secure atmosphere. Hochschild (1983) explored in detail the emotion work that is required from flight attendants and bill collectors. Flight attendants, for example, are trained to be empathic, to smile, even when dealing with a grouchy passenger, and to conceal feelings of anger or fear. In contrast, in some professions the experience and expression of negative emotion is required when there is a need to intimidate another individual or to solicit another's cooperation. Bill collectors, for example, are trained to feel suspicious of debtors, to deflate debtors' status, and to express anger by behaving in a harsh way, and by raising the voice for the purpose of breaking a debtor's resistance to pay. According to Hochschild (1983) both flight attendants and bill collectors are expected to control not only their overt expressions (so-called "surface acting") but also to work on their feelings (so-called "deep acting"). Their *emotion work* consists of inducing or suppressing feelings in order to create an outward appearance that produces specific states of mind in others. Many other professions require their employees to regulate their feelings and expressions in order to regulate the feelings of others, as, for example, firemen, policemen, nurses, salespersons, secretaries, and waiters. Some professionals, for example, lawyers and doctors, control their emotions by referring to professional ethics and to client expectations.

In conclusion, emotion regulation is driven by personal, hedonic as well as social motives involving the desire to avoid unwanted consequences for the self and for others, and to conform to emotion norms that are specific to culture, gender, social roles and different professions. Emotion norms change over time, and in western cultures emotional authenticity and emotional sensitivity are increasingly considered as important capacities that render communication meaningful (Fischer et al., 2004). The capacity to regulate one's emotions by conforming to emotion norms but also by taking into account the feelings of others is a core component of *emotional intelligence* (Feldman Barrett & Gross, 2001; Salovey, Hsee, & Mayer, 1993). Emotional intelligence encompasses the abilities to perceive, appraise and express emotions accurately, to access and generate emotional states that facilitate cognitive processing, to understand, analyze and to employ emotional information, and to manage emotions in oneself and others (for a review see Mayer, Salovey & Caruso, 2000; Salovey, Bedell, Detweiler, & Mayer, 2000). The last ability refers specifically to the ability to regulate one's emotions.

Now that we know why individuals are motivated to control their emotions, we can ask *how* do they do it? As we discuss in the following section, individuals employ a variety of different strategies that are more or less efficient in changing their emotions.

How do People Control their Emotions? Emotion Regulation Strategies

In Chapter 1, we described emotions as component processes that include the appraisal of events as emotionally meaningful and a coordinated set of emotional response tendencies such as experiential, physiological, and expressive responses. The implication of this view is that emotions can be regulated by the operation of different processes that occur at different moments in the entire experience. Gross (1998a, 1999) proposed a process model of emotion regulation in which two types of emotion regulation strategy are distinguished. *Antecedent-focused* emotion regulation refers to strategies that occur very early in the generation of an emotion, that is, before the emotion itself has been fully elicited, and consists of modifying the emotional impact of an object or event. *Response-focused* regulation refers to the modification of the experiential, expressive, or physiological aspects of the emotion once it has been elicited (see Figure 5.2).

Antecedent-focused emotion regulation consists of anticipating and controlling emotional responses by actively selecting and influencing situations and cognitions in order to prevent unwanted emotions and to enhance desired emotions. Gross (1998a, 1999) distinguished four subtypes of antecedent-focused regulation strategy. First, situations or persons that might evoke unpleasant feelings can be avoided, and those that are likely to evoke pleasant feelings can be approached (*situation selection*). An individual

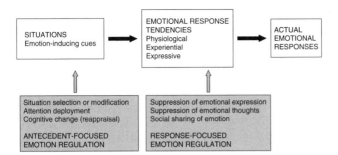

FIGURE 5.2. A process model of emotion generation in which emotion regulation can operate on the emotion-inducing situation or on the emotional response tendencies. Adapted from Gross, J. (1998a). The emerging field of emotion regulation: An integrative view. *Review of General Psychology, 2,* 1–29.

can, for example, decide not to attend a party in order to avoid a particular person who might make her feel sad or angry. Or, an individual can seek out the company of a person who makes her feel good. Second, individuals can also change a situation in order to alter its emotional impact (*situation modification*). Asking a friend to keep his dog on a leash during a visit, or asking a housemate to turn his music down are examples of this. Third, the emotional impact of a situation can also be influenced by selectively attending to or ignoring certain features of the situation (*attention deployment*). Individuals may, for example, reorient their attention to the nonemotional features of the situation or can evoke thoughts and memories that are inconsistent with the undesired emotional state. Fourth, individuals may also modify how they think about a situation (*cognitive change or reappraisal*) in order to increase or to decrease the occurrence of specific emotions. A potentially emotion-eliciting stimulus can for example be re-evaluated (reappraised) in a way that modifies its emotional meaning. For instance, an individual might feel anger over not having been greeted by a neighbor if he interprets the behavior as intentional ignoring. However, the neighbor's behavior could be interpreted as due to chronic impoliteness (directed at everyone), as due to her preoccupation with personal problems, or even as due to her poor eyesight!

Response-focused regulation occurs later in the emotion process, once an emotion has actually been evoked, and involves attempts to modify its specific experiential, physiological, and expressive components. The saying that "feeling is not always revealing" suggests that the activated emotion response tendencies are not necessarily expressed and that they are potential targets of regulation (Gross & John, 1997). The *regulation of expressive behavior* involves the suppression (inhibition) or enhancement (amplification) of ongoing expressive behavior that should modulate emotional experience. Conscious concealment of expressive behavior, along with the strategy of cognitive reappraisal, is one of the most studied emotion regulation strategies and is presented more in detail below. The *regulation of physiological arousal* can be effected by medication such as tranquilizers, which decrease muscle tension, or beta-blockers, which inhibit the adrenergic beta-receptors thereby reducing sympathetic arousal. Beta-blockers are frequently used in the treatment of hypertension but also for fighting stage fright and exam nerves. Other drugs that affect muscle tension and/or physiological arousal include alcohol, coffee, marihuana, and cigarettes. The regulation of physiological arousal may also be achieved through self-induced muscle relaxation and biofeedback, or through exercising (Thayer, Newman, & McClain, 1994).

The *regulation of experience* involves focused concentration on, or suppression of, emotional thoughts that accompany feelings. The first, often called *rumination*, consists of consciously drawing attention to (especially) negative thoughts and feelings with the goal of making sense of them, and thus reducing their unpleasant impact. Rumination has primarily been studied in the context of depression, and has been found to worsen the depressive symptoms (Nolen-Hoeksema, McBride, & Larsen, 1997; Nolen-Hoeksema & Morrow, 1993). Gross (1999) suggested that rumination about anger-, guilt-, and anxiety-related thoughts should have the same consequences in terms of producing longer lasting and more intense emotions. The second, the conscious suppression of emotional thoughts is illustrated by the familiar experience of trying not to think of a former lover in order not to feel bad. As we will see below, *emotional thought suppression* may produce ironic effects similar to those produced by thought suppression in general (Wegner, 1994), that is, it may paradoxically facilitate the return of the suppressed emotions. A final strategy used to regulate emotions is emotional disclosure or the so-called *social sharing of emotions*. Immediately following intense positive or negative emotional experiences people are inclined to talk about their feelings to others, which, in turn, may influence their emotions.

In the rest of this chapter, we discuss in detail the efficacy of four emotion regulation strategies: emotion-expressive suppression, cognitive reappraisal, emotional thought suppression, and emotional disclosure. We also consider their cognitive and social consequences as well as their implication for mental and physical health.

Suppression of Expressive Behavior: Trying Not to Show It

One well-studied response-focused emotion regulation strategy is the voluntary suppression of the outward facial expression of emotion.

According to facial feedback theories (see Chapter 4), amplifying or suppressing the mere expression of emotion modulates, that is, increases or decreases, the individual's experience of emotion. While many studies have experimentally manipulated participants' facial expressions through detailed muscle contraction instructions, only a few have had participants explicitly inhibit their spontaneous expressive behavior, and then assessed the impact of suppression on participants' emotional experience and physiological arousal. The inhibition of pain expressions was found to decrease self-reported feelings of pain (Kopel & Arkowitz, 1974) and to decrease physiological arousal (Kleck et al., 1976; Lanzetta et al., 1976). McCanne and Anderson (1987) showed that expressive suppression while imaging pleasant or unpleasant emotional situations impaired participants' capacity to feel the corresponding emotions. The instruction to suppress laughter while watching an amusing film has been shown to cause less positive evaluations of the film (Leventhal & Mace, 1970).

However, there is little evidence that the suppression of spontaneous emotional expression leads to decrease in *emotional experience* and *physiological arousal* apart from manipulation of pain expressions. Zuckerman and colleagues (1981) used three expressions modes (suppression, amplification or non-manipulated expression) and pleasant, unpleasant and neutral filmclips as emotion elicitors and found that, compared to the non-manipulated expression, exaggerated expression intensified participants' emotional feelings and physiological arousal while inhibited expression did not significantly decrease it. Similarly, Bush and colleagues (1989) found that participants whose expressive responses to amusing filmclips were amplified through the insertion of a laugh track, reported feeling more amused and showed increased physiological arousal compared to control participants. However, the inhibition of expressive behavior did not decrease participants' self-reported amusement, nor did it affect physiological arousal. These findings suggest that exaggeration rather than suppression of expressive behavior influences emotional experience and physiological arousal.

In the emotion regulation literature, the inhibition of emotional expression has largely been studied in minimal social situations, in which participants were exposed to emotion-inducing films or slides and were instructed to suppress their overt emotional reactions. Gross and Levenson (1993), for example, videotaped participants' facial expressions while they watched, first, a neutral film and then two unpleasant films showing burn victims and amputations. Half the participants were instructed to suppress outward expressions of emotion during the third, upsetting, film, while the other half viewed all three films without specific instructions. Suppressors expressed less disgust, and experienced decreased heart rate and a general decrease in somatic activity compared to control participants. However, suppression of expressive behavior did not affect self-reported disgust, and led to increased sympathetic arousal (as measured by finger pulse amplitude and electrodermal reactivity). We now take a closer look at the expressive-behavioral, the affective-experiential, and the physiological consequences of expressive suppression.

Expressive-behavioral Consequences of Suppression

Suppression has been found to reduce the facial expression of positive and negative emotions, but not to completely inhibit it. Gross and Levenson (1997) for example, had participants watch a sad, an amusing, and a neutral film, either with the instruction to suppress facial expressions, or without specific instructions. As presented in the upper part of Table 5.1, the suppression instruction led to less expressive behavior compared to the no-instruction group. However, suppressors were still more expressive during emotion-arousing films than during the neutral film. This finding indicates that suppression does not completely inhibit emotion expression (Gross & Levenson, 1993, 1997; Richards & Gross, 1999).

Affective-experiential Consequences of Suppression

Suppression has been found to have little or no impact on suppressors' self-reported feelings. In the above-cited Gross and Levenson (1997) study, suppressors reported feeling less amused during an amusing film compared to no suppressors. However, suppression of expressive behavior during a sad film did not decrease the self-reported feeling of sadness (see middle part of Table 5.1). Similarly, suppression of disgust during the viewing of films showing surgical amputations did not decrease the subjective experience of disgust (Gross & Levenson, 1993). Thus, suppression seems to reduce the experience of positive emotions but not the experience of negative emotions. The absence of an influence of suppression on emotional experience may be a methodological artifact. Izard (1990) pointed out that experimenter-manipulated facial expressions usually produce smaller feedback effects than self-regulated facial display. Self-induced suppression that occurs in a natural setting may actually decrease the corresponding emotional feelings.

Physiological Consequences of Suppression

The expressive suppression of positive and negative emotions has been found to increase physiological arousal during the exposure to emotion-arousing stimuli. In particular, suppression produced an increase in the

TABLE 5.1

Mean Change Score (Prefilm Score Subtracted from Film Score) in Self-rated Emotional Experience, Coder-rated Expressive Behavior, and Sympathetic Activation of the Cardiovascular System During Amusement, Neutral, and Sadness Films for Suppression and No-suppression Participants

	Amusement		Neutral		Sadness	
	Suppression	No Suppression	Suppression	No Suppression	Suppression	No Suppression
Expressive behavior						
Happiness	2.29 <	4.62	0.04	0.21	0.26	0.76
Sadness	0.27	0.06	0.65	0.50	1.23 <	1.96
Smiling	1.39 <	4.81	−0.07	0.03	−0.03	0.21
Crying	0.07	0.00	0.02	20.02	0.38 <	0.92
Subjective experience						
Amusement	4.04 <	4.70	0.22	0.21	0.07	0.61
Sadness	−0.37	−0.16	−0.8	−0.27	3.79	4.09
Physiology						
Sympathetic arousal	0.43 >	0.11	−0.09	−0.12	0.30 >	0.13

<, > signs indicate that means differ significantly at $p < .05$.
From Gross, J., & Levenson, R. (1997). Hiding feelings: The acute effects of inhibiting negative and positive emotions. *Journal of Abnormal Psychology, 106*, 95–103.

sympathetic activation of the cardiovascular system, which included a decrease in pulse transit time to the finger and to the ear, a decrease in finger pulse amplitude and in finger temperature. The heartbeat rate was measured by the cardiac interbeat interval, and its decrease signifies heartbeat acceleration. Heart rate generally reflects the sum of antagonistic sympathetic and parasympathetic activity and was therefore not included in the composite sympathetic activation measure (Gross, 1998b; Gross & Levenson, 1993, 1997; Richards & Gross, 1999). As can be seen in the lower part of Table 5.1, suppression produced increased sympathetic arousal only during emotion-arousing films, but not during a neutral film suggesting that the physiological changes are due to the suppression of emotion-related expressions and not to the act of suppression of any ongoing facial behavior.

As we have seen to this point, experimenter-induced suppression decreases the outward expression of emotion, but it does not seem to be an efficient strategy for reducing negative feelings and emotional arousal. Nevertheless, people spontaneously inhibit their facial expressions of emotions, especially in public situations. For example, the simple presence of an observer was found to attenuate participants' facial expression of pain during the reception of electric shocks (Kleck et al., 1976), and the presence of a co-competitor inhibited the facial expression of pride and happiness after success in a problem-solving task (Friedman & Miller-Herringer, 1991). At this point, we may ask why people use expressive suppression at all. One possible answer is that suppression of facial display is not intended to enhance or inhibit inner feelings. In the laboratory, people inhibit their facial expressions in order to conform to experimenter demands. In everyday life, suppression may serve to conform individuals' outward appearance to emotional norms in a given situation, and to facilitate social interaction. Inhibiting the expression of socially undesirable emotions may prevent conflicts with others and being negatively judged or blamed by others, and help to protect others' feelings.

Germane to this issue, Carstensen and colleagues examined the specific emotional behavior (verbal content, tone of voice, facial expression, gesture and body movement) expressed by spouses during discussion of marital problems. Marital dissatisfaction was shown to be associated with more expression of negative emotions and less expression of positive emotions, while marital satisfaction was found to increase with decreased exchange of negative emotions (Carstensen, Gottman, & Levenson, 1995; Levenson, Carstensen, & Gottman, 1994). Successfully modifying the facial expression of emotion may thus be important in people's social and marital relationships, but it does not much help to decrease one's negative feelings. So what can people do to change their feelings? One possibility is to change the way they think about a situation.

Cognitive Reappraisal: Thinking about It Differently

As we saw in Chapter 1, emotions are often generated by an individual's evaluation of the situation. Changing the way that a potentially emotion-arousing situation is evaluated, so-called cognitive reappraisal, is an antecedent-focused emotion regulation strategy that operates before an emotion becomes full blown. Reappraisal of the situation may result in a change of emotional responses, that is, in less or more intense feelings, physiological arousal, and expressive behavior. Cognitive reappraisal was initially investigated for its capacity to reduce the experience of negative emotions and to decrease physiological arousal. For instance, Lazarus and Alfert (1964) showed that the reinterpretation of an upsetting, stressful film concerning a tribal circumcision ceremony, in a non-emotional way modified the participants' emotional and physiological responses. Reappraisal was experimentally manipulated by "denial" instructions that minimized the harmful, painful aspects of the surgical operation and emphasized its positive aspects, such as the pride experienced by the boys over their participation in the tribal ceremony. Participants who were given the denial instructions showed fewer signs of physiological arousal (as measured by skin conductance and heart rate), and reported feeling less depressed and more pleased and concentrated than those who watched the film without the denial instructions.

Similarly, Stemmler (1997) showed that the way people interpret an anger-provoking situation can change its emotional impact. In his study, participants were blamed by the experimenter's assistant for their lack of cooperation, and for their poor performance on an experimental task. The assistant was either initially presented to the participants as not very reliable and credible (*excuse condition*), or participants were told that the criticism was faked (*ignore condition*), or no specific information was given (*control condition*). Self-reported anger, physiological arousal (diastolic blood pressure and heart rate), facial expression of anger, and anger-related thoughts (perceived seriousness of the provocation, perceived difficulty to control anger-related aggressive action tendencies) were lower in the ignore and excuse conditions than in the control condition. Reappraisal seems thus an efficient way to reduce negative feelings as well as the accompanying physiological arousal (see also Gross, 1998b).

Does this mean that students can reduce unpleasant feelings of worry and stress concerning an upcoming exam by thinking of the situation in a more detached or positive way, for example, by seeing the exam situation as an occasion to show what they know rather than what they do not know? This is exactly what was found in a study by Tomaka, Blascovich, Kibler, and Ernst (1997). They showed that the experimentally induced reappraisal of a math task as *threatening* (emphasizing accuracy and potential evaluation) or as challenging (emphasizing effort and doing one's best) influenced participants' emotional experience and physiological arousal. In particular, interpreting the math task as challenging rather than threatening decreased participants' self-reported anxiety and stress, and produced more adaptive physiological arousal characterized by intense cardiac reactivity and a decrease of vascular resistance.

Reappraisal of emotion-inducing events not only influences emotional meaning and physiological arousal, it may also reduce the cognitive costs that normally arise when individuals process emotionally stressful stimuli. In particular, Kramer, Buckhout, Fox, Widman, and Tusche (1991) showed that the appraisal of an upsetting target slide (i.e., a dead man disfigured by a claw hammer) as depicting an actor rather than a real crime victim not only reduced self-reported anxiety and arousal, but also reduced the memory impairment for neutral slides that were presented after the stressful target slide (Kramer et al., 1991). The latter, memory finding, suggests that cognitive effort was reduced by the more benign appraisal.

Taken together, research on reappraisal suggests that this emotion regulation strategy is quite successful in reducing negative emotional experience, expression, and physiological arousal. The study by Kramer and colleagues suggests, furthermore, that reappraisal does not consume cognitive resources in that it does not impair memory. But does this mean that emotion regulation is an effortless task that requires no cognitive resources? Several studies that directly compared expressive suppression and cognitive reappraisal showed that not all kinds of emotion regulation are cognitively inexpensive and that some may come with cognitive costs.

Cognitive Consequences of Expressive Suppression and Cognitive Reappraisal

The suppression of emotion-expressive behavior is a deliberate and effortful act that not only changes outward appearance and bodily arousal, but that also influences individuals' cognitive functioning. First, some evidence for the cognitive costs of expressive-behavioral suppression comes from a study by Gilbert, Krull, and Pelham (1988) showing that the inhibition of gaze behavior impairs cognitive performance. Participants who were asked to suppress gaze, that is, to avoid looking at certain words, made less accurate social inferences about a target person than those who did not regulate their gaze. Similarly, the inhibition of emotional expression has been found to be cognitively taxing. Richards and Gross (1999) showed that suppression of emotional expression impairs memory for information encountered during the suppression period. In their study, participants watched slides depicting people with severe or no apparent injuries paired with orally presented biographical information. Participants who were instructed to suppress their expressive behavior, as compared to no instruction participants, showed reduced emotional expressiveness, but increased sympathetic arousal, and poorer recall of the biographical information that accompanied the high and low emotional slides. Furthermore, suppressors reported being less confident in their memory for slide information than nonsuppressors, indicating that they were aware of their memory impairment.

In a related study, Richards and Gross (2000) had participants watch a filmclip depicting a marital conflict that induced negative emotions of sadness, anger, and anxiety. Again, suppression did not affect subjective experience, but it decreased the expression of negative emotions and impaired recall of details of the film. Suppressors also felt less confident in their memory than nonsuppressors. At this point, it is reasonable to ask if all emotion regulation strategies are cognitively costly.

To address this question, in a second study, Richards and Gross (2000) had participants view negative emotional slides depicting severely or mildly injured persons either under suppression instructions, reappraisal instructions, or with no special instruction. Again, expressive suppression led to decrease in expressive behavior and impaired memory for verbal information that was presented with the slides. Suppression did not affect self-reported emotional experience. Reappraisal, by the same token, decreased self-reported emotional feelings as well as expressive behavior, but did not impair memory. These findings were confirmed in a third diary study in which respondents using suppression reported poorer conversational memory and poorer recall of emotional episodes they experienced during a two-week period in which they kept a diary. Reappraisal, in this instance, did not impair subjective or objective memory.

Similar results were found in a more complex interactive situation. Richards, Butler, and Gross (2003) asked married couples to discuss a relationship conflict with the instruction either to reappraise the situation in positive terms or to suppress any emotional expression. As predicted, suppression impaired memory for the verbal content of the conversation, whereas reappraisal did not. Interestingly, memory for the emotional reactions during the conversation was increased in suppressors, a finding that indicates that expressive suppression facilitates the accessibility of the suppressed emotional reactions. But why does concealing one's feelings impair memory for events?

Regulatory Depletion Account

According to the *regulatory depletion* (Muraven, Tice, & Baumeister, 1998) or *ego-depletion* hypothesis (Baumeister, Bratslavsky, Muraven, & Tice, 1998) conscious, deliberate regulation efforts draw on the individual's limited cognitive and attentional resources, and temporarily reduce the individual's capacity to perform another cognitive demanding task. In this view, the deliberate regulation of one's expressive behavior should deplete the cognitive resources, which impair subsequent self-regulatory acts or otherwise cognitive costly tasks. This is exactly what was found in a study by Muraven and colleagues (1998). In the study, participants who were asked to amplify or inhibit the expression of their feelings while watching an upsetting film performed more poorly on a subsequent muscular endurance task than no instruction participants. Similarly, Baumeister and colleagues (1998) found that participants who were instructed to suppress and conceal their feelings while watching an amusing or sad film performed worse at solving anagrams than no suppression participants. That emotion suppression requires cognitive resources was also supported in a study in which expressive suppression was the dependent variable (Muraven et al., 1998). Participants who were first asked to perform a thought regulation task (suppress thoughts of white bear) were less able to suppress their emotional expression while watching an amusing filmclip than participants who engaged in a first task with no regulation demands (solving easy math problems). Taken together, these findings indicate that suppression of expressive behavior depletes cognitive resources, undermines self-regulation in other tasks and is detrimental to performance.

The memory impairment for information encountered during the suppression period may thus be due to reduced cognitive and attentional resources imposed by suppression. In particular, it has been suggested that the deliberate suppression of expressive behavior involves changes in self-focus and self-monitoring (Richards & Gross, 2000). Suppression instructions draw attention to the internal aspects of the self and reduce attentional resources for encoding the external event. Furthermore, suppression heightens self-monitoring, that is, suppressors' concern whether they are successful in concealing their feelings. This language-based, "subvocal" monitoring ("Do I show anything?" or "I must try to keep my face still") impedes the encoding of verbal information, which explains why suppression impairs above all the verbal memory. By contrast, there is no evidence that reappraisal impairs memory. This may be due to the fact that reappraisal is cognitively inexpensive, as it does not require constant self-monitoring. Indeed, once the situation is reappraised in non-emotional terms it does not require further self-regulatory efforts, and leaves attentional and cognitive resources intact for the processing of information.

Different emotion regulation strategies have thus different cognitive consequences, that is, suppression but not reappraisal impairs memory for details of an emotional event. This finding may have implications for individuals' social functioning. Those who tend to conceal their feelings during a social encounter are prone to forget details of what has been said, which could influence social judgments. Expressive suppression during social interactions, which impairs encoding and memorizing of individuating information about the interaction partner, may enhance stereotyping or may lead to inaccurate social inferences. In interactive social encounters, keeping a "poker face" is not only cognitively costly, it has also social costs. The reduced memory for the content of an animated conversation may lead to misunderstandings and to frustration in the interaction partner.

Social Consequences of Expressive Suppression and Cognitive Reappraisal

As we have seen, suppression leads to changes in self-focus and self-monitoring, and produces an attentional shift away from the situation to internal aspects of the self. It is therefore reasonable to suspect that suppression distracts attention from the interaction partner. Suppression may impair the suppressor's responsiveness in a social encounter, that is, it may impair appropriate contingent responses and hamper coordination with the interaction partner. Furthermore, expressive suppression conceals the feelings, social motives, and behavioral intentions of an individual, and this ambiguity concerning the suppressor's needs and intentions may produce stress and reduced feelings of closeness and connectedness in the partner. Evidence for the disruptive effect of expressive suppression on interpersonal communication comes from a study by Butler, Egloff, Wilhelm, Smith, Erickson, and Gross (2003) in which pairs of unacquainted women were asked to discuss their thoughts and beliefs concerning an upsetting war documentation film they had just seen. In each pair, there was always one uninstructed person and one person who was instructed either to respond naturally (free expression dyad), or to perceive the situation in such a way to remain calm and dispassionate during the discussion (reappraisal dyad), or to conceal her feelings from the partner during the conversation (suppression dyad). Although both suppressors and reappraisers were less facially expressive, suppressors alone showed

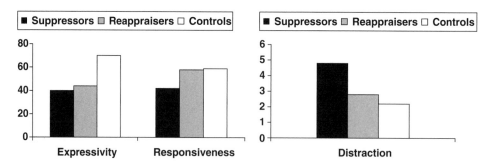

FIGURE 5.3. Actor effects: Expressivity (%), responsiveness (%), and self-rated distraction on a 0–10 scale. From Butler, E. et al. (2003). The social consequences of expressive suppression. *Emotion, 3,* 48–67.

reduced responsiveness to the partner and reported increased feelings of distraction during the conversation (see Figure 5.3).

More importantly, only suppressors' partners experienced a larger increase in blood pressure, indicating that interacting with an inexpressive person is physiologically stressful. Finally, suppression diminished the partners' feeling of closeness, decreased liking, and reduced their willingness to affiliate and become friends (see Figure 5.4).

Contrary to the effects of reappraisal, expressive suppression seems to disrupt social exchange and to hamper the development of social bonding. Some additional support for the detrimental effects of suppression on social relationships comes from research on marital interaction. Low expressiveness in married couples has been found to be associated with negative feelings and reduced marital satisfaction in both spouses (Gottman & Levenson, 1986) while responsive listening (as indicated by attention to and comprehension of partner) has been found to be beneficial for marital satisfaction (Pasupathi, Carstensen, Levenson, & Gottman, 1999).

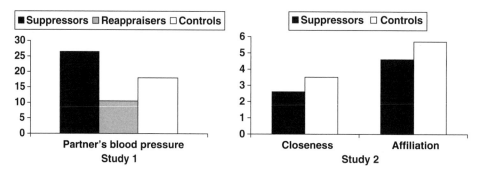

FIGURE 5.4. Partner effects: Physiological arousal (blood pressure in mmgh), experienced closeness, and willingness to affiliate on a 0–10 scale. From Butler, E. et al. (2003). The social consequences of expressive suppression. *Emotion, 3,* 48–67.

Of course, as we have noted previously in this chapter, concealing one's feelings, and in particular one's negative feelings, during social exchange can also have positive social consequences because it protects others' feelings and prevents interpersonal conflict. When expressive suppression is beneficial and when it is detrimental depends on the specific emotions that are concealed, on the situation in which the suppression occurs, and also on the frequency with which the emotions are suppressed. Suppression should be beneficial when it prevents the build-up of negative, disturbing emotions such as anxiety, anger, or hostility. Suppression may also be desirable in situations in which interpersonal distance is required, such as in interactions with a superior. Hiding one's feelings may be adaptive when it is used as temporary tool that allows the individual to conform to personal needs and social demands in a given context. Not expressing one's anger about a close person in public will doubtless be beneficial for their relationship.

Chronic suppression, contrariwise, may put existing relationships at risk, and hinder the development of new ones, and it may perpetuate the feelings one is concealing. Suppression of the anger caused by recurrent, unfair, and insolent remarks of a colleague will prevent the colleague from realizing the harmful impact of his remarks, and instead of correcting the behavior by apologizing he may continue to make them, which will further enflame the anger and cause a deterioration of the relationship.

To conclude, expressive suppression has physiological as well as cognitive and social costs whereas reappraisal does not. Reappraisal appears thus to be a more efficient emotion regulation strategy, with more adaptive consequences for the individual. Reappraising a situation in unemotional terms is quite successful in short-circuiting unwanted emotions and is thus preferable to suppressing an emotion. But what can we do once the unwanted feelings have been activated? Recall the example at the beginning of the chapter. What could Sophie do to control her fear of the dog? She could decide to ignore it and not to think of it any more in the hope of forgetting her fear as well. Emotion regulation through the suppression of emotional thoughts and feelings is the topic of the next section.

Emotional Thought Suppression: Trying Not to Think about It

The suppression of unwanted thoughts is quite common and may involve the inhibition of thoughts that elicit unwanted feelings or behavior. People try not to think of cigarettes when they want to stop smoking, and try not to think of food when they want to lose weight. In the same way, people try to regulate their emotions by suppressing thoughts that elicit unwanted painful, unpleasant feelings. Who has not tried to overcome the pain of the breakup of a romantic relationship by actively avoiding thoughts of the ex-lover? But unwanted emotions are not necessarily negative ones. People sometimes also try to suppress pleasant thoughts that may elicit emotions that are unwanted in a particular situation. For example, an individual may try to suppress thoughts of an exciting, upcoming date while a close friend is talking about a serious health problem. However, as has perhaps been observed by those who have tried to diet or tried to stop smoking, as well as those who have tried to overcome the pain of a lost love, trying to avoid thinking of cigarettes, food, or an ex-lover may paradoxically increase the frequency with which these thoughts come to mind!

Rebound of Suppressed Thoughts

The ironic and counterproductive effect of active suppression of an unwanted thought is called the *rebound effect* and was first demonstrated in an experiment that concerned the suppression of an emotionally neutral thought (Wegner, Schneider, Carter, & White, 1987). In the experiment, participants were asked to verbalize their thoughts in a stream-of-consciousness task, that is, to talk aloud about whatever came to their mind. After this initial period, the stream-of-consciousness task continued; however, half the participants were instructed to avoid thinking about a white bear, which constituted a suppression period for these participants. In the last phase of the experiment, called an expression period, all participants were encouraged to think of a white bear. Analysis of the content of the expression period showed that those who had previously suppressed thoughts of a white bear now mentioned this thought much more often than those who had not been instructed to suppress thoughts of a white bear. Why do suppressed thoughts come back to mind after suppression, and how can their rebound in consciousness be avoided? And, even more importantly for the present concerns, is there also a rebound after suppression of emotionally arousing thoughts?

According to Wegner's model of mental control (Wegner, 1994), thought suppression recruits two processes. The first is an *automatic monitoring process*, which is effortless, involuntary, functions outside of conscious awareness, and does not require cognitive resources. The second is a *controlled operating process*, which is conscious, intentional, and which requires cognitive resources for its operation. The monitoring process searches mental content for instances of the unwanted thought. Every time it detects the presence of the to-be-suppressed unwanted thought, the operating process is then activated with the goal to seek out other thoughts, so-called *distracter* thoughts, that capture conscious attention and serve to keep the unwanted thought out of mind.

Wegner's model of mental control proposes different explanations for the rebound of suppressed thoughts. The *association explanation* holds that the distracter thoughts that are used to replace the unwanted thought become strongly associated with the unwanted thoughts. Distracters then serve as memory cues that prompt the unwanted thought whenever they come to mind or appear in the environment. This explains why rebound effects are stronger when the suppression and subsequent expression periods take place in the same physical or emotional environment (Wegner, Schneider, Knutson, & McMahon, 1991; Wenzlaff, Wegner, & Klein, 1991). Wenzlaff and colleagues (1991), for example, found a stronger rebound of a previously suppressed thought (of a white bear) for suppressors who were in the same mood during the suppression and the final expression period, that is, who listened to the same happy or depressive music. Being in the same mood facilitated the return of the unwanted thought (mood-dependent rebound). In a second study, they showed that the rebound of the suppressed thought induced the emotional state experienced during suppression. These findings indicate that suppression creates a strong association between the unwanted thought and the mood experienced during suppression. Later on, the activation of one will instigate the other.

There is still another account of the rebound of suppressed thoughts. The *accessibility explanation* holds that suppression increases the accessibility of the to-be-suppressed thoughts because the automatic monitoring process continues to search for the unwanted thought even when suppression is no longer required. Suppression increases thus the likelihood that the previously suppressed thought rebounds, without being cued by a distracter (Macrae, Bodenhausen, Milne, & Jetten, 1994; Page, Locke, & Trio, 2005). Furthermore, according to the *cognitive load explanation* the rebound effect is more likely when cognitive resources are minimized due to a concurrent task, time pressure, or stress. Cognitive load undermines the cognitively costly operating process, and so enhances the ironic effects of the monitoring process. Under cognitive load, the monitoring process will continue to search for the to-be-suppressed thought, but because the operating process is no longer able to replace the thought with distracters, the unwanted thought will become even more accessible (for a review, see Wenzlaff & Wegner, 2000).

Rebound of Emotional Thoughts

Now that we have described possible explanations for the rebound of suppressed thoughts, we may turn to our initial question concerning the rebound of emotions and emotion-related thoughts. Only one study directly addressed the question of the regulation of emotions through mental control. Wegner, Erber, and Zanakos (1993) had participants recall happy or sad past events with the instruction either to feel or not to feel the emotion, or with no regulation instruction. Additionally, half the participants had to perform the recall task under cognitive load (rehearsing a nine-digit number). Results showed that cognitive load impaired the capacity to regulate the emotions in the intended direction, and ironically produced the opposite effect, that is, the rebound of the unwanted emotion. Participants who had been instructed to change their emotions in a negative direction (i.e., to feel sad or to not feel happy) reported feeling happier than those who had been instructed to change their emotions in a positive direction (i.e., to feel happy or to not feel sad), with control participants falling in between. Participants who were not under cognitive load, however, were quite successful in regulating their emotions: self-reported happiness was greater for those who engaged in positive mood regulation and weaker for those who engaged in negative mood regulation compared to the control group (see Figure 5.5).

Unfortunately, the strategy of suppression (not feel an emotion) and expression (feel an emotion) was confounded and it is therefore difficult to say if suppression of emotion produces a stronger rebound of the suppressed feelings once the suppression is released. The authors reported suggestive support for the idea that the ironic effects under cognitive load were stronger for those who had to suppress their feelings (i.e., those who tried not to feel happy or sad) than those who concentrated on the desired feeling (i.e., those who tried to feel happy or sad). However, without cognitive load no signs of rebound of the regulated emotion were observed.

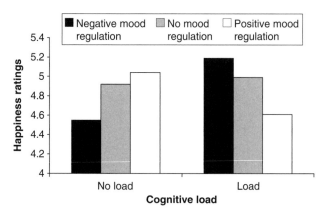

FIGURE 5.5. Self-rated happiness on a 7-point scale as a function of mood regulation instruction and cognitive load. From Wegner, D. et al. (1993). Ironic processes in the mental control of mood and mood-related thoughts. *Journal of Personality and Social Psychology, 65*, 1093–1104.

Several other studies have shown that the classical rebound effect cannot be generalized so easily to the suppression of emotions and emotional thoughts. For instance, Muris, Merkelbach, van den Hout, and de Jong (1992) had participants read either an emotional or a non-emotional version of a story about a car accident and to try to identify with the main character. In the emotional version, the main character was responsible for the accident in which a baby died while in the non-emotional version all emotional elements were replaced by neutral ones. Next, participants performed a stream-of-consciousness task either with the instruction not to think of the story they just read (suppression) or to think of whatever they like including the story (free expression). Finally, all participants were instructed to freely express their thoughts. The classical rebound effect was observed only for suppression of thoughts concerning the neutral, non-emotional story version. That is, neutral story suppressors reported more thoughts about the accident after the suppression period than neutral story expressors during the initial free expression period. However, the suppression of the emotional story version did not affect the frequency with which it came back to mind in the final free expression period.

A study by Kelly and Kahn (1994), which compared the effects of suppression of self-generated emotional thoughts and experimenter-induced neutral thoughts of a white bear, suggests that the suppression of personal emotional thoughts may even help to decrease their occurrence. Participants were first asked to write down their most pleasant/unpleasant personal intrusive thought (or the neutral thoughts about a white bear). Then, half of them were invited to write down whatever came to their mind but suppressing the personal thought (or the neutral thought), followed by a period of expression of this same thought (suppression–expression condition). For the other half, the order was reversed (expression–suppression condition). As can be seen in Figure 5.6, participants who were instructed to avoid thinking of personally intrusive thoughts mentioned these thoughts slightly less frequently in the post-suppression expression period compared to those without previous suppression instruction. By contrast, the suppression of a neutral thought of a white bear produced the classical rebound effect, that is, more intrusive thoughts in the expression period that followed suppression compared to intrusive thoughts in an initial expression period.

Germane to this issue, Wegner and Gold (1995) found that participants who had suppressed an emotionally involving thought, a still-desired ex-lover, later talked less about the ex-lover than those who had not suppressed. By contrast, participants who had suppressed a less involving thought, a no longer desired ex-lover, experienced more intrusive thoughts compared to those who had expressed.

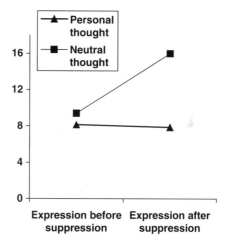

FIGURE 5.6. Mean number of thoughts as a function of type of thought and expression condition. From Kelly, A., & Kahn, J. (1994). Effects of suppression of personal intrusive thoughts. *Journal of Personality and Social Psychology, 66,* 998–1006.

Availability of Distracters

The efficacy of suppression in reducing the reappearance of emotional thoughts in consciousness may be due to people's prior experience with controlling intrusive thoughts. In particular, individuals may have a variety of distracters they normally use to avoid personal intrusive, emotional thoughts. These previously used "outside" distracters are not linked to the laboratory context. In the laboratory, such distracters are therefore less likely to come to mind to cue the to-be-suppressed thought. By contrast, to-be-suppressed thoughts that are provided by the experimenter (i.e., a white bear) are generally novel and not personally relevant for participants, and participants probably do not have "outside" distracters at hand. Participants must therefore search potential distracters in the immediate suppression environment, that is, in the laboratory. These "inside" distracters become paired with to-be-suppressed thoughts and cause their subsequent rebound. This account was supported by the finding that participants who expressed or suppressed self-generated emotional thoughts mentioned more outside distracters, while those who thought or suppressed thinking of a white bear mentioned inside distracters more often. Furthermore, the frequency of intrusive thoughts was positively correlated with inside distracters and negatively correlated with outside distracters. This indicates that cues from inside the laboratory prompt the suppressed thoughts and make their reappearance more likely while outside distracters prevent the rebound of intrusive thoughts (Kelly & Kahn, 1994).

Defensive Suppression

The absence of a rebound of suppressed emotional thoughts has also been explained in terms of a *defensive suppression mechanism* (Wegner & Gold, 1995). In everyday life, thought suppression is more common for emotional than for neutral thoughts because people are motivated to avoid the painful, unpleasant, or inappropriate feelings they evoke. The instruction to suppress such thoughts enhances the natural tendency to avoid unwanted emotional thoughts. The instruction to freely express emotional thoughts in the free expression period goes against the natural tendency to suppress and provoke a defensive suppression reaction against the unwanted intrusive thoughts, and active suppression of the unwanted thoughts and feelings is practiced even when the instruction to suppress is no longer applied.

Physiological Rebound

Unlike the suppression of emotionally neutral thoughts, the suppression of emotional thoughts seems quite successful. But one might then ask whether the suppression of emotional thoughts also prevents the individual from experiencing the undesirable emotions. Several studies suggest that the inhibition of emotional thoughts may calm the mind but not the body. In particular, Koriat, Melkman, Averill, and Lazarus (1972) showed that the instruction to suppress the emotional feelings and thoughts induced by an emotionally upsetting film about accidents in the workplace reduced participants' self-reported emotional distress, but did not decrease their physiological arousal. In fact, participants manifested a weak (nonsignificant) *increase* in electrodermal reactivity and heart rate compared to a control group that watched the upsetting film without specific instructions.

Similar physiological costs were also found for self-imposed emotional suppression. Martin (1964) had college men watch sexually arousing slides of nude women. Male participants who had just been instructed to think about their parents and to recall memories of parental discipline (suppression context) looked at the film for a shorter period of time, but were more aroused than those who were not reminded of their parents just before viewing the film (permissive context).

Wegner, Shortt, Blake, and Page (1990) showed that increased physiological arousal after the suppression of exciting thoughts is not due to an increase of intrusive thoughts, but to the close relationship between intrusive thoughts and emotional arousal. In their study, participants were invited to verbalize their thoughts in a stream-of-consciousness task with the instruction either to think or not to think about several topics, one of which was exciting (i.e., sex) as indicated by an increase in skin conductivity for this topic only. The suppression of the exciting thought decreased the frequency with which it was mentioned but did not decrease the physiological arousal during the suppression period. That is, those who suppressed thinking of sex became even slightly more aroused than those who, to the contrary, had been instructed to think of sex. Furthermore, suppressors' skin conductance level increased every time they experienced the intrusion of the exciting thought. For participants who were allowed to express the exciting thought, or for those who thought or suppressed thinking about an emotionally neutral topic (the weather), thought intrusion was not related to arousal.

The suppression of emotionally exciting thoughts may thus be counterproductive because even though it diminishes the frequency of intrusive thoughts, it causes people to become aroused each time the suppressed thought returns to mind. Does this mean that the more one tries, for example, to put a past relationship out of mind the more one will be disturbed by unpleasant bodily arousal? Research by Wegner and Gold (1995) that we mentioned briefly before, suggests that this may be the case. These researchers examined the effects of the suppression of thoughts of a past close relationship, on the frequency of thinking and talking about the ex-lover (an "old flame"), and on physiological arousal. In an initial expression period, participants were invited to think aloud about a past romantic relationship that still affected them emotionally (i.e., a "hot flame") or that was no longer desired (i.e., a "cold flame"). Half the participants were then instructed to suppress thoughts of their old flame, while the other half continued to express thoughts of the old flame. In the final expression period, participants were all invited to think aloud about the old flame. The rebound effect, that is, an increased frequency of thoughts about the old flame, was found only for cold flame suppressors. Hot flame suppressors did not manifest a rebound of the previously suppressed thought. They talked less about their still-desired old flame during the expression period compared to those who freely expressed. Hot flame suppressors, however, did show an increased electrodermal response, a physiological rebound. This finding indicates that the rebound of thoughts is more likely after the suppression of neutral or non-emotional thoughts while a physiological rebound is more likely when the target of suppression is emotionally involving.

Most of the studies we have reviewed investigated emotional thought suppression in situations of social isolation. But what happens when emotionally involving thoughts or feelings are suppressed in more complex, interaction situations? Imagine that you plan to get together with a friend because you need to talk to her about your recent relationship problems.

When you arrive at the agreed-upon time and place, you find that your friend has brought along an acquaintance of hers whom you do not know. There is no way to talk about your problems, and so you half-heartedly engage in a discussion of a new film. You might feel especially aroused because you have to avoid thinking about what you really want to discuss. This is exactly what was found in an experiment by Mendes, Reis, Seery, and Blascovich (2003). In their study, participants were instructed to think of either an emotionally involving topic (i.e., a past embarrassing situation) or of emotional neutral topics (e.g., duties and responsibilities in a job) in order to discuss it with a research assistant later on. However, only half the participants actually had the opportunity to discuss the prepared topic with the assistant. Unexpectedly for them, the remaining participants had to discuss an unrelated neutral topic that they had not thought about before. That is, they had to inhibit thoughts of the topic they intended to talk about. Participants who had to suppress thoughts about emotional topic exhibited greater physiological arousal compared to baseline arousal and to the non-emotional suppressers. The arousal pattern of emotional suppressors was characterized by moderate cardiovascular reactivity and increased vascular resistance (vasoconstriction that is related to increase in blood pressure), which is, as we will discuss below, characteristic of a threat response (see Figure 5.7).

The increased physiological reactivity after suppression of emotional thoughts and feelings can be accounted for by an *accessibility explanation* according to which suppression increases the accessibility of

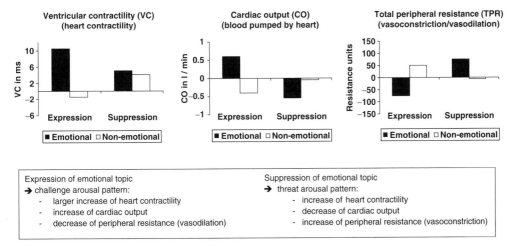

FIGURE 5.7. Cardiovascular responses (VC, CO, TPR) during expression or suppression of non-emotional vs. emotional topics. From Mendes, B. et al. (2003). Cardiovascular correlates of emotional expression and suppression: Do content and gender context matter? *Journal of Personality and Social Psychology, 84,* 771–792.

the to-be-suppressed thoughts, which in turn facilitates their rebound. Suppressed emotional thoughts, although highly accessible, tend to be less intrusive because of the availability of distracters and of defensive suppression. But the few times the suppressed emotional thoughts come back to mind intrusively, they produce strong emotional reactions in the form of bodily arousal.

Another account of increased physiological arousal following suppression of personally involving emotional thoughts and feelings was proposed by Mendes and colleagues (2003). According to the *challenge and threat theory* (Blascovich & Mendes, 2000; Blaskovich & Tomaka, 1996), situations may be appraised as challenging or threatening depending on the situational demands (including uncertainty or required effort) and personal coping resources (including knowledge, abilities, dispositions, and external support). Challenge and threat appraisals are associated with specific challenge and threat responses including specific cardiovascular arousal (Tomaka et al., 1997). *Challenge responses* are more likely when the situational demands are within the individual's personal coping resources. Challenge is associated with positive affect, approach orientation, enhanced performance, and an arousal pattern characterized by intense cardiovascular reactivity and decreased vascular resistance (vasodilation). *Threat responses*, by way of contrast, are more likely to occur when the situational and task demands exceed the individual's resources and capacities to cope with them. Threat is linked to negative affect, poorer task performance, behavioral inhibition, avoidance orientation, and an arousal pattern characterized by moderate cardiovascular reactivity and increased vascular resistance (vasoconstriction). Within the challenge and threat theory, the increased emotional reactivity associated with emotional suppression can be explained as follows: suppression in general is associated with mental effort that strains psychological resources. Emotional, as compared to non-emotional, suppression is particularly demanding and effortful because it involves the inhibition of self-relevant, emotional thoughts. In this case, the suppression demands may easily exceed the individual's resources and therefore elicit strong threat arousal.

To conclude, suppression of emotional thoughts may prevent their coming back to consciousness, but tend to produce increased physiological arousal. A gradual confrontation with the unwanted emotional thought may be a remedy against the physiological rebound because it facilitates habituation to the unwanted emotional thought, which also reduces the other concomitant emotional responses (i.e., bodily arousal) over the course of time. This helps the individual face the unwanted emotional thought long enough to be able to process and re-evaluate its emotional content in order to make it manageable and bearable (Wegner, 1989).

Social Sharing of Emotions: Talking about It

Within the psychoanalytic tradition (Bucci, 1995; Freud 1920/2005) the accumulation of non-expressed emotions is associated with mental and physical disorders. The revocation and verbalization of traumatic events and the associated emotions play a central role in the psychoanalytic cure and are considered as beneficial for the individual. Common sense too holds that it is helpful and good to talk about one's problems, emotions, and feelings because it makes one feel better. In addition to emotional recovery, revealing one's feelings to others is considered to be beneficial for physical and psychological health. People's beliefs about the salutary effects of talking about their emotions, and their ideas about the intrapersonal and interpersonal consequences of such disclosure, were directly investigated in a questionnaire study by Zech (reported in Zech, 1999). Results showed that a large majority of participants believed that talking about emotions is beneficial because it put things in order, and helped to solicit comfort and the creation of confidence relationship. But do people really talk about their emotions and feelings so easily? And what are the emotions people share, and with whom do they share them? And finally, why do they talk about them, that is, what are functions and consequences of social sharing? All these questions will be addressed in the next sections.

Frequency, Duration, and Partner of Social Sharing

Social sharing consists of communicating one's emotions and the emotion-eliciting event to others either verbally or in written form, as for example in a diary or in a letter, and involves "the re-evocation of an emotional experience in a socially-shared language and at least at the symbolic level, some addressee" (Rimé, Mesquita, Philippot, & Boca, 1991a, p. 438).

Initial studies of the social sharing of emotion were mainly concerned with quantitative aspects of social sharing, that is, with what emotional events people share when, how often, and with whom. And four different methods were largely employed to investigate the occurrence of spontaneous social sharing after an emotional episode. In *recall studies*, participants were instructed to recall a personal emotional episode concerning a specific emotion (e.g., joy, sadness, anger) and to answer questions about the occurrence, frequency, duration, and the partner of social sharing (Rimé et al., 1991a; Rimé, Noël & Philippot, 1991b; for a review see Rimé, Finkenauer, Luminet, Zech, & Philippot, 1998). In general, the vast majority of participants (about 90–95%) reported having talked to someone, most of them on the very day of the emotional event, and nearly half of

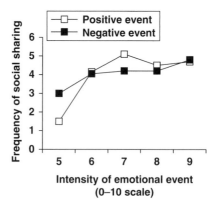

FIGURE 5.8. Mean number of times of initial social sharing as a function of the initial intensity level and the valence of recalled emotional events. From Rimé, B. et al. (1998). Social sharing of emotion: New evidence and new questions. In W. Stroebe, & M. Hewstone (Eds.), *European review of social psychology* (Vol. 9, pp. 145–189). Chichester: John Wiley & Sons.

them reported having talked about the emotional episode several times, which emphasizes the repetitive character of social sharing. Parents, close family members, spouses, and best friends were the preferred persons with whom emotions were shared. The frequency of social sharing was positively correlated with the intensity and disruptiveness of the emotional experience indicating that people are more inclined to talk about intense and disturbing emotional episodes (see Figure 5.8).

In *diary studies*, conducted over several weeks, participants reported the most important emotional episode of the day and answered questions about the social sharing of the described emotional event. The findings of four diary studies, reported in Rimé and colleagues (1998), replicated the findings of the recall studies. The majority of participants reported having talked about the emotional event to others the day it happened. Furthermore, social sharing did not vary as a function of specific emotions except for shame and guilt, which tended to be less shared and talked about. This last finding is not surprising because shame- and guilt-related events are often caused by transgression of social norms and keeping these episodes secret prevent social disapproval and rejection (Finkenauer & Rimé, 1998a).

In *follow-up studies*, participants were first contacted immediately after an emotional episode, and then again several days or weeks later, and asked questions about event-related social sharing. Rimé and colleagues (1998) reviewed seven follow-up studies on social sharing of emotional events including traffic, domestic or working accident, child birth, bereavement, anxiety-arousing exams, first blood donation, and attending or performing the dissection of a human corpse. In general, the proportion of participants who reported having talked about the emotional event within the first and/or second week after the event was very high (90–100%) and comparable to proportions found with recall or diary method (see Figure 5.9).

Experimental studies used filmclips to induce specific emotions that varied in intensity and assessed participants' spontaneous social sharing after exposure to the film. In three studies by Luminet, Bouts, Delie, Manstead, and Rimé (2000), participants who came with a same-sex friend, watched one of three filmclips that induced high, moderate, and low emotions, involving tourists eating a monkey's brain, a cockfight, and a life in the Himalayas, respectively, while their friend performed an irrelevant task in a separate room. Participants' facial expressions were filmed with a hidden camera and later rated for intensity of facial expression and duration of gaze aversion. After the film, participants and their friends were brought together in a waiting room and left alone for five minutes. Two independent judges rated their taperecorded conversation for the time they talked about the film.

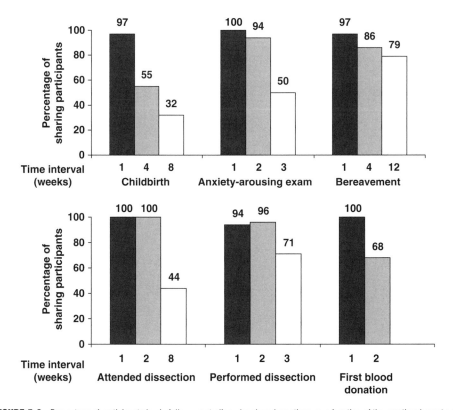

FIGURE 5.9. Percentage of participants in six follow-up studies who shared emotions as a function of the emotional event and the time interval. From Rimé, B. et al. (1998). Social sharing of emotion: New evidence and new questions. In W. Stroebe, & M. Hewstone (Eds.), *European review of social psychology* (Vol. 9, pp. 145–189). Chichester: John Wiley & Sons.

Results showed that social sharing was influenced by the emotional intensity of the viewed film. Participants talked more about the highly emotional film than about the moderately emotional and the neutral film, which did not differ from each other. Social sharing was also positively correlated with the intensity of the participants' facial reactions. The more the participants were emotionally aroused as measured by the intensity of their facial reactions, the more they later talked about the film to their friend. The finding that experimentally induced intense negative emotions elicited more social sharing compared to moderate or low intensity emotions suggests that social sharing of an emotional experience is more likely to occur when the emotional intensity exceeds a certain threshold.

Emotional Recovery and the Content of Social Sharing

In most studies on social sharing, emotional recovery has been assessed by comparing the initial emotional intensity of the emotional episode with the emotional intensity elicited by the recall of the same episode (*residual intensity*). The recovery score (i.e., initial intensity minus residual intensity) is then correlated with the extent of sharing. Typically, no significant relationship between spontaneous social sharing and emotional recovery has been found, indicating that recalling and talking about an emotional event does not decrease its emotional impact (Finkenauer & Rimé, 1998a; Rimé et al., 1991a). On the contrary, social sharing has been found to reactivate the shared emotion, that is, talking about a past emotional event was reported to re-instigate concomitant mental images, bodily sensations and subjective feelings (for a review, see Rimé et al., 1998). However, the disclosure of negative emotional episodes is not perceived as unpleasant (Rimé et al., 1991a).

Several studies have shown that it is the *content* of social sharing that may be critical for emotional recovery. Pennebaker and Beall (1986) found that writing about the emotional aspects, compared to writing about the factual aspects, of a traumatic event increased physiological arousal on the first day of writing, but decreased it on the following days. Similarly, Mendolia and Kleck (1993) found that the content of social sharing, that is, talking about one's emotional reactions and feelings or about the objective facts concerning a stressful film about accidents in the workplace influenced participants' emotional responses immediately after having talked about it with the experimenter, and also during a second exposure to the same stressful film. Participants who had talked about their emotional reactions and feelings after the first exposure to the film exhibited more physiological arousal during immediate re-exposure to the film, a result that is in line with the general finding of the absence of immediate emotional recovery after sharing. However, emotional sharers, compared to those who talked about the facts of the film, manifested less physiological arousal during a delayed re-exposure that took place two days later. Interestingly, emotional sharers reported also more intrusive thoughts and more discussions about the film in the period between the two sessions. This self-induced, repeated mental exposure to the film may enable them to process the emotional information and to re-evaluate its personal relevance. Emotional sharing has thus negative short-term effects because it tends to increase arousal immediately after the first sharing, but it has long-term benefits because it reduces physiological reactivity, and facilitates emotional adjustment due to the repeated confrontation with and reprocessing of the emotional information. Overall, these findings suggest that emotional recovery takes place only after repeated thinking of and talking about one's feelings and emotions.

Emotional change after talking about an emotional event has also been found to be related to specific features of the sharing context, including the sharers' goal and gender as well as the listeners' behavior (Pasupathi, 2003). The emotional benefit increases with the responsiveness and agreeability of the listener, and the more the sharers' motive for disclosure was to regulate their emotions. Moreover, men tended to benefit more from sharing than women.

Functions of Social Sharing

The above cited studies suggest that people are quite willing to talk about negative emotionally arousing events even though the disclosure tends to reactivate the negative emotional responses. At this point, we may ask why people are so inclined to share their negative emotions. Is the widespread belief that talking about negative emotions reduces their emotional impact and facilitates emotional recovery wrong? Or do people tolerate re-experiencing the negative emotions during social sharing because of other, more delayed, long-term benefits? According to Rimé and colleagues (1991a) social sharing not only plays an important role in the processing of emotional information, but it may also serve important psychological and social functions. Specifically, they suggest that social sharing is a source of social comparison, of social support, of social integration, and of social affirmation or approval (for a review see Rimé et al., 1998; Pennebaker, Zech, & Rimé, 2001).

Emotional Information Processing

Emotions, and in particular negative ones, may challenge people's belief about the world and lead them to see the world as unfair, or unsafe or out of control. Individuals' willingness to talk about emotional events is motivated by a desire to feel better, but also by a need to understand the meaning of the emotional event and to adapt to it. By verbalizing and putting their emotional experience into words, people distance themselves from the emotional experience, which enables them to reprocess the emotional information and to restore the threatened beliefs about the world. This *working through* the emotional experience allows people to integrate the emotional event in their existing emotional schemas and scripts (*assimilation*), or to modify them (*accommodation*) in order to adjust them to the new reality, especially in the case of a major emotional life event (Horowitz, 1976/1992).

Social Comparison

Emotional events may induce complex and ambiguous sensations and feelings that need to be clarified and interpreted. Social comparison is a means to better understand and identify ambiguous feelings (Festinger, 1954). Talking with others about one's emotions, sensations, and feelings enables individuals to compare themselves and their emotional reactions with others. Social sharing is thus a means to evaluate the appropriateness and the relevance of one's own feelings in a given situation, and to clarify the meaning of the emotional event. According to Festinger's social comparison theory, social comparison is a selective process, that is, people do not compare themselves with just everybody, they generally prefer to compare themselves with similar others. This explains why individuals share their emotions mainly with members of their reference group (e.g., close family members, friends, or spouses).

Social Support

Social sharing of emotion may also be motivated by the search for external social support and assistance in coping with emotions. Individuals therefore talk about their feelings and emotions primarily with a person who can provide the expected assistance and support for their emotional work. Others can help to reappraise the situation, or to distract from the stressful aspects of the event. Talking to others about intense emotional events often causes the listener to comfort the other not only with understanding words and supportive actions but also with nonverbal behavior, such as touching and hugging. Social sharing may thus decrease the physical and interpersonal distance, and contribute to the development of close relationships (Thoits, 1984).

Social Affirmation

Confiding one's emotions and feelings in others has still other benefits. Besides the receipt of support and assistance, it provokes interest, attention and sympathy in the listener. Consistent with this idea, Collins and

Miller (1994) found that people who share their emotions and feelings with others are more liked than those who hold them back. In addition, being chosen as a confidant is also affirming for the listener because he is considered as trustworthy and his advice as valuable. Social sharing therefore enhances social cohesion.

Social Integration

Strong emotional events tax the individual's attentional and cognitive resources and often produce increased self-focused attention, which induces dissociation between the individual and the social environment. Social sharing enables the individual to preserve and to restore the social integration. By communicating one's emotions and feelings, members of the social environment come to better know and to understand the inner feelings of the person, and are able to provide socially accepted ways to interpret the emotional event and the associated emotions and feelings.

To conclude, across studies and methods, emotional events have been found to be shared by a vast majority of research participants. Social sharing appears to be repeated often and involves different partners, mostly intimates, such as close family members, friends, spouses, or companions. The degree of social sharing depends on the disruptiveness and intensity of the emotional episode; the more intense and disruptive the emotional episode the more it is likely to be shared. However, social sharing has also been found to be independent of the valence and type of emotion (with the exception of shame and guilt). Talking about one's emotion does not vary substantially with age, sex, and culture (Rimé, Philippot, Boca, & Mesquita, 1992; Rimé et al., 1998). With regard to individual differences, social sharing has been found to be negatively correlated to alexithymia, a personality trait that is characterized by difficulty in identifying and expressing emotions (Luminet, Zech, Rimé & Wagner, 2000; Paez, Velasco, & Gonzalez, 1999).

Although social sharing does not result in immediate emotional recovery, it is beneficial in the long term because it enables people to re-experience the emotional event in a more positive way. Furthermore, emotional sharing is evaluated as more meaningful and interesting than talking in an objective and descriptive way (Zech & Rimé, 1996).

Emotion Regulation and Health

Emotion regulation is commonly considered as central to and even necessary for mental and physical health. Emotional dysregulation is held to be responsible for clinical problems such as eating disorders, alcohol abuse, anxiety and mood disorders, in particular depression (for a review see Gross & Munoz, 1995). In correlation studies, chronic emotional suppression (as compared to reappraisal) has been found to be associated with more self-reported depressive symptoms, with lower life satisfaction, weaker self-esteem, and lower overall well-being (Gross & John, 2003). Several studies have explored the relationship between cognitive emotion regulation strategies and measures of depression and anxiety (Garnefski, Kraaij, & Spinhoven, 2001; Garnefski, van den Kommer, Kraaij, Teerds, Legerstee, & Onstein, 2002). Several "maladaptive" cognitive regulation strategies such as *rumination* (recurrent thinking about negative feelings), *catastrophizing* (explicitly emphasizing the negativity of the event), *self-blame* (blaming oneself for what has happened), and *other blame* (blaming others for what has happened), are positively related to depression and anxiety. More adaptive strategies such as *positive reappraisal* (interpretation of a negative event in a positive way in terms of personal growth), *positive refocus* (thinking about pleasant, joyful things that distract from negative event), *putting into perspective* (emphasizing the relativity of the event compared to other events), *acceptance* (accepting and resigning to what has happened), and *refocus on planning* (thinking about the steps to take in order to deal with the negative event), are negatively related to anxiety and depression.

The negative effect of inhibition of emotions was illustrated in a study about keeping secrets. Individuals who reported having memories of unshared, secret emotional events also reported more health problems and lower life satisfaction compared to those who did not have secret memories (Finkenauer & Rimé, 1998b).

In addition to psychological problems and mood disorders, emotion dysregulation can also cause somatic illness. It has been shown quite consistently that avoidance, inhibition, suppression, and holding back of negative emotions has deleterious consequences for physical health. Emotion inhibition may increase the risk of cancer and accelerate cancer progression (Gross, 1989; Kune, Kune, Watson, & Bahnson, 1991). Chronic inhibition of anger and hostility has also been found to be associated with hypertension and coronary heart disease (Smith, 1992).

The adverse effects of emotion inhibition may be due to the increased sympathetic nervous system activation that it produces. According to Pennebaker and colleagues' *inhibition theory*, the conscious effort to inhibit one's emotional thoughts, feelings and emotion-related behavior generates physiological arousal (Pennebaker, 1989; Pennebaker & Beall, 1986; Pennebaker, Hughes, & O'Heeron, 1987). Chronic inhibition produces cumulative physiological arousal and increases the likelihood of stress-related psychological and physical health problems. Another mechanism through which emotional suppression affects health is its selective inhibitory effect on immune functioning (Petrie, Booth, & Davidson, 1995; Petrie, Booth, & Pennebaker, 1998). Disclosure of stressful, traumatic events, by the same token, appears to enhance the immune functioning (Esterling, Antoni, Fletcher, Margulies, & Schneiderman, 1994; Pennebaker, Kiecolt-Glaser, & Glaser, 1988).

Of course, based on what we have learned about emotion regulation and health we should not infer that the less we inhibit or the more often we express our emotions, the healthier we are. As Gross and Munoz have noted: "It is the ability to flexibly adjust the way one regulates one's emotions to environmental exigencies that is related to [. . .] health, not how often one regulates one's emotions" (Gross & Munoz, 1995, p. 160).

Summary

Although emotions have evolved for their adaptive value, they are not always desirable because they may be inconsistent with social norms for a given situation, or because they can cause physical or psychological suffering. Individuals may therefore regularly attempt to inhibit or reduce emotions that are painful and/or inappropriate, and to generate or enhance emotions that are pleasant and/or socially desirable. We have seen that individuals have at their disposal a wide variety of emotion regulation strategies, which are differently effective, and which have different costs and benefits over the long run. A comparison of the strategies of cognitive reappraisal and of suppression of expressive behavior, feelings and thoughts suggests that these two means of emotion regulation have different affective, physiological, cognitive, and social consequences.

Research has generally demonstrated that reappraisal of an emotional situation is more effective than avoiding, inhibiting, and suppressing emotional responses. Reappraisal may be quite difficult in the first place, but when it can be done, it may diminish the subjective experience and the expressive aspects of an emotion without impairing memory, indicating that reappraisal is not cognitively taxing. Suppression of expressive behavior, feelings and thoughts, contrariwise, is successful in decreasing behavioral expression and keeping thoughts out of consciousness. However, suppression does not decrease emotional experience and it is associated with increases in sympathetic activation in both the suppressor and the interaction partner, and at the same time it impairs memory for information encountered during suppression. Thus, suppression can be a physiologically, cognitively, and socially costly strategy. It is likely for this reason that individuals who habitually suppress negative emotions tend also to suffer both minor and more permanent health consequences. Emotional disclosure, or talking about one's emotions and sharing them with supportive listeners, may produce short-term adverse effects but facilitates emotional adjustment in the long term, and promotes psychological and physical health.

Emotion in Social Cognition 6

Most languages have expressions that convey the everyday belief that emotions can affect how we see things and how we think about them. Edith Piaf, the famous French singer, sang that happiness makes us see life through rose-colored glasses, for example. We hear that love can blind people, that when angry people are unable to see straight, and that sadness can make the whole world look bleak. One of the authors of this book once boarded a train in Cracow, bound for Warsaw. A Polish man sitting in the same compartment, who wanted to speak English, asked her what she did in life. When he learned the answer, he asked her to describe the topic of her psychological research and its implications. She explained that it concerned the ways in which emotions affect cognition. On hearing this, the man bolted to his feet and exclaimed: "You should study the Poles! We have very strong emotions, and these emotions affect the way we think!" Emotions affect the way almost all people think.

Try to recall the last time you were feeling angry. Maybe you were angry because you were fined for parking your car momentarily on the sidewalk, or in front of a garage door on which there was a sign specifying that parking was forbidden. "But everyone, everywhere, parks illegally," you whine, generalizing pessimistically about human nature. You drive home, highly irritated with the other drivers. "All of them, they are so incompetent behind the steering wheel," you mutter to no one in particular, honking at an older woman whom you believe is taking much too much time to turn left. At home, you notice that your roommate did not clean up after his lunch, and left all the dishes in the sink. He is such a pig. You were going to go to a party with him over the weekend, but now you think you won't. It would probably be a bad party, anyway . . .

Does this sound familiar to you? Once in a particular emotional state, your perceptions and thoughts are not unaffected. Often, as we shall see, they are congruent in tone with your feeling state. Perception, memory, categorization, decisions, and judgments. These are all cognitive processes that are affected by current emotional states, or perhaps more accurately, accompany them, in the sense of constituting part of that emotional state. Although relationships between emotion and cognition are in and of themselves important, psychologists are particularly interested in these relationships because, as we shall see, thoughts are assumed to affect behavior. Maybe in an angry state, in which you assume that everyone drives poorly, you drive poorly too, or at least worse than usual. Perhaps the belief that other people do annoying things enhances your tendency to do so. Because emotions are so often provoked in social interaction, and because cognitions are instrumental for guiding behavior, the relationships between emotion and cognition are fundamental for understanding human social behavior.

In this chapter, we will show that specific emotional states influence the way individuals think and make judgments about everything from attitude objects to other individuals. To this end, we will first show that emotions influence the content of thought, and then that they also influence the strategies that are used to process information, suggesting that emotional states should be considered an integral part of inform ation processing models (Damasio, 1994).

The experimental strategy used in many of the studies we will describe involves two phases. In the first phase, an emotional state is induced. In the second phase, participants perform an ostensibly unrelated task in which the main measures of attending, perceiving, thinking, or judging are measured. In studies of this type, emotional states have been induced with the use of numerous procedures that produce states of different intensity, and make participants more or less aware of the real source of the state. Because experimental participants often do not know the source of their state, in the remainder of this chapter, we will use the terms *affective state* and *mood state* instead of emotional state. As we mentioned in Chapter 1, emotions are reactions to specific eliciting objects or events, and affective states or moods are the longer term consequences of these objects or events. Thus, many of the experiments that employ a two-phase procedure can be said to be investigating the effects of affective state, rather than emotion, on subsequent cognition and behavior.

Affective State and the Content of Cognitive Processes

How could affective states influence the content of perception and cognition? This has been one preoccupation of psychologists particularly in the past 30 years. As we mentioned in our opening illustrations, one very likely hypothesis is that affective state is associated with an increase in perceptions and thoughts that have the same emotional tone as the affective state. This idea is called the mood congruence hypothesis, and the hypothesis has received enormous empirical attention, in part due to its importance for understanding depression and other affective disorders. In this section, we start by introducing one of the most influential accounts of the way in which affective states influence the content of information that appears in (mostly conscious) thought, specifically in a mood congruent way, the *associative network models* of emotion.

Associative Network Models of Emotion

Associative network models of human memory posit that memory can be modeled as a web of interconnected informational nodes or units, which represent semantic concepts, as well as procedural knowledge about the use of these concepts (e.g., Anderson & Bower, 1973; Collins & Loftus, 1975). The importance of the connections among units of information is that it allows the use of one concept to influence the probability that a connected concept will also come to mind. The influence occurs through a process of spreading activation, or excitation, within the network. When an informational unit, or a concept, is activated through exposure to an example of the concept or through intentional thinking about the concept, activation spreads throughout the network via associative links. When activation exceeds some threshold, the part of the network that has been activated reaches consciousness. For example, the concept of "dog" may be linked through a "part of" semantic relation to the concept of "tail." When we see a dog or think of one, this idea will therefore also bring the idea of a tail to mind. This is why when we are asked to name the features of a typical dog, we can easily and quickly bring to mind the idea that a typical dog has a tail.

Bower (1981, 1991), who was one of the leading researchers in the area of human associative memory, extended such models to emotion by suggesting that emotions are represented in the network as specific informational nodes (see also Ingram, 1984; Niedenthal, Setterlund, & Jones, 1994a; Teasdale, 1983, for related models). The number of emotions represented in the network differs according to different authors, but generally includes the following five emotions: anger, disgust, fear, happiness, and sadness. According to all such accounts, however, each emotion node is linked by associative pointers to the representation of emotionally related objects and events, as well as autobiographical memories. Figure 6.1 illustrates a schematic representation of the happiness node and its links.

Associative network models of emotion thus make the straightforward prediction that when an emotion unit, for example the unit that represents "happiness," is activated above some threshold, activation spreads throughout the network to associated information. These excitatory links are represented by the solid lines in Figure 6.1. Autonomic reactions, expressive behaviors, emotion-related events and personal memories are thereby excited and may enter the individual's consciousness. For instance, when one is feeling happiness, the material in memory related to happiness becomes activated. As a consequence, one may experience an increase in heart rate and in blood pressure, an activation of the *zygomaticus major* muscle, and a heightened accessibility to the words and memories associated with happiness. In some versions of this model, the nodes that represent "opposite" states, such as happiness and sadness are connected by inhibitory links such that the activation of one emotion node leads to the inhibition of the other one (Bower, 1981). These inhibitory links are

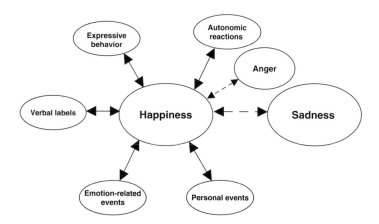

FIGURE 6.1. Spreading activation model. From Bower, G. H. (1981). Mood and memory. *American Psychologist, 36,* 129–148.

represented by dotted lines in Figure 6.1. For instance, activating happiness is expected to inhibit the activation of sadness.

The mood congruence prediction made by the associative network models has been tested with regard to many cognitive processes, including perception, memory, and judgments about events, other persons, and the self.

Visual Perception

When applied to perception, the mood congruence hypothesis states that objects and events that have the same emotion significance as the current affective state of the individual (i.e., are affect congruent) are perceived by that individual with greater efficiency than other stimuli, such as neutral or emotion-incongruent stimuli. By "efficiency," we mean that less perceptual information from the object is required before it is consciously perceived, because the representations that support its perception have already been *preactivated* by the affective state (Gerrig & Bower, 1982). Very often the perception of emotional words has been studied because it is easy for experimenters to match the meaning of a word, such as "gloomy" to an emotional state such as *sadness*. Initial tests of mood congruent perception hypothesis, which employed many different tasks for measuring perception, failed to find supportive evidence, however, casting doubt on Edith Piaf's notion of rose-colored glasses (e.g., Bower, 1987; Clark, Teasdale, Broadbent, & Martin, 1983; Gerrig & Bower, 1982; MacLeod, Tata, & Mathews, 1987). Other studies found mixed results. For instance, Challis and Krane (1988) found more efficient perceptual processing of

positive words by happy than sad and neutral participants, but they did not find any difference for negative words.

According to Niedenthal and colleagues (Niedenthal, Halberstadt, & Setterlund, 1997; Niedenthal & Setterlund, 1994), the initial failure to demonstrate mood congruence in perception was due to vagary in the understanding and experimental realization of the predictions of the associative network models. In most of the studies that failed to find facilitated perceptual processing of emotion congruent information, researchers compared participants' perception of words of the *same valence* as the affective state they were currently experiencing with their perception of words of the *opposite valence*. For example, participants in whom happiness and sadness had been induced performed tasks that involved the perception of words with positive and negative meanings. Such a design would make sense if a given state could activate above a certain threshold all words that shared the valence of that state. Almost all words have a valence, so this would require the activation of many words. Although in theory this may be the case, empirically it may be difficult to detect such an effect. According to a discrete emotions conception of emotion structure and the semantics of emotion (as discussed in Chapter 2), affect congruency in perception may only be observed when the perceived stimuli are associated with the same discrete affective state as the one experienced by the perceiver. For example, happiness should facilitate perceptual processing of happiness-related information, such as words, but not necessarily all positive information.

Niedenthal and colleagues reported findings consistent with this reasoning in a series of studies using a lexical decision task (Niedenthal & Setterlund, 1994) and also in studies using a word-naming task (Niedenthal et al., 1997; see Balota & Chumbley, 1985; Klinger, Burton, & Pitts, 2000, for a comparison of these tasks). For example, in one such study, participants who had been put into a sad, a neutral, or a happy affective state with the use of classical music completed a word-naming task (Niedenthal et al., 1997). To perform the task they had to pronounce words presented on a computer screen as quickly and accurately as possible. So, if they saw the word "smile," their task was to say "smile" out loud. The words that participants had to pronounce were related to sadness, anger, happiness, and love, and the remaining words had neutral meanings. The time from word presentation to pronounciation by the participant was the response of interest. An affect congruence effect is supported if individuals in happy states can name happy words faster than other words, and if sad individuals can name sad words faster than other words.

Facilitation scores were computed by taking the difference between latencies to pronouncing emotion words (for each of the four categories)

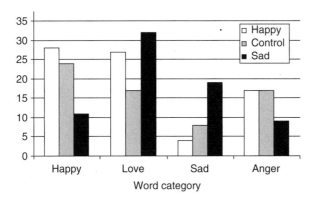

FIGURE 6.2. Facilitation (in milliseconds) in naming emotional words compared to neutral words by participants in happy, sad, and neutral states. From Niedenthal, P. M. et al. (1997). Being happy and seeing "happy": Emotional state mediates visual word recognition. *Cognition and Emotion, 11,* 403–432.

and to pronouncing neutral words. Results are presented in Figure 6.2. They reveal that indeed happiness facilitated the time to name happy compared to neutral words, whereas sadness facilitated the naming of sad compared to neutral words. However, compared with neutral and sadness conditions, happiness did not facilitate word naming for love words, neither did sadness facilitate responses to anger words compared with neutral and happy conditions. Thus, these results suggest that affective states facilitate the perceptual processing of words categorically associated with the induced affective state activated, not all the words of the same valence. Other studies have reported similar findings for the perceptual processing of facial expression of emotion (e.g., Niedenthal, Halberstadt, Margolin, & Innes-Ker, 2000).

Memory

Associative network models of emotion also predict two different biases in the retrieval of information from long-term memory, which have been called mood state-dependent and mood-congruent memory. *Mood state-dependent memory* is a phenomenon characterized by enhanced retrieval during a particular affective state of any information that was learned, or *encoded*, during that same affective state (i.e., compared to another state). The information can be neutral in meaning itself; the important factor is the match between the affective state at encoding and recall. *Mood-congruent memory* refers to enhanced retrieval of information whose affective meaning itself matches, compared to mismatches, an individual's current affective state.

Mood state-dependent memory

The reason that associative network models of emotion predict mood state-dependent memory is that, as we have seen, an affective state involves a complex set of psychological and physiological mental events, the representations of which are interconnected in memory. The entire set of representations that can potentially be active during a mental state, such as an affective state, is sometimes called the *mental context*. When an individual learns a new piece of information during an affective state, the representation of the new information is integrated into the currently activated mental context. Importantly, then, all the other representations in the context can serve as *cues* for later retrieval of the new information from long-term memory. Specifically, when the affective state is reactivated, activation will spread to the associated memories, such as the information that has been learned during that affective state. In this way, information that has been encoded in a specific affective state can be better recalled during the same than under another affective state.

In an early demonstration of mood state-dependent memory, participants first learned a list of words (list A) in either a happy or a sad affective state that was induced with hypnosis (Bower, Monteiro, & Gilligan, 1978). Then, they learned a second list (list B) either in the same or in the opposite affective state (e.g., sad for those who were happy first, and happy for those who were sad first). Finally, participants completed a free recall test of the words on list A while in either the same affective state as they were during the learning of list A, or the same affective state as they were in when they learned list B. This complex design, illustrated in Table 6.1, allowed the researchers to compare the recall performance of control participants who performed all three tasks in the same affective

---

TABLE 6.1
Design of a Mood-congruent Memory Study

List A	List B	Recall (List A)	
Happy	Happy	Happy	Control condition
Happy	Sad	Sad	High interference
Happy	Sad	Happy	Low interference
Sad	Sad	Sad	Control condition
Sad	Happy	Happy	High interference
Sad	Happy	Sad	Low interference

From Bower, G. H. et al. (1981). Selectivity of learning caused by affective states. *Journal of Experimental Psychology: General, 110,* 451–473.

state (e.g., sad–sad–sad) to participants who recalled list A in a different affective state than they were in during the learning of list A, but in the same affective state as they were in during the learning of list B (e.g. sad–happy–happy, a condition of high interference for the recall of list A). Control participants were also compared to participants who recalled list A in the same affective state that they were in during the learning of list A, but a different affective state than they were in during the learning of list B (e.g., sad–happy–sad, a condition of low interference for the recall of list A).

Results revealed that participants were best at recalling the words on list A when they had learned and recalled that list in the same affective state, and had learned list B in a different affective state. Apparently this condition provided the strongest mood context effect for recall of list A, and the lowest interference from words on list B. Similar results have been found for young children with affective states induced by asking participants to imagine a sad versus a happy event (Bartlett, Burleson, & Santrock, 1982) and by having participants watch happy versus sad videofilm sequences (Forgas, Burnham, & Trimboli, 1988).

Despite these initial suggestive demonstrations, the conditions of occurrence of mood state-dependent retrieval have appeared rather puzzling, and there have been numerous failures to replicate the effect (e.g., Bower & Mayer, 1985; Isen, Shalker, Clark, & Karp, 1978; Nasby & Yando, 1982; Wetzler, 1985). Recent reviews of the state of the literature on mood state-dependent memory have suggested that the effect is limited by at least two factors: the nature of the to-be-learned information, and the nature of the retrieval task.

Regarding the nature of the to-be-learned information, it is important to note that affective state is only one of numerous contextual cues that the to-be-remembered information is associated with during learning. Other cues such as the experimenter and the experimental room are also associated with the new information, and they may also be used as retrieval cues, thus minimizing the cues provided by the affective state (Mayer & Salovey, 1988). As a result, mood state-dependent recall should be more robust if the to-be-remembered information is *generated* by the participant rather than *furnished* by the experimenter, because in the latter case the information is more likely to be associated only with external cues (not with the current mental state).

Consistent with this idea, Eich and Metcalfe (1989) instructed participants in sad and happy induced affective states to read pairs of examples of categories ("precious metal: silver – *gold*"), or to generate the second example from its first letter ("precious metal: silver – *g*). Two days later, participants in either sad or happy induced affective states recalled the

Bower 1981
Sad happy Sad
Control, high, low

Eich + Metcalf 89
self generated words
retrieved better -
found effect on free call but not on recognition

words they had read or generated during learning. Results revealed better recall of information learned and recalled in the same affective state than information learned and recalled in mismatching states. Although this was true both for words that had been read and those that had been self-generated, the effect was more marked for generated words.

With regard to the *nature of retrieval*, mood state-dependent memory should be more likely in free recall tasks than in cued recall or recognition tasks (e.g., Eich, 1995; Eich & Metcalfe, 1989; see also Bower, 1981; Forgas et al., 1988). This is because, since the learned words are presented (for recognition) in the task itself, recognition tasks explicitly provide cues for the retrieval of the information. Consequently, again, participants use their internal state as retrieval cues to a lesser degree. In contrast, there are no cues provided in a free recall task, in which the participants are merely asked to recall previously learned items. In the absence of other cues, individuals therefore rely much more on cues from their internal state for recall. Indeed, Eich and Metcalfe (1989) found the mood state-dependence effect on a free recall task but not on a recognition task. In fact, this is why we most often talk of mood state-dependent recall rather than mood state-dependent memory.

Mood-congruent memory

Mood-congruent memory is straightforwardly predicted as the superior retrieval of memories or ideas associated with the current affective state in memory because such ideas receive activation from the representation of the affective state itself. As with our everyday beliefs about the relationship between emotion and perception, it seems almost axiomatic that when in different emotional states we tend to think thoughts and retrieve memories that have the same emotional tone.

Indeed, in a very oft cited early study, Snyder and White (1982) found that participants who had been put in induced happy or sad affective states recalled more happy or sad events of the previous week of their lives, respectively, than control participants. Since that demonstration, mood-congruent memory has been demonstrated with affective states induced by music (Eich, Macaulay, & Ryan, 1994), hypnosis (Bower et al., 1981), recall of personal events (Fiedler & Stroehm, 1986), odors (Ehrlichman & Halpern, 1988), and naturally occurring emotional states (e.g., Mayer et al., 1995). Such studies show either a greater number of mood-congruent memories recalled, or a decrease in latency for recalling these memories compared with incongruent memories (e.g., Teasdale & Fogarty, 1979; Teasdale et al., 1980).

Despite the initial enormous enthusiasm for the importance of this effect, however, plenty of inconsistent findings and null results pepper the empirical literature (e.g., see specific studies in Bower & Mayer, 1985; Bower et al., 1981; Clark & Teasdale, 1985; Nasby & Yando, 1982). The inconsistency in findings could be explained by the same factors that influence the observation of mood-state dependent recall. For instance, Fiedler and colleagues have proposed that the effects of affective state on memory are stronger for information that cannot be structured by means other than its affective meaning (Fiedler, Pampe, & Scherf, 1986; Fiedler & Stroehm, 1986). Structured material is material that can be encoded economically with the use of already oft used mental representations such as categories and scripts, which will mask or render less important its affective meaning. In a demonstration of this idea, Fiedler and Stroehm (1986) presented experimental participants with a set of positive and negative pictures that could be grouped into categories (structured information; e.g., "comedians," "beautiful landscapes," "accidents," or "environmental pollution") or had no particular relation or theme in common (unstructured information). Later, participants were exposed to a happy or sad mood induction procedure. And then they completed a free recall task. Happy participants recalled more positive than negative events and these effects did not occur for neutral participants. However, and consistent with their hypotheses, this pattern of data was found only when participants were provided with unstructured material, for which, presumably, the affective meaning became the single unifying theme. This type of finding is reminiscent of the reasoning for why free recall tasks reveal stronger mood state-dependent memory effects than do recognition tasks.

Judgment

Mood-congruent judgment is the most robust effect in the literature on affect and cognition, and early observations of this effect in part inspired the development of associative network models of emotion. Razran (1940), for instance, found that students and unemployed participants judged sociopolitical slogans more positively when they had just received a free lunch than when they had to evaluate the slogans in a room inundated by an unpleasant odor.

Mood-congruent judgment could be explained by the impact of mood on the way incoming information is encoded and interpreted. In this account, the judgment is mood congruent because the information on which the judgment is based is mood congruent. Support for this interpretation was found in a study by Halberstadt, Niedenthal, and Kushner (1995). The researchers exposed participants, in whom different affective states had been induced, to *homophones* (words that sound alike, but that have different meanings) that were pronounced out loud. The participants were instructed to write down the words as they heard them. The critical homophones had one emotional and one neutral meaning. Results showed that individuals tended to access the emotion-congruent meaning of the homophones. Thus, for instance, sad participants tended to write down the sad meaning of a word that sounded like "morning" (i.e., *mourning*) while those in other states accessed the neutral meaning (i.e., *morning*). This suggests that emotion-congruent information is preferentially learned (Bower, 1981). Later judgments based on this information would then also be mood congruent.

It is also possible that information is not encoded in an entirely biased way, but that mood-congruent judgments are due to selective retrieval of mood-congruent information, which we illustrated in the previous section. Naturally, both processes probably occur to some degree. Most research in this area, which examines likelihood estimation, judgments of objects and persons, and judgments about the self, does not tease apart these two mechanistic accounts.

Likelihood estimations

In the illustration of your being angry at the beginning of this chapter, you estimated that most people engage in the same disruptive behavior (parking on the sidewalk) as you. This tendency to judge probabilities differently in different emotional states has also been shown empirically. Johnson and Tversky (1983) put experimental participants in a negative affective state by having them read a short, rather depressing text. Compared to control participants, these individuals later estimated that diseases (e.g., leukemia, lung cancer), hazards (e.g., fire, electrocution), and violence (e.g., homicide, war) were more likely to occur in general than participants in a neutral affective state. In contrast, participants in a positive affective state were more optimistic in their risk estimates than neutral participants. This tendency was observed whether the text used to induce affective state was related to the risk estimates or not. For example, even if the depressing text specifically concerned incidences of cancer, it affected all other health estimates.

Several authors recently extended these findings by showing that mood-congruence effects on likelihood estimations are a function of discrete emotions and not just valence (e.g., DeSteno, Petty, Wegener, & Rucker, 2000; Lerner & Keltner, 2001). For instance, DeSteno and colleagues (2000) predicted and found that individuals gave greater estimates for events congruent with their current affective state than for other events of the same valence but eliciting another emotion. More precisely, they found that sadness increases estimates of sad events (e.g., "Of the 60,000 orphans in Romania, how many are malnourished due to food short-ages?") more than estimates of angry events (e.g., "Of the 2,000,000 people in the U.S. who will buy a used car this year, how many will intentionally be sold a 'lemon' by a dishonest car dealer?") whereas the reverse was true for anger.

Lerner and Keltner further refined this idea by applying appraisal theory (described in Chapter 1) in accounting for the effects of specific emotions on judgments of likelihood. They reasoned that activation from the appraisals associated with different discrete emotions leads to predictable effects on likelihood estimates. For instance, anger (and happiness) are associated with the appraisal of future events as predictable and under individual control whereas fear is associated with the appraisal of future events as unpredictable and under situational control. As a result, angry individuals should estimate risks as less likely whereas fear should lead to more pessimistic judgments. Lerner and Keltner (2001) found results consistent with this hypothesis with dispositionally angry, happy and fearful participants as well as with anger and fear being induced in the laboratory. As Figure 6.3 illustrates, Lerner and Keltner found that people made angry, compared with fearful, estimated the situation as more controllable, and more predictable. Consequently, they made more optimistic risk evaluations.

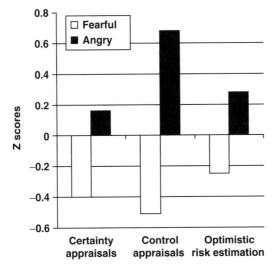

FIGURE 6.3. Findings showing that fear and anger can have opposite effects on cognitive appraisals and on optimistic risk estimates. From Lerner, J. S., & Keltner, D. (2001). Fear, anger, and risk. *Journal of Personality and Social Psychology, 81,* 146–159.

Judgments of objects and persons

The effect of mood on judgments of objects and persons has received enormous empirical attention, and mood congruence is precisely the effect that has been most often observed (e.g., Abele & Petzold, 1994; Esses & Zanna, 1995; Forgas, 1992a, 1993, 1995b; Forgas & Bower, 1987; Forgas, Bower, & Krantz, 1984; Gouaux, 1971; Gouaux & Summers, 1973; Griffitt, 1970; Stapel & Koomen, 2000). In a classic demonstration of the effect, Gouaux (1971) had female participants watch either an elating or a depressing film. Then, participants received a 20-item survey questionnaire ostensibly filled out by another person. They were asked to read the questionnaire and then to evaluate the person who had completed it on a number of personality trait scales. Participants who had watched the elating film felt better and evaluated the target person more positively than participants who had watched the depressing film.

Innes-Ker and Niedenthal (2002) put individuals into a happy, sad, or neutral emotional state with the use of a combined music and film procedure (described in Chapter 1), and then asked them to read a hypothetical story about a woman, called M, who engaged in a number of activities, the emotional impact of which was somewhat open to interpretation. Afterwards, all participants rated M's feelings and the emotional nature of a number of the events in the story. Results showed that people in happy moods evaluated M's feelings and experiences as happier than did the participants in the other experimental groups. Meanwhile, sad individuals tended to read M as being sadder and as having experienced more sadness.

Mood-congruent social judgments have also been observed in the field. For instance, Forgas and Moylan (1987) approached 980 people, selected at random, as they left a movie theater after having seen a happy, an aggressive, or a sad movie. Individuals were asked to answer questions about their satisfaction with political issues, about the likelihood of several events, about the severity of punishment required for several offences (e.g., drunken driving, heroin trafficking), and about their satisfaction with their own lives. Individuals having watched a happy movie made more positive judgments for all four types of item than both participants who had seen an aggressive or a sad movie (these two groups did not differ from each other).

Furthermore, research on *affective priming* has demonstrated that individuals do not have to be aware of the affective stimuli to be influenced by them in their judgments. Several studies have found that the suboptimal presentation of emotional stimuli produces congruent judgments. Participants exposed without awareness to human faces expressing disgust just before the presentation of a cartoon character make more negative judgment about the cartoon than participants primed without awareness with happy faces (Niedenthal, 1990). Similarly, Murphy and Zajonc (1993; Murphy, Monahan & Zajonc, 1995; see also Stapel, Koomen, & Ruys, 2002; Winkielman, Zajonc, & Schwarz, 1997) found that participants exposed for a very brief period of time to smiling faces just before Chinese ideograms (or other stimuli), judged these ideograms more positively than when primed with frowning faces. These results suggest that the affective dimension of the stimuli has probably a special status, which is extracted very early in the processing of incoming information, and is not assimilated to the other semantic features of the stimuli.

Judgments about the self

If one's affective state can influence the perception and judgment of others, it is likely that affective states can influence judgments about the self, too. Consistent with this hypothesis, it has been repeatedly found that individuals in happy states rate themselves as having high levels of self-esteem, at least at the moment (see also Wright & Mischel, 1982).

Sedikides (1995) also found that affective states cause mood-congruent self-descriptions. Participants in that study who had been induced to feel happiness nominated more positive (less negative) behaviors and traits as descriptive of themselves than participants who had been induced to feel sadness. However, these effects were restricted to peripheral aspects of the self and not to the central ones (i.e., information about the self that is high in both personal descriptiveness and importance). Furthermore, Forgas et al. (1984) found that mood-congruence effects on evaluation of one's own behaviors were even greater than on evaluation of the behavior of others.

Mood Regulation Influences on Congruence Effects

So far things might sound relatively clear to the average reader: people have ideas stored in memory that are related because they are all related to a specific emotional state. When that state reoccurs, activation in the associative network makes such "mood-congruent" ideas and memories more likely to come to consciousness and be used in thought and reasoning. But things are not as straightforward as they may seem. A number of findings are also inconsistent with such a neat conclusion.

First of all, some studies on the impact of affective states on memory have found mood-congruent information processing in happy but not in sad states, or else stronger influences of mood in happy than sad states. Other findings suggest that happiness increases the recall of happy events and inhibits the recall of negative events, while sadness inhibits the recall of positive events but does not increase the recall of sad events (Eich et al.,

1994; Isen et al., 1978; Mayer, Gayle, Meehan, & Haarman, 1990; Nasby & Yando, 1982; Natale & Hantas, 1982; see Blaney, 1986, for a review).

Some of these inconsistencies in the mood-congruence effect have been explained by the operation of *mood regulation processes* aimed at putting the sad individual in a happier state, and keeping the already happy individual in a happy state too (Blaney, 1986). Mood regulation may indeed account for a number of studies in which mood-incongruent judgment was observed. In a study by Parrott and Sabini (1990), for example, participants in sad moods recalled autobiographical events that were more positive than those recalled by happy individuals when mood was induced in real life by participants' midterm grades, or by the weather. In order to avoid any misinterpretation of this finding due to confounds inherent to field studies, Parrott and Sabini also replicated their findings in more controlled experimental studies, in which affective state was induced with the use of music. Taken together, these findings suggest that when in sad states people try to improve their mood by retrieving pleasant thoughts and memories (see also, e.g., Erber & Erber, 1994; Josephson, Singer, & Salovey, 1996; Rusting & DeHart, 2000).

The importance of mood regulation processes in mood-incongruent recall has also been illustrated in studies exploring stable personality factors related to mood regulation. For instance, Smith and Petty (1995) investigated the way in which people's general ability and motivation to regulate their affective state was related to mood-congruent recall. Specifically, they compared individuals who were identified as low versus high in *negative mood regulation* (NMR, i.e., individuals who believe that they successfully regulate negative moods; Catanzaro & Mearns, 1990). Findings showed that participants low in NMR recalled more negative autobiographical memories when in a sad mood than when in a neutral mood. These participants thus exhibited mood-congruent recall. In contrast, participants high in NMR recalled more positive memories when in a sad mood than in a neutral mood, suggesting that they were engaging in mood regulation (see Rusting and DeHart, 2000, for related results).

In another study of individual differences, Boden and Baumeister (1997) found that *repressors*, defined as individuals who show a strong tendency to try to prevent thoughts of threatening experiences or information from reaching consciousness (Weinberger, Schwartz, & Davidson, 1979), were faster at recalling happy memories after experiencing an unpleasant event than after experiencing a neutral event, suggesting that mood-incongruent recall is a mood regulation strategy used by repressors to cope with negative events. In contrast, nonrepressors were faster to recall happy memories after a neutral event than after an unpleasant one.

It thus appears that mood-incongruent recall often occurs in the service of mood regulation. In particular, individuals in negative affective states may try to improve their feelings through mood-incongruent recall. However, mood-incongruent processing may sometimes reflect an attempt to neutralize one's affective state. Indeed, in many social situations, such as before an interaction with a stranger (Erber et al., 1996), it would be maladaptive to be in an intense affective state. Therefore, one may try to recall events that would neutralize one's affective state. Such processes could explain why mood-incongruent recall has also been found among participants in a positive affective state (e.g., Erber & Erber, 1994; Erber et al., 1996; Forgas & Ciarrochi, 2002; Parrott & Sabini, 1990).

In an illustration of this, Erber and Erber (1994) induced sad or happy affective states in individuals by the means of the retrieval of an autobiographical event. The individuals were then asked to recall another event of their choice. The experiment took place either at the beginning of a class, when participants might perceive their affective state as possibly interfering with coursework, or at the end of the class, when participants would not perceive their affective state as an interference with coursework. Consistent with predictions, Erber and Erber found evidence for mood-congruent recall when the experiment took place at the end of the class and for a mood-incongruent recall when the experiment took place at the beginning of the class. In a similar vein, Erber et al. (1996) demonstrated that individuals tend to retrieve mood-incongruent material when they anticipate an interaction with another person. Moreover, they found that sad participants did not try to neutralize their affective state (did not engage in mood-incongruent activity) when they anticipated interacting with a sad person but they did when they anticipated interacting with an individual in a neutral mood. These results suggest that mood regulation processes, that are often expected to underlie mood-incongruent recall, may operate in the service of facilitating a social interaction.

It is worth noting that mood regulation accounts of mood-incongruent recall are not inherently incompatible with the phenomenon of mood-congruent recall as predicted by associative network models of emotion (e.g., Isen et al., 1978; Parrott & Sabini, 1990). It may well be that mood-congruent memory is a robust phenomenon, but can be altered by experimental situations that specifically promote mood regulation processes. Therefore, what these studies suggest is that the associative network model proposed by Bower must be combined with accounts of subsequent processes that are guided by motivational states, allowing one to predict the conditions in which participants attempt to activate a given part of the associative network.

The Affect-as-Information Model

One of the earliest accounts of the relationship between affective states and judgment was stated in terms of conditioned responses (Staats & Staats, 1958; see, for a more recent formulation, Krosnick, Betz, Jussim, & Lynn, 1992). Specifically, the idea was that when an object is frequently associated with an affectively charged stimulus, the object itself acquires the same affective meaning. For instance, Staats and Staats (1958) found that individuals evaluated names of nationalities (e.g., German, Italian, Swedish) that had been previously presented paired with positive words more positively than names of nationalities that had been previously presented paired with negative words. Based on this general account of the learning of affective meaning through conditioning, it could also be hypothesized that one's affective state (i.e., the unconditioned response) in reaction to some affective stimulus (i.e., the unconditioned stimulus; e.g., the weather) becomes associated with a specific object frequently encountered in the situation (i.e., the conditioned stimuli). As a result, objects that are frequently associated with one's positive affective state would be judged more positively than the objects frequently associated with negative affective states.

The affect-as-information model can be considered as a refinement of this hypothesis and an alternative account of mood-congruence effects in memory and judgment (Clore, Wyer, Dienes, Gasper, Gohm, & Isbell, 2001). Proposed by Schwarz and Clore (e.g., 1983, 1988; Clore et al., 2001; Schwarz, 1990) on the basis of an idea initially articulated by Wyer and Carlston (1979), the model holds that individuals use their affective states as relevant information to use when making evaluative judgments. For example, if someone asks you whether you like your psychology professor, you may rely on your feelings about or affective reaction to her to make the judgment. Sometimes feelings are at the heart of the judgment; feeling good about someone and liking them are likely related. However, we may also use our feelings as *heuristics*, or simple "tricks" for making an efficient judgment, even if our feelings are not the best or only information we have for making the judgment. For instance, if the evaluation task is complex because there is a lot of information about the target, or if one does not want to invest in the judgment task, one may ask oneself "How-do-I-feel-about-it (or 'her' in the present example)?" If the answer is that one feels good, the judgment will be positive, whereas it will be negative in case of a negative affective state. For example, if the judgment concerns whether one should take a course at the university offered by a particular professor, and we have a wealth of information to use to make this decision, a positive feeling may indeed lead us to take the course if we want to simplify the decision-making process.

Importantly, the use of affect as information is held to be minimized when individuals realize that their affective reactions have nothing whatsoever to do with the object of judgment at hand. According to the affect-as-information account, if the affective state is consciously perceived as having been induced by some external incidental event (e.g., the weather), the affective state should no longer be taken into account and thus should no longer influence judgment. This is an important limitation to the effect, and provides a way to account for null results and even mood incongruence in studies of memory and judgment, as discussed below. Furthermore, the limitation is not clearly predicted by associative network models of emotion, and is thus a test that distinguishes between the models.

A study that specifically tested the tenets of the affect as information model was conducted by Schwarz and Clore (1983). Under the guise of a telephone survey on life satisfaction, these researchers called participants on either rainy or sunny days. On the basis of past findings of the impact of weather on mood, they expected that participants would be in a more negative mood on rainy than on sunny days. Participants answered a series of questions concerning their level of life satisfaction, and findings strongly suggested that participants used their feelings (due, in fact, to the weather) to make these evaluations. Thus, participants who were called on sunny days reported being more satisfied with their life than participants who answered on rainy days.

In two other conditions of the study, however, Schwarz and Clore focused the attention of the participants on the likely source of their affective state (i.e., the weather). They did so by either asking explicitly about current weather in the city of the participant, or by telling them that the study was about the effects of the weather on mood. Consistent with the model, Schwarz and Clore (1983) found that when participants explicitly attributed their affective state to something other than their life, in this case the weather, the effects of mood on life satisfaction judgments disappeared (see, for similar findings, Hirt, Levine, McDonald, Melton, & Martin, 1997; Lantermann & Otto, 1996).

Further refinements of the affect-as-information model have defined boundary conditions for the occurrence of mood-congruence effects. They have also proposed other processes underlying the disappearance of these effects when individuals are made aware of the irrelevance of their affective state for the judgment at hand.

First, because the "How-do-I-feel-about-it?" heuristic is likely to be used when individuals try to simplify the judgment task, when the judgment domain is very specific, when criteria for evaluation are well defined, or when comparative information is easily available (e.g., satisfaction with one's present income or with one's housing; Schwarz, Strack, Kommer, & Wagner, 1987), this heuristic will be of no use. Therefore, mood congruence should not appear in such situations.

With regard to the correction processes, Schwarz and Clore proposed that individuals are able to disregard the irrelevant sources of their affective reactions when elaborating their judgment. This "discounting process" requires identification of the source of the affect before information integration and also that affective reactions triggered by these irrelevant sources can be clearly distinguished from affective reactions triggered by the target itself. However, it is often difficult to make such a distinction. Therefore, in these conditions, individuals' attempts to block out the unwanted influence may result in attenuation (i.e., in case of partial correction), contrast (i.e., in case of over-correction), or in the disappearance of the effect of affective states depending on whether the irrelevant influence is under-, or overestimated, or estimated with accuracy, respectively (Ottati & Isbell, 1996; Wyer, Clore, & Isbell, 1999).

Moreover, correction processes imply controlled, resource-demanding mental processes (e.g., Gilbert, 1989; Wegener & Petty, 1995). As a result, individuals need both motivation and cognitive resources in order to overcome the influence of their affective state. Consistent with this view, Ottati and Isbell (1996; see Isbell & Wyer, 1999, for related results) found that participants' affective state influenced judgments of a political candidate in a congruent way among those who invested limited cognitive resources in judgment tasks (i.e., participants whose recall performance of information about the target fell in the lower quartile). However, a contrast effect was found among the participants who invested resources (i.e., participants whose recall performance was in the upper quartile). Albarracín and Kumkale (2003) extended these demonstrations to the processing of a persuasive message.

It is worth repeating that such effects are difficult to explain with an associative network model (Bower, 1981). Associative network models do not make predictions concerning the manipulation of the relevance of affective information, and they do not predict that the effects of mood on the judgmental domain depends on the specificity of the judgment. These models predict that the effects of affective state on judgment should be the same whether the affective state is or is not perceived as informative for the judgment at hand and as long as the judgmental domain involves information linked to the relevant emotion node.

Affect Infusion Model

In the wake of a relatively complex literature on the relationship between affect and cognition, Forgas (1992b, 1995a) proposed a multiprocess model of the impact of affective states on judgment, called the affect infusion model (AIM). The model attempts to reconcile the two major aforementioned models, that is affect priming and affect-as-information models, and to go beyond the predictions of each.

The AIM is based on two major assumptions concerning social judgment. The assumption of *effort minimization* posits that individuals attempt to preserve their cognitive resources and that they prefer to use the simplest and least effortful processing strategy as long as it satisfies the minimal processing requirements demanded by the situation (Forgas, 1995a). The *process mediation* assumption posits that the effects of one's affective state are moderated by the kind of processing strategy individuals are engaged in.

The AIM distinguishes four processing strategies, as summarized in Figure 6.4. The *direct access* strategy, the simplest strategy, refers to the straightforward retrieval of a prestored evaluation or judgment. The *motivated* strategy operates in the service of a directional goal (for instance, maintaining one's own positive affective state). When using such a strategy, individuals engage in highly specific and targeted information search and information use strategies designed to support a specific goal. These two first processing strategies are considered as "low infusion" strategies, in which affect should have relatively low impact.

In contrast, the two remaining strategies, *heuristic* and *substantive processing*, are considered "high affect infusion" strategies, meaning that they are vulnerable to influence by affective state. Heuristic processing refers to the use of a small subset of the available information that allows for the use of simple rules aimed at formulating a judgment without careful examination of the available information. Numerous rules of that kind have been identified in the literature on persuasion (Chaiken, Liberman, & Eagly, 1989). For instance, knowing that 80% of the consumers are satisfied with a product will lead to a more favorable evaluation of the product than knowing that only 20% are satisfied. In such a condition, participants can formulate a judgment without examining all the features of the product or comparing them with those of other concurrent products. They rely on a heuristic rule of the kind "the number makes the truth," which implies that if 80% of the owners are satisfied, the product should be good. In the present case, one of the heuristics people could rely on would be the "How-do-I-feel-about-it?" rule. If they feel good, individuals will make more positive judgments than if they feel bad. Therefore, when participants engage in the heuristic strategy, the processes at stake could be similar to those

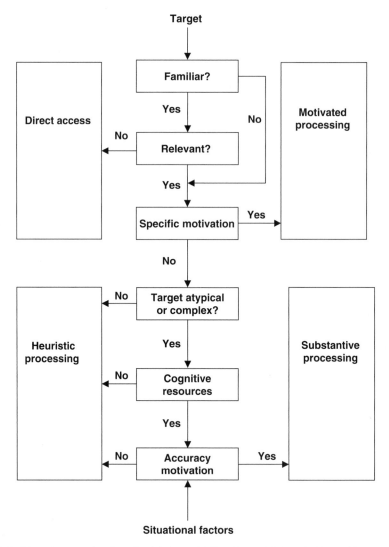

FIGURE 6.4. Schematic presentation of the affect infusion model. From Forgas, J. P. (1995a). Mood and judgment: The affect infusion model (AIM). *Psychological Review, 117,* 39–66.

proposed by the affect-as-information model (Schwarz & Clore, 1983, 1988).

The last and most demanding processing strategy is *substantive processing*. This strategy consists in a careful search, selection, and interpretation of incoming information. According to the AIM, affect can have a great influence under substantive processing through its impact on the information selected to be integrated in the judgment – that is, through mood-priming processes (Bower, 1981).

Therefore, the AIM holds that one's affective state affects judgment as long as the strategy in which one is engaged is constructive (that is either heuristic or substantive processing). Otherwise, one's affective state should not affect judgment in a mood-congruent manner. Thus, in this account, affect priming and affect-as-information processes are not incompatible with each other; they both could operate depending of the processing strategy people engage in.

In the AIM, the use of a particular strategy is a function of three factors: the target of judgment, the individual, and the situation. Some factors decrease the extent to which one must rely on incoming information to make a judgment. For instance, if the target of the judgment is highly familiar, highly typical, or very simple, the judgment requires less processing effort than if the target is unfamiliar, atypical, or complex. Concerning the individual him or herself, investment in information processing will be a function of personal relevance of the judgment, of motivational goals, and of cognitive capacity. Moreover, according to this account, the affective state of the judge could also increase (if negative) or decrease (if positive) the processing of incoming information (e.g., Schwarz, 1990; see "Influences on the structure of cognitive processing" in this chapter). Finally, situational constraints also have an impact on the strategy that individuals use. For instance, depending on the situation, individuals may try to be more accurate, thus more careful in information processing.

Forgas (1992a) put participants in a positive or a negative affective state. Then, participants received categorical information about a person (e.g., David is a surfer). In the typical condition, all the remaining information was consistent with the category (e.g., "he has bleached blond hair") whereas half was inconsistent with the category in the atypical target condition (e.g., "David is not very fit"). Consistent with his model, Forgas found that mood-congruency effects in impression of person were more marked for atypical than for typical target. Similar results were found on judgment of atypical (i.e., nonmatched in attractiveness) against typical (i.e., matched in attractiveness) couples (Forgas, 1993, 1995b). Happy participants estimated that the couples had better relationships, and judged the individuals as more likeable, than sad participants. And these effects were stronger for atypical couples than for typical couples.

Other studies revealed findings consistent with those mentioned above. Petty, Schumann, Richman, and Strathman (1993) showed that participants low in need for cognition (i.e., who are reluctant to invest in information processing) were directly influenced by their affective state when being exposed to a persuasive message whereas the same effect on attitudes of participants high in need for cognition were mediated by the content of their thoughts.

Sedikides (1995) found comparable results on judgments about the self. As mentioned earlier in the chapter, central self-conceptions are accessed frequently, are highly structured, and are of high importance for oneself. Therefore, they are more likely processed by either direct access or by motivated processing. In the study, central self-conceptions were unaffected by individuals' affective state whereas less central, or peripheral self-conceptions were affected in a mood-congruent manner. Moreover, latencies to express a judgment (an indicator of investment in processing) mediate these effects: the longer the time the stronger the effects of affective state, suggesting that the impact of mood is greater when processing is careful. A follow-up study furthermore suggested that these effects are more probably due to substantive than to heuristic processing because mood-congruency effects were greater under instruction leading to high elaboration than under conditions leading to low elaboration.

This integrative model has generated much research activity, and provides a good description of the conditions of occurrence of the effects of affective states on social judgment. One of the major problems with the model is related to the hypothesized moderation of the effects of affective states by processing strategy. It is difficult on a priori ground to evaluate whether an individual engages in either heuristic or substantial processing (see, e.g., Chaiken et al., 1989). Therefore, in the absence of a clear a priori characterization of the processing strategy people engage in, all the results can be expected, and could thus be interpreted as consistent with the model.

Influences on the Structure of Cognitive Processing

In addition to demonstrations that affective state influences what people think about, research has repeatedly documented another way that affect influences cognition. Specifically, affective states seem to affect how people think about things; how they organize and use information, not only what information they pay attention to, store, and retrieve from memory.

The idea that affective state may be related to the structure of thought was initially suggested by research showing that happy individuals are often more efficient in performing tasks that require the use of broad categories and elimination of superfluous detail (Isen & Means, 1983). Based in part on this observation, Isen and Daubman (1984) proposed that positive affect increases reliance on broader categories, categories that include more members, because there is more positive information in memory per se, and accessing it (as during a positive state) requires chunking the extensive information into larger, more inclusive categories in order to manage the wealth of available information.

In a direct test of the hypothesis that individuals use more inclusive categories during happy states, Isen and Daubman had participants who had been put in happy, neutral, and sad affective states complete a categorization task. In the task they received four category labels (i.e., "tool," "clothing," "vehicle," and "weapon") and nine category members of each of the four categories. Of the nine members, three had been previously rated as excellent examples of the category, three were moderately good, and three were poor examples of the category according to Rosch's (1975) norms (e.g., "crane," "scissors," and "rags," were poor examples of the category "tool"; "purse," "elevator," and "feet" were poor examples of the category "vehicle"). Participants' task was to rate the extent to which each member was a "good" example of the category. All participants, regardless of mood, rated excellent exemplars as good examples of category members. However, consistent with their hypothesis, Isen and Daubman found that happy individuals rated the poor exemplars as significantly better exemplars of the category than did those in a neutral mood. That is, the individuals in a happy mood seemed to extend the category boundaries, allowing borderline cases to have clear category status. Isen et al. (1992) extended this finding to the study of social categories. Furthermore, perhaps as a consequence of the expansion of category boundaries during happy states, in many cases happiness also leads individuals to perceive social groups as more homogeneous (Dovidio, Gaertner, Isen, & Lowrance, 1995; Stroessner & Mackie, 1992; see also Park & Banaji, 2000).

The notion that happy affective states are associated with a tendency to use larger cognitive units of information, broader categories, and sometimes, by consequence, the tendency to ignore differences or details, generated an enormous amount of research devoted to the exploration of differences in the structure of cognitive processes during different affective states. Moreover, the basic ideas have been used to further understand two complex social cognitive processes, namely, persuasion and stereotyping. We focus the remainder of this chapter on these two processes, the role of affect state in them, and various theoretical accounts of the extant findings.

Examples: Persuasion and Stereotyping

Persuasion

Early studies of the impact of individuals' affective state on their reactions to persuasive messages demonstrated a simple, and perhaps intuitively plausible effect: individuals in positive affective states were more influenced by a persuasive message than individuals in a neutral or negative affective state (e.g., Dabbs & Janis, 1965). This finding can be and has been interpreted as a demonstration of mood congruence; that is, perhaps individuals in a happy state see the positive features of presented arguments and therefore are more receptive to them (e.g., Petty et al., 1993). However, the reality is not so simple. Subsequent research showed that individuals in a happy state are less influenced by the strength of persuasive messages, and more influenced by cues allowing them to use *heuristics*, or simple *rules of thumb*, than participants in sad states (e.g., Bless, Bohner, Schwarz, & Strack, 1990; Bless, Mackie & Schwarz, 1992; Bohner, Crow, Erb, & Schwarz, 1992; Mackie & Worth, 1989; Schwarz, Bless, & Bohner, 1991; Worth & Mackie, 1987). Therefore, on some occasions, such as when a heuristic cue indicates that the arguments are bad, individuals in a happy state are less persuaded than those in a sad state.

In one of the first studies demonstrating this phenomenon, Mackie and Worth (1989) induced happy and neutral moods in their participants by the use of films. The participants then read a text about handgun control. Participants' attitude toward this issue had actually been measured in the first part of the experiment (1 = strong disagreement; 9 = strong agreement), and thus the experimenters were able to present them with counterattitudinal message: pro handgun control for those who were anti and anti handgun control for those who were pro. The experimenters also manipulated the strength (or quality) of the arguments, such that they were strong or weak, and also manipulated the source to which the arguments were attributed. The source was either said to be an expert on gun control (i.e., an eminent legal scholar at an American university) or a non-expert (i.e., a freshman at the same university). Using a heuristic – or rule of thumb – would dictate that the expert was right and the non-expert was wrong. After they had read the text, participants again reported their attitude toward handgun control. As Figure 6.5 illustrates, the findings indicate that happy participants were less affected by the strength of the argumentation (top panel) and more affected by the source's degree of expertise (bottom panel) than were neutral participants. This means that they were more likely to use a heuristic if one were available.

In another series of studies, Bless et al. (1990) showed that these effects were due specifically to happiness. They found that sad participants were more influenced by the argumentation than were happy participants. Moreover, Bless and colleagues (1992) demonstrated that the tendency for individuals in happy moods to be impervious to argument quality was due to the presence of affective state at encoding (i.e., before they read the text) and not at time of judgment. When participants were not put in a

a Attitude change as a function of mood and argument quality

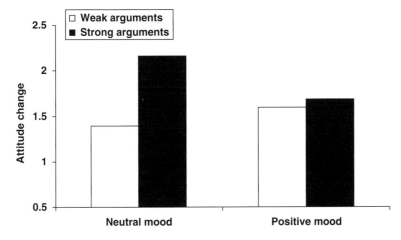

b Attitude change as a function of mood and source expertise

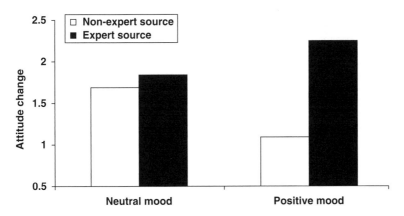

FIGURE 6.5. Findings showing that individuals in a happy mood are less sensitive to argument quality and more persuaded by experts than individuals in a neutral mood. From Mackie, D. M., & Worth L. T. (1989). Processing deficit and the mediation of positive affect in persuasion. *Journal of Personality and Social Psychology, 57,* 27–40.

specific affective state at encoding but at judgment, the effects were reversed. The attitude of happy individuals reflects more the strength of the arguments than the attitude of other individuals. According to Bless et al., in such cases individuals happy at time of judgment rely heuristically on their global attitudes elaborated in a systematic way (at encoding) when they were in a neutral affective state.

Research on persuasion has mainly studied the effects of happiness and sadness as prototypical positive and negative affective states, respectively. However, it is interesting to note that studies that have manipulated other discrete emotions have found results indicating that theoretical explanations based on the valence of affective state are too general. For instance, in contrast with sadness which is typically associated with careful processing, fear has been found to lead to superficial processing of social information (Baron, Inman, Kao & Logan, 1992; but see Baron, Logan, Lilly, Inman, & Brennan, 1994).

Stereotyping

Similar findings have been observed in research on the impact of affective states on reliance on stereotypes in social judgment. Although it may seem counterintuitive, or inconsistent with the mood-congruence effect, Bodenhausen et al. (1994a) found that happy individuals rely more on stereotypes in a guilt judgment task than participants in a neutral affective state (see also Stroessner & Mackie, 1992; see Abele, Gendolla, & Petzold, 1998, for observations of increased ingroup/outgroup differentiation). Bodenhausen and colleagues also demonstrated that these effects were not attributable to distraction associated with happy state as the same results were found when happiness was induced with the use of facial contractions (see Adelmann & Zajonc, 1989; Strack et al., 1988) that minimize the activation of distracting thoughts. And they also showed that these findings could not be attributable to an increase in arousal associated with happiness as they found the same results whether music used to induce happiness was energetic or calm. Krauth-Gruber and Ric (2000) replicated the basic effect and also found that sadness decreases the individual's reliance on stereotypes (see also Bless, Schwarz, & Wieland, 1996a; Lambert, Khan, Lickel, & Fricke, 1997).

In related research, Park and Banaji (2000) found that happy individuals were more likely to attribute a stereotypical trait to members of the group. For instance, happy individuals compared with neutral participants were more likely to categorize individuals with an African American name as criminals, and individuals with a European American name as politicians. Moreover, in additional work they demonstrated that these effects were attributable to a reduced sensitivity of happy individuals to differences between members of a stereotyped group (see also Stroessner & Mackie, 1992). In contrast, sad participants adopted a more stringent criterion to apply the categorical knowledge (stereotype) to a specific individual.

Again in contrast with a general valence conception of affective state, Bodenhausen et al. (1994b) found that anger increases reliance on stereotypes (see DeSteno, Dasgupta, Bartlett, & Cajdric, 2004) and promotes heuristic thinking (Lerner, Goldberg, & Tetlock, 1998).

Theoretical Accounts

Here we describe several theoretical accounts of the influences of positive and negative affective state on the structure of information processing just reviewed. Before doing so, it must be acknowledged that we restrict our presentation to the most frequently evoked and/or tested theoretical explanations. Moreover, the theoretical accounts presented in this part must not be considered as mutually exclusive. Some of the accounts are compatible, but more likely applicable in some specific situations. In addition, none of these theoretical propositions explains the full range of effects described in the literature. It will be the aim of future research to specify the boundary conditions of the theoretical explanations available.

Cognitive Decrement Hypothesis

In order to account for the differences in processing strategy used by individuals in positive and negative moods, Mackie and Worth (1989) proposed that positive affective states activate related material in memory (e.g., Bower, 1981). Considering that memory contains much more positive than negative material, Mackie and Worth proposed that happiness makes accessible so many ideas that working memory is overloaded, resulting in a decrease in processing capacity (Isen, 1987). According to these authors, happy individuals are not less motivated to process incoming information in a careful manner than others, they just lack the capacity to do so.

Consistent with this hypothesis, research by these authors found that happy participants were less influenced by the strength of the argumentation of a persuasive message and more influenced by heuristic cues than participants in a nonmanipulated affective state, but only when time of exposure to the persuasive message was limited. When the participants were given as much time as they wanted to read the persuasive message, and could thus spend more time in reading the text to compensate for their reduced cognitive capacity, they did not differ from the neutral ones (Mackie & Worth, 1989).

Although the findings of Mackie and Worth appear convincing, several other studies have reported findings inconsistent with such an account. For example, it has been found that providing happy participants with a motivational impetus makes them process the incoming information as carefully as others (e.g., Bless et al., 1990; Bodenhausen et al., 1994a; Wegener et al., 1995) and sometimes outperform other participants on tasks requiring attentional resources (e.g., Bless et al., 1996b; Isen et al., 1987; Murray, Sujan, Hirt, & Sujan, 1990). For instance, Bless et al. (1990) demonstrated that even though happy participants were less influenced by the strength of the arguments in a persuasive message than sad individuals, this difference disappeared when they were explicitly asked to concentrate on the message.

Hedonic View

The hedonic view encompasses two main theoretical positions that both suggest that the processing strategy used by individuals is a direct effect of mood regulation strategies or processes.

Mood repair hypothesis

According to the mood maintenance/repair hypothesis (Isen, 1984, 1987; Isen et al., 1978), a positive affective state is a pleasant state that individuals want to experience or to maintain. When individuals are already in a positive affective state, they will avoid engaging in any task that could alter their current affective state, especially if this task could have potential detrimental consequences on their affective state (Carlson, Charlin, & Miller, 1988). As a result, happy individuals do not engage in careful information processing and rely on heuristics that allow them to preserve their current affective state.

In contrast, individuals in a negative affective state experience an unpleasant state. Thus, they are likely to engage in the task proposed in order to find a way to change their current affective state. As a result, they process the incoming information in careful manner.

Hedonic contingency hypothesis

The hedonic contingency hypothesis (Wegener & Petty, 1994; Wegener, Petty, & Smith, 1995) is based on the same premise as the mood repair hypothesis, that individuals attempt to manage their affective state. However, this model specifically proposes that one's current affective state influences the degree to which individuals engage in an evaluation of the hedonic consequences of their actions. When people are in a positive affective state, much of what they would have to do in a persuasion context (e.g., thinking about difficult or problematic states of affairs) has potential negative hedonic consequences, and would make them feel worse. As a consequence, happy individuals engage in a careful examination of the hedonic consequences of their potential actions. If they are offered a text to read about acid rain (Worth & Mackie, 1987), increases in student service fees (Bless et al., 1990; Bless et al., 1992), handgun control (Mackie & Worth, 1989), a violation of the law (Bodenhausen et al., 1994a), or other similar depressing topics, happy individuals will process the information very superficially in order to avoid being influenced, emotionally, by the content of the message. In contrast, if the activity has positive hedonic consequences, happy individuals are likely to engage in careful processing of the incoming information. For instance, they would happily read, in detail, a message about income tax reduction, a successful cure for cancer, or about "the easy ways to improve one's life."

In contrast, for individuals in a negative affective state, most tasks could improve their affective state, because they can at least distract them from their own negative thoughts and feelings, and thus have positive hedonic consequences. Therefore, sad individuals do not consider the specific potential hedonic consequences of their actions, and they invest in careful processing of most incoming information. Thus, an interesting and original feature of this model is that the use of mood management strategies per se, in the sense of being implemented depending on the hedonic consequences of the current situation, is thought to be more prevalent in happy than in sad participants.

A study by Wegener and colleagues (1995) provided good support for this model. In the study, participants watched 10 minutes of either a happy or a sad video, and then read a short article ostensibly for pretest for future research. The text was about the implementation of a university service. Its presentation was preceded by a statement indicating that that text typically made people feel happy and had positive implications for students (uplifting hedonic expectancy condition), or a statement that the text typically made people feel sad, and had negative implications for students (depressing hedonic expectancy condition). Argument quality was also manipulated. For half of the participants the arguments were weak whereas they were strong for the other half. Consistent with the hedonic contingency model, results showed that sad participants were strongly influenced by argument quality whatever the hedonic consequences of the text. By the same token, happy individuals were strongly influenced by the quality of the arguments when the text was presented as having potential positive hedonic consequences, and not when it was presented as having negative hedonic consequences.

Informational Models

Most of the informational models can be considered as extensions of the affect-as-information model. All such models share the basic assumption that affective states inform the organism about the state of the environment. The state of the environment evaluated in this way has implications for how much attention should be allocated to processing new information, and how much one can rely on information one already possesses. In what follows, we will first present the original mood-as-information model and then some of its extensions.

Original mood-as-information model

On the basis of the affect-as-information model, Schwarz (1990) proposed that one's affective state not only provides direct information for the judgment at hand, but also indicates to the organism the state of the environment (see, Clore, Schwarz, & Conway, 1994; Schwarz, 2001). A positive affective state informs the organism that the environment is secure and that no action is needed to make things right. Because there is no threat, a positive state therefore signals to the individual that there is no need to engage in careful processing of the incoming information, unless this would be required by other situational demands (Bless et al., 1990). As a result, happy individuals should naturally tend to engage in heuristic processing of information.

In contrast, a negative affective state (like sadness) indicates that the environment is problematic and that individuals should invest resources in information processing in order to resolve what is problematic. This motivational impetus should lead individuals in a negative affective state to process incoming information carefully, allocating attention to details, and to avoid the use of heuristic strategy as it could have detrimental consequences.

In support of this account, Sinclair, Mark, and Clore (1994) asked individuals on rainy days and sunny days to take part in a survey about the implementation of university comprehensive exams. Before completing the survey, half of the participants were asked to evaluate the weather to control for "any mood–weather effects that could affect other responses" (external attribution condition) while the remaining participants completed the survey without considering the reason for their current affective state (no attribution condition). Both groups then read a text arguing for the implementation of comprehensive exams, but that differed according to the strength of the arguments presented (strong vs. weak). Finally, they answered several questions related to their attitude toward the implementation of comprehensive exams. The results are depicted in Figure 6.6. Consistent with previous findings, in the control condition, participants in a pleasant affective state (i.e., those who were approached when the weather was pleasant) were less affected by the arguments' strength than participants in an unpleasant affective state (i.e., those who were approached when the weather was unpleasant; see right-hand panel). However, consistent with the affect-as-information model,

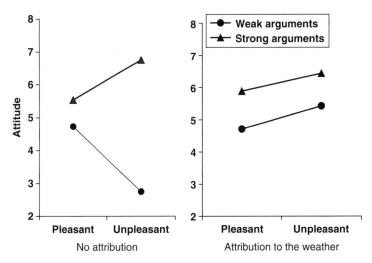

FIGURE 6.6. Effects of mood states on the influence of argument strength on attitudes when an attribution for the mood is present (right panel) and absent (left panel). From Sinclair, R. C. et al. (1994). Mood-related persuasion depends on (mis)attributions. *Social Cognition, 12,* 309–326.

when participants were led to attribute their affective state to the weather, the impact of their affective state on processing disappeared (see Figure 6.6, left-hand panel).

Mood-and-general knowledge model

In a refinement of the original model, Bless and colleagues (Bless, 2001; Bless & Fiedler, 1995; Bless et al., 1996b; Bless et al., 1996a; see also Fiedler, 1990, 1991, 2001, for related propositions) proposed that affective states do not directly influence the amount of effort that individuals invest in the processing of incoming information. They suggest instead that the affective states inform individuals about the extent to which they can rely on their general knowledge structures, that is, ideas and beliefs that they already possess, such as stereotypes.

According to this extension, happiness causes individuals to be particularly confident in these preexisting ideas and beliefs. Therefore, they examine incoming information in relation to their general knowledge structures and try to resolve discrepancies. As a result, the judgmental outcome depends on the degree of discrepancy between the knowledge structure (e.g., a given category or stereotype) and incoming information (e.g., pieces of behavioral information). In case of slight contradiction (for instance in case of ambiguous information), happy individuals will interpret the incoming information so as to make it consistent with the activated knowledge structures in which they are currently confident. So, for example, if happy individuals have to express a judgment about another person, they will be likely to express stereotypic judgments – and this will *resemble* heuristic processing (Bodenhausen et al., 1994a; Krauth-Gruber & Ric, 2000). As the discrepancy becomes greater, happy individuals can resolve it by correcting the potential impact of the knowledge structures. This correction may take the form of a contrast effect. For instance, if they learn something negative about another person, they might judge the person more negatively if he is a member of a positive category than if he is a member of a negative category (Bless et al., 1996a). The correction may also take the form of the absence of an effect of the general knowledge structure (Krauth-Gruber & Ric, 2000). Thus, what seems important in this refinement is that happiness does not lead to superficial processing, but it does make people confident in their knowledge structures (see also Bless & Fiedler, 1995). Happy people do process incoming information and, only if necessary, take it into account in their judgments.

In contrast, negative affective states decrease people's confidence in their general knowledge structures because relying on such structures in a problematic situation could have detrimental consequences. As a result, individuals engage in careful processing of incoming information and may eventually correct for the anticipated influence of general knowledge structures, especially when they are perceived as inappropriate (Lambert et al., 1997).

Bless and colleagues (1996a) found some support for this idea in a series of experiments. In one experiment they asked happy, neutral, and sad participants to perform a concentration task on several occasions during the experimental session. Results of the concentration task performed just after the induction of affective states revealed no difference in performance between conditions, suggesting that happiness does not reduce either capacity or motivation. Moreover, on another occasion, participants were asked to perform the concentration task while simultaneously completing a concurrent task. The concurrent task could be completed by relying on a specific *script*. A script is a general knowledge structure that contains information about the typical sequence of events in a given situation; in the present experiment, either "a ride on a tramway," or "a telephone call from a public telephone booth." As hypothesized, happy participants relied more on scripts in order to complete the concurrent task than other participants. They also performed better on the concentration task. According to Bless and colleagues, their superior performance on the concentration task was due to the fact that they relied on scripts to perform the concurrent task, and thus had more cognitive resources available with which to complete the concentration task.

Mood-as-input

Similar ideas are echoed in the thinking of Martin, Ward, Achee, and Wyer (1993). When individuals complete a performance task they frequently think of their own position with respect to the goal that has to be reached. In such condition, individuals' affective state can be used to evaluate this position. Negative affect may be interpreted as a failure to reach the goal, therefore effort should be invested. In contrast, a positive affective state would indicate that the goal has been reached and that no more efforts are required.

However, in other tasks, the question is not whether the goal has or has not been attained but whether one enjoys the task. In such conditions, a positive affect could be interpreted as indicating that the task is enjoyable and thus that one can persevere in this task whereas a negative affective state could be interpreted as indicating that the task is unpleasant and that it is time to stop. In sum, depending on the question we have in mind (e.g., "Have I done enough?" or "Do I enjoy the task?") the use of the affective state to provide an answer would lead to opposite answers.

Martin and colleagues (1993; see for related results, Hirt, Melton, McDonald, & Harackiewicz, 1996) found results illustrative of this point. They put participants in either a happy or a sad affective state by means of filmclips. After an interpolated task, participants completed an item generation task. In this task, they had to generate a list of birds from memory. In the control condition, participants were asked to stop listing "whenever they feel like stopping." In the two other conditions, participants were told to ask themselves whether if it was a good time to stop (time-to-stop rule) or if they felt like continuing the task (enjoyment rule). The results are presented in Figure 6.7.

Consistent with the hypothesis, when participants asked themselves whether it was a good time to stop, happy participants stopped sooner (Figure 6.7a) and listed fewer birds (Figure 6.7b) than sad participants. Participants in the control condition did the same but to a lesser extent, suggesting that the rule used in this task is the one used implicitly in many tasks used in previous experiments. However, when they were told to ask themselves if they felt like continuing, happy participants listed more birds and spent more time doing the task than sad participants.

Summary

Research reviewed in this chapter suggests that individuals' affective states influence both the content of their thoughts and the way that information is subsequently processed. One of the most thoroughly studied

a Time spent listing birds

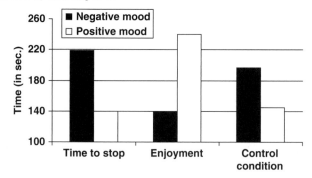

b Number of birds listed

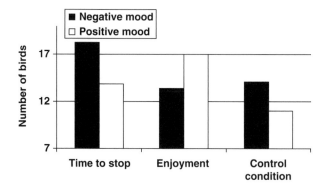

FIGURE 6.7. Influence of mood on time devoted to a task as a function of stop rules. From Martin, L. L. et al. (1993). Mood as input: People have to interpret the motivational implications of their moods. *Journal of Personality and Social Psychology, 64,* 317–326.

phenomena is that of mood congruence. It appears that individuals perceive information, recall memories and ideas, and judge objects and events in a way that is congruent with their current affective state. Thus, a happy person tends to see happy things, recall happy times, and make more or less optimistic judgments and estimations of likelihood. Perhaps this is why we like to be around happy people! When mood congruence is not observed, this is likely due to times when individuals in sad states are trying to change their moods, and become happier. For example, sad individuals might try to recall more pleasant memories in order to improve their present mood.

Affective states also cause, or are accompanied by, changes in the way in which individuals process information per se. In general, when in a happy mood, individuals seem to rely on simplifying rules, or heuristics, in order to render a judgment or adopt a specific attitude. They seem less likely than individuals in sad states to pay close attention to the details of incoming information. One surprising consequence of this is that when in happy moods people tend to rely more on their stereotypes than when in sad or neutral states. We suggested that there are many explanations for these tendencies. Happy moods seem to signal that the environment is safe and benign. When feeling happy, therefore, individuals feel no need to process information carefully. They also feel confident of their own pre-existing knowledge, and in general feel that they are doing pretty well on any task that they are performing. Sad moods seem to signal that the environment is not safe or benign. When feeling sad, therefore, individuals examine new information more carefully, and they have doubts in the usefulness or accuracy of their preexisting knowledge, and even doubts in whether they have done enough on a task.

Due, in part, to the fact that happy and sad mood are relatively easy to induce in the lab (see Chapter 1), much existing research has focused specifically on these states. The exceptions are studies by Bodenhausen and colleagues (1994a, 1994b), DeSteno and colleagues (2000), and Lerner and Keltner (2001). An avenue for future research is therefore a more careful mapping of discrete emotional states to facets of cognitive processing.

Emotion and Group Processes 7

The title of this chapter may appear paradoxical to the careful reader of the preceding chapters. Emotions have indeed been presented, and are generally considered, as intra-individual phenomena – processes that do not occur at the level of the group. Emotions, it would seem, happen to individuals, not groups. Or do they? It is not hard to imagine that group membership and group dynamics are fundamental in the generation and differentiation of emotion. For instance, imagine attending the final of the 100-meter race of the Olympic Games. Do you think you would feel the same way if you were in a stadium with 40,000 other people as you would if you were alone in front of your television screen? Would your emotions differ depending on whether one of the competitors was from your country, your family, your ethnic group, or if none of them had any particular relationship to you? Do you think your feelings would be the same if you were actively involved in track and field, played sports in general, or if you were not interested in sports at all? The emotions you would experience and their intensity before, during, and after the race, would probably be very different as a function of each and every one of these social, group-related factors. Imagine now that a competitor from another country tripped your favorite sprinter. What would your reaction be? How would you feel toward this clumsy competitor? Toward the members of his group?

As our questions about your emotional experience while watching the 100-meter race imply, there are at least two important ways in which emotions can be called group processes, and not only individual processes. First, there is the idea that emotions can be shared – and shaped – by a group, such as the 40,000 people in the stadium, or by the individuals in the stadium who come from the same country as the winner (or the loser!). Second, there is the idea that emotions can be felt by a group of individuals toward another group of individuals, importantly determining the ways in which the members of the two groups act toward each other. Of course, although these two group processes may seem to be separate phenomena, they are in fact highly intertwined in daily life. Furthermore, such phenomena are of extreme importance because a deeper understanding of emotion and group processes can help explain, and generate potential solutions for group conflict in which emotions play an integral role. It is indeed in intergroup contexts that we generally have the unpleasant experience of observing the most intense anger, hatred, or fear among individuals. And these feelings are often pervasive and long lasting. For instance, many years after the end of World War II, and in spite of the reconstruction of Europe, some older French people who experienced Nazi occupation still have very negative and hostile reactions toward the Germans as a group.

The present chapter focuses on these issues. First, we consider emotional experiences at the group level, that is, we consider the possibility that an entire group can share or experience the same emotion for the same reason. These are called "group-based" emotions, although under certain conditions they are sometimes also called emotions "on behalf of the group." We discuss both the measurement of group-based emotions and the mechanisms through which emotions can spread throughout a group. In the second part of the chapter, we examine the role of emotions in intergroup relations. We discuss the relationship between prejudice and emotions, as well as more general links between emotion, perception of others, and intergroup behavior. Finally, in the last part of the chapter, we present research indicating that emotions can lead to actions taken toward an outgroup.

The Group as a Place for Emotions

Although we suggested that the notion of group-based emotions is somewhat inconsistent with the idea that emotions are private or intra-individual experiences, there is considerable evidence that emotions are "social" in the sense of being influenced by social factors (Parkinson, 1996; Parkinson, Fischer, & Manstead, 2004). First, the cause of an emotional experience lies frequently in other people. It seems obvious that much of the time, we feel sad, happy, angry and so forth *because of* the actions of a significant other. Second, other people may significantly influence the way we interpret our emotional experience (Schachter & Singer, 1962). Other people, that is, may help us understand what we are feeling and the cause of our feelings in situations in which these are ambiguous. Finally, our expression of emotion, and thus potentially the intensity of our emotional experience, is also affected by the presence of others. As we saw in Chapter 4, we as individuals are more likely to smile when someone is around to see us, and especially if that other person is our friend (Hess, Banse, & Kappas, 1995).

Furthermore, the idea of group-based emotions has been around for a long time. Le Bon (1895/1963), a pioneer in social psychology, proposed that groups provide contexts for intense contagious emotional experiences. His analysis of group emotions was however restricted to what he called "psychological crowds," which he defined as groups of people in which the individual's conscious, unique personality disappears, and in which feelings and ideas of each component of the group are directed at the same target. As examples of psychological crowds, Le Bon cited members of a court jury, or groups of voters. The position of Le Bon reflects the dualist approach that views emotion and reason as opposing forces and according to which reason is a better guide for action than emotions. He suggested that one of the main characteristics of the crowd is that the reasoning of its members is strongly compromised and that the members are governed by their feelings, which he held was also true of the members of primitive tribes and children. This position probably seems somewhat ludicrous and highly dated, of course, because it is marked by the dominant ideology of his time. Nevertheless, some of these ideas are still apparent in the commonsense theories of groups. Groups or crowds are considered capable of extreme emotional movements such as hatred, love, fear (i.e., panic) or exhilaration, directed at a single cause of concern to their members.

Although the study of group-based emotions all but disappeared for many decades, the pendulum has swung back again, and currently there is much interest in the topic. Still, the very concept of group-based emotion remains problematic because there exists no clear, consensual means to define and measure it. One possibility is that by group emotions we mean the "average level" of the emotions felt by the individuals composing a group. But this is not a very good indicator of group-based emotions, because it does not express anything about the variability of the emotional experience within the group. It could be that some group members feel very strongly one way and that other members do not feel much of that emotion at all. The average of the group emotion does not convey this variability. The variability of group members' emotions is obviously important for being able to characterize the emotion or even say that it defines the group at all (George, 1990). In fact, one could argue that low variability, thus high homogeneity, in the emotions experienced by members of a given group is a good indicator of the existence of a group-based emotion because it suggests that the whole group is experiencing a similar state. Following this reasoning, George (1990) concluded that salesperson workgroups experienced group emotions because the participants' evaluations of their own emotional state were highly consistent within workgroups. The agreement between individual members of a group, measured by interrater reliability coefficient (an indicator of the extent to which people's ratings are similar) was higher than .70 in 50 of the 52 group estimates. Totterdell, Kellett, Teuchmann, and Briner (1998) reported findings consistent with this idea in workgroups of community nurses and accountants.

Although the "group" part of group-based emotions poses some conceptual difficulties as noted in the preceding paragraph, the "emotion" part of group-based emotion does not seem to differ fundamentally in its definition from the definition we presented in Chapter 1. That is, most researchers of group-based emotions use the same emotion categories, study the same psychological processes, as those that are the subject of the scientific study of individual emotions. Thus, for now and as long as no other evidence is offered for the uniqueness of group-based emotions, the group can be seen as another source of (individual shared) emotion or a modulator of the intensity or expression of individual emotion. For instance, group-based emotions may be both more intense and more long lasting than emotions at the individual level.

In the next section, we describe how emotions arise and spread through the group. It is obvious that emotions can be induced in the members of a group if they are exposed to the same eliciting event at the same time (say, for instance, the victory or defeat of one's favorite football team or a natural disaster). However, it is far less obvious how group processes might intensify and maintain these emotions. Neither is it obvious how the emotion could propagate in a group in which members were apparently not exposed to the primary eliciting event. We therefore address these questions and present several mechanisms held to underlie such phenomena.

Emotional Contagion

Emotional contagion is defined as "the tendency to 'catch' (experience/ express) another person's emotions (his or her emotional appraisals, subjective feelings, expressions, patterned physiological processes, action tendencies, and instrumental behaviors)" (Hatfield, Cacioppo, & Rapson, 1992, p. 153). This phenomenon may occur without any intent or awareness of transmitting (for the target) or of "catching" (for the perceiver) the target's emotion. Hatfield and her colleagues (Hatfield, Cacioppo, & Rapson, 1993; Hatfield et al., 1992, 1994) have placed specific emphasis on what they have called "primitive emotional contagion," which appears especially relevant for group emotions, and which they have defined as "the tendency to automatically mimic and synchronize movements, expressions, postures, and vocalizations with those of another person and, consequently, to converge emotionally" (Hatfield et al., 1992, pp. 153–154).

Emotional contagion is familiar to lay people, psychologists, as well as people working in marketing and advertising, as evidenced by the canned laughter that is so often used in television shows and commercials. Canned laughter is intended to provoke the audience's mirth, positive affective state, and ultimately a positive attitude toward the series or the product. An experiment by Bush, Barr, McHugo, and Lanzetta (1989) is particularly relevant in demonstrating the contagious effect of canned laughter. Bush and colleagues had participants watch video excerpts of comedy routines. For half of the participants these video excerpts contained short close-up inserts of the faces of different people laughing, and for half of the participants the excerpts contained no inserts. The activity of participants' facial muscles implicated in the production of smiles, those in the eye and cheek regions, were measured. And participants' amusement while they were watching the video excerpts was also assessed. Findings of the study indicated that both muscle activity associated with happiness and self-reported amusement were greater in the condition in which the videos contained close-up inserts of people laughing than when the inserts were not presented. This shows that emotional states can propagate rapidly and automatically between individuals, presumably even many individuals. Moreover, because of its automatic component, emotion can perpetuate itself, each individual influencing and being influenced by the others.

Emotion contagion may also occur in less intrusive situations, in the absence of obvious and explicit measures of emotion, and thus without any intention to imitate. For example, Hsee, Hatfield, Carslon, and Chemtob (1990) led experimental participants to believe that they were going to interact via television monitors with another participant who was supposedly stationed in another room. In reality, the other participant was a confederate of the experimenter, and had been previously videotaped. Before the experiment began, the experimenter explained that an interview would be conducted with each of the participants in order for them to get them acquainted with each other. The (prerecorded) interview with the confederate was presented first. At one point in the interview, the confederate expressed intense feelings of happiness in his facial expressions and gestures, and he expressed intense feelings of sadness at another point in the interview. The facial expressions of the real participant were unobtrusively taped as he or she watched the interview with the confederate, and subsequently the tapes were evaluated by independent naive judges who knew nothing of the nature of the confederate interview or the experimental hypotheses. Findings of this study showed that the facial expressions of the confederate strongly influenced both the expression displayed by the "real participant" and his or her feelings. That is, when participants saw the confederate exhibiting happiness, they displayed more happiness and less sadness in their facial expressions than when they saw the confederate exhibiting sadness. Moreover, they retrospectively rated their emotional state as congruent with the one expressed by the "other participant" at that time.

Recently, Neumann and Strack (2000; see also Neumann, Seibt, & Strack, 2001) demonstrated a similar contagion effect with the use of emotional voices. In the first of a series of ingenious experiments, they found that participants who had listened to a neutral philosophical text read in a slightly happy voice were in better moods than those who had listened to the same text read with a slightly sad voice. It is important to note that the affective tone of the voice was not consciously detected by the participants. Subsequent studies in the same series showed that the effects were largely automatic because they were not affected when cognitive resources were taxed. That is, the same mood contagion effects were obtained whether participants were only asked to listen to the text, or if they had to perform another task (i.e., to insert three metal pins in each of the 100 holes of a wooden board) while they were listening to the philosophical text (see Figure 7.1). Just being exposed to an emotional voice, even when one is cognitively "busy," appears, then, to affect one's mood.

Moreover, emotional contagion is not limited to the laboratory. Not surprisingly, similar contagion effects have been found in more naturalistic settings, suggesting that these processes are quite ecologically valid. As an

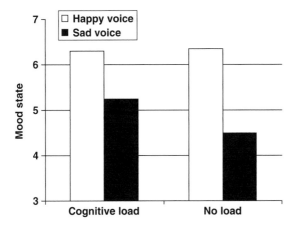

FIGURE 7.1. Mean mood state (0 = very bad; 9 = very good) as a function of vocal emotional expression and cognitive load. From Neumann, R., & Strack, F. (2000). "Mood contagion": The automatic transfer of mood between persons. *Journal of Personality and Social Psychology, 79,* 211–223.

example, Totterdell et al. (1998) had community nurses working in 13 teams complete daily measures of their mood, work hassles, team commitment, and team climate over a 3-week period. Analyses of these diaries indicated that a nurse's mood on a particular day was significantly predicted by the mean of their teammates' mood on the same day. Moreover, this relation remained significant even when controlling for the effect of work hassles, suggesting that the relation between the moods of the nurse and the mood of the rest of her team was not entirely attributable to work shared problems. Similar findings were reported by Totterdell (2000) who found that the mood of professional cricket players varied as a function of the happiness of the players teammates during a session of play, independently of the match situation and hassles.

Accounts of Emotional Contagion

Several accounts have been proposed to explain the contagion of emotion between individuals and group members. These explanations run the gamut of relying on basic principles of learning theory to more complex psychological phenomena such as empathy. What we believe importantly distinguishes the accounts is whether they suggest that the mechanisms underlying what we observe to be emotional contagion are automatic (in the sense of happening unconsciously, effortlessly, and without intention) or due to controlled processes (in the sense of processes that are engaged consciously, effortfully, and with intention). Suggesting that emotional contagion happens automatically versus in a more intentional way implies that different processes would be necessary to change or counteract the contagion of it were it undesirable or destructive.

Automatic processes in emotional contagion

Learning processes According to one explanation that relies on the notion of conditioned responses, individuals learn to have an emotional feeling whenever they see particular signs of emotions expressed by others in the social environment (Bandura, 1976). For instance, if you have learned that when people express fear, something frightening generally happens in the following seconds, fear and escape behavior can be automatically associated with your perception of fear on the face of others. It may also be that reactions of others, for instance in a situation of high anxiety or of irritation, produce behavioral changes (agitation, rapid movements, noise) that irritate you. If learned over years, it is likely that as soon as the first signs of these emotional states are detected in others, they will elicit the conditioned response in you. However, it is also possible that the stimulus eliciting the emotion in the person observed has no direct impact on the perceiver. For instance, individuals may learn that when other people are happy, they act kindly and generously, which leads the individuals in turn to feel positive feelings. As a result, the individuals may automatically experience joy as soon as they detect the smallest indicator of other people's happiness. This may occur while the stimulus inducing happiness in the actor is even not known to the observer.

Hard interface approach As we have already mentioned, Hatfield and colleagues proposed that facial expressions, postures, and vocal expressions are automatically imitated by the observers (Adelmann & Zajonc, 1989; Dimberg, 1982; Izard, 1977; Neumann & Strack 2000). Hatfield and colleagues' account has much in common with the hard interface theory of representation of Zajonc and Markus (1984). According to this theory, objects (e.g., a person experiencing a particular emotion) are represented as a specific arrangement of muscular and skeletal sensations in memory. For instance, the perception of a sad person could be represented in the observer as the muscular sensations associated with the production of a face similar to the one displayed by the observed person.

Therefore, if you observe a person exhibiting sadness, you will imitate his or her behavior and thereby activate the representation of a sad person by your imitation. The pattern of skeletal musculature you have adopted will in turn influence your emotional experience. According to this approach, such processes would help us to understand the inner emotional state of other persons.

Perceptual symbol systems approach   A similar account relating emotional expression and emotion feelings has been recently proposed by Niedenthal and colleagues (Niedenthal, Barsalou, Ric, & Krauth-Gruber, 2005a; Niedenthal, Barsalou, Winkielman, Krauth-Gruber, & Ric, 2005b). Their ideas are based on Barsalou's perceptual symbol systems theory (PSS; Barsalou, 1999), a theory of "embodied cognition" that proposes that knowledge is grounded in specific sensory-motor states, or patterns of neural activation, that occur in interaction with the object or event being referred to (see also Damasio, 1989). A way to understand the idea of this theory is to understand that often information processing has been thought of as the manipulation of abstract "files" of information stored something like computer files in the brain, and these files contain *redescriptions* of the initial perceptual information. Theories of embodied cognition propose that knowledge in the brain is not abstract but is in part a replay of the actual physical experience of the object. According to this account, the perception of a person experiencing an emotion activates in perceivers the same sensory-motor states, that is, the same patterns of activation in the brain, that are implicated in the production of the emotional response that is being observed. Thus, the perception of an emotion, and its imitation, causes a partial reenactment of the emotion state in the perceiver. Furthermore, it is more likely that the state will be fully or partially reenacted if individuals are observing people with whom they want to empathize and have a close understanding, such as members of one's own group.

Controlled processes in emotional contagion

Self-perception   Self-perception theory (Bem, 1972) offers another potential explanation of the phenomenon of emotional contagion (Laird, 1974; Olson, 1992). As discussed in Chapter 4, according to this theory individuals have limited access to their inner states, and they therefore infer their states in the same way as they infer the state of others, that is by relying on external clues. For instance, individuals may infer that they are experiencing a specific emotion from the perception of the contractions of their *zygomaticus major* muscle. Applied to emotional contagion, then, an individual might imitate the behavior of others and then infer from her own behavior what her emotional state is. According to a self-perception view, although mimicry may be automatic, inferences from mimicry to specify one's own affective state require at least a minimum cognitive work.

Communication   Researchers have also proposed that motor mimicry is a communicative act to show other people that we know how they feel and that we feel the same as they do. In support of this position, Bavelas, Black, Lemery, and Mullett (1986; see also Buck et al., 1992; Fridlund, 1991, for related findings) found that facial mimicry of an experimenter who dropped a television monitor on his already injured finger and displayed pain was more marked among participants who could make eye contact with the experimenter than among those who could not. Moreover, participants' facial reactions to the experimenter's injury were unobtrusively videotaped and shown in a second experiment to another group of participants (observers). The observers were informed about the experimenter's injury but were blind to the former participants' experimental condition. Observers judged that participants in the eye contact condition had a better understanding of how the experimenter felt and cared more about what happened compared with participants in the no-eye contact condition. Kraut and Johnston (1979) reported similar observations of bowlers who did not smile as a function of their performance if they were facing the bowling pins, but who did it if they were facing friends (after taking their turn). Thus, emotional contagion may be a consequence of emotional communication among group members. And it may be propagated in a very conscious and intentional way.

Social comparison　In a similar vein, Sullins (1991) and Wrightsman (1960) hold that emotional contagion is often caused by social comparison processes. That is, emotional contagion, or "convergence" (i.e., the fact that the affective states of members of a given group tend to converge), is due to a pressure toward uniformity that results from comparing with others who are relatively similar to us (Festinger, 1954). Members of groups are by definition similar in that they share the same group identity. In cases in which appropriate feelings in a situation are not clearly defined, group members compare with each other and tend to interpret their feelings and emotional reactions as similar.

Consistent with this view, in a study by Wrightsman (1960) participants were divided into groups of four. Participants were placed in separate individual rooms in which they were ostensibly told that the study was about "glucose level and mental activity," and that they would receive a painful injection that could have a strong unpleasant impact on their behavior. At this point, participants were asked how they felt "at this moment" (0 = completely at ease; 100 = completely ill at ease). Then, participants were asked to wait 5 minutes before the injection. In the two first conditions, the four participants waited together. However, in one group the participants were allowed to talk to each other (together talk condition) whereas in the second, they were not (together not talk condition). In the third condition, participants waited for the injection alone.

Participants were subsequently again asked to indicate how at ease or ill at ease they felt. Homogenization of mood was evaluated in each four-person group by the ratio of the range of mood evaluations after the waiting period divided by the range of evaluations the period before the waiting period. Consistent with work on mood contagion, the results indicated that participants waiting in a group, whether they were allowed to speak together or not, showed more mood convergence after a 5-minute wait than individuals who waited alone. Consistent with social comparison theory, the convergence effects were more marked for groups composed of individuals who were relatively similar to each other, as evaluated by the range of the within group mood evaluations before the waiting period.

Also consistent with a social comparison interpretation of these findings, Sullins (1991) found that participants who had a 5-minute wait in the presence of another participant, and were not allowed to talk to them, tended to converge emotionally with that other participant, but only if the other participant was said to be participating in the same experiment as they were.

Empathy Finally, emotion contagion may also be accounted for by processes of empathy (e.g., Kelly & Barsade, 2001) that we deWne here as the process by which an observer places him- or herself in the place of the actor. It is worth noting that this deWnition departs from those that consider "empathy" and "emotional contagion" as equivalent, and those that consider empathy as an outcome that is explained by emotion contagion processes (e.g., Eisenberg & Miller, 1987; Levenson, 1996; Vaughan & Lanzetta, 1981). In the present chapter, empathy is thus restricted to taking the perspective of someone else. Such a process requires that when observing an individual experiencing an emotional state, the observers give up their own perspective and attempt to place themselves in the same situation as the actor (see Davis, 2004). By doing so, the individuals should be able to appraise the situation in the same manner and to experience an emotion similar to the one experienced by the actor.

As an example, think of a situation in which you are watching an extremely sad movie in which the character's beloved dies just after she learned she was expecting his baby. As a result, you feel the same emotional experience the actor is supposed to feel, that is sadness. Eventually, your eyes may fill with tears. Recent evidence from neuroimaging research provides support for these effects. For instance, Ruby and Decety (2004) found that the amygdala (i.e., a brain structure involved in emotion processing) was activated to a greater extent when participants were reading sentences describing emotion-eliciting situations than when reading neutral sentences.

More important for our purpose, these differences were obtained whether participants answered from their own perspective or answered as they thought their mother would.

Two processes have been proposed that could at least partially underlie empathy. The first one is the activation of autobiographical memories (Davis, 2004). It may be that the actor or something in the situation activates relevant memories that make individuals remember similar situations in which they felt the same emotions. The second process is the reliance on implicit theories of emotions. That is, individuals may rely on implicit theories (acquired through socialization or from one's own experience) concerning the way people feel emotions and for what reasons. Note that the latter process may or may not actually involve taking the perspective of the actor.

Reconciling automatic and controlled process views

As we have seen, depending on the account, the explanation of emotion contagion stresses the importance of either automatic or controlled processes. At first pass, these two views might be contradictory. However, they are not necessarily incompatible because automatic processes are often subtle and vulnerable to being overridden by more controlled processes (Bargh, 1997). For instance, although you can automatically, and even without awareness of doing so, display a smile when you see someone else smiling, it is possible that you will intentionally accentuate your facial expression if you see that the other person is watching you. You might do so in order to communicate your feelings. You might also attempt to control your facial expression, consciously mask a smile for instance, if the situation called for the expression of negative or neutral emotional expression.

Relatedly, recent research by Neumann and Strack (2000) on emotional contagion caused by voices, described earlier, suggests that the observation of others' affective state has different effects as a result of automatic or of more controlled processes. Specifically, Neumann and Strack suggested that the perception of others' emotional behavior induces mood, but not discrete emotions, in the perceiver so long as the perceiver is not conscious of the source of the induced feeling state. In their studies, participants' mood but not their discrete emotion state (measures related to either happiness or sadness) was affected by the affective tone of the voice of the message they listened to. However, when the participants' attention was directed toward the emotional state of the speaker, they could imagine his or her emotion state as well as its source. As a result, in such conditions the tone of the voice altered emotion states of the participants in addition to their mood in a congruent manner (Study 4).

Therefore, according to Neumann and Strack, there exists automatic contagion of mood, but the transfer of emotions among individuals requires additional cognitive resources directed to the appraisal of the observed person's situation.

Finally, some of these accounts can be considered as complementary rather than mutually exclusive, because for emotion contagion, as for many other phenomena, there is not one unique determining cause. Depending on the conditions, it is probable that one of the several accounts of emotional contagion explains the phenomenon.

Intentional Emotion Propagation in the Group

We have thus far discussed emotional contagion that occurs with no particular intention to share a common emotional experience on the part of members of the group, or the group as a whole. That is, we have considered the situation in which emotions are transferred to others while the transmitter is neither aware of the transmission of emotion nor is intending to do so. In other situations, however, changes in a group affective state can be the consequences of deliberate attempts to modify the others' affective state.

A consideration of deliberate attempts to cause emotional contagion in a group immediately brings to mind the notion of the charismatic leader. A leader may indeed have the potential to induce group-based emotions. And this influence may be used intentionally, as a way to modify the behavior of the members of the group. For instance, imagine that a coach of a rugby team wants to make his players display more competitive spirit. In this situation, he or she may try to induce anger in the players. On other occasions, a leader may attempt to induce fear in the members of his or her group in order to justify a particular political position, to engage in war with another country, or to justify an important loss of ingroup members. Such Machiavellian examples suppose that the leader knows what affective state should be induced to produce the outcomes expected and how it can be induced. It is likely that leaders are often aware of the desired outcome. Whether he or she is aware of the use of emotion induction is less clear.

Intentional influence on group emotions is obviously not restricted to leaders. Within a group, members may attempt to modify the emotions of group members who are particularly influential in an effort to change a group-based decision. And, finally, there is evidence that emotions are sometimes transmitted from one to another for reasons of emotion regulation. That is, individuals attempt to share their emotional experience with the aim of regulating their own affective state (e.g., Rimé et al., 1992; Rimé et al., 1998). These ideas were already discussed in detail in Chapter 5, on emotion regulation. Yet, it is probable that this regulation goal may be achieved on some occasions without the individual's intention or awareness of doing so.

Emotion on Behalf of a Group

The idea that individuals experience emotions on behalf of a group even when not involved in or present for the emotion-inducing event is not new. Young Germans have expressed shame and guilt for the atrocities committed in their country and neighboring countries during World War II. Young French adults also felt shame on behalf of French people after learning, for example, about the trial of Maurice Papon, who was responsible for the exportation of Jews to Nazi extermination camps, also during World War II. When the Portugese national soccer team lost the final of the European Soccer Championship, in 2004, the whole of Portugal cried, while the Greeks, whose team had won, celebrated in wild group ecstasy. Many young Germans and French were not born during World War II, and many Portuguese and Greek citizens do not even play soccer or were not at the final game. They felt these emotions on *behalf* of the country, on *behalf* of the national teams. Despite the ease with which examples of emotions on behalf of a group can come to mind, however, theoretical accounts of and experimental evidence for this phenomenon are surprisingly recent (Doosje, Branscombe, Spears, & Manstead, 1998; Mackie, Devos, & Smith, 2000; Smith, 1993; Yzerbyt, Dumont, Wigboldus & Gordijn, 2003).

Classic studies by Cialdini et al. (1976) demonstrated that individuals feel pride or shame as a function of the success or failure, respectively, of their group members. Specifically, Cialdini and colleagues showed that American university students wear their university apparel (e.g., buttons, jackets, sweatshirts, tee shirts) more frequently after a victory of their university team than after a loss. Individuals also use the pronoun "we" to describe a team victory more frequently than when describing a loss. Subsequent studies addressed this point more directly. Hirt, Zillman, Erickson, and Kennedy (1992), for example, had basketball fans watch the broadcast of a game that the team they supported either won or lost. Not surprisingly, the game outcome strongly affected their affective state. Participants were in a better mood when their team won than when it lost. Moreover, the effects were more pronounced for participants who identified most with the basketball team.

Such findings suggest that individuals can experience an emotion even when not directly confronted with the cause of the emotion. In such situations, the individual experiences a given emotion *because members of his or her group experienced the eliciting event.* In contrast to emotional contagion, which is automatic and does not require awareness of the eliciting stimulus, the experience of an emotion on behalf of a group requires both consciousness of the emotion-eliciting situation and an explicit sense of identification with the group in question. However, recent work has gone much deeper into the study of emotions on behalf of a group.

Doosje and colleagues (1998) replicated and extended the findings by Hirt el al. (1992), using novel groups that were constructed in the laboratory. Specifically, these researchers led experimental participants to believe that they were "inductive thinkers," whereas other participants had been ostensibly identified as "deductive thinkers." Then, participants completed an evaluation task in which they had to judge figures created with a finite set of geometric pieces (i.e., "tangram" game) supposedly created by members of their group (inductive thinkers) or by members of the other group (deductive thinkers). They learned that their group was generally unfair (vs. fair) when evaluating the other group and that they were personally more (vs. less) discriminating than the norm. Measures of guilt revealed that when participants were members of a discriminating group (low group fairness condition; see Figure 7.2), they felt more guilt than if they were members of a nondiscriminating group (high group fairness condition). Moreover, this effect occurred only when the participant him- or herself was not doing the discriminating (high personal fairness condition). Otherwise, group fairness had no impact on the level of guilt experienced (low personal fairness condition; see Figure 7.2).

In another study testing the role of group identification, Doosje and colleagues (1998) manipulated the presentation of facts concerning the history

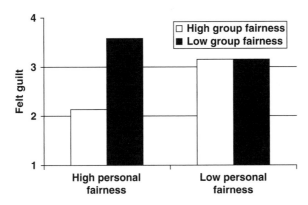

FIGURE 7.2. Mean collective guilt as a function of group and personal fairness. Scores could range from 1 to 7 with higher numbers indicating greater acceptance of collective guilt. From Doosje, B. et al. (1998). Guilty by association: When one's group has a negative history. *Journal of Personality and Social Psychology, 75,* 872–886.

of the relationship between Dutch people and Indonesians (the Netherlands have had a long history of colonial occupation of Indonesia). In one condition, the presentation emphasized the positive aspects of the occupation such as the resulting improvements in the Indonesian infrastructure, and the introduction of a solid legal system. In another condition, the presentation emphasized the negative aspects of occupation, such as the exploitation of Indonesian land, and the death of many Indonesians. Finally, in a third condition, information was balanced and therefore the global evaluative tone of the presentation was mixed. Consistent with previous findings, when the presentation was negatively framed, participants experienced more guilt than when the presentation was positively framed, regardless of the participant's level of identification with the Dutch. The impact of group identification was revealed in case of ambiguity. In that case, high identifiers experienced less guilt than low identifiers, probably because those who identified the most with the group attempted to defend their group, a strategy that was unnecessary when the presentation was positively framed, and difficult to use by high identifiers when the presentation was negatively framed (see Branscombe, Doosje, & McGarty, 2002, for a review of these studies).

Another way to understand emotions on behalf of a group can be found in the research by Bizman, Yinon, and Krotman (2001). With an approach relatively similar to the one of Doosje and colleagues, these researchers applied self-discrepancy theory (Higgins, 1987, 1989) to understanding emotions at the group level. The theory developed by Higgins holds that inconsistencies between features of different self-concepts, especially between the actual self (what one is really like) and the ideal (desired) or ought (prescribed) selves can lead to the experience of specific negative emotions. Bizman and colleagues extended the theory to discrepancies related to the group-based aspects of the self. Consistent with self-discrepancy theory, they showed that in Israeli students a discrepancy between the perceived attributes of the actual group and the attributes of the ideal group (i.e., the attributes the participants wished the members of their group possessed) triggered specifically dejection-related affective states (e.g., sadness, disappointment, hopelessness) whereas a contradiction between the perceived attributes of the actual group and the attributes of the ought group (i.e., the attributes their group members should possess, considering their responsibilities and duties) triggered agitation-related affective states (e.g., tension, nervousness, apprehension). These effects paralleled those predicted by Higgins at the level of individual emotions. Interestingly, these group-level effects on emotions were independent of self-discrepancies at the individual level. Such findings are important because they suggest that parallel effects could occur at the individual and at the group level, supported by similar processes that do not interfere with each other.

Therefore, it appears that individuals, because of their identification with the ingroup, can experience emotions that are elicited in other members of their group, without being directly confronted with the emotion eliciting events. According to Smith (1993), such effects occur because of the significance of group membership for the definition of one's self-concept among those who are highly identified with the group. Moreover, these studies suggest that group-based emotions can be triggered by processes parallel to those that appear to trigger individual emotions, each operating at different and not necessarily interacting levels.

Emotions in Intergroup Context

Emotion as a Predictor of Intergroup Attitudes and Behavior

Emotions should be an important factor in intergroup relations and prejudice. After all, prejudice, which is typically conceptualized as a global negative attitude toward an outgroup, contains an evaluative dimension that resembles one of the two fundamental dimensions of affective states (i.e., pleasantness). Also, in some theories of prejudice emotional factors have been considered as central. For instance, the "scapegoat theory" holds that negative attitudes toward outgroups are the result of a displacement of hostility toward powerful others (Allport, 1954; Dollar, Miller, Doob, Mowrer, & Sears, 1939). By the same token, social psychologists have often emphasized the role of beliefs about outgroup characteristics in prejudice (e.g., Hamilton, 1981), suggesting that prejudice could derive from individuals' beliefs about the group, that is, strictly from the content of their stereotypes (e.g., Eagly & Mladinic, 1989). According to such a view, the negative attitude toward members of the outgroup results from global negative beliefs about the group. Therefore, a reduction of the prejudice toward an outgroup would require a change in the beliefs concerning the group.

In a more inclusive approach, attitudes, and therefore prejudice, have been conceptualized as being composed of three distinct components: cognitions, behavior, and affect. In such an approach, an attitude is based on beliefs about the group, but also on observations of one's own behaviors as well as on one's affective reactions, including emotions, to the attitude object, that is in the present case, outgroup members (Zanna & Rempel, 1988). On the basis of this "tripartite" conceptualization, several studies have attempted to measure the affective (emotional) component of prejudice and its relative contribution to prejudice, in comparison with the belief component. Stangor, Sullivan, and Ford (1991) measured affective responses, stereotypes, and attitudes toward several social groups (e.g., white people, Jews, homosexuals, Arabs). In two studies, they found that affect was a better predictor of participants' attitudes than was the content of their stereotypes. This effect remained unchanged whether stereotypes measures were individual (i.e., the belief one personally endorses about members of a specific social group) or consensual (i.e., belief about members of a specific social group that is shared among members of a social group). Similarly, Jackson, Hodge, Gerard, Ingram, Ervin, and Sheppard (1996) found that intergroup affect was among the best predictors of intergroup attitudes toward African Americans, Hispanic Americans, and Asian Americans.

In a related set of studies, Jussim, Nelson, Manis, and Soffin (1995), had participants read 20 word definitions apparently provided by 20 individuals (10 "rock performers" and 10 "child abusers"). Each definition appeared on one page with the category of the target person at the top of the page. After they had read the word definition, participants were instructed to evaluate the mental illness as well as the creativity of the author. At the end of the experiment (or at the beginning in another condition), participants were asked to complete a questionnaire aimed at assessing their liking as well as their beliefs (i.e., stereotypes) of the two groups. Individual targets labeled as "child abusers" were evaluated as more mentally ill than targets labeled as "rock performers." More important for our purpose, the impact of category membership ("child abusers" vs. "rock performers") on judgments of mental illness was for a large part determined by the participants' affective reactions to these groups and not by beliefs about the two groups (i.e., stereotypes). Comparable results were found in a subsequent study using homosexuals versus heterosexuals as target group instead of "child abusers" and "rock performers."

Several accounts of the predominant role of affect in prejudice have been advanced. First, Esses, Haddock, and Zanna (1993) proposed that stereotypes, in part, determine an individual's emotional reactions to outgroup members, and the emotional reactions determine in turn their attitudes toward these people. We will call this account the "stereotype-emotion-prejudice hypothesis" (Figure 7.3; model B). This account is based on findings showing that stereotypes sometimes predict intergroup attitudes, but that this relationship is generally weakened when emotions and symbolic beliefs (i.e., "all thoughts about the relation between social groups and basic norms, whether the relation is negative or positive," Esses et al., 1993, p. 147) are taken into account. Furthermore, for some groups, emotions and symbolic beliefs may uniquely predict prejudice (Esses et al., 1993). Thus, according to such a hypothesis, the traditional view according to which stereotypes directly determine prejudice (see Figure 7.3, model A) requires the addition of an emotion mediator between stereotypes and prejudice. So, for example, if you have a stereotype of French people that is mainly negative (e.g., they are arrogant, egocentric, and unfaithful), this stereotype will trigger negative affect toward French people, and it is this resulting emotion that will constitute your overall prejudice toward the French (Figure 7.3, model B).

However, even the pattern we just mentioned can also be accounted for by another model (Figure 7.3, model C). It is indeed possible that an individual's current emotional state increases the likelihood that emotion-congruent aspects of the stereotype come to mind (e.g., Bower, 1981; see Chapter 6). These aspects of the stereotype determine the valence of the content of the stereotype at least for the moment (Esses & Zanna, 1995), and ultimately the individual's present attitude toward the group. As an example, imagine that Sabine is in a negative emotional state when she encounters a number of outgroup members. According to this hypothesis, Sabine's current emotional state will influence her stereotype of the group such that it will be more negative in content. As a result, she will express a more negative attitude toward members of this group. Alternatively, Smith (1993) has proposed a prejudice-as-social-emotion account, described in more detail later in the chapter, that equates prejudice with emotions triggered by appraisals of the intergroup situation and that can be considered as a refinement of the model B in Figure 7.3. According to this account, prejudice is not a global more or less negative attitude toward the outgroup. Rather, prejudice is conceptualized in terms of discrete emotions and their components. For instance, if an individual's ingroup is threatened by another group that is perceived as powerful, then the prejudiced emotion experienced by this individual will be related to anxiety or fear, and to the action tendencies of moving away to protect.

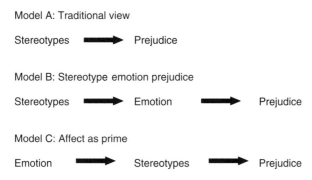

Model A: Traditional view

Stereotypes ➡ Prejudice

Model B: Stereotype emotion prejudice

Stereotypes ➡ Emotion ➡ Prejudice

Model C: Affect as prime

Emotion ➡ Stereotypes ➡ Prejudice

FIGURE 7.3. Models of relationships between emotion, stereotypes and prejudice.

Findings of research by Cottrell and Neuberg (2005; Neuberg & Cottrell, 2002) provide strong support for the role of discrete emotions in prejudice. Participants in their studies rated their global attitude toward several groups and reported the extent to which they experienced several discrete emotions (anger, fear, disgust, resentment, pity, and envy) when thinking of the group or of its members. Although the participants possessed equally negative attitudes (measured as global positive and negative feelings toward the group) toward African Americans, Asian Americans, and Native Americans, these three groups widely differed in the emotions they elicited in the participants. As shown in Figure 7.4, all three groups evoked some level of anger/resentment but only African Americans and Native Americans evoked pity, and only African Americans evoked fear and anxiety. Importantly, the kind of emotions that were experienced appeared to be related to the kind of threat posed by the outgroup. For instance, African Americans were the only group in the sample that evoked threats to physical safety, personal property, that are hypothesized to provoke fear.

An early study by Dijker (1987) reported findings consistent with the prejudice-as-social-emotion account in a study of both attitudes and action tendencies. In his study, the attitudes of Dutch people toward Surinamese and immigrants from Morocco and Turkey were predicted by different emotions, positive emotions for the former and irritation and concerns for the latter, these emotions being perceived as having been elicited by

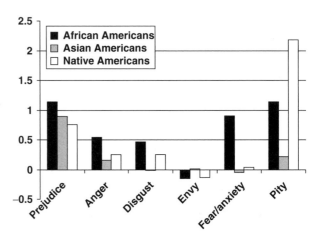

FIGURE 7.4. Level of prejudice and of specific emotions felt toward African Americans, Asian Americans, and Native Americans (on 9-point scales; e.g., 1 = I do not experience this feeling at all; 9 = I do experience this feeling extremely). The reported data represent the mean differences between the evaluation of the individuals' group (European Americans) on these dimensions and the three target outgroups. From Cottrell, C. A., & Neuberg, S. L. (2005). Different emotional reactions to different groups: A socio-functional threat-based approach to "prejudice". *Journal of Personality and Social Psychology, 88*, 770–789.

salient different antecedents (Dijker, Koomen, van den Heuvel, & Frijda, 1996), and leading to specific action tendencies. For instance, Dutch natives experienced irritation toward immigrants from Morocco and Turkey and, as a result, were likely to experience readiness to engage in verbal and physical aggression toward the group.

If we consider, consistent with the appraisal model of emotions (see Chapter 1 and "Intergroup emotions theories," below), that each emotion motivates a distinct set of behaviors, then discrete emotions should better predict intergroup behavior than do global evaluations.

Finally, a more elaborated version of the stereotype-emotion-prejudice hypothesis, which includes some features of Smith's model, has been presented by Fiske and colleagues (Fiske, Cuddy, & Glick 2002; Fiske, Cuddy, Glick, & Xu, 2002). In their stereotype content model (SCM), specific features of the stereotypes generate discrete emotions, and actions, toward the outgroup. In line with the stereotype-emotion-prejudice hypothesis (see Figure 7.3, model B), this account holds that stereotypes determine the appraisals of the outgroup and their behavior, which in turn results in specific emotions characterizing the nature of prejudice felt toward that group.

Fiske and colleagues argue further that the content of the stereotypes is organized by two central dimensions: *competence* and *warmth*. Competence is positively correlated with the perceived status of the group, whereas warmth is negatively correlated with the perceived competition of the outgroup. The specific emotions, and the related prejudice, felt toward one group depend in turn on the perception of the group on these two dimensions. If the group is appraised as warm (noncompetitive) and not competent (low status), this should produce feelings of sympathy and/or pity, which lead to prosocial behavior. Examples of such groups are retarded or disabled individuals. If the group is perceived as cold (competitive) and not competent, this should produce feelings of contempt, which lead to lack of assistance or to aggression. An appraisal of a group as cold and competent will produce envy and jealousy, and will promote aggression tendencies. Finally, groups appraised as competent and warmth (generally ingroups) elicit pride and lead to contact seeking. Similar to the preceding models, this model holds that prejudice should not be conceptualized as general antipathy toward outgroup members. Rather, there are different kinds of prejudice characterized by different emotions toward the outgroup. In contrast to the other models, however, the SCM emphasizes the fact that emotions toward a group are generally mixed, that is both positive and negative emotions may be felt simultaneously toward a group, and that these emotions occur as a function of the perceived warmth and competence of group.

In sum, the different accounts of prejudice just reviewed emphasize the emotional component of prejudice. The relative failure to consider emotions in theorizing and reseach on prejudice for many years may help to explain why previous research generally observed weak relationships between the extent to which stereotypes content is negative and the degree of self-reported prejudice, on the one hand (e.g., Brigham, 1971; Jussim et al., 1995; Stangor et al., 1991), and between prejudice and behavior, on the other hand (e.g., LaPiere, 1934). In all such work, prejudice was measured as a general antipathy to, or dislike of, the outgroup. Clearly, it is something more complex than reported dislike.

Intergroup Contact and Emotions

Intergroup contact is often problematic. Even though more frequent contact between groups has been suggested as a useful way to reduce intergroup conflict and prejudice (e.g., Tropp & Pettigrew, 2004), in fact such contact frequently enhances prejudice (e.g., Amir, 1969; Worchel, 1986). Most importantly, intergroup contact seems to increase anxiety among the individuals of the interacting groups (Islam & Hewstone, 1993; Stephan & Stephan, 1985). And this anxiety may increase for a variety of reasons (Stephan & Stephan, 1985). First, individuals may fear negative consequences of the contact for their sense of self-worth. For instance, they may anticipate feeling embarrassed about not knowing what to do or what to talk about with an outgroup member. This is especially likely when an individual encounters someone with a different cultural background. In addition, on some occasions, and depending on the relationships between the groups in question, the individual may also fear negative behavioral consequences, for example, being harmed physically. Finally, individuals may more simply anticipate negative evaluations by the outgroup members, and also from the ingroup members, either because they have agreed to have contact with an outgroup member, or because their behavior toward the outgroup member has been evaluated as inadequate. Their behavior could be judged as, for instance, either too friendly or too discriminating depending of the norms of the ingroup.

Imagine the situation of a white individual who has had very little experience with black individuals. In a contact situation with black people, even if the white person has good intentions, he may feel anxious about not doing things "right" in the interaction situation. He may wonder how to act (e.g., not too friendly, but not with too much distance either). He may also wonder what conversation topics might be of interest to the others. Which topic would risk making them ill at ease? In such a situation, and because of the high level of uncertainty of the person, it is likely that the white person may anticipate receiving a negative judgment from the outgroup as well as from the ingroup members. In addition, the intergroup context of interaction could also contribute strongly to the level of anxiety aroused by the situation. For instance, situations of competition with another group, or involving self-disclosure, are particularly anxiety arousing (Wilder & Shapiro, 1989b).

What are the consequences of anxiety? First, because the individual is preoccupied with the situation he may express fewer than expected positive emotions, and may express serious or somewhat negative facial expressions of emotion, even without, or especially without, being aware of doing so. Therefore, it is possible that in intergroup contact situations, individuals exhibit negative facial displays, triggered by either the situation (e.g., attempt to control one's responses) or by outgroup members themselves (e.g., Vanman, Paul, Ito, & Miller, 1997). Outgroup members may interpret these expressions, accurately or inaccurately, as an indicator of negative attitude toward their group. Of course, it could be proposed that, at least if they are conscious of possible negative emotional expressions, individuals try to control and attenuate their expressions in order to look natural and avoid direct negative reactions from outgroup members. But in general individuals fail at this. This is because, as already mentioned, individuals are frequently unaware of their facial expressions. Moreover, even in situations in which they are conscious of potentially expressing negative emotions toward the outgroup, their efforts to control these emotional expressions are likely to backfire and to have unexpected negative consequences.

Research by Leyens, Demoulin, Désert, Vaes, and Philippot (2002) is particularly relevant here. These researchers found that white Belgian participants who posed emotions for a photographer thought they did better when the photographer was a black African (outgroup member) than when he was a white Belgian. In contrast, independent judges rated the performance of the "models" as better when the photographer was an ingroup member than when he was an outgroup member (and, importantly, the judges were not aware of the photographer's group membership). Moreover, results of a second study suggest that these effects were attributable to participants' attempts to look natural and undiscriminating, that is to control their emotional expression. In this experiment, Leyens and colleagues asked the participants to either act as if the black photographer were white (color-blindness condition), or to act as a white person would in front of a black photographer (color-consciousness condition). In a control condition, no specific instructions were given. The authors reasoned that if problems of emotional communication to out-group members were attributable to individuals' attempts to look natural and undiscriminating, the worst performance in posing would be found in the color-blindness condition, because their efforts to be natural would interfere with their expression of emotion. In contrast, allowing people to freely be different from outgroup members, as in the color-consciousness condition, should increase performance because participants would not have to control their emotional expression. The findings of the study were consistent with these hypotheses. Individuals acting like white Belgians in front of a black African photographer expressed the most natural emotions. They appeared to be relieved of their concern about presenting themselves naturally.

Another negative consequence of anxiety in intergroup situations is that it may increase the degree to which the outgroup members appear similar to each other. This has been called *perceived homogeneity*. In a series of studies, Wilder and Shapiro (1989b) induced high (vs. low) levels of anxiety in participants by having them compete (vs. cooperate) with another group. For example, some participants first had to complete an urban planning task in four-person groups. They then watched another four-person group give them feedback on their own performance through a TV monitor. Although the "real" group of participants did not know it, this second group was actually composed of confederates of the experimenter who had been prerecorded. Three of the four members of the ostensible other group gave negative feedback whereas one gave positive feedback, and thus was atypical of the group. Later the real participants evaluated the members of this fictitious group. Evaluations of the atypical person were *assimilated* toward the evaluations of the other three group members, such that high anxiety participants evaluated that person more negatively than did low anxiety participants.

Interestingly, these findings have been replicated whether the source of anxiety was caused in some way by the other group (Wilder & Shapiro, 1989b), or the anxiety was induced through a laboratory manipulation that was unrelated to the other group. For example, Wilder and Shapiro (1989a) induced anxiety in their participants by having them anticipate an embarrassing (vs. non-embarrassing) speech, being photographed in ridiculous clothing, or receiving electric shocks (Wilder & Shapiro, 1989a). Moreover, Wilder and Shapiro demonstrated that their findings could not be interpreted as mood-congruence effects. They found indeed that being highly anxious leads individuals to see an atypically *negative* group member as more similar to an otherwise positively evaluated group, and thus rate him more *positively* (Wilder & Shapiro, 1989a). However, because in competitive settings outgroup members are generally perceived negatively, anxiety created by intergroup contact is likely to strengthen the perceived negativity of the outgroup, prejudice and thus conflict.

Other studies have generalized these findings to more realistic settings. As an example, Islam and Hewstone (1993) conducted a survey of Hindu and Muslim students in Bangladesh. The student participants answered a series of questions about quantitative (e.g., amount of contact with outgroup members at college) as well as quantitative aspects of outgroup contact (e.g., whether the contact was perceived as equal), intergroup aspects of contact (e.g., contact as individuals or members of one's group), and perceived outgroup homogeneity. Moreover, the participants completed the intergroup anxiety scale (Stephan & Stephan, 1985). In this study, intergroup anxiety was negatively related to the number of intergroup contacts and to quality of intergroup contact, and was positively related to the level of intergroup (as opposed to interpersonal) contact. In turn, an increase in intergroup anxiety was associated with an increase in perceived outgroup homogeneity and to more negative attitudes toward the outgroup.

In a related study on the relationship between British and Japanese nationals, Greenland and Brown (1999) found that intergroup categorization, favoritism toward the ingroup, and negative affect toward the outgroup were predicted by intergroup anxiety. Intergroup anxiety was also found to be one of the best predictors of negative attitudes towards outgroup in whites vs. Native Canadians relationships (Corenblum & Stephan, 2001), toward African Americans (Britt, Boniecki, Vescio, Biernat, & Brown, 1996), or children with HIV (Greenland, Masser, & Prentice, 2001; see also Stephan et al., 2002).

However, interestingly and consistent with the research presented in Chapter 6, it has been shown that happiness can cause somewhat similar ways of perceiving and judging the outgroup as does anxiety. For instance, Stroessner and Mackie (1992; see, for more detailed presentations, Mackie, Queller, Stroessner, & Hamilton, 1996) made participants feel happy, sad, or a neutral state, with the use of videoclips, and then asked them to read behavioral descriptions of the members of a fictitious group. Depending on the condition, the behaviors were high (vs. low) in variability such that the members were described as not very similar, or very similar. The results indicated that only participants in a neutral state were sensitive to the objective variability of the group members in their judgments of similarity. Both happy and sad participants did not seem to notice that group members were similar, or homogeneous, in one condition and quite variable in another.

In a related experiment, Queller, Mackie, and Stroessner (1996) had happy and neutral mood participants read descriptions of eight "surfers" (i.e., individuals who spend much of their time surfboarding) and form an impression of each individual. The descriptions contained six behavioral statements. Some of the behavioral statements were associated with traits stereotypic of surfers (e.g., "casual," "clique-ish"), others were associated with counterstereotypic traits (e.g., "success oriented," "intellectual") and the remaining were unrelated to the stereotype of surfers. In one condition, the 12 counterstereotypic statements were concentrated in the descriptions of two individuals (*concentrated* condition), whereas they were dispersed across six out of the eight surfers in the other condition (*dispersed* condition). In the dispersed condition, happy participants made higher estimates of stereotype consistent behaviors as well as lower estimates of behavioral inconsistencies than participants in a neutral mood. No difference was found in the concentrated condition. These results suggest that, like anxiety, happiness increases the perceived homogeneity of the outgroup but only when there are no highly atypical members. In a second study, happy participants perceived the group as more homogenous than the neutral participants when they had been instructed to form an impression of the members of the group. However, this effect disappeared when the participants' attention was drawn to the differences between the targets by instructing them to sort the descriptions of the target into piles that represented differences among them. Finally, completing this view, Abele, Gendolla, and Petzold (1998) demonstrated that happiness can increase discrimination toward outgroup members in minimal group context (i.e., the groups were defined for the experimental session on the basis of a bogus criterion; e.g., overestimators vs. underestimators on a dot estimation task).

It appears, therefore, that emotions triggered in intergroup contact situations, whether they are negative (e.g., anxiety) or positive (e.g., happiness), increase the perceived homogeneity of the outgroup. By most accounts, the increase in perceived homogeneity is due to a reduced attention to inconsistent information. This explanation is consistent with the one offered by Gudykunst and colleagues (e.g., Gudykunst & Shapiro, 1996; Hubbert, Gudykunst, & Guerrero, 1999; Stephan, Stephan, & Gudykunst, 1999) in accounting for problems of intergroup communication. According to this account, when anxiety exceeds some threshold, communication between groups becomes less effective because anxiety reduces attentional focus and leads people to process information in a simplistic manner. As a result, individuals exaggerate the similarities between members of outgroups and treat their message superficially, and are thus more likely to engage in discriminatory behavior toward them. However, having these individuals focused on differences between groups could help weaken the impact of emotions (e.g., Queller et al., 1996).

The similarity between the effects of happiness and anxiety is intriguing. What is common to happiness and anxiety? One common feature is the level of arousal that characterizes the two states. Indeed, even though happiness and anxiety differ in valence they are both characterized by a relatively high level of arousal. Arousal may produce a cognitive load that causes a failure to perceive differences among outgroup members and even produces negative impressions. However, recall that Stroessner and Mackie (1992) also found that sadness produced the same effects as happiness. These two affective states are generally considered as differing in their level of arousal, which is typically low for sadness. This thus casts some doubt on arousal as the explanatory mechanism.

Another account can be offered at least for the impact of negative emotions on intergroup perception. As we have already mentioned, the contact situation may be perceived as anxiety inducing because individuals may anticipate an unpleasant interaction due to the fact that they do not know exactly how to act in such a situation. It is then possible that such negative feelings may be misattributed to the outgroup members following the mood-as-information processes described in Chapter 6 (Britt et al., 1996). Thus, such processes could lead to increased negativity, that is, prejudice and discrimination, toward the outgroup. However, as we have mentioned, this explanation would not be easily applicable to the effects of positive emotions.

A first look at the effects of emotions on intergroup perception and intergroup relations may lead to a pessimistic view of the situation. We have shown that emotions are frequently aroused in intergroup situations, and that whether positive or negative, they would lead to a more stereotyped perception of the outgroup. Moreover, negative emotions have been shown to strengthen prejudice.

These results may also be considered in a more optimistic way, however. If happiness decreases attention allocated to inconsistent information, it may have at least two potential positive consequences on intergroup perception. First, happy, but also anxious individuals should be more prone to consider members of two groups (ingroup and outgroup) as belonging to the same group (Dovidio et al., 1995), at least if attention is directed toward group similarities and not group differences (Dovidio, Gaertner, & Loux, 2000). Second, happiness and anxiety should interfere with the production of distinctiveness-based illusory correlations (Stroessner, Hamilton, & Mackie, 1992), a phenomenon that has sometimes been considered as involving processes at stake in the formation of social stereotypes (Hamilton & Gifford, 1976). Finally, a positive consequence may arise from the recent conceptions of prejudice (see "Emotion as a predictor of intergoup attitudes and behavior" in this chapter). If we consider that prejudice is a main cause of the failure of intergroup relations, and if we acknowledge that prejudice is largely determined by emotions elicited by outgroup members, then factors increasing positive affect toward the outgroup, such as cooperation or observation of an outgroup member being a victim of discrimination, may ultimately reduce prejudice and intergroup conflict (Miller, Smith, & Mackie, 2004), as suggested by recent meta-analyses (Tropp & Pettigrew, 2004), and may also increase individuals' willingness to engage in contact with outgroup members (Esses & Dovidio, 2002).

Emotions on Behalf of One's Group and Intergroup Behavior

We have already discussed the role of emotions in intergroup contact. However, it is often the case that individuals develop attitudes toward an outgroup and behave toward members of this group without having ever been in direct contact with outgroup members. For instance, on September 11, 2001, extremist Muslim terrorists attacked the World Trade Center in New York and the Pentagon in Washington, killing thousands of people. Americans as well as people from some European countries supported the decision by the United States to go to war against Afghanistan. It seems that inhabitants of these countries developed a negative attitude toward Afghans, and yet most of them had never encountered one. In a similar way, the refusal of the French president Jacques Chirac to engage France in the coalition that went to war in Iraq two years later led numerous Americans to engage in discrimination toward French people and products imported from France. However, the refusal of the French president did not affect many of them personally, and the persons who were the object of prejudice had nothing to do directly with their president (some of the French believed, for instance, that France should go to war in Iraq too). How can we explain such behaviors?

Anger and Fear

Research by Doosje and colleagues, discussed earlier, suggests that individuals can experience emotions on behalf of their group. We can now complete this picture by adding that emotions on behalf of one's group are often directed toward an outgroup and that such emotions guide behavior toward the outgroup. For instance, anger is considered to be an emotion that typically occurs when someone feels threatened but also feels strong enough to confront the threat (Frijda, 1986; Smith, 1993).

Recent research has found that individuals who were not the object of aggression or of direct threat may experience anger if members of a group to which they identify are under threat. As an example, Mackie and colleagues (2000) had participants categorize themselves as either members of a group in favor of equal rights for homosexual couples, or as members of a group opposed to that position. All participants then read a list of newspaper headlines. Depending on the condition, the majority of the headlines (16 out of 19) supported the position of their group (strong position condition) or opposed it (weak position condition). Consistent with the hypotheses, participants reported more anger and more action tendencies to act out against the outgroup in the strong than in the weak position condition.

In similar vein, Gordijn, Wigboldus, and Yzerbyt (2001) used a clever means to manipulate the salience of group membership or self-categorization in order to test more thoroughly its impact. They described to students from Amsterdam University an unfair decision that professors of another university (Leiden) had made regarding increases in study load for students at that other university. Half the participants were led to categorize themselves as members of the same group as the students who were the targets of the unfair decision by having them focus on the differences between students and professors. The other half were led to categorize themselves in a different group from the students who were the targets of the unfair decision by having their attention drawn to differences between the two universities, Amsterdam and Leiden. In a control condition, the attention of the participants was not manipulated. As expected, after hearing about the unfair decision participants felt more anger and less happiness if they had been led to categorize themselves as students than if they had been led to categorize themselves as different from the other students or than the individuals in the control condition. Moreover, as was the case in Mackie and colleagues' studies, the effects were only apparent on anger-related but not on anxiety-related measures, suggesting that the reactions were emotion specific.

These findings have been generalized to emotions other than anger, including fear. For instance, Dumont, Yzerbyt, Wigboldus, and Gordijn (2003) had Belgian and Dutch students complete a questionnaire approximately 10 days after September 11 terrorist attacks. Participants were informed that the aim of the study was either to compare the emotional reactions of Europeans as opposed to Americans, or the attitude of Arabs as opposed to westerners toward the September 11 terrorist attacks. In this way, a common social group including both the victims and the participants (ingroup) was made salient in the second condition whereas it was not in the first one. Again, participants experienced more intense emotions, and in the present case fear, when they were led to think of the victims as members of the ingroup (i.e., westerners) than when they were led to think of them as an outgroup (i.e., Americans).

Finally, Yzerbyt and colleagues (2003) extended these findings by showing that the effects were moderated by ingroup identification. That is, the salience of a similar group membership with other persons led participants to experience more intensely the emotions experienced by ingroup members (anger in the present case) to the extent that the individuals identified strongly with the ingroup. It is worth noting that parallel effects were observed on intentions of action. That is, participants in conditions eliciting the most anger were also the most prone to engage in action tendencies related to anger, thus to aggress against the outgroup. Complementary analyses revealed that the effects of identification with the victims on intentions to engage in aggressive action tendencies were mediated by anger. That is, if self-reported anger was statistically controlled, the impact of identification on offensive action tendencies was no longer significant (see also Yzerbyt, Dumont, Gordijn, & Wigboldus, 2002). Therefore, group-based emotions, like anger, are a basis for collective action in situations in which individuals strongly identify with an ingroup facing an unfair decision but who perceive themselves as having the power of changing the state of affairs (Van Zomeren, Spears, Fischer, & Leach, 2004).

In spite of their importance, these studies need to be generalized to real behaviors. Up to now, behavior is mainly assessed in these studies by measures of behavioral tendencies. There are two limitations of this approach. First, we cannot be completely sure that people would indeed engage in behaviors such as collective action, physical aggression, prosocial behavior, in real-life situations. Moreover, in paper-and-pencil studies, because there is no necessity for them to engage in real behavior, participants may have relied on naive theories concerning the elicitation of social emotions and their role in social behavior. Given the potential implications of such research, studies exploring the impact of social emotions on real behaviors would be very useful.

Schadenfreude

Of the intergroup emotions studied in social psychology research, Schadenfreude is at the same time somewhat obscure and of particular interest. A German word, Schadenfreude refers to the malicious pleasure one may feel when seeing someone suffer. This emotion is of importance because, even though it cannot explain why members of some groups have persecuted members of other groups (e.g., Jews, homosexuals during World War II; Tutsis in Rwanda), it may help explain why a vast majority of people did not intervene to stop the process (see Spears & Leach, 2004).

Not surprisingly, Schadenfreude is likely to be observed in situations of rivalry. For example, Dutch people see Germans as rivals in numerous domains, especially in soccer. Therefore, the passive observation of a defeat of the German national soccer team should produce in Dutch individuals a sensation of pleasure, even if the Germans were not specifically defeated by the Dutch team. Leach, Spears, Branscombe, and Doosje (2003) observed exactly this in Dutch participants who had been reminded of Germany's loss to Croatia in the quarterfinals of the 1998 World Cup championship. This example of Schadenfreude is particularly interesting, in that it refers to an emotional experience in conditions in which neither the individuals nor their ingroup directly experienced the emotion-eliciting event.

Intergroup Emotions Theories

Smith's intergroup emotions theory has been recently proposed to integrate and account for many of the findings presented thus far in the chapter (IET, Smith, 1993; see also Devos, Mackie, Silver, & Smith, 2002; Mackie et al., 2000). The IET stresses the importance of specific emotions in prejudice and intergroup behavior by trying to wed important ideas from social identity theory (Tajfel, 1982) and its extensions in self-categorization theory (Turner, Hogg, Oakes, Reicher, & Wetherell, 1987) with appraisal theories of emotion (e.g., Frijda, 1986; Smith & Ellsworth, 1985; see Chapter 1).

Based on principles of social identity theory, the IET assumes that a part of the self, referred to as "social identity," is determined by one's social category memberships and their affective implications. Depending on the situation, this part of the self is more or less salient and thus differentially affects self-perception as well as behavior. If no category membership, thus no social identity, is salient, an individual will think of herself as a unique individual characterized by idiosyncratic properties, and will act toward others on this basis. However, when one of an individual's group memberships becomes salient, the related social identity of the individual becomes salient too. The individual perceives herself as a member of the group, characterized by the attributes of the group. In such a condition, her behavior toward others is guided by group membership.

According to appraisal theories of emotion, the self must be involved in the emotion-eliciting situation in order for the individual to experience an emotion. Smith and colleagues propose that, because social identity becomes an integral part of the self when social identity is salient, appraisal theories of emotion are applicable at the group level in such conditions. Therefore, events or situations in which appraisals elicit a specific emotion among members of the ingroup should also affect other members of the group who are not directly confronted with the eliciting events. In such cases, individuals may experience emotions on behalf of their (in)group as predicted by appraisal theories of emotions as well as the corresponding actions tendencies directed toward the outgroup (see Table 7.1). For instance, if an individual who identifies strongly with his group believes that fellow ingroup members are hindered in the attainment of a goal by outgroup members, and he also believes that he has sufficient resources to confront the outgroup, he will likely feel anger and engage in offensive behavior toward outgroup members (see, for instance, Mackie et al., 2000). In contrast, if the same person believes he is unable to change the situation, the emotion felt is more likely to be anxiety or fear, which is associated with defensive intergroup behavior (i.e., avoidance).

TABLE 7.1

Examples of Emotions, Main Causes, Their Associated Action Tendencies, and Related Intergroup Behaviors

Emotion	Cause	Action Tendencies	Intergroup Behavior
Anger	Obstacle in goal attainment (e.g., by a powerless outgroup)	Approach to aggress and suppress the obstacle (i.e., move against)	Aggression; discrimination
Disgust	Contamination (e.g., by a low-status outgroup)	Rejection	Avoidance of outgroup members
Fear	Threat to group safety (e.g., by a powerful outgroup)	Escape the situation; protection	Avoidance of outgroup members
Guilt	Perception of one's own (group) unfairness	Reparation	Reconciliatory behavior
Sadness (pity)	Others in need; object of unfairness	Self-contemplation, reflection; apathy	Pro-social behavior

From Neuberg, S. L., & Cottrell, C. A. (2002). Intergroup emotions: A biocultural approach. In D. M. Mackie, & E. R. Smith (Eds.), *From prejudice to intergroup emotions: Differentiated reactions to social groups* (pp. 265–283). New York: Psychology Press; Smith, E. R. (1993). Social identity and social emotions: Toward new conceptualizations of prejudice. In D. M. Mackie, & D. L. Hamilton (Eds.), *Affect, cognition, and stereotyping: Interactive group processes in group perception* (pp. 297–315). San Diego, CA: Academic Press.

As already mentioned, the IET can be used to account for the apparently weak links between prejudice and behavior that have been observed in previous studies in which prejudice is measured in a very general way (e.g., I don't like this group) and then used to predict many different negative behaviors (e.g., discrimination, avoidance, rejection). The IET suggests that prejudice must be conceptualized as a specific emotion (e.g., anger, fear, disgust) that causes related specific behaviors (e.g., aggression and discrimination, avoidance, or rejection, respectively). Therefore, in contrast with the more traditional view that holds that the content of the stereotypes (i.e., beliefs; e.g., they are dirty, stupid, hostile) determines attitudes toward the outgroup (i.e., prejudice; e.g., I don't like them), which in turn lead to intergroup behavior (e.g., discrimination), Smith proposes that appraisals of the situations produce social emotions that guide behavior toward the outgroup, irrespective of the stereotype content.

Neuberg and Cottrell (2002; Cottrell & Neuberg, 2005) propose a related model based on a functional approach to emotions. This "biocultural approach" relies on two basic assumptions. According to the first, emotions serve individuals in the attainment of their basic human motives, which concern survival in order to mate and to reproduce (see Chapter 2). Anything that interferes with the individual's ability to satisfy these motives is considered as a threat. Neuberg and Cottrell also propose that emotions activate the action program adapted to respond to this threat.

The second basic assumption is that humans have evolved as a group-living species, life in cooperative groups having higher survival and reproductive values than solitary life. Because group life facilitates access to opportunities as well as a successful management of threat, individuals are very concerned by group-level threats. These group-level threats concern both the resources of the group (e.g., physical safety, territory) as well as its integrity (e.g., trust, social coordination, values). As in previously seen theories, depending on the threat, different appraisals will be aroused that will activate the corresponding emotion and the associated action tendencies. For instance, a threat to group safety will elicit fear in individuals who will then feel a need to escape the threat, whereas if possessions are threatened by another group, individuals will experience anger and probably aggress the other group.

The model proposed by Neuberg and Cottrell thus shares many features with the IET. They both consider that parts of the self-concept can be defined at the individual as well as the group levels and that prejudice corresponds to specific differentiated emotions that lead to specific actions toward the outgroup, depending on the appraisals of the situation. However, the model proposed by Neuberg and Cottrell differs from the IET mainly in the fact that they consider that the connection between the self and the group is biologically grounded rather than learned as assumed by social identity theory.

Emotional Consequences of Prejudice and Discrimination

Although without a doubt prejudice toward some groups of people is more explicit and pervasive than is prejudice toward other groups, most people have been the target of prejudice at some time in their lives. Being the target of prejudice is a very unpleasant and emotionally charged experience (see Major, Quinton, & McCoy, 2002, for a presentation of the effects of prejudice on wellbeing). But exactly what kinds of emotion are elicited by such treatment, that is, of perceiving oneself as being the object of prejudice, whether real or imagined? Most of the studies related to the impact of prejudice on people's feelings have looked at its effect on self-esteem (see, for overviews, Major et al., 2002; Schmitt & Branscombe, 2002), but very few have directly explored the emotional consequences of prejudice. As an exception, Major and colleagues (e.g., Kaiser & Major, 2004) proposed that prejudice triggers different negative emotions depending on whether the self or others are considered responsible for the negative treatment. When the self is perceived as responsible for the treatment, self-directed emotions (e.g., shame) are more likely aroused. When it is attributed to others, other-directed emotions (e.g., anger, resentment) are more likely to be felt.

Moreover, as is assumed in other research that has already been presented in this chapter (Doosje et al., 1998; Smith, 1993), this approach holds that group memberships constitute important parts of the self (i.e., social identity) that are activated in situations in which they are made salient (Tajfel, 1982). As a result, whereas individuals feel emotions directed to a specific individual (self or other, depending on the attribution for the negative treatment) when no particular group membership is salient, in situations where the social identity is salient, they are particularly attentive to outcomes at the group level, and are more likely to experience emotions at this level, either on behalf of the ingroup or toward the outgroup depending on the self/other direction of the emotion.

In sum, Major and colleagues predict that prejudice and discrimination are more likely to engender sadness or shame in individuals when the treatment is perceived as deserved. These emotions can be experienced at the group or at the individual level depending on whether individuals' social identity is or is not salient, respectively. In contrast, if prejudice is perceived as undeserved, individuals experience anger and resentment toward either the individual or the group responsible for this behavior.

Therefore, it appears that the perception of deservedness of the discriminatory behavior is an important determinant of the effects of prejudice and discrimination on emotions (Kaiser & Major, 2004).

Consistent with this model, Crocker, Cornwell, and Major (1993) found that overweight women who were refused as a partner by an attractive man (who knew their weight) attributed the refusal to their weight and not to the man's personality, and felt more depressed than average weight women who received the same treatment. An explanation of this finding is that because weight is typically considered to be controllable, overweight participants perceived the treatment as deserved and thus experienced self-directed emotions. In contrast, individuals who were treated negatively (i.e., they were denied participation in an important course by the professor) because of their gender, that is, an uncontrollable factor, experienced less sadness than participants who were treated in a similar way because of their personal characteristics (i.e. the professor thought they were unintelligent). However, participants in the two conditions did not differ in their level of anger (other-directed emotion) which was significantly greater than in a third condition in which everyone was rejected (Major, Kaiser, & McCoy, 2003).

Schmitt, Branscombe, and Postmes (2003) identified another important factor that determines the intensity of emotional reactions to prejudice: the pervasiveness of the discriminatory behavior. They reasoned that a specific act of discrimination should affect individuals more strongly when it is generalized, or perceived as pervasive, and therefore not attributable to an isolated act of hostility. In such cases, the negative treatment (i.e., discrimination) is perceived as being potentially recurrent in the future, as uncontrollable.

In order to test the role of pervasiveness of the prejudice, Schmitt and colleagues (2003) had undergraduate women take part in a study about "employment interview process." They were told that they would participate in a mock job interview with one of 20 business people, who constituted a representative sample of people conducting employment interviews. Participants were asked to act as if they were applying for a job. When the interview was over, the participants waited for their evaluation. The experimenter then confided to them that the interviewer was different from the 19 others in that he was either giving everyone a negative evaluation (nonsexist condition), or in that he was giving women a negative evaluation while he was giving a positive evaluation to men (rare sexism condition). In a third condition, the experimenter said that all the 20 interviewers gave negative evaluations to women and positive evaluations to men (pervasive sexism condition). Finally, the participants received their evaluation forms, which were negative, and completed several measures including a composite measure of affect. Results indicated that women felt more negative affect when the negative feedback was attributed to general prejudice against women (i.e., sexism) than when it could be attributed to idiosyncratic features of the interviewer himself (i.e., negativity in the nonsexist condition or sexism in the rare sexism condition), thus highlighting the role of the perception of pervasiveness of discrimination in affective reactions to this kind of behavior.

These studies thus support the idea that prejudice and acts of discrimination elicit different negative emotions of different intensities depending on specific features of the situation as for example the perceived deservingness and pervasiveness of the prejudiced treatment. However, this research is recent and this issue has not yet received the attention it deserves. More research is needed to further explore these fascinating and socially important issues.

Summary

In the introduction to this chapter, we posed several questions about emotions in groups. These questions were related to the nature, measure, and propagation of emotions in the group as well as to the role of emotions in intergroup relations. The research we reviewed suggests that emotions play a central role in social life, both within the group, and in intergroup perception and behavior.

First, we saw that emotions propagate rapidly within the group due to a number of processes including imitation, empathy, and communication. Even though group-level emotions so far have not been demonstrated to differ in nature from individual emotions, they may have specific features depending on the social context in which they are aroused. For instance, we have suggested that emotion contagion mechanisms cause emotions experienced at the group level to be more intense and longer lasting than individual emotions, and that group-level emotions could be induced in the individual while he or she is not in direct contact with the emotion-eliciting event.

Emotion also plays a crucial role in intergroup perception and intergroup conflict. The intensity of the emotions felt toward the outgroup, for example, appears to be one of the most powerful predictors of prejudice and intergroup behavior. And emotions that are felt on behalf of one's group can also lead to both prosocial and aggressive behaviors, particularly when one is highly identified with the group.

In conclusion, although having the potential to provide a fuller understanding of group performance and intergroup relations, and suggesting means of reducing intergroup conflict, research on group-level emotions has remained relatively marginal until recently. The number of studies published on this area has dramatically increased in recent years. We are convinced that this is a research area that will provide important contributions to social psychology literature in the coming years.

Gender Differences in Emotion Processes

8

▶ *Contents at a Glance*

In the repertoire of American country and western music there are literally thousands of songs about men and women and their emotions. What might those songs say? If you were to guess, perhaps you would wager that the words likely tell stories of women falling in love, completely losing control of their emotions, and of men putting on their hats, squaring their shoulders and their jaws, and riding into the sunset without looking back. Perhaps even going off to ride in the rodeo. If that is what you guessed, you would be relying on the stereotype that women are emotional and emotionally expressive, and that men are stoic and slightly overwhelmed by expressions of emotion by women. But then you might listen to the words of a song sung by country and western star Randy Travis, entitled "What'll you do about me?" Here is how it begins: All you wanted was a one-night stand/The fire of the wine and the touch of a man/But I fell in love and ruined all of your plans/Now what'll you do about me?

Well, well. Who lost control of his emotions here?

In western cultures, the belief in the emotional woman and the rational (as in unemotional) man is well documented, and largely endorsed by both men and women. Women are held to be the more tender sex, having greater emotional insight, that is, being more emotionally responsive, and also being more empathetic and sensitive to the feeling of others. Women are also believed to be more inclined to express their feelings without constraint, with the exception of anger, which is generally associated with men. And, women are thought to be moody, emotionally unstable, to cry a lot, or even to be hysterical, while men keep cool and maintain self-control. Men are also believed to be stoic, to not grieve openly, and more generally, to control their feelings and inhibit the expression of their feelings.

But what about those wildly gesticulating men, shouting with joy over the victory of their favorite soccer team, and those who insult or physically attack the referee for having called an unjustified penalty? And what about those men in the supermarket who bristle with impatience and annoyance in the long line at the checkout, and those fathers who melt with love and affection at the mere sight of their own baby? And what, finally, about those men in so many country and western songs? Everyone can recall examples of men seemingly in the throes of strong emotion. Is the belief in the emotional woman and the unemotional man a myth?

In this chapter, we will try to disentangle the complex relationship between gender and emotion. We will first examine the content of stereotypic beliefs about men's and women's emotions, and how they generalize across specific emotions and social contexts. Then we turn to the question of whether these gender stereotypes accurately reflect sex differences in emotions, or to the contrary if they create them. In other words, do men and women actually differ in their emotional experience and expressions, and in their judgment of others' emotions, or are all such processes biased by stereotypical beliefs? In the last part of the chapter, we will discuss how social roles, socialization history, and culture contribute to gender differences in emotions beyond biological sex.

Having used both the terms sex and gender, we should stop to clarify our terminology. Some authors have argued that sex and gender should be clearly distinguished (Deaux, 1993; Shields, 2000, 2002), with sex referring to the biological attributes of a person with respect to being male and female (i.e., a biologically defined category), and gender referring to the psychological and sociocultural characteristics associated with maleness and femaleness (i.e., a social category). Gender can thus be viewed as sex put into social terms. In this chapter, we use these two closely related terms interchangeably, because they have been so used in much of the empirical literature. However, we do try to follow the recommendation of Deaux (1993) and Shields (2002) by using terms such as gender identity, gender stereotypes, and gender roles, where judgments and inferences about the social nature of maleness and femaleness are fundamental.

Stereotypical Beliefs about the Experience, Expression, and Judgment of Emotion

The stereotype that women are more emotional than men seems to be strongly embedded in western culture. But what does "more emotional" really mean? In general terms, individuals understand "being emotional" as the tendency to respond too quickly – without control – and too much – too intensely – to emotion-eliciting events. Furthermore, individuals tend to interpret the meaning of "emotional" per se differently for men and women. A man's "emotional" reaction in response to an upsetting event (e.g., his car has been stolen) is typically attributed to excusable situational factors while a female's "emotional" reaction to the same upsetting event is attributed more to her personality (Shields, 2002). Therefore, given the same reaction to the same event, the man is not labelled "emotional" whereas the woman is.

The folk concept of "emotionality" can thus be criticized as too simple because it implies that (women's) emotional reactions are based on a general stable personality trait (Fischer, 1993a). As we have seen throughout this book, emotions are not only determined by personal emotional style but also by the social environment. Emotions are experienced and expressed in specific social and cultural contexts, which provide norms that prescribe the emotions that are appropriate to a given situation. The concept of emotionality is also too global because it does not specify the component of the emotion that is supposedly exaggerated in women, or the specific emotions contained in the stereotype. When we say that women are "emotional," do we mean that they express emotion more easily and intensely than men or do we mean that they feel these states more easily and intensely than men? Similarly, do women experience all emotions more easily and more strongly than men? Or are certain emotions

The emotional lives of men and women?

prototypic to the concept of "emotionality"? And finally, why are women compared to men as a baseline? Could it not be that men are emotionally "handicapped" (see the notion of restrictive male emotionality; Jansz, 2000)? It is to these questions that we turn next.

Specific Gender Stereotypes

Component-specific Gender Stereotypes

Stereotypical beliefs about sex differences in emotions have been documented for both emotional experience and emotional expression, but the stereotype tends to apply more to emotional expressiveness. Thus, men and women are considered to differ more in their overt emotional display than in their feelings, again such that women express their emotions more than men (Fabes & Martin, 1991; Grossman & Wood, 1993; Johnson & Shulman, 1988). Women are also thought to be more sensitive to others, to pay more attention to others' body language and to possess better decoding skills, that is, they are thought to be better at judging others' emotions from nonverbal cues (Briton & Hall, 1995).

Emotion-specific Gender Stereotypes

A closer examination of the content of adults' beliefs about sex differences in emotionality indicates that stereotypes not only vary with regard to the emotional components, but also with respect to specific emotions. Fabes and Martin (1991), for example, had male and female participants rate the frequency with which men and women typically experience and express basic emotions (anger, fear, sadness, happiness, surprise) as well as nonbasic emotions (i.e. sympathy, pride, jealousy, hate, guilt, admiration). They compared the aggregate scores for basic and for nonbasic emotions and found that for both kinds of emotion women were rated as expressing, but not as experiencing, the states more often than men. Furthermore, analyses revealed sex differences in emotional expression within basic emotions. Women were believed to express more sadness, fear, and love, while men were believed to express more anger.

Similar emotion-specific stereotypes concerning sex differences in emotional expression have been found in several other studies. Results of these studies suggest that women are believed to smile, laugh, and gaze more (Briton & Hall, 1995) and to express emotions that communicate submissiveness – often called "powerless emotions" – such as sadness, fear, shame. Men, by way of contrast, are believed to be less emotionally expressive overall, but more expressive of emotions that communicate dominance – often called "powerful" emotions – such as anger, contempt, disgust, and pride (Brody & Hall, 1993, 2000; Fischer, 1993b; Grossman & Wood, 1993; Hess, Sénecal, Kirouac, Herrera, Philippot, & Kleck, 2000; Timmers et al., 2003). These gender stereotypes concerning emotional display have also been observed in preschool children (Birnbaum, 1983; Birnbaum, Nosanchuk, & Croll, 1980). Birnbaum and colleagues (1980) had 3- to 5-year-old children and adults identify the sex of gender-neutral puppy dogs depicting happy, angry, fearful, and sad emotions. Children as well as adults associated the drawings of happy-, sad- and fearful-looking puppies with femaleness and angry-looking puppy dogs with maleness (see Figure 8.1).

Situation-specific Gender Stereotypes

The nature of the situation in which an emotion is experienced, for instance, one in which the focus is other-directed versus self-directed, or the basic concern is interpersonal versus achievement, has been found to determine people's stereotypical beliefs about men's and women's emotional expression. Johnson and Shulman (1988) had participants try to imagine a male or female friend in several situations that elicited pleasant and unpleasant other-directed emotions, or so-called *communal* emotions (e.g., being content while relaxing with friends, or being fearful about the

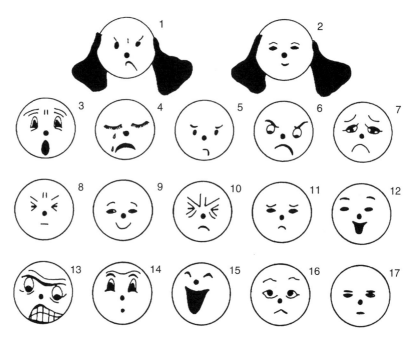

FIGURE 8.1. "Is this a boy puppy or a girl puppy?" Gender-neutral facial stimuli used to measure children's stereotypes about sex differences in emotional expression. From Birnbaum, D. et al. (1980). Children's stereotypes about sex differences in emotionality. *Sex Roles, 6,* 435–443.

health of a relative) and pleasant and unpleasant self-directed emotions (e.g., being proud after receiving the highest grade in the class, or being envious of the superior grade that someone else had received). Participants then evaluated the likelihood with which the male or female friend would experience and overtly express these emotions. Participants judged the likelihood of female friends expressing other-directed emotions as higher, and of expressing self-oriented emotions as lower than male friends. In contrast, male friends were judged to be more likely to express self-oriented emotions and less likely to express communal emotions than female friends.

In a related study, a gender-neutral target person expressing pride over a personal success was rated as more likely to be a man, while the target person expressing pride over another person's success was rated as more likely to be a woman (Stoppard & Gunn Grunchy, 1993). Furthermore, women are expected to be more expressive in interpersonal, relationship-oriented situations, while men's expressivity is associated with achievement situations, and with situations where their autonomy is challenged (Brody, 1997; Kelly & Hutson-Comeaux, 1999). Findings such as these indicate that stereotypical beliefs concerning emotional expression are differentially linked to gender depending on the specific situation in which a given emotion is expressed.

Prescriptive and Descriptive Nature of Gender Stereotypes

Stereotypes about men and women's emotions not only describe what people generally believe about sex differences. Stereotypical beliefs can also represent prescriptive norms that specify the emotional reactions that are appropriate for men and women. Indeed, gender-stereotype-consistent emotional reactions are likely to be socially approved while gender-stereotype-inconsistent emotional behaviors are disapproved and sanctioned (Graham, Gentry, & Green, 1981; Stoppard & Gunn Grunchy, 1993). As an illustration of this, in one study participants were asked to imagine a situation of personal success, such as winning a sports competition or receiving a top exam mark, that occurred either to themselves (*self context*) or to a friend or acquaintance (*other context*) and where the positive feelings over the success were either expressed (self-congratulation or congratulating the friend) or not expressed at all. Participants then rated the likelihood that others would engage in positive, rewarding or negative, costly behavior towards them (being complimented, polite, generous behavior vs. disapproval, social rejection). Female, but not male participants expected more social disapproval for failing to express positive emotions in the other context, but they did not expect different social consequences for the expression and nonexpression of positive emotions focused on the self (Stoppard & Gunn Grunchy, 1993).

Furthermore, women have been found to anticipate more negative social consequences for expressions of anger and aggression, and to be more concerned about how the expression of such emotions might be detrimental for their social relations (Davis, LaRosa, & Foshee, 1992; Eagly & Steffen, 1986). These findings indicate that the gender-specific prescription of the expression of positive emotions is limited to other-directed situations, that is, women are particularly required to express positive emotions towards others, which facilitates social relationships. By the same token, the expression of anger, which may harm relationships with others, tends to be unacceptable for women.

Gender stereotypes have also been found to create expectations that determine the informative value of emotional behavior and its social acceptance. Hutson-Comeaux and Kelly (2002) presented participants with short stories depicting male and female protagonists who displayed exaggerated expressions of typical male (e.g., anger) and typical female (e.g., happiness) emotions. Participants had to evaluate the social appropriateness and sincerity of the protagonists' emotional overreactions.

Examples of these behaviors included distributing one's autographed photo because one's school basketball team won the state title, tearing apart one's best friend's clothes because that friend borrowed and was then careless with one's favorite shirt, and discrediting one's company in public after having been overlooked for a promised promotion. The exaggerated expression of stereotype-consistent emotions was judged as less socially appropriate and less sincere than stereotype-inconsistent expressions. That is, women's happy overreactions were perceived as less socially appropriate and less sincere while the same happy overreactions by men were judged as more sincere. The inverse was true for angry overreactions, which were rated as less appropriate and less sincere when displayed by men for whom the expression of anger is typical, while the same anger overreactions were considered as more sincere when displayed by female protagonists. Consistent with correspondent inference theory (Jones & Davis, 1965) stereotypical emotional behavior was perceived as less informative about the protagonist's dispositions than counterstereotypic behavior.

Zammuner (2000) examined participants' beliefs about the typical (descriptive beliefs) and appropriate emotional reaction (prescriptive beliefs) in response to hypothetical emotion-eliciting situations. Consistent with existing gender stereotypes, the typical man was believed to express more anger, but overall to control his emotions more and to rationalize, while the typical women was perceived as expressing her emotions more – especially powerless or submissive emotions – and as having difficulties in coping with the emotional event. Prescriptive beliefs, however, were found to be less gendered. Interestingly, the powerless emotion of sadness, which was considered as typical for women, was consensually judged as more appropriate for men while the typical male reaction of rationalization was judged as more appropriate for women, indicating that men are allowed to display sadness while women should try to become more rational (and less emotional) when confronting emotional situations.

The direct comparison of descriptive and prescriptive beliefs – comparison of the ratings of how "typical" and how "appropriate" the emotional reactions were – served as an indicator of their social desirability. Negative emotions (e.g., jealousy, envy, sadness, anxiety, disappointment, and anger) as well as the emotion-related behavior of isolation and withdrawal, emotional expressivity, and having difficulties facing the event were rated as more typical than appropriate emotional reactions, indicating that these reactions are socially undesirable. Positive emotions (e.g., joy, gladness), as well as emotional control and rationalization were rated as more appropriate than typical emotional reactions, and thus perceived as more socially desirable. Overall these findings illustrate that the typical male reactions of rationalization and emotional control are still perceived as appropriate and desirable reactions to emotional events in general; in other words, that emotions, and especially negative emotions, should be regulated.

A recent study by Timmers and colleagues (2003) suggests that in western cultures gender emotion stereotypes have recently become less prescriptive in nature. In this study, which was briefly described in Chapter 4, participants had to indicate their agreement with several prescriptive statements (i.e., "men should not cry") and descriptive statements (i.e., "women cry more than men") concerning the emotional behavior of men and women. Overall, participants agreed more with descriptive beliefs than with prescriptive norms. That is, participants agreed that men typically display more powerful emotions of anger and pride, and that women typically express more powerless emotions such as sadness and fear (descriptive beliefs), but they did not prescribe them in the way that past research had shown. Rather, the prescriptive beliefs concerning emotional displays of men and women were quite gender neutral. For instance, participants did not prescribe the masculine stereotype of intolerance of displays of powerless emotions to men and women differentially, suggesting that they believe that men should be allowed to express sadness and fear as much as women. An exception was the feminine stereotype of intolerance of expression of powerful emotions, which was more prescribed for men than women. That is, participants tended to agree that men should not express anger and aggression, probably because men are perceived as more likely to engage in aggressive behavior.

The greater endorsement of stereotypical beliefs about women than men indicates that women are still perceived as the more emotional sex, expressing and sharing their emotions more than men, in particular powerless emotions. Interestingly, this does not imply that stereotypic women are actually more *liked*. Indeed, participants reported stronger negative attitudes towards emotional women than emotional men. The greater tolerance for emotional expression in men may indicate a change in prescriptive norms. Males' emotional expression is perceived less as sign of weakness and irrationality and is considered more as a socially skilled, adaptive behavior that is important in social and working life. The expression of powerless emotions by men gives them extra value, making them suitable for typical female roles without making them unsuitable for male roles (Fischer et al., 2004; Timmers et al., 2003).

Women more than men are thus confronted with a dilemma, because both their emotional expressions, often judged as excessive and exaggerated, and their emotional control may lead to negative evaluations (Hutson-Comeaux & Kelly, 2002; Kelly & Hutson-Comeaux, 2000). In reviewing parenting advice books, Shields, Steinke, and Koster (1995) found that women face an emotional double bind. Mothers, on the one hand, are warned against excessive emotional expression that may be detrimental for the child's development, while at the same time a mother's lack of emotional expression is described to be potentially harmful too. Fathers' emotional expressions, on the other hand, are perceived as more justified because their stereotype-inconsistent emotional behavior reveals their veridical emotional feelings. Moreover, fathers' emotional control is perceived more positively too because it demonstrates their greater objectivity. For women, there exists thus a narrow range concerning the amount of emotional expression that is perceived as appropriate and socially approved.

Do Gender Stereotypes of Emotion Reflect Reality or Create It?

Many studies have found that stereotypes about gender differences in the experience and display of emotions correspond to actual gender differences in emotional experience and expression. Roughly speaking, women report experiencing emotions more intensely and expressing them more and with greater frequency than men. This is particularly true for the powerless emotions of sadness, fear, shame, and guilt as well as socially desirable other-oriented positive emotions such as empathy, sympathy, and love. Men, contrariwise, report expressing more powerful emotions such as anger, contempt, disgust, and pride. These findings seem to indicate that gender stereotypes mirror reality.

However, stereotypes shape reality because they create expectancies about men and women's emotional reactions which may influence one's own behavior, creating self-fulfilling prophecies (Brody & Hall, 2000). As we have seen, gender stereotypes function as social and cultural norms that prescribe how and when and by whom emotion can be expressed; stereotype-consistent emotional reactions are socially approved while stereotype-inconsistent emotional behaviors lead to social disapproval, which may motivate individuals to behave in a stereotype-congruent way. Consequently, stereotypes may bias self-reports of emotional experience and expression under certain conditions, especially when they involve global ratings rather than specific feelings (LaFrance & Banaji, 1992), when they involve retrospective, memory-based rather than momentary, online ratings (Feldman Barrett, Robin, Pietromonaco, & Eyssell, 1998), and when they involve ratings of emotional reactions of others rather than of themselves and in hypothetical rather than actual emotional situations (Robinson, Johnson, & Shields, 1998). In the next part of the chapter, we first review the literature on actual observed and self-reported gender differences in emotional experience and expression. We then discuss in more detail the conditions under which gender stereotypes are used to describe the emotional reactions of the self and others.

How do Men and Women Experience and Express their Emotions?

Sex Differences in Emotional Experience

Gender differences have been found in individuals' self-reports of the intensity of their affect in general, in their self-reports of specific emotions, and in self-reported emotional experience in response to imagined/recalled emotional situations. Women report greater overall intensity of positive and negative affect than men as measured with an affect intensity measure (AIM) (Fujita, Diener & Sandvik, 1991). Women also report experiencing more intensely and more frequently the positive emotions of joy, love, and affection, as well as the negative emotions of sadness, fear, anger, distress, embarrassment, shame, and guilt (Brebner, 2003; Brody, 1999; Brody & Hall, 2000; Ferguson & Crowley, 1997; Ferguson & Eyre, 2000; Fischer & Manstead, 2000; Tangney, 1990). However, men report experiencing pride more frequently and more intensely than women (Brebner, 2003).

Similar results have been found when participants are asked to rate the intensity of their emotional experience in hypothetical emotion-inducing situations. Women rate the intensity with which they feel sadness, fear, disappointment, and anger in imagined emotional situations as higher than men (Timmers et al., 1998). In one study, women reported more fear in imagined frightening situations (e.g., "one night you are alone at home and a stranger is walking towards your house") and in situations that involved a male's hostile and aggressive behavior (e.g., "he's getting angry and throwing things at you"). Women also reported more intense feelings of anger in anger-eliciting situations (e.g., "a friend promised but forgot to pick up an important package for you"), and in frightening situations, especially when a male protagonist was involved (Brody, Lovas and Hay, 1995).

The general finding of women's more intense emotional experience may be explained by differences in the cognitive strategies that men and women use to cope with emotional situations. Nolen-Hoeksema (1987) for example explains women's greater proneness to depression as due to their tendency to ruminate about the causes of negative feelings, while men tend to distract themselves when they experience negative feelings.

Larsen, Diener, and Cropanzano (1987) found that individuals with high affect intensity, a general personality characteristic, tended to interpret events in a self-referential manner, to overgeneralize specific events as representative of their whole life, and to selectively focus their attention on the emotional aspects of events. Women's greater affect intensity may also make them more prone to self-referring, overgeneralizing, and selective attention to emotional information, which may lead to more intense emotional reactions (Fujita et al., 1991).

Women's greater emotional experience may also be due to their greater awareness of emotions in both themselves and others (Feldman Barrett, Lane, Sechrest, & Schwartz, 2000), and in particular to their greater susceptibility to emotional contagion, that is, the tendency to automatically "catch" the emotions of others and to respond in an emotion congruent way (Hatfield, Cacioppo, & Rapson, 1994; see also Chapter 7). For instance, women were found to score higher on the emotional contagion scale and to report being more susceptible than men to others' positive, as well as negative, emotional expressions. That is, women more than men reported being cheered up when with happy people, and feeling nervous when listening to a screaming child at the doctor's office (Doherty, 1997). Furthermore, participants high in emotional contagion who watched a videotape of an emotionally expressive happy or sad stimulus person reported stronger feelings congruent with those of the stimulus person (Doherty, 1997).

The reviewed sex differences in self-reported emotional experience are dependent on the type of emotion under study, and are generally smaller than those found for emotional expression. Indeed, studies that directly compare emotional experience and expression often find fewer sex differences in emotional experience compared to overt emotional display, or else none at all (Kring & Gordon, 1998; Wagner, Buck, & Winterbotham, 1993).

Sex Differences in Emotional Expression

Female's greater overall emotional expressivity is well documented, and has been shown across different measures of expressivity, including electromyography recordings (EMG), observer ratings, and self-ratings of emotional expression. However, sex differences in emotional expressivity have been found to depend on the specific emotions expressed, as well as on the context in which the expressions occur.

EMG

As we saw in Chapter 4, activation of the facial muscles above the eyebrows (*corrugator occulis*) is associated with the perception of unpleasant stimuli, while facial muscle activity in the lower cheek (*zygomaticus major*) is associated with the perception of pleasant stimuli. Studies that have measured facial expressivity by means of EMG generally find greater activation of facial muscles in women compared to men. Greater corrugator activity in females compared with males has been observed in response to imagined negative situations, as for example, driving a car and realizing that the brakes no longer function correctly (Schwartz, Brown, & Ahern, 1980), and in response to unpleasant emotional slides (Bradley, Codispoti, Sabatinelli, & Lang, 2001; Grossman & Wood, 1993). Greater zygomaticus activity in females compared to males has also been observed in response to pleasant emotional slides, especially those depicting family scenes and babies (Bradley et al., 2001). Dimberg and Lundqvist (1990) found greater zygomaticus activity in females compared to males in response to happy faces, but no sex differences in corrugator activity in response to angry faces. In the case of faces as emotional stimuli, it is not clear if the participants' EMG activity reflected their emotional reaction to the depicted face or a simple imitative response.

Finally, the finding that women are more successful than men at enhancing their emotional expressions when asked to do so, as indicated by a significant increase in female EMG activity, further supports the idea that females have a greater facility to express their emotions. Men, by way of contrast, are more successful than women in inhibiting expression when asked to do so (Grossman & Wood, 1993, Study 2).

Observer Ratings of Emotional Expressivity

Sex differences in emotional expressivity have been observed in studies that compared observers' ratings of men's and women's facial displays in response to emotion-inducing slides and films (i.e., the *slide-viewing paradigm*, see Buck et al., 1974; Kring and Gordon, 1998; Wagner et al., 1993). For instance, Buck and colleagues had male and female undergraduates ("senders") view pleasant, unpleasant, sexual, scenic, and unusual slides with the instruction to describe their feelings and to rate the pleasantness of each slide. Participants' facial expressions were unobtrusively videotaped during the entire experiment and their physiological reactions (skin conductance, heart rate) were measured continuously. Observers watched each sender's videotaped facial expressions with no attendant sound, and made judgments about the nature of the slide and the sender's feelings towards it. Observers were more accurate in identifying the type of slides female senders were viewing as well as their reaction towards it, indicating that women were better at communicating their emotions through their facial expressions than men. Furthermore, female senders' facial displays were judged as overall more expressive than those of male senders

(Buck et al., 1974). Similarly, observers rated females' videotaped facial expressions induced by emotion-eliciting happy, sad, disgusting, anger- and fear-evoking films as more expressive than males' facial expressions across all films, with the smallest sex difference for anger (Kring & Gordon, 1998). However, another study showed that male participants' facial expressions while recalling past anger-provoking events were better identified than those of female participants (Coats & Feldman, 1996). In conclusion, studies that relied on observers' ratings of accuracy of facial display suggest that women's facial expressions of emotions are better and easier to "read" than those of men, except for the expression of anger.

Greater expressivity in females has not only been found in minimal social situations in which the impact of participants' sex is maximized because of the absence of possible context-related display rules, but also in situations involving social interaction. In conflictual marital interactions, for example, women tend to express their emotions more while men tend to react with so-called stonewalling, that is, with withdrawal from the situation, inhibited emotional display and an avoidance of eye contact (Levenson et al., 1994). Hall and Friedman (1999) examined the nonverbal behavior of employees of a company as a function of their sex and their status within the company. Employees' dyadic interactions were videotaped while they performed two standard tasks (i.e., a discussion about a nonwork-related topic, and a creativity task involving the construction of a tower). Videotapes were rated by undergraduates for the personality characteristics conveyed by the members of the dyads (i.e., their dominance, warmth, submissiveness, expressiveness) and the frequency of nonverbal behavior including smiles, head nods, self-touching, and hand gestures.

The results generalize the classical sex differences found mostly with college students to an adult sample of employees, age 25 to 64 years. Women were not only rated as warmer, less dominant, and more expressive, they were also found to smile more, to nod more, to touch others more, and to interrupt others less often. Similarly, women were found to display the more authentic "Duchenne" smiles during same-sex dyadic interactions in which they discussed high-involving political topics (Merten, 1997). There are, however, only few studies such as this that have investigated males' and females' emotional expressions in interactive social situations. Most studies have relied on self-reports to examine sex differences in emotional expression.

Self-reported Emotional Expression

Self-report measures of emotional expression can take quite different forms. They can measure dispositional emotional expressivity, or they can assess self-rated expressions of specific emotions out of context or in a given hypothetical situation, and, finally, they can solicit self-reports of specific incidents of the expression of emotion that occurred in the past.

Global dispositional expressivity scales, as for example the emotional expressivity scale (EES; Kring, Smith, & Neale, 1994), the emotional expressivity questionnaire (EEQ; King & Emmons, 1990), and the Berkely expressivity questionnaire (BEQ; Gross & John 1995) measure an individual's general predisposition to express emotions without taking into account the type of emotion expressed and the channel of emotional expression. Studies that have assessed individuals' self-reported dispositional expressivity have generally found that women report being more expressive than men, that is, that women report being more disposed to outwardly display their emotions (Kring & Gordon, 1998).

Greater self-reported female expressivity has also been documented in questionnaire studies in which male and female participants report on the frequency and intensity with which they express particular emotions, independent of a specific social context. In general, the sex differences in self-reported emotional expression parallel those of stereotypical beliefs. For instance, women report expressing the typical feminine emotions of happiness, love, sadness, and fear more intensely and with greater frequency than men, while men tend to report more intense and frequent expressions of the typical masculine emotion of anger than women (Grossman & Wood, 1993; see Figure 8.2). Male participants also report expressing contempt and pride more frequently and more intensely than female participants (Stapley & Haviland, 1989).

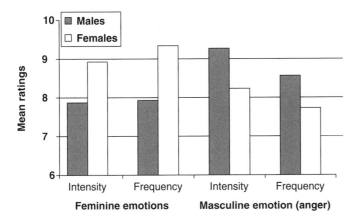

FIGURE 8.2. Self-reported intensity and frequency of typical feminine and masculine emotions in function of participants' sex. From Grossman, M., & Wood, W. (1993). Sex differences in intensity of emotional experience: A social role interpretation. *Journal of Personality and Social Psychology, 65,* 1010–1022.

It is noteworthy that sex differences in self-reported expression of anger are somewhat contradictory. When situational information is provided, women may report that they would express equal or even more anger than men, and also more hurt and disappointment in response to anger-eliciting situations than men (Frost & Averill, 1982). However, sex *differences* are typically found in the way that men and women express their anger. Men typically react physically by hitting and throwing *objects*, and verbally by name calling, while women express their anger more by crying. Furthermore, men tend to express anger more towards males and strangers, and when the target is the cause of their anger (such as expressing anger at a colleague for his being late). Meanwhile, women express anger more towards close others, males or females, who are not the cause of their anger (such as expressing anger about unfair treatment by superior to a friend) (Timmers et al., 1998; for a review, see Kring, 2000).

Moreover, sex differences have been found in self-reports of emotional expression in response to hypothetical emotion-evoking events. In three studies, Hess, Sénecal, Kirouac, Herrera, Philippot, and Kleck (2000) had participants rate the likelihood with which men and women in general, and with which they themselves, would express different emotions and emotion-related behavior in hypothetical situations inducing anger, fear, sadness, disgust, shame, guilt, and happiness. Women reported a higher probability of displaying sadness, fear, shame, and guilt as well as sadness-related and fear-related behavior (i.e., crying, trembling) than men. Men reported a higher probability of displaying serenity and happiness, and the corresponding emotional behavior (i.e., relax, smile, laugh) than women in disgust-, fear- and guilt-inducing situations, and of engaging in anger- and contempt-related behavior (i.e., hit, insult, stare at). Overall, participants' self-reports of emotional reactions to hypothetical emotion-inducing situations were consistent with stereotypical beliefs. The gender-stereotypic beliefs were also reflected in participants' descriptions of freely chosen negative autobiographical emotional situations involving their family. Women chose and described more sad events while men chose and recalled more anger events. Women also reported more intense sad feelings during the recalled negative autobiographical events. However, men and women appraised the recalled negative emotional events in the same way, that is, no sex differences were found in the perceived pleasantness and fairness of the causes, in the event's contribution to goal attainment, in the event's effect on self-esteem and self-confidence, and in the event's impact on the relationship. This finding indicates that sex differences in self-reports were not due to different ways in which men and women appraise emotional events, but that they reflect the prevailing gender stereotype.

The idea that sex differences found in self-reported emotional experience and expression may not reflect actual differences in men and women's emotional reactions but the conformity to gender stereotypes is suggested by the results of several studies. For instance, Grossman and Wood (1993) had male and female participants rate the intensity and frequency with which they themselves (i.e., self-reports) and the typical man and the typical woman (i.e., stereotypical belief) experience and express "feminine" emotions of joy, love, sadness, and fear, and the "masculine" emotion of anger. Participants' self-reported emotional experience and expression of feminine and masculine emotions were related to the extent to which they endorsed the gender-stereotypical beliefs. In particular, the more female participants endorsed the stereotype that women express feminine emotions more, and that men express anger more, the more they themselves reported expressing joy, love, sadness, and fear and the less they reported expressing anger. And this same relationship between stereotypic beliefs and self-reports of expressed emotions held for men. Furthermore, more traditional men who more strongly endorsed the masculine gender roles reported lower overall affect intensity than less traditional men (Jakupcak, Salters, Gratz, & Roemer, 2003). Since these findings are correlational in nature, we cannot draw causal conclusions. It could be that self-reported sex differences are in part determined by participants' endorsement of gender-stereotypical beliefs about emotions, but endorsement of the stereotypes might also be determined by personal experience.

Gender Stereotypes as Heuristic Devices

At this point, we can turn to the question of the conditions under which people use gender stereotypes of emotions to make judgments about the emotional experience and expression of themselves and others. There is some evidence that people rely more on gender stereotypes when they lack concrete emotional information on which to base their judgments (LaFrance & Banaji, 1992; Feldman Barrett et al., 1998; Robinson et al., 1998).

In two studies, Robinson and colleagues (1998) investigated the impact of the availability and accessibility in memory of specific emotional information on the application of the gender stereotype to others and to oneself. Participants in the study were assigned either the role of a player or of an observer in a competitive word game that they actually played or watched (*actual game* condition), or that they imagined playing or watching (*hypothetical game* condition). Players had to evaluate their (actual or imagined) emotional experience while observers were asked to rate the players' emotions based on their (actual or imagined) emotional display. These emotional ratings included typical feminine emotions such as the positive other-directed emotions of sympathy, friendless, gratefulness, as well as the negative self-directed emotions of disappointment, guilt, and embarrassment. Also included were typical masculine emotions such as the positive self-directed emotions of pride, self-satisfaction as well as the negative other-directed emotions of anger and hostility. Emotional ratings of the actual game condition were either completed immediately after the game (*online rating*), or one day to one week later (*delayed rating*).

Results showed that observers in the hypothetical condition who did not watch the actual game based their emotional ratings more on gender stereotypes, probably because they lacked concrete information concerning the players' facial displays. Observers in the hypothetical condition believed that male players would express more masculine emotions and that female players would display more feminine emotions. However, observers who actually watched the players and who had access to concrete expressive information disregarded the gender stereotypes in both their online ratings and the delayed ratings. That is, they did not evaluate male and female players' emotions differently (see Figure 8.3).

Concerning players' self-ratings, male and female players in the online condition did not differ in their ratings of their own emotional experience, indicating that men and women that are placed in the same situation experience similar emotions. However, in the delayed rating

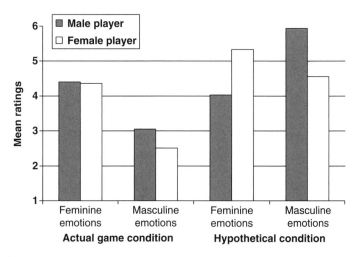

FIGURE 8.3. Observers' mean rating of feminine and masculine emotions expressed by male and female players in the actual vs. the hypothetical competitive word game condition. From Robinson, M. et al. (1998). The gender heuristic and the database: Factors affecting the perception of gender-related differences in the experience and display of emotions. *Basic and Applied Social Psychology, 20,* 206–219.

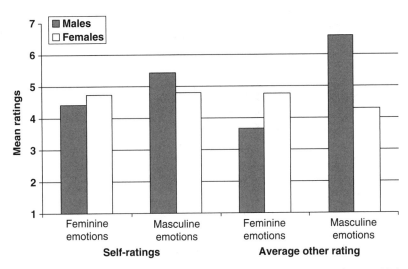

FIGURE 8.4. Male and female participants' self-reported expressions of feminine and masculine emotions and their mean ratings of the emotional expressions of the average man and woman in an imagined competitive word game. From Robinson, M. et al. (1998). The gender heuristic and the database: Factors affecting the perception of gender-related differences in the experience and display of emotions. *Basic and Applied Social Psychology, 20*, 206–219.

condition as well as in the hypothetical condition male players reported that they would experience more masculine emotions, while female players reported that they would experience more feminine emotions. Furthermore, participants relied more on gender stereotypes when they imagined the emotional reactions of the average man or woman than when they imagined their own emotional reactions in the word game (see Figure 8.4). Taken together, these findings suggest that gender stereotypes are more likely to influence self-reports and judgments of others' emotions in hypothetical compared to actual experienced situations, when the emotional judgments are delayed in time rather than immediate, and when people are judging others' emotion compared to judging their own emotional reactions. In situations where people have no or reduced access to relevant emotional information, they rely on gender stereotypes that function as a heuristic device to fill in the missing information.

Another condition that promotes reliance on gender stereotypes in self-reported emotions is the use of global retrospective ratings (Feldman Barrett et al., 1998; LaFrance & Banaji, 1992). Specifically, sex differences in self-reported emotions have been shown to depend on the degree to which participants must rely on their memory when describing and rating their emotional reactions. In the study by Feldman Barrett and colleagues, for example, sex differences emerged in global retrospective self-reports of emotional experience, but not in online self-reports of momentary emotional experience (Feldman Barrett et al., 1998). Consistent with the gender stereotype, women reported higher affect intensity, and more happiness, sadness, and fear on global self-report scales than men. However, men and women did not differ in their momentary, online ratings of specific emotional reactions measured immediately after dyadic social interactions.

The lack of correspondence between global, retrospective reports and momentary reports of affective experience may be explained by a reconstruction and recollection bias. In order to provide a global summary of one's experience of sadness, fear, and so forth, individuals must retrieve, summarize, and integrate information about numerous prior emotional experiences. Because this is a difficult task, they may rely on stereotypical beliefs concerning the emotional reactions of men and women to produce their global account. Retrospective reports of previous emotional experiences are also biased by the individual's emotion knowledge. Indeed, women have been found to have more complex and differentiated general emotion knowledge than men. Not surprisingly, they also describe their own emotional experiences and those of others in a more differentiated and integrative way than men (Feldman Barrett et al., 2000). Women also recall more and more differentiated emotional experience than men. Women's superior recall of autobiographical emotional memories has been found to be linked to their more detailed encoding of autobiographical events (Seidlitz & Diener, 1998). Sex differences in global, retrospective ratings may thus be due to sex differences in emotional knowledge and to men and women's conformity to gender stereotypes rather than to sex differences in emotional experience and expression per se. This does not mean, however, that sex differences in actual emotional reactions do not exist at all, but suggests that in situations where no or few sex differences actually exist, memory-based reconstruction may create or enhance them.

Gender-based vs. Context-based Emotion Norms

Gender stereotypes prescribe the emotional behavior appropriate for women and men. Emotional behavior inconsistent with these gender-based norms is perceived to have social costs, leading to social disapproval, social rejection and feelings of guilt and anxiety and motivates people to behave in a stereotype consistent way (see LaFrance & Hecht, 2000; Stoppard & Gunn Grunchy, 1993). But as we have noted, people's emotional behavior is also determined by the context in which it occurs. Context-based emotion norms (display rules, feeling rules) prescribe emotional experience and expressions in specific situations like a wedding or a funeral, independent of the expresser's sex. In these situations sex differences are smaller, because the emotion norms that are activated apply to whomever is in this situation and thus constrain everyone. In contrast, sex differences tend to be more pronounced in situations in which situational demands are minimal or absent and in situations that are ambiguous with respect to the appropriate behavior because in this case gender norms are the default option that prescribes emotional behavior. Gender norms are also particularly salient in public situations, in which people are aware of being observed, monitored, or evaluated by others (Deaux & Major, 1987; Eagly & Wood, 1991; LaFrance, Hecht, & Levy Paluck, 2003).

LaFrance and colleagues' meta-analysis of gender and smiling showed that smiling was not only determined by gender norms but also by situational demands. Larger sex differences in frequency and amount of smiling were found in studies that used situations in which gender norms were especially salient, that is, in situations in which participants' expressions were filmed by a camera that was visible rather than hidden, situations in which participants were engaged in interactions with others rather than alone, and situations in which participants were explicitly instructed to share their thoughts and feelings with others. Reduced or no sex differences in smiling were found in studies in which male and female participants were given identical goals such as explicit deception instructions or where expressive behavior was guided by situational demands to deceive or to compete with others (LaFrance & Hecht, 2000; LaFrance et al., 2003).

The finding that sex differences in emotions vary with the presence or absence of context-based norms received further support in a study that directly manipulated the normative expectations concerning participants' emotional responses (Grossman and Wood, 1993). In this study, participants had to evaluate their pleasant and unpleasant feelings induced by emotion-inducing positive, negative and neutral slides. Before performing the task, they were informed that emotional expression is either beneficial or detrimental for psychological adjustment, or they received no information. The furnished information was intended to establish normative pressure to enhance or attenuate emotional reactions. In the absence of explicit information concerning the appropriate emotional response (control condition) participants' self-reported emotions were in accordance with the gender stereotype of greater female emotionality. However, in the conditions in which normative beliefs were made comparable for male and female participants (enhance/attenuate information), no sex differences in self-reported emotions were found. Context-based emotion norms (i.e., experimenter-provided norms) may thus outweigh the impact of gender norms and reduce sex differences in emotional responses.

Differences in Status and Power

Status is an important determinant of how people express emotion, and which emotions they express. For instance, superiors are typically perceived as expressing more anger and disgust, while subordinates are typically perceived as expressing more fear and embarrassment (Algoe, Buswell, & DeLamater, 2000). Sex differences in emotional expression have been linked to men's and women's relative status and power in society (Kemper, 1978; LaFrance & Henley, 1994). Differences in status and power may affect the way men and women appraise situations and may determine which emotions are adaptive for them to express (Brody, 1997). Women, who typically possess less power and who generally occupy lower status positions in society, tend to express emotions that are well adapted with their lower power and status, that is, they display more powerless emotions of fear, sadness, shame and guilt that signal their vulnerability and their submission. Because of their lower status, women are also more inclined to interpret situations as uncontrollable and threatening, which leads to greater experience and expression of fear. Women smile more in order to accommodate and to appease those higher in status and power, and they express less anger in order to avoid conflict with others and to maintain social relationships. Men, who possess more power and hold higher status positions in society, typically avoid the expression of powerless emotions because they are incompatible with the status associated to their masculine identity. Men express emotions such as anger, contempt, and pride, which signal their independence, their dominance and their capacity to cope with conflictual and challenging situations. Moreover, males' aggressive behavior and expression of anger allow them to maintain their power over others.

If females' greater disposition to express powerless emotions is due to their lower status then low status persons should display similar emotions independent of their sex. However, stereotype-consistent sex differences in emotional expression are found to persist even when controlling for status, indicating that differences in men's and women's emotional expression cannot be explained by differences in status alone (Hall & Friedman, 1999).

Externalizer–Internalizer Distinction

Sex differences in emotional expressivity may be due to men's and women's different emotional response style. The idea that people differ with regard to the emotional channel through which they respond to an emotional situation is not new. Jones (1935) introduced the term "internalizer" to describe a person exhibiting a high physiological response accompanied by a low level of emotional expression. "Externalizers," in contrast, exhibit a high level of emotional expression while manifesting only low physiological reactivity. Several studies have found negative correlations between the overt facial expression of emotion and physiological responses, supporting the externalizer–internalizer distinction (Buck, Savin, Miller & Caul, 1972; Buck, Loslow, Murphy, & Costanzo, 1992; Buck et al., 1974). The more individuals experienced physiological arousal in response to emotional stimuli, the less they facially expressed their emotions (internalizers), and the more they were facially reactive the more weakly they responded at the physiological level (externalizer). It is worth noting that these negative correlations were found between participants. For a given individual, however, the correlation between facial expressivity and physiological reactivity was positive. Consistent with the readout view of facial expression of emotion, the more an individual experiences an emotion the more it is overtly displayed, regardless of the individual's specific emotional response style.

The hypothesis that women's greater expressivity is due to their greater tendency to externalize their feelings was tested and supported in several studies (Buck et al., 1974; Kring and Gordon, 1998). Using the slide-viewing paradigm, which was described in greater detail earlier in the chapter, Buck and colleagues found negative correlations between participants' facial display and their physiological responses to emotionally loaded slides. As expected, participants who exhibited greater physiological reactivity in response to the slides were those who expressed their emotions the least.

In order to identify individual differences in emotional response style, Buck and colleagues distinguished participants who scored above or below the median on the facial expressivity measure and who exhibited skin conductance reactivity above or below the median. Participants scoring high in facial expressivity and low in skin conductance were classified as externalizers and those scoring low in facial expressivity but high in skin conductance were considered as internalizers. Results revealed that the externalizer category included mainly women (64%) while the internalizer category included mainly men (73%). It is worth noting that Buck (1977) failed to find such a relationship between gender and the externalizer–internalizer dimensions among 5-year-old children.

Kring and Gordon (1998) partially replicated and extended these findings. They had male and female participants watch emotional video clips. In addition to self-reported emotions, measures included emotional facial expression (coded by three independent judges) and skin conductance. Women were found to express their emotions more overtly than men, although they did not differ in their self-reported emotional experience. More importantly for our concerns, more women than men were found to

TABLE 8.1
Number of Male and Female Participants Classified as Internalizer, Externalizer, High Responder, and Low Responder

	Emotional response style			
	Internalizer	Externalizer	High responder	Low responder
Men	11	4	3	10
Women	4	10	9	2

From Kring, A. M., & Gordon, A. H. (1998). Sex differences in emotion: Expression, experience and physiology. *Journal of Personality and Social Psychology, 74,* 686–703.

be in the externalizer category and in the high responder category (high expressivity and high physiological reactivity), while more men than women were in the internalizer category and in the low responder category (low expressivity and low physiological reactivity) (see Table 8.1). According to Brody and Hall (2000) men's tendency to internalize their feelings enables them to preserve control and independence while women's externalizing style characterized by the expression of emotion in different emotional channels ("generalizer") facilitates their social interactions and favors interdependence with others.

Taken together, these findings suggest that differences in the emotional response style and in particular the externalizer–internalizer dimension might account for some sex differences in emotional expression, and that this relationship is established over development.

Three main accounts have been offered concerning the processes underlying the externalizer–internalizer distinction (see Manstead, 1991, for a thorough discussion). First, the "discharge model" proposes that individuals have to express their emotion through one channel or another. If the expression by one channel is impeded, expression will occur through other channels. According to the discharge account, children would naturally externalize their affective states, but socialization processes would then tend to promote the inhibition of affective display. In western culture, this inhibitory demand is directed more markedly at boys, who are discouraged from expressing their emotions. As a result, boys are expected to exhibit more marked physiological responses (i.e., discharges) than girls (e.g., Jones, 1960).

The second model, the "innate arousability model," reverses the pattern of causality and suggests that men, who have a greater innate arousability, are more sensitive to socialization and consequently inhibit their affective reactions to a greater degree.

Finally, the "response conflict model" (Lanzetta & Kleck, 1970) proposes that individuals learn through socialization to inhibit their emotional facial reaction. However, because these responses are continuously stimulated by affective stimuli, individuals experience response conflict. Response conflict is expressed as increasing autonomic activity. Thus, those who have faced the strongest socialization pressure to inhibit their emotions should experience the greatest response conflict and should thus exhibit the greatest autonomic activity.

How Well do Men and Women Decode Others' Emotions?

Decoding refers to the capacity to judge, to interpret and to identify others' emotions from nonverbal cues including facial, vocal, and postural information. In emotion recognition studies participants are usually presented with slides, drawings or films of facial expressions, bodily postures or tapes of speech samples and asked to judge their emotional meaning.

Decoding Accuracy

Women have typically been found to be more accurate in decoding the emotional meaning of nonverbal cues (see reviews by Hall, 1978, 1984; Hall, Carter, & Horgan, 2000). Hall and Matsumoto (2004) for example, had participants judge photographs of posed facial expressions of anger, contempt, sadness, happiness, fear, surprise, and disgust which were presented either for 10 seconds or, in a second study, for 200 ms embedded in the same target person's neutral face that was presented for 1 second each. Women were found to show more variability in their ratings, that is, they used a wider range on the rating scales than men. Furthermore, women rated the target emotion (the emotion expressed by the face) higher than men for both long and short stimulus presentation. No sex differences were found in the ratings of nontarget emotions (the six other emotions not expressed by the face).

Similarly, Thayer and Jonsen (2000) found women to be more accurate in correctly identifying the emotions in faces depicting happy, sad, angry, disgusting, fearful, surprised and neutral emotional expressions. Women were also faster at correctly identifying happy, sad and neutral faces (Rahman, Wilson, & Abrahams, 2004). These results indicate that women are faster and more accurate in their emotional judgments.

Developmental research, however, has found no or only weak sex differences in decoding accuracy of children, which suggests that the sex differences in the capacity to correctly identify others emotions are not innate but strongly shaped by socialization processes (Brody, 1985; McClure, 2000). We will discuss the role of socialization as well as other potential causes for sex differences in emotions in more detail at the end of the chapter.

Several factors have been found to influence men and women's decoding capacities: poser's sex, poser's status and perceived dominance and affiliation.

Poser's Sex

Males' anger expressions are typically recognized more accurately than females' anger expressions while sad and fear expressions are better recognized when displayed by a female poser (Goos & Silverman, 2002; Rotter & Rotter, 1988). Indeed, several studies suggest that poser's sex may bias decoding of facial expressions in a gender-stereotype-consistent way. Women's facial expressions are more likely to be identified as expressing feminine emotions, such as sadness and fear, while men's facial expressions are more likely to be perceived as displaying masculine emotion of anger. In their classic study, Condry and Condry (1976) showed that the same records of an infant's emotional reaction to a Jack-in-the-Box was interpreted either as fear or as anger depending on whether the infant was presented as being a girl or a boy. A gender-stereotypic perception of emotional expressions was also found for adults' emotional display. Equally intense anger expressions were rated as more intense when expressed by a male poser, while equally intense happy expressions were rated as more intense when displayed by a female poser (Hess, Blairy and Kleck, 1997).

Similarly, Plant, Hyde, Keltner and Devine (2000) found gender-stereotype-consistent interpretation of facial expressions that were matched in emotional content, that is, a blend of sad and angry expression, but that differed in poser's sex. The same sad–angry expression displayed by a female poser was rated as sadder and less angry than when displayed by a male poser. In another study, Plant, Kling, and Smith (2004) used identical expressions that consisted of morphed faces depicting a blend of sadness and anger. Posers' sex was manipulated by choosing male or female hairstyle and clothing. Results revealed gender-stereotype-consistent interpretation of the ambiguous sad-angry facial expressions. The same facial expression was judged as sadder and less angry when dressed up as woman than when disguised as a man. The finding that ambiguous facial expressions are interpreted consistent with gender stereotypes was also supported in a study by Mignault and Chaudhuri (2003) that investigated the impact of poser's sex and head position on perceived dominance. Females' neutral faces were more likely perceived as expressing happiness and powerless emotions including sadness, shame, guilt, regret, embarrassment and respect, and as expressing less dominance. Males' neutral faces were more likely perceived as expressing anger and powerful "superiority" emotions including contempt, pride, haughtiness, and self-assurance.

Poser's Status

Job status (superior versus subordinate status) was found to be associated with gender-specific personality characteristics and emotional behavior. Algoe et al. (2000) had participants read a short description of a workplace interaction: a superior inquiring about a duty assigned to an employee who had not finished it. They were also shown a photograph of the target person expressing either fear, anger or disgust. The target person held either the role of the superior or of the subordinate and was either presented with a male or a female name. Participants rated the emotion expressed by the target person, as well as several personal characteristics including dominance, submissiveness, affiliation, cold-heartedness. Participants' attributions of personality traits were strongly affected by the target person's status, that is, the high status target person was found to be associated with masculine characteristics of dominance, self-assertiveness and self-confidence, while the low status person was shown to be related to feminine characteristics of submissiveness and affiliation.

More interestingly, participants' interpretation of the target person's facial expression was not only affected by the displayed emotion but also by the target's job status and target's gender. Female and subordinate targets received higher fear and embarrassment ratings while male and superior targets were rated as expressing more anger and disgust and contempt.

In conclusion, poser's sex as well as poser's status, which are often confounded because men, typically occupying higher status positions than women, may influence people's interpretation of facial expressions of emotion. Sex and status are contextual cues that activate gender stereotypes, which serve as a heuristic device in the case of ambiguous or incomplete information.

Perceived Dominance and Affiliation

Specific emotional expressions have been found to be linked to perceived dominance and affiliation. In particular, happy facial expressions are perceived as high in dominance and in affiliation, anger and disgust expressions are perceived as high in dominance and low in affiliation, and sadness and fear expressions are perceived as low in dominance (Hess, Blairy, & Kleck, 2000; Knutson, 1996). Hess and colleagues further showed that the morphological features that are associated with dominance (square face, high forehead and heavy eyebrows) and with affiliation (round face and large eyes) are confounded with poser's sex. Male faces typically possess dominant-related morphological features, while female faces possess more affiliation-related morphological features.

The impact of poser's sex on judgments of emotional expressions – an identical anger expression rated as more intense when expressed by a "male" poser and an identical happy expression rated as happier when displayed by a "female" poser – was found to disappear or even to be reversed when the poser's facial expressions were controlled for morphological cues, that is, when interior facial cues were moderate in dominance and affiliation with gender-specific hairstyle indicating poser's sex (Hess, Adams, & Kleck, 2004). The same angry expression with moderate dominance and affiliation features was rated as angrier when associated with female than male hairstyle. Similarly, the same smiling expression was rated as happier when dressed up with a male than female hairstyle (see Figure 8.5). Furthermore, a person's disposition to display specific emotions was found to be determined by perceived dominance and affiliation and not by poser's sex per se (Hess, Adams, & Kleck, 2005). The tendency to perceive women as more disposed to express happiness and surprise

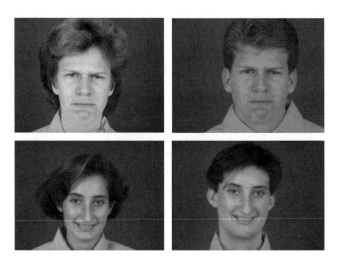

FIGURE 8.5. Examples of angry and happy facial expressions with the same morphological features and gender-specific hairstyle. From Hess, U. et al. (in press). When two do the same it might not mean the same: The perception of emotional expressions shown by men and women. In U. Hess, & P. Philippot (Eds.), *Group dynamics and emotional expression.* New York: Cambridge University Press.

was determined by perceived high affiliation, while women's proneness to express fear and sadness was determined by perceived low dominance. And the tendency to perceive men as more disposed to express anger, disgust and contempt was determined by both perceived high dominance and low affiliation. Together, these findings suggest that the decoding of emotional expressions in a gender-stereotype-consistent way is, in part, caused by morphological facial cues associated with perceived dominance and affiliation.

Why Men and Women Differ in their Emotions: Origins of Gender Differences

Gender differences in emotional experience, expression, and recognition have been explained by the differential socialization of boys and girls, by the different social roles that men and women occupy in society, and by their cultural background. We discuss each of these possible determinants of sex differences in emotion in the next sections.

Socialization of Emotion

Gender differences in emotions are, for the most part, explained by the socialization of girls and boys to behave in accordance with the culturally prevailing gender stereotypes and norms. Consistent with the gender stereotype, girls are taught to express emotions that facilitate their relationships with other people. Girls tend to be taught to be nice, friendly and smile, and not to behave aggressively and wildly. Boys, contrariwise, tend to be taught to behave in a "manly" way – that is, to be strong and brave, and to defend themselves, and not to express sadness, fear, pain, or other signs of weakness and vulnerability.

These norms are transmitted by parents and peers and by other socialization agents such as the school and the media. For example, boys and girls who behaved in a gender-consistent masculine-competitive-aggressive and feminine-cooperative-friendly manner, respectively, were found to be more popular and more liked among their peers than those who violated gender norms (Adler, Kless, & Adler, 1992). Furthermore, parents were found to encourage their daughters to express feminine emotions and to inhibit the expression of anger and aggression, and to encourage their sons to express anger but otherwise to control the expression of their feelings (Birnbaum & Croll, 1984).

Parental reactions to their sons and daughters are not only guided by gender stereotypes but also by sex-related characteristics such as the child's temperament, language skills and sociability (for a review see Brody, 1985, 2000; Brody & Hall, 1993, 2000). The child's temperament, that is, the child's innate reactivity to internal and external stimulation may elicit different responses from parents and caretakers. Male infants tend to have a higher level of arousal than girls and to be more irritable, more startled, and less consolable than girls. Boys' higher arousal and activity level may incite parents to teach them to inhibit the expression of their emotions and to control their feelings. Boys will thus become less expressive with age because they experience more socialization pressure to control their emotions that are perceived as *too* intense. Mothers have also been found to exaggerate their facial expressions when interacting with their sons, probably to get their attention and to regulate their behavior. In the long run, such behavior may prevent boys from learning to identify subtle emotional expressions, and may thus explain males' inferior decoding skills.

Girls, by way of contrast, have better and earlier language skills, a more extensive emotion vocabulary, and they are more responsive to others. They thus show stronger empathic responses than boys when faced with another person's pain, and they react more strongly to their mother's fearful facial display. When interacting with their responsive and language-skilled girls, parents tend to express more positive emotions and to use more emotional language. Parents also tend to discuss emotions more with their daughters than with their sons, except for the emotions of anger and disgust (Kuebli & Fivush, 1992).

Boys and girls are socialized to conform to the culturally dominant gender stereotypes and to behave in accordance with their gender roles. However, a child's endorsement of gender stereotypes has been shown to depend on their *fathers'* implication in childrearing and household tasks (Brody, 1997). The time fathers spend with their children is negatively correlated with the children's expression of gender-stereotypical emotions. Girls with more involved fathers express more competition, more aggression, more positive emotions, and less sadness compared to girls with less involved fathers. And boys with highly involved fathers express more affiliation, warmth, and fear, and less competition, anger, and aggression. These results illustrate that changes in socialization processes may alter gender differences in emotions.

Social Role Interpretation

Eagly's (1987) social role account explains sex differences in social behavior in terms of gender roles, that is, the social roles that men and women hold in society. Women's social roles involve childrearing, domestic work, and caring professions (e.g., nurses, teachers), that strongly determine the content of the female gender role. Men's social roles typically involve those of the provider, protector, and are related to more dominant, power-related positions in the family as well as in professional life and in society. The different social roles of men and women create gender role expectations, that is, expectations concerning the appropriate behavior for men and women. Women are expected to possess communal qualities such as being friendly, being sensitive to the needs of others, being warm and nurturing, and behaving in a affiliative and relationship-oriented way. Men are expected to possess agentic qualities including attributes such as independence, assertiveness, and instrumental competence. The enactment of their different social roles causes men and women to develop different skills (i.e., more or less sensitivity for others, more or less emotional responsiveness). According to the social role account, sex differences in emotions are thus due to men's and women's conformity with their gender role as well as to their different emotional skills, which cause them to behave differently.

Support for the social role interpretation comes from the observation of sex differences concerning the type and the nature of men and women's activities. Women occupy more caretaker activities with children and the elderly, and they provide more personal care and support while men provide more technical and administration help. Women have thus more opportunities to practice emotion-related skills (Grossman & Wood, 1993). Similarly, studies examining gender stereotypes have found that the typical woman is judged as more likely to occupy the homemaker and caretaker role requiring emotional sensitivity and expressivity, and thus to possess higher communal traits than the typical man. However, when men and women hold the same roles, no sex differences in the attribution of communal traits are observed (Eagly & Steffen, 1984).

The impact of gender role identity on emotional expression was examined in the study by Kring and Gordon (1998). Participants were classified as masculine, feminine or androgynous (i.e., neither masculine nor feminine, but, rather, having both qualities) on the basis of their score on the Bem sex role inventory (BSRI; Bem, 1979). Androgynous participants were those who endorsed a high number of both masculine-instrumental and feminine-expressive characteristics, feminine participants scored high on feminine traits and low on masculine traits, and masculine participants scored high on masculine traits and low on feminine traits. Results revealed that androgynous participants reported the highest dispositional expressivity on a self-report measure of expressivity and were judged as the most expressive while masculine participants were judged as the least expressive, with feminine participants falling in between. A similar finding comes from a study that examined individuals' proneness to cry.

Independent of their biological sex, masculine participants more than participants with a feminine gender identity tended to be reluctant to cry (Ross & Mirowsky, 1984). These findings suggest that gender role identity determines emotional behavior at least as much as, if not more than, their biological sex.

Emotion, Gender, and Culture

Most of the studies of gender and emotion that we have reviewed in this chapter were conducted in western cultures (North America and western Europe), and found overall greater female emotionality. Although sex differences in emotionality vary with type of emotion, with the component of emotion, and measurement of emotional response as well as with the social context, they are mainly characterized by differences in the extent to which men and women outwardly express or control their emotions. Studies that have examined gender and emotions across cultures have found sex differences to be more pronounced in western cultures, especially in North America, compared to, in particular, Asian cultures (for reviews see Brody, 1997; Fischer & Manstead, 2000).

For example, whereas Caucasian women are perceived as expressing more happiness than men, no sex differences are found for Japanese posers (Matsumoto, 1992). Likewise, female Americans report more intense emotions and more emotional expressive behavior than men while Japanese males and females do not differ significantly (Matsumoto, Kudoh, Scherer, & Wallbott, 1988). Sex differences in crying frequency and overall crying proneness also tend to be greater in western countries compared to African and Asian countries (Vingerhoets & Becht, 1996; Vingerhoets & Scheirs, 2000). And women's greater tendency to report shame, fear, and nervousness in response to emotion-eliciting stories is more pronounced in American European samples than in American Asian and Asian samples (Copeland, Hwang, & Brody, 1996).

The impact of culture on sex differences in emotions may be explained by the different social roles that men and women occupy across cultures, by the relative status and power they hold in society, and by differences in cultural values. The hypothesis that differences in cultural values and in the division of labor promote culture-specific patterns of sex differences in emotions was tested in a study by Fischer and Manstead (2000). These researchers examined the relationship between three cultural measures, that is, the actual division of labor (as listed by the gender empowerment measure (GEM), which reports the extent to which women actively participate in economic and political life), sex role ideology (a measure of masculinity–femininity), a measure of individualism–collectivism (the degree to which the culture values individual achievement versus group harmony and interdependence, as discussed in the next chapter), and the self-reported intensity, duration, and nonverbal expression of seven emotions (joy, fear, anger, sadness, disgust, shame, guilt) of participants from 37 countries on five continents (using the ISEAR cross-cultural database).

Women in all countries reported experiencing the target emotions more intensely and for longer durations, and expressing them more overtly than men. Unexpectedly, sex differences in emotional reactions were greater in countries with *less* traditional divisions of labor (high GEM) and with prevailing individualistic values (western European countries, USA, Australia) than in more traditional, collectivistic countries (African, Asian, South American countries). These findings suggest that sex differences in emotionality cannot be reduced to the traditional division of labor between men and women as suggested by social role theory. To the contrary, the less traditional labor division in individualistic countries seems to be related to a *need* for gendered emotional differentiation.

One explanation for this unexpected finding is that the search for independence and autonomy that characterizes individualistic cultures threatens the basic human need for social relations. Thus, in order to establish a balance between the need for independence from others and the need for relatedness, men are socialized to become specialists in independence and women to become specialists in social relations. In particular, men are socialized to control their emotions, mainly those that threaten their independence, power and status, while women are encouraged to express positive other-directed emotions and powerless emotions that foster relations with others. Collectivistic cultures, which emphasize the search for interdependence with others and adjustment to others are less in need of this gendered emotional differentiation. The dichotomy of the emotional woman and the unemotional man seems to be largely a "western dichotomy" that cannot be generalized to collectivistic cultures (Fischer & Manstead, 2000). The impact of culture on emotions will be treated more in detail in Chapter 9.

Summary

In reviewing the literature on gender and emotion it appears that the belief in the emotional woman and the unemotional man exists more strongly in people's mind than in their actual feeling and doing. Most studies have revealed that differences in men and women's emotional experience, expression and recognition depend on the components of emotion, on the type of emotions, and on the specific social context in which emotions occur.

In particular, sex differences are found to be larger for overt expression compared to experience. Furthermore, women appear to experience and express more positive other-directed emotions (joy, love, sympathy, empathy) and powerless emotions (fear, sadness, shame, guilt) while men express more powerful emotions (anger, contempt, pride) that signal and protect their independence, power and status. However, these observed sex differences in emotions, which are consistent with people's stereotypical beliefs, are restricted to specific contexts and to specific emotional measurements.

Gender stereotypes contribute to sex differences in emotions because they prescribe how and when it is appropriate for men and women to experience and express specific emotions. They create expectancies about men and women's emotional reactions, which may influence their emotional behavior generating self-fulfilling prophecies. Men and women may be motivated to behave in conformity with the gender stereotype because it is socially approved while stereotype-inconsistent behavior tends to be socially sanctioned. Gender stereotypes are used as heuristic devices and influence people's judgment of emotions of the self and others in a stereotype-consistent way, particularly when emotional information is ambiguous or scarce. Finally, gender stereotypes indirectly contribute to sex differences in emotions because they provide the basis for the socialization of "gender-appropriate" emotional behavior in girls and boys.

Sex differences in emotions are not invariant and universal, but have been shown to be linked to the differences in men and women's social roles, to their relative status and power, to their socialization history and to culture. Brody (1997) suggested that changes in these processes may also produce changes in the emotional experience and expression of men and women.

Emotion and Culture

9

The authors of this book know a man who is Polish, grew to adolescence in Poland, but who has lived in the United States now for more than 50 years. Quite frequently, the man admits: "I have lived here for many years, but I am still not completely comfortable with Americans' emotions. They smile all the time, and say that they are 'happy.' I hardly ever use this word." A Dutch friend says: "You know, the Americans and the British, when they do something wrong, they always say that they are sorry. But they do not really feel sorry." Many Europeans and European Americans think that Asians are inscrutable; they tend to mask their true feelings. What are their true feelings? And individuals from Mediterranean countries think that Scandinavians do not actually experience much emotion at all, an accusation to which a Swede might respond: "Yes, but still waters run deep." Meanwhile, a Finnish man once told one of us that Finns are in general suspicious of adults who do not control their expression of emotion, especially in public. Dramatic displays of emotion are seen as immature or slightly out of control.

What is going on here? These comments and beliefs seem to suggest that there are differences in the ways in which people from different countries or continents feel, express, or label emotions. Or perhaps all three. Are there significant cultural differences in the experience of emotion, or do the above comments merely reflect stereotypes and values that mask underlying similarity? This is a very difficult question to answer in a simple way, because, as we have seen, emotions have many components. Evaluating cultural differences and similarities requires that research attention be directed to all the components (Mesquita & Frijda, 1992; Scherer, 1997). Of course, even if we agree that an assessment of cultural differences in emotion must involve assessment of many or all components of emotion, one might still wonder whether some components are more important or fundamental than others. The unsatisfactory answer to that question is that it depends on which theory of emotion is adopted. For example, as we saw in Chapter 1, while the strongest tests of the evolutionary theory of emotion may not involve examination of emotional language or the existence of words for the same "feelings" in different languages (see Frijda, Markam, Sato, & Wiers, 1995; Hess, 2001, for a discussion of this point), the social constructionist theory was, in part, developed on the basis of analysis of these lexical items (Wierzbicka, 1986, 1992). Therefore, cultural variation in emotional language has somewhat different meanings for the two theories.

So here is a thought, or an illustration, to orient us as we delve into the issue of cultural differences in emotion. As you recall again from Chapter 1, evolutionary theory assumes that there are some very important objects and events that, universally, evoke specific emotions and resulting actions or action readiness because they are recognized as biologically relevant. Let us consider one such object. As it turns out, dead bodies – those not yet prepared for viewing, of course – provoke the emotion of disgust, as evidenced by self-reports and facial expression, and related behaviors such as vomiting, in European and North American countries (Rozin, Haidt, & McCauley,

2000). Because dead bodies can spread disease, this seems to be a biologically prepared reaction. But disgust does not, according to most accounts, accurately label the feelings with which the Navajo Indians of North America reacted to dead bodies, at least before their assimilation to the now dominant European American culture. According to traditional Navajo spiritual beliefs, dead bodies house potentially dangerous spirits that can wreak all sorts of havoc on the living. The treatment of the body is believed to influence the likelihood that an evil spirit of the dead will return to pose a danger. Consequently, to the traditional Navajo, dead bodies are intensely feared, and are treated with a care and ritual that is motivated by this intense fear. For example, in traditional families, four mourners are typically hired to prepare the body of a deceased for burial. In this way, the family avoids coming in contact with the body themselves. The mourners cleanse the body and dress it in fine clothes. They also put the moccasins of the deceased on the wrong feet in order to ensure that the dead would have trouble walking back to the village from the burial site (Schwarz, 2001).

Now the questions to keep in mind as we examine cultural differences in emotional experience are, do traditional Navajos not feel disgust when faced with a dead body, and, indeed, fear, suggesting that the emotion itself is different? Or do traditional Navajos actually respond with disgust to the dead body, and with fear to their deeply held belief of the potentially dangerous spirit and its consequences for the group? Or, finally, do the Navajo react with something that looks, perhaps even biologically, like disgust, which they then label as fear because this label for the emotion makes sense in light of their beliefs and practices surrounding dead bodies? The only answer we will be able to provide for this series of questions is that all accounts describe cultural differences in emotion that are very important (Solomon, 1995). Why this is so is that these differences, while located in different components of the emotion process, all lead the Navajo to engage in cultural practices that are related to the emotion of fear. *Not disgust*. So, if we want to predict their behavior and understand their conscious feelings, we need to know that this difference exists. Sanitizing and then embalming the body, which is performed in so-called western cultures, would in no way address the feelings of the Navajo, because this way of handling the body aims at making it less disgusting, and would do little in the way of making it less fearful. In fact, embalming the body would probably only enhance the Navajos' fear, because such treatment is at odds with their beliefs about the sacred nature of the body and their rituals for dealing with death.

In the beginning of this chapter, we trace the history of the study of the cross-cultural study of emotions, noting that the endeavor initially began with a search for similarities, and has evolved toward a theory of cultural differences (Mesquita, 2001a). As will become apparent from this history, in looking for cultural differences in emotion, we need to know what culture is and how it can be conceptualized and measured. If no theory of culture is adopted it is difficult to be able to predict whether individuals on one continent will be different from individuals on another continent, and to understand why they are different when relevant data are obtained. Or, if we define each ethnic group and each nationality as, by definition, a separate culture, then we spend all of our time learning about each country's unique beliefs and practices, and trying to formulate hypotheses based on its idiosyncrasies (which is perfectly acceptable in ethnographic and anthropologic research). Although it unquestionably provides important ideas from which general hypotheses can be generated such an idiosyncratic approach makes the development of general psychological knowledge about emotion and culture difficult (Shweder, 2002). In the second part of this chapter, therefore, we define culture and the ways in which cultural differences have been conceptualized generally, with important implications for emotions, and also more specifically with regard to emotion processes. Finally, in the remainder of the chapter, we review the scientific literature that investigates possible cultural differences in different components of the emotion process.

The Cross-cultural Study of Emotion: A Brief History

The same problems of definition and measurement that characterize the study of emotion in general become very acute when a researcher wants to compare the emotional experiences of members of two or more cultures. How in the world can we know if two people are experiencing a similar or a different internal state? Or, as it has been rhetorically asked:

> How sure are we that we can judge what veiling, polygamy or circumcision means to women in other cultures? Can we judge the affective tone of parent–child relations in other cultures? Do we understand the emotional expressions of our non-Western business partners correctly when we are at the negotiation table with them? Is it possible to counsel people from other cultures? Are we able to interpret the aggressive threats or the populist emotional address of the leaders of antagonistic countries in other parts of the world? Or, perhaps more importantly, do we know how to increase the likelihood that those leaders would agree to negotiation to peaceful solutions? (Mesquita, 2001a)

Well, do we? The research base does not allow us to say that we do just yet.

Looking for the Fundamentals

The history of the cross-cultural study of emotion within experimental psychology started with the search for basic, therefore universal, emotions (Mesquita, 2001a; Mesquita & Haire, 2004). The underlying idea was that if there are universal facial expressions, there are presumably evolved emotion programs (Tomkins, 1962, 1963). Thus, the existence of universal facial expressions would provide evidence for the existence of basic emotions. As we saw in Chapter 4, there is strong evidence for universal facial expressions of emotion (Ekman & Friesen, 1971; Haidt & Keltner, 1999). This conclusion, as was noted, is based on the fact that recognition rates in the different cultures are substantially better than chance (see Camras, Oster, Campos, Miyake, & Bradshaw, 1997 for evidence of cross-cultural similarity in the spontaneous production of facial expression). The same is true of vocal affect. A number of studies have examined the recognition of vocal affect across cultures (e.g., Albas, McCluskey, & Albas, 1976; Scherer, Banse, & Wallbott, 2001; Van Bezooijen, Otto, & Heenan, 1983). The results of all such studies suggest that the recognition of emotions, expressed in the same vocal stimuli, is above chance, suggesting a universality of vocal affect.

But the recognition of facial expression and vocal affect have never been demonstrated to be perfectly accurate, not even within a culture. How does one explain the variability in the accuracy of the recognition of facial expression of emotion? One account points to the imperfection of the stimuli and the measurement methods used in such research: neither the stimuli nor the measurement methods in such studies can ever be ideal representations or indicators, respectively, of the process of interest. Therefore, perfectly accurate recognition of every facial expression (or emotional utterance) by every individual in every culture could never, in reality, be observed. This, in fact, is entirely true. But, there is also systematic variability in accuracy that appears to be due to culture. For instance, there are robust cultural differences in overall recognition rates such that members of western cultures tend to be more accurate than those of literate nonwestern cultures, and members of illiterate nonwestern cultures show the poorest recognition (e.g., Biehl et al., 1997; Matsumoto, 1992; Russell, 1994). There also exist systematic cultural differences in the accuracy of recognition of, and in confusions among, specific emotional expressions, including expressions considered indicative of basic emotions (e.g., Haidt & Keltner, 1999; Izard, 1977). Very similar to findings in the literature on the recognition of facial expression of emotion, there are also cultural differences in the recognition of vocal affect. For instance, which emotions are recognized from the voice with the highest accuracy varies across cultures (Van Bezooijen et al., 1983). Thus, although psychologists have largely concluded that there is strong evidence in favor of universal facial and vocal expressions of emotion, many have also concluded that there is a portion in the variability that is probably accounted for by culture (e.g., Matsumoto et al., 2002, for an example of this approach).

The initial quest for experimental evidence in favor of the existence of basic emotions initially limited the focus of cross-cultural research on emotion to similarities – which it was intended to do, of course. More inadvertently, however, the approach tended to promote a certain inattention to ways in which differences could conceivably occur (Mesquita, 2001a; Mesquita & Haire, 2004). Also, the research tended neither to take into account the social situations in which emotions unfold nor their everyday practice in the sense of their prevalence and their significance across cultures.

Looking at the Components

Theories of basic emotions precede, in the history of the scientific study of emotion, the component process account, described in Chapter 1. The relatively more recent claim by some researchers that emotions are not tightly coordinated innate programs but rather are events that are composed of loosely coordinated components (e.g., Frijda, 1986; Lang, 1977; Ortony & Turner, 1990; Scherer, 1984), focused researchers on the possible existence of different amounts and types of cultural variation across the specific components (Mesquita & Frijda, 1992; Mesquita, Frijda, & Scherer, 1997). Much initial research from this perspective admitted that rather than similarity or difference, emotional experience across cultures could reveal similarity and differences in a more continual, less all-or-none fashion (Mesquita, 2001a).

One of the signature programs of this type of research is the enormous study of the emotional experiences of university students from 37 countries comprising six geopolitical regions, including northern and central Europe, Mediterranean countries, Anglo-American New World countries, Latin American, Asian, and African countries (Scherer, 1997; Scherer & Wallbott, 1994; Scherer, Wallbott, Matsumoto, & Kudoh, 1988). The advantage of the program of research, in addition to its cultural and geographic/geopolitical breadth, is that it is one of only a handful of studies that attempted to examine a number of components of emotion simultaneously.

The method used in the study was to instruct participants to recall situations in which they felt certain emotions. The emotions of interest to

Scherer and colleagues were joy, anger, sadness, fear, shame, guilt, and disgust. Then, the participants had to answer a number of questions about the experienced emotion itself. Some of the questions concerned their appraisal of the situation that brought about the emotion. Others assessed specific aspects of the experience, such as how long it lasted, its intensity, their efforts to control it, and the effects the emotion had on other relationships. Still other questions concerned physiological components of the emotion, such as whether they experienced changes in heart rate, muscular tension, or temperature, and whether they experienced classic symptoms of certain emotions such as stomach trouble or a lump in the throat.

Cultural differences were found in all component processes. These differences were on average, however, smaller than the differences between the seven emotions, suggesting overall similarity as well. For example, Scherer (1997) found very similar patterns of appraisal, across cultures, for the emotions of joy, fear, anger, sadness, disgust, shame and guilt. The pattern of appraisal for situations conducive of anger, for instance, were ones that were evaluated as unpleasant, unexpected, obstructing goals, unfair, and caused by other people. However, in comparison to other geopolitical regions, individuals in African countries appraised situations conducive of all negative emotions as significantly more unfair, as more consistently externally caused, and as more immoral. This makes sense in light of the fact that individuals from African countries have more elaborated beliefs in spirits and other supernatural powers that can cause and otherwise control situations that bring about negative experiences, such as pain and suffering. Individuals in Latin American countries, in contrast, rated situations conducive of negative emotions as less immoral than the other regions.

We should note that the methodology in this study, as well as other studies with similar aims discussed later in the chapter, could be considered limited because it consists of collecting retrospective accounts of emotional experience, and may thus be an indication of how people construct and remember their emotional experience, rather than a close reflection of the experiences that people have online (Robinson & Clore, 2002). Still, this and similar studies influenced a new generation of research on emotion and culture in its insistence on studying emotions in all their complexity.

Looking for Culture

The research on emotion and culture within scientific psychology briefly mentioned in the previous two sections can be criticized for not having been guided by a theory of culture (Shweder, 2002). Posing the question, "Do people all over the world recognize the same expressions of emotion?"

presupposes a theory of emotion, the basic emotions account. Posing the question, "Do people all over the world vary substantially in how they experience the different components of emotion?" presupposes a different account of the emotion process, a component process account. But who should differ (and be similar) and why? Asking the question in this way requires that the researcher adopt a theory of the relationship between the groups under study and their emotions. As Kitayama and Markus (1994) noted: "Emotions observed in everyday life seem to depend on the dominant cultural frame in which specific social situations are constructed and, therefore, cannot be separated from culture specific patterns of thinking, acting, and interaction" (p. 4). More recently, therefore, the cross-cultural study of emotion has been approached from the perspective of different theories of culture and cultural models of emotion, not only from the perspective of different theories of emotion.

Specifically, cross-cultural research on emotion is increasingly influenced by theories of cultural differences within anthropology and ethnography (Lutz, 1987, 1988; Shweder, 1993, 1994, Shweder & Haidt, 2000) and linguistics (Wierzbicka, 1986, 1992). Consistent with the social constructionist theory of emotion, presented in Chapter 1, theories of cultural difference challenge, to greater or lesser extent, the nativist position on emotion that holds that emotion is a natural category of experience, and suggest that culture and emotion are interactive processes such that culture influences how emotions are expressed, managed, and understood, and emotions influence the development of cultural meanings and practices (Mesquita, 2003; Shweder, 1994, 2002; Solomon, 1995; see also Barrett, 2006). The focus is thus on the ways in which people interpret their world, their relationships, and the meaning of their lives, and the ways in which these beliefs are embodied in cultural practices, including those that provide an outlet for the experience and expression of emotion. In the next section, we examine the constructs of culture, and cultural models of emotion that have been most generative of psychological research to this point.

Defining Culture and Cultural Differences

When in Europe or the United States we say that there is not a lot of culture to be found in a certain city, we are saying that there is not much institutionalized theater, music, art, or dance to be experienced there. But culture in the sense used in this chapter is transmitted in more ways that those that have come to be called institutions of "culture." Culture is composed of a large number of symbolic processes, which include lay theories, interpretive schemas, images, and icons that are shared by members of a group and revealed in daily rituals, habits, and customs, which we refer to as cultural practices (Kitayama, 2002; Sperber, 1996). According to Shweder and Haidt (2000): "A culture is that subset of possible or available meanings which, by virtue of enculturation (informal or formal, implicit or explicit, unintended or intended), has become active in giving shape to the psychological processes of the individuals in a group" (p. 398). These meanings and the practices that embody them are efficient ways to impute social imperatives, including what people are expected to do in their lives, the ways in which they carry out those expectations, and how well or poorly they are likely to do so. What is also important about these meanings is that they can be so automatic as to seem to be "raw" or "uninterpreted" experience. For example, that a corpse causes fear may seem to the individual feeling this fear that it is an unmediated emotional experience that is determined by nature itself (e.g., Geertz, 1984). Contrary to what it feels like, however, many such experiences are mediated by culture-specific conceptual systems or "cultural models" (Markus, Kitayama, & Heinman, 1996; Nisbett & Cohen, 1995). It is often only when members of one culture are confronted by the cultural understandings of another culture that they realize that their experiences are not raw and uninterpreted, but in fact open to interpretation.

In order to make sense of cultural conceptual systems or models, at least as they might relate to emotional experience, it is useful to combine cultural meanings into groups of meanings that are somehow related and shown to be fundamental (Matsumoto, 2003; Mesquita & Markus, 2004; Smith & Schwartz, 1999). In this way, we can then cluster individuals and groups together into larger cultural categories. As Matsumoto (1990), among others, has noted: "Cultures transcend national borders and require researchers to use meaningful dimensions of variability rather than physical boundaries [in conceptualizing them]" (p. 196).

Of course, this does not make studies of and comparisons of different national groups unimportant or uninteresting. Because there is typically a dominant language, educational system, political system, shared mass media, as well as national symbols such as sports teams and flags, it is not unreasonable to assume that there is at the least reasonable cultural homogeneity within a country, and important differences from other countries (Smith & Schwartz, 1999). But it is still important to characterize nations in ways that hope to make them comparable. In the next sections, we discuss a number of ways in which cultural beliefs have been grouped together and systematized into constructs, also called cultural models, that help the researcher compare emotional experiences around the world. We begin by discussing some general constructs that make general predictions about emotion, and then discuss some accounts of cultural models of emotion in particular.

General Culture Constructs

Individualism and Collectivism

One way in which researchers have categorized cultures is in terms of the degree to which individuals in a given group think of themselves as fundamentally separate from other individuals, versus as an integral part of the larger group (Hofstede, 1980; Mead, 1967; Triandis, 1972, 1995). In this approach, individualist cultures are ones in which important meanings concerning relationships, identity, power, and ambition converge to promote individual needs, wishes, and desires over those of the group and collective needs, wishes, and desires. In such cultures, and North American culture is assumed to be a prototype, hierarchical power and status differences are minimized, and equality and the possibility of personal attainment are encouraged. People are viewed as autonomous from the groups of which they are members, with separate destinies and outcomes. They are thus encouraged to express themselves and develop their individuality (Markus & Kitayama, 1991; Triandis, 1994). This is in rather sharp contrast to cultures defined as collectivist, in which important meanings concerning relationships, identity, power, and ambition involve the group. The needs, wishes, and desires of the collectivities in which individuals find themselves (e.g., castes, families, businesses) are emphasized and the notion of individuality is minimized or even absent from the cultural model. In collectivist cultures, hierarchy and status are widely recognized and formalized, and roles and normative behaviors are clearly defined by social position. These cultures, and some Asian cultures are prototypes, encourage relationship harmony, and discourage individual ambition and direct threats to authority (Kitayama & Markus, 1995).

Another culture construct, that of independent versus interdependent self-concepts is largely overlapping with the distinction between individualist versus collectivist cultures (Markus & Kitayama, 1991). The former analysis, however, focuses more on the ways in which the meanings and values intrinsic to the two cultures result in the development of different ways of thinking about and defining one's identity, including beliefs about agency or who is responsible for and determinant of specific actions (Markus & Kityama, 2004; Mesquita & Markus, 2004). For the purposes of this book, we tend to use the terms individualist and collectivist cultures, noting that the relation to independent and interdependent selves is an intimate one.

Broad hypotheses involving cultural variation in emotion fall naturally out of this distinction. For example, emotional moderation in general might be expected to be observed in collectivist cultures more than in individualist cultures, since strong emotions and emotional expression could disrupt intra-group relations and smooth social functioning (e.g., Matsumoto, 1989, 1990; Tsai & Levenson, 1997). A specific example of this general prediction focuses on the emotions of anger and shame. Because individualistic cultures show less concern for social structure and group cohesiveness, anger might be expected to be more frequently expressed in such cultures than in collectivist cultures, in which respect for authority and group harmony is, as mentioned, fundamental. And a respect for authority and group harmony might be associated with a greater tendency to express shame, which acknowledges deviations from accepted norms and group-defined goals (Cole, Bruschi, & Tamang, 2002).

Cultures of Honor

The notion of honor refers to an individual's self-respect or sense of self-esteem as determined by his own reputation or status, and by the reputation of his own group, especially his family. In so-called cultures of honor, family members are obliged to uphold the reputation of the family, especially through their public behavior and avoidance of humiliation (Miller, 1993). Mediterranean and South American countries have been described as honor cultures (Pitt-Rivers, 1965), as has the culture of the American South and the American West (Cohen, 1998; Nisbett, 1993). The value of honor in such cultures is not trivial, but is a defining one that influences much social behavior and social organization.

A number of specific hypotheses about differences in the experience of emotion in cultures of honor compared mostly to northern European (as represented both in Europe and in the American North) cultures, in which honor is not an inherent value, have been investigated (e.g., Cohen, Nisbett, Bowdle, & Schwarz, 1996; Fischer, Manstead, & Rodriguez Mosquera, 1999; Rodriguez Mosquera, Manstead, & Fischer, 2002). One such hypothesis is that anger and violence as responses to insults to honor are both more often felt and more often expressed by individuals in honor cultures (Cohen & Nisbett, 1994; Cohen et al., 1996).

Much support for this hypothesis has now accumulated. For instance, in a series of three elegant studies, Cohen et al. (1996) invited male university students who had grown up in the American South or the American North into the laboratory. In the context of completing some questionnaires, the experimenters arranged that all participants inconvenienced another person, who was actually a confederate of the experimenter, by making him move aside to let them walk down a hallway. When obliged to let the participant pass by a second time, the confederate bumped into the participant and called him an "asshole." Other confederates of the experimenter sitting in the hallway discretely observed and noted the behavior of the participant as a function of the insult. In addition, some hormonal measures were taken under the guise of a concern with physiological correlates of general performance. Specifically, the stress hormone cortisol was measured to assess the degree of anger or upset, and testosterone was measured to assess the participants' physiological readiness for aggression (levels of both were measured simply by obtaining a saliva sample). Among other things, compared with Northerners, who were relatively impervious to the insult, Southerners were more likely to engage in aggressive and dominant behaviors (as observed by the confederates), were made more upset by the insult (as indicated by a rise in cortisol levels), and were more physiologically readied for aggression (as indicated by a rise in testosterone levels). Anger has also been reported to be elicited by insults to honor more in Spain (an honor culture) than in the Netherlands (Fischer et al., 1999; Rodriguez Mosquera et al., 2002).

Power Distance

Yet another pertinent culture construct comes from analyses of pancultural values. Theorists who study cultural values assume that values reflect solutions to the fundamental problems or issues that societies confront in order to regulate the activities of their members (Hofstede, 1980; Schwartz, 1994a). Values thus are overarching goals, to which specific shape is given by policy and decision makers, and that serve as guiding principles in individuals' lives (Rokeach, 1973; Schwartz, 1992, 1994a). Power distance refers to how much hierarchical inequality the culture encourages individuals to accept and regard as legitimate. By examining values and relationships in the workplace, specifically among individuals employed by the company IBM, Hofstede (1983) was able to measure and report power distances for a large number of countries. A low power distance indicates that employers and employees work closely together, try to apply democratic practices, and consider each other equals even in the face of differences in education level. In contrast, a high power distance indicates that relations between employer and employee are strictly ruled and dependent on the decisions of the employer, that the company organization is centralized and hierarchical, and that employees expect to be told what to do from their superiors because they consider each other as unequal. In the most recent analysis, Hofstede (2001) reported that Austria, Israel, and Denmark had the lowest power distances, whereas the Philippines, Guatemala, and Malaysia had the highest.

The notion of power distance is related to Schwartz's (Schwartz, 1994a, 1994b) analysis of cultural values. Schwartz identified three bipolar dimensions that express value typologies. These include cultures that value conservatism (i.e., maintenance of the social structure and the traditional order) versus autonomy (i.e., uniqueness of the individual, importance of individual rights and expression); hierarchy (i.e., unequal distribution of power and goods, socially prescribed roles) versus egalitarianism (i.e., voluntary cooperation, concern with public welfare); and mastery (i.e., active self-assertion, the effecting of change in the natural and social world) versus harmony (i.e., harmonious assimilation into the natural world, unity with nature). Cultures that value hierarchy and conservatism are likely to be similar to those showing high power distance.

Some general predictions about the experience and expression of emotion can be generated from an analysis of power distance and related values such as conservatism versus autonomy and hierarchy versus egalitarianism. These predictions largely concern who is expected to and allowed to express which emotions to whom. One would expect that individuals in high power distance cultures express strong, sometimes called dominant, emotions such as anger and pride, to individuals who are in subordinate positions to them. And one would also expect that individuals in such cultures express submissive emotions such as appreciation, sadness, and shame in the presence of superiors. Indeed, some research has shown that individuals from countries high in power distance tend to behave submissively and to be afraid in the presence of their superiors (Bochner & Hesketh, 1994). Furthermore, the notion that superiors express dominant, and inhibit submissive, emotions in such cultures was recently suggested by a cross-national study by Mondillon, Niedenthal, Brauer, Rohmann, Dalle, and Uchida (2005). In that study, university students in Japan, the United States, France, and Germany described what they believed being in a position of power means in their society in terms of dimensions related to control (over others versus the self) and in terms of the obligation to uphold social norms (requirement to uphold versus liberty to transgress). Compared to the United States and Japan, European respondents conveyed a more conservative view of power as involving control over others as well as personal liberty from the constraints of social norms. Respondents in European countries also reported that powerful people were expected to display dominant emotions and to inhibit submissive ones to a greater degree than those from the other two countries.

Cultural Models of Emotion

Working from these larger culture constructs, some theorists have recently proposed specific ways to conceptualize different cultural models of emotion; coherent systems of beliefs about the meanings of potentially emotional situations; and the resulting emotions and expression of emotion.

Dialetical vs. Optimizing

One such conceptualization of cultural models of emotion focusses on the ways in which positive and negative experiences and feelings are related. In this approach, the comparison is between the Asian cultural model of emotion versus the European American one (e.g., Bagozzi, Wong, & Yi, 1999b; Leu, Mesquita, & Ellsworth, 2005; Peng & Nisbett, 1999, 2000). In the Asian model of emotion, extremes are shunned. The ideal of moderation in emotional experience and expression has already been suggested by the previous discussion of collectivist cultures. Furthermore, however, in this account of the cultural model of emotion, moderation involves a tolerance of, even a philosophical requirement for, a fundamental positive relationship between positive and negative feelings (Leu et al., 2005). The cultural basis for this belief is seen as residing in the teachings of the dominant religions of Daoism, Buddhism, and Confucianism. Daoism, for example, holds that "happiness is unhappiness." This expression conveys the important idea that good feelings and experiences imply, are fundamentally linked to, bad feelings and bad experiences (Ji, Nisbett, & Peng, 2001). Consistent with this, Lu (2001) reported that Chinese college students characterized happiness as a positive feeling that was very often followed by or otherwise associated with unhappiness. In a related way, Buddhism and Confucianism view striving for happiness, and for rewards more generally, as undesirable. In Buddhism, such a pursuit interferes with an individual's ability to resist succumbing to desire, which is taught as the way to overcome basic human suffering. In Confucianism, the pursuit of happiness can disrupt group harmony because it can elicit jealousy in others (Edwards, 1996) or threaten the maintenance of the social order through its emphasis on individualism (Heine et al., 1999). As a result of these fundamental beliefs, and teachings, the Asian cultural model of emotion involves a need for balance between positive and negative feelings, where each moderates the extent of the other (Leu et al., 2005).

Such a model is by contrast to the European American model. This model has been recently called an optimizing cultural model of emotion (Leu et al., 2005), and has been linked to the humanist philosophy of the Renaissance (e.g., Lukes, 1973). In that perspective, which describes morality as individualistic, the person is encouraged to be self-defining and self-determined. The right to the pursuit of happiness, ultimately made explicit in the American constitution, follows naturally from such a philosophy. Furthermore, in this philosophy, happiness is viewed as a personal characteristic that should be a defining feature of one's identity (Bellah, Madsen, Sullivan, Swidler, & Tiption, 1985). Since the individual is self-defining and self-determined, and since happiness is part of one's identity, expressions of unhappiness are seen as signs of failure (e.g., D'Andrade, 1984). Therefore, happiness in this model is a desired state and endpoint, in contrast with the Asian model; it is at odds with unhappiness and is not related to negative emotions in a fundamental dialectic (Bagozzi et al., 1999b).

The basic hypothesis about cultural differences in emotion that falls naturally from this way of defining cultural models of emotion is that Asians in general ought to report feeling more moderated positive and negative feelings, and to more often feel both in a given situation, whereas European Americans should report feeling more positive feelings, and only positive or negative feelings – but not often both – in any given situation. Some support for this idea was reported in a study by Kitayama and colleagues (Kitayama, Markus, & Kurokawa, 2000). In that study, the researchers compared the frequency of reported positive and negative emotions in American and Japanese participants. The Americans reported feeling more positive emotions than negative ones, and the Japanese reported feeling as many positive as negative emotions. In related work, Mesquita and colleagues (for example, Mesquita & Karasawa, 2002) showed that on scales ranging from very pleasant to very unpleasant, Asian participants tended to use the midpoint of the scale when reporting their feelings. Americans tended to report high pleasant feelings, more often using the extreme positive end of the scale. Finally, Schimmack, Oishi, and Diener (2002) showed that the correlation between the frequency of experiences of positive and negative emotions was significantly less negative for members of Asian cultures than were experiences of such emotions among American and other western cultures. The stronger negative correlation between the frequency with which positive and negative emotions were experienced in the latter cultures means that the experience of positive emotion implied the absence of negative emotions.

Engaging and Disengaging Emotions

Another way to characterize Asian and European American models of emotion has referred to engaging and disengaging emotions. This construct relies in part on the distinction between independent and interdependent self-concepts (Kitayama et al., 1995; Markus & Kitayama, 1991), which reflect the processes of identity development and relating in individualist and collectivist cultures, respectively. According to Kitayama, Mesquita, and Karasawa (2004), in collectivist cultures, individuals interpret many situations as ones in which social interdependence is salient, and in which their interdependent identity may (or may not, if things go wrong) be affirmed. For instance, a social interaction may be largely understood as a context in which social harmony can and should be realized. If harmony has been disrupted in some way, then a concern with failed repayment may result. Linked to and resulting from this way of understanding social interaction, certain positive emotions, such as friendliness and respect, and certain negative emotions such as guilt and shame, become constitutive of the Asian cultural model of emotion. That is, the cultural model of emotion includes interpretations, based in fundamental values and meanings that are very often applied, and thus establish the prevalence of specific emotions. These have been called *socially engaged emotions* (Kitayama et al., 2004).

In contrast, members of individualist cultures tend to interpret many situations in terms of individual self-expression and achievement, and thus as situations in which their independent self can be affirmed. Or, in the case of the confrontation by an obstacle, the independent self can be harmed by the disruption of important goals. Linked to and resulting from this way of understanding social interaction, certain positive emotions, such as pride, and certain negative emotions such as anger and frustration, become constitutive of the European American cultural model of emotion. Again, the cultural model of emotion includes interpretations, based in fundamental values and meanings that are very often applied, and thus establish the prevalence of specific emotions. These have been called *socially disengaged emotions* (Kitayama et al., 2004).

In a diary study in which Japanese and American university students recalled the "most emotional episode of the day" for 14 consecutive days, Kitayama and colleagues indeed found that the Japanese felt more intense socially engaged positive emotions than socially disengaged positive emotions in positive situations. They also felt socially engaged negative emotions more intensely than socially disengaged emotions in negative situations. The American students showed the opposite effect in both situations (see Figure 9.1). The same basic effect was also found in a second study in which participants rated their likely emotions in experimenter-provided situations.

Recent years have seen the formulation of ways in which cultures can be conceptualized and compared. Cultural models of values, interpersonal relationships, and identity development and maintenance, as well as specific cultural models of emotion, provide researchers with means to pose specific hypotheses about how members of different cultures experience their emotions. In the remainder of this chapter, we examine the roles of culture in three components of emotion. The first has to do with the antecedent events to emotion, both concrete descriptions of those situations

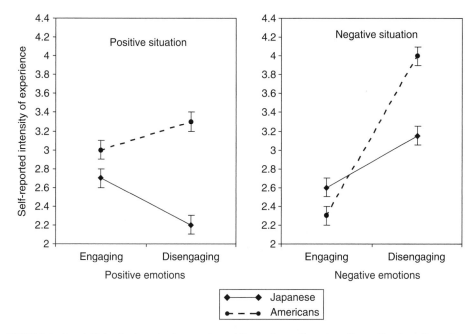

FIGURE 9.1. Reported intensity of experiencing engaging and disengaging positive and negative emotions in positive and negative situations, respectively. From Kitayama, S. et al. (2004). *Culture and emotional experience: Socially engaging and disengaging emotions in Japan and the United States.* Unpublished manuscript, University of Michigan, Ann Arbor, MI.

and also individuals' appraisals of the situations. Are the situations that lead to the experience of discrete emotions in one culture roughly the same as those that lead to the experience of the same emotion in another culture? Second, we examine the way that emotions look across culture. Specifically, we examine in more detail the ways in which individuals in different cultures perceive others' emotional expressions and the ways in which they display their own emotions. Finally, we summarize research on physiology and physical sensations. Here the question is whether, across cultures, individuals experience the same physiological changes when they are exposed to the same emotional events and report also having the same emotion. We explore this question looking both at changes in physiology and in people's self-reports of their bodily sensations.

Do Emotions Occur in the Same Places?

When and where do members of different cultures experience emotions? This question is difficult to address easily because we have already seen that the same apparently objective situation can have very different meanings for people in different cultures. So, although we can pose the simple question "do the same emotions arise in the same situations?" if there are differences across cultures, we cannot be sure why. An analysis of the appraisals of situations that systematically elicit different emotions might then shed light on the differences. In the next sections, we first examine the situations that seem to elicit certain emotions across cultures, and then we discuss analyses of the appraisals that seem to underlie the experience of emotions in different cultures.

Antecedent Events

In a study of Americans, Europeans (from eight countries) and Japanese, Scherer and colleagues sought to identify the antecedent events for four emotions, including anger, sadness, happiness, and fear (Scherer et al., 1988). Participants in the study were asked to describe the situations in which the four emotions were experienced, and the nominated situations were later coded as falling into a number of possible categories or having specific themes. Although the researchers expected quite high similarity in the frequency with which different types of situations and themes were nominated across the three groups, this was not the case. The results are reported in Table 9.1.

As can be seen in the table, joy was associated with quite different events to different degrees, especially for the Japanese. For instance, while cultural pleasures, births, and bodily pleasures were important for the Europeans and Americans, all were much less frequent antecedents of joy for the Japanese. In addition, as expected by other work on the difference between individuals in individualist versus collectivist countries, achievements were antecedents of joy for Americans and Europeans far more than for the Japanese.

The antecedent events of sadness were also quite different across cultures. Death, for instance, was a much less common antecedent event for sadness for the Japanese than for the Americans and Europeans. The authors note that this may be related to beliefs about death in Japan, which link the person's soul to the remaining family in a more peaceful and lasting way. Americans were much more often saddened by separation and the Japanese much more saddened by relationship problems, with the Europeans somewhere in between for both type of situations. This finding was interpreted as being due to the relative greater mobility of Americans, making separation more likely and perhaps more salient than relationship problems caused by other factors.

Fear was caused often by strangers and a failure of achievements in the United States. In Japan, fear was often caused by the situation of confronting

TABLE 9.1
Percentages of Participants Reporting Categories of Antecedent Events
for Joy, Sadness, Fear, and Anger

	Europe	Japan	USA	p
Joy				
News	9.9	4.6	10.3	ns.
Relationships	29.4	33.3	23.6	ns.
Social institution	4.7	.6	10.3	***
Temporary meetings	19.6	13.2	17.6	ns.
Birth	8.3	.6	6.1	**
Body	12.8	2.9	16.4	***
Achievement	16.0	13.8	26.1	**
Sadness				
News	9.5	2.3	14.5	***
Relationships	27.1	36.2	20.0	**
Temporary separation	6.5	2.3	12.7	**
Permanent separation	8.9	2.3	12.1	***
Death	22.2	5.2	22.4	***
Body	10.1	5.2	10.3	ns.
Fear				
Relationships	4.6	9.8	3.6	*
Death	6.5	6.9	4.2	ns.
Body	7.2	4.6	3.0	ns.
Strangers	14.9	5.2	20.0	***
Achievement	11.7	16.7	18.8	ns.
Supernatural	3.9	4.6	6.7	ns.
Risky situations	11.2	5.3	14.5	*
Traffic	20.0	14.4	11.5	ns.
Novel situation	14.5	17.2	13.3	ns.
Anger				
Relationships	38.5	29.3	58.2	***
Strangers	19.9	52.3	14.5	***
Achievement	6.7	10.3	8.5	ns.
Injustice	20.9	4.0	20.6	***
Inconvenience	8.5	9.8	6.1	ns.

a (listed only if at least 5% in at least one sample); ns. not significant.
*$p < .05$; **$p < .01$; ***$p < .001$
From Scherer, K. R. et al. (1988). Emotional experience in cultural context: A comparison between Europe, Japan, and the United States. In K. R. Scherer (Ed.), *Facets of emotions* (pp. 5–30). Hillsdale, NJ: Lawrence Erlbaum Associates, Inc.

novel situations, although a fear evoked by failure in achievement situations was also very frequent. Fear also arose in the context of relationships more in Japan than in the United States or Europe, which was interpreted as a fear of failing to maintain social relationships and harmony.

Finally, anger was also associated with different antecedent events. Americans and, to some degree, Europeans experienced most anger within close relationships, while Japanese experienced most anger in the context of strangers. Injustice also caused anger in Americans and Europeans significantly more often than in Japanese. Both of these findings are predicted from a view of individuals in collectivist cultures as more concerned about harmony within close relationships and as tolerant of accepted hierarchy and inequalities.

The differences in the antecedent events for emotion in different countries are in and of themselves interesting. However, we cannot really know *why* these differences exist. Perhaps they exist because the same situations have very different meanings in the different countries. In order to know if that is the case, it is therefore important to study the appraisals and the meanings of emotional situations.

Appraisals

Initial studies of possible cultural differences in appraisals of emotional situations asked participants to rate on a number of fundamental appraisal dimensions the ways in which they evaluated the antecedent conditions of a specified emotion (e.g., Frijda et al., 1995; Roseman, Dhawan, Rettek, Naidu, & Thapa, 1995; Scherer, 1997). As mentioned earlier in the chapter, such studies found both important similarities and differences in the role of appraisal dimensions in predicting specific emotions. Similar to the study by Scherer (1997), Mauro, Sato, and Tucker (1992) investigated the differentiation of 14 emotions along 14 appraisal dimensions, based on dimensions proposed by Roseman (1984), Scherer (1984a), and Smith and Ellsworth (1985) (see Chapter 1 for a review of these dimensions). The participants came from the United States, Japan, the People's Republic of China, and Hong Kong. Mauro and colleagues predicted and found little cultural variability in the extent to which pleasantness, certainty, and goal conduciveness differentiated specific emotions. These dimensions were predicted to show less cultural variability because they are more "primitive" in that they presumably occur earlier in the evaluation process and/or require fewer cognitive resources. There was significant cultural variation, however, in the differentiation of specific emotions by the more cognitively demanding appraisal dimensions. Such appraisals included the extent to which the event could be controlled, responsibility, and anticipated effort. The observed variability in the ways in which these dimensions contributed to the experience of specific emotions is consistent with other analyses (e.g., Scherer, 1997), and highlights the fact that western conceptions of control, responsibility, and effort have strongly shaped appraisal theories of emotion.

More recently cultural analyses of appraisals have sought to examine the importance of meanings or evaluations that do not necessarily appear in existing lists of fundamental appraisal dimensions for emotions, but which can be extracted from of cultural models of emotion.

Interpretations of Social Meaning

We have seen that there is a tendency for individuals from collectivist cultures to view many situations as affording possibilities to affirm (or disrupt) in some way the interdependent sense of self, or group harmony, while those from individualist cultures might see the same situations as affording the possibility to affirm (or disrupt) the independent sense of self. This further suggests that many situations, even if they have objectively similar characteristics, have different meanings for individuals from different cultures and can result in the experience of different emotions (Kitayama et al., 2004).

Other findings that are consistent with this idea come from a study comparing the emotions of individuals from individualist and collectivist cultures residing in the Netherlands (Mesquita, 2001b). Participants representing a collectivist culture came from the Surinamese and Turkish minority populations in the Netherlands, and individuals representing an individualist culture came from the majority Dutch population. Participants in the study were instructed to recall positive, offensive, and immoral experiences from their past. Results showed that participants from collectivist cultural contexts were more aware of how the situation would be perceived by others than were participants from the individualist cultural context. Very interestingly, the Turkish and Surinamese participants reported, moreover, that the emotional meanings of the situations were more "obvious" than did the Dutch participants. This indicates that they assumed that other individuals would interpret, feel, and act in the same way as they had in the same situation. In this sense, there was social consensus, or at least an assumed social consensus. Dutch participants were more likely to think that their interpretations, feelings, and actions were personal. And they did not think that these were necessarily obvious or likely to be shared by other individuals. Thus, in this sense, the appraisals of members of collectivist cultures were more social and consensual than were appraisals of members of an individualist culture.

The importance of social meaning in situational appraisals is further supported by another study by Mesquita and colleagues (Mesquita &

Haire, 2004; Mesquita & Markus, 2004), which assessed the appraisals of American and Japanese participants in different emotional situations. In the study, participants were interviewed about times when they had been offended, humiliated and valued. They self-nominated situations from their pasts that fit these themes, described them in detail, and the descriptions were recorded and later coded for content including the implications of the situation for other people. Analysis of the content coding revealed that, in the negative situations in particular, Japanese appraised the situation in terms of its meaning for other people. For example, more than 40% of the Japanese described the situation from the perspective of a third person or a generalized other, whereas none of the Americans did so. This suggests again that members of collectivist cultures appraise emotional situations in ways that reflect concern with the general social implications.

Compared to those from individualist cultures, members of collectivist cultures also interpret emotional situations in terms of the meaning for their own social position and the social status of their own group As an example of this, in the study of Surinamese, Turkish, and Dutch participants just described (Mesquita, 2001b), the individuals from the collectivist cultures appraised positive situations as more important to their status and respectability in the group than did Dutch respondents, and they also appraised positive situations as sharingmore positive implications for their families or relevant social groups than did the Dutch. These specific appraisals of social worth are similar to those displayed by individuals from cultures of honor. In those cultures, too, the meaning of an emotional situation for social position and stature is often far more central than in cultures in which honor is not a salient value (Fischer et al., 1999).

When taken together, the research on appraisals suggests that there are quite large cultural differences in the ways in which emotional situations are interpreted. Although across cultures, some of the fundamental dimensions of appraisals that produce and differentiate emotions are certainly observed, a cultural analysis provides further insight into the meaning of emotional situations. Specifically, individuals from collectivist cultures and cultures of honor tend to appraise situations that give rise to emotion in terms of their implications for the group and in terms of affirmation of or threats to social status and position. Furthermore, emotional situations involve the whole group, relationships within the group, and consequences for the group. In contrast, members of individualist cultures seem to see emotions as their own and involving their own personal internal states and needs. Thus, consensus about what should be felt when it is not achieved and concerns about the implications of the situation for the whole group rarely enter into appraisals.

To summarize, the limited research on this topic suggests that somewhat different antecedent events provoke emotions in individuals across cultures. Furthermore, although several common appraisal dimensions predict quite well the emergence of specific emotions, more recent cultural analyses suggest that the meaning of emotional situations for the group and the individual differ quite substantially. Future research will be required to further clarify the links between the meanings of emotional situations and the specific emotions that result.

Do Emotions Look the Same?

As we have already seen elsewhere in this book, there is high agreement, across cultures, in the recognition of anger, disgust, fear, happiness, sadness, and surprise (Ekman, 1972; Ekman & Friesen, 1971; Izard, 1971). However, as we have already noted in this chapter, there are also some general cultural differences in the accuracy with which different cultures recognize these expressions, and even in the way they make confusions among them. In the following sections, we discuss some other systematic differences both in how emotions are recognized and how they are expressed, with particular reference to differences that were predicted by specific cultural models or theories of culture.

Recognizing Facial Expressions

In one demonstration of cultural differences in the recognition of facial expression of emotion, Matsumoto (1989) examined the intensity ratings of facial expressions of negative emotions (anger, fear, and sadness) as a function of the power distance ranking of the country (Hofstede, 1983). The intensity ratings came from a cross-national study of different countries, including Estonia, Germany, Greece, Hong Kong, Italy, Japan, Scotland, Sumatra, Turkey, and the United States, conducted by Ekman et al. (1987). Matsumoto noted that high power distance countries have a hierarchical and unequal structure, and that the expression of negative emotions is threatening to the existing social order. Thus, it would be protective of the social order to not express or see expressed in faces a high degree of negative emotion. Indeed, when he correlated the average perceived intensity of the negative expressions with the power distance ranking of the countries, he found a negative correlation. This suggests that individuals in high power distance countries reported seeing less intense negative emotions expressed on the same faces as those judged by individuals in low power distance countries.

A more recent study also considered the importance of social relationships and the social context, so important to the collectivist cultural model of emotion, in the perception of emotional expression (Masuda, Ellsworth, Mesquita, Leu, & Veerdonk, 2005). Specifically, these researchers proposed that the perceived intensity of facial expressions of emotion by individuals from collectivist cultures should be affected by social context more than the perceived intensity of expressions by individuals from individualist cultures. The Japanese and American university students who participated in the study were presented with pictures, such as the one presented in Figure 9.2. As can be seen, the pictures showed a central figure, a child, expressing anger, sadness, happiness, or neutral emotion. The central figure was surrounded by a crowd of children who were all expressing either the same emotion or another emotion (the figure shows an example of an inconsistency between the emotion expressed by the central figure and the emotion expressed by the crowd of children). Participants had to judge the intensity of the emotion felt by the central figure by rating the degree to which he or she felt anger, sadness, and happiness for each picture. As expected, Japanese but not American, perceivers were influenced in their judgments by the emotions expressed by the crowds surrounding the central figure. So for example, if the central figure was expressing anger (sadness, happiness) Japanese participants rated the central figure as more angry (sad, happy) if the surrounding crowd was also expressing that emotion. Furthermore, the Japanese, but not the Americans, tended to see more of the (inconsistent) emotion expressed by the crowd in the expression displayed by the central figure.

FIGURE 9.2. A sample cartoon image. From Masuda, T. et al. (2005). *Putting the face in context: Cultural differences in the perception of emotions from facial behavior.* Unpublished manuscript, University of Michigan, Ann Arbor, MI.

So, for example, if the central figure was expressing happiness but the others were expressing sadness, the central figure was rated as expressing happiness, plus some sadness.

The importance of a concern with the social context was also revealed in a study of the recognition of facial expression by Canadians of Asian and European descent. In that study, participants were instructed to recall an emotional event from the past in which they had experienced one of six target emotions: sadness, sympathy, fear, anger, shame, and contempt (Cohen & Gunz, 2002). The six emotions were chosen because they comprise three complementary pairs of emotions, in that when an individual experiences one emotion, a relating person would be expected to feel the complementary emotion (e.g. contempt–shame). After they had recalled and relived one of the six target emotional events, participants were exposed to a number of facial expressions and had to rate the extent to which each expressed the six target emotions. Participants of Asian descent who had just recalled one specific emotion tended to rate the faces as expressing more of the complementary emotion. In contrast, those of European descent had a slight tendency to see their own emotional state in the expressions of others, rather than the complementary state. Cohen and Gunz (2002) suggest that collectivist cultures emphasize the ability to see the impact of one's own emotions on others. Individualist cultures, in contrast, emphasize the importance of one's own internal state and this leads to a tendency to project one's feelings onto others.

A Cultural Ingroup Advantage

It has recently been suggested that individuals recognize emotional expressions displayed by members of their cultural ingroup more accurately than expressions displayed by individuals from other cultures. This cultural ingroup advantage was initially supported by a meta-analysis of the results of 97 studies involving 182 different samples of participants (Elfenbein & Ambady, 2002a). The ingroup advantage appeared to hold, moreover, independent of the emotional expression or of the experimental method used in the study. The meta-analysis also provided evidence of a cultural ingroup advantage in the recognition of emotion from other nonverbal signals of emotion including the voice and body language. Subsequent studies designed to test the implications of the meta-analysis found evidence in favor of an ingroup advantage among American, Japanese, and Indian observers and expressers (Elfenbein, Mandal, Ambady, & Harizuka, 2002), and among non-Asian American and Chinese observers who recognized Caucasian and Chinese expressions (Elfenbein & Ambady, 2003b).

A *dialect theory* of facial expression has been proposed to account for the ingroup advantage (Elfenbein and Ambady, 2003b). Drawing on accounts of dialects in linguistics, this theory holds that there is a universal, perhaps innate, language of emotion, which underlies the better-than-chance recognition of a set of facial expressions (and other nonverbal behavior) across culture. But then, similar to variations in accent, grammar, and vocabulary within a language (for instance, the differences between American and British English), different cultures add accents and "vocabularies" of emotional expression that are unique to that culture and result in slightly different signals of the emotion. These dialects are the result of learning, in the sense that they develop in the context of the attunement of expression between individuals within the culture (Leach, 1972). But they are held to differ from display rules in that they are not necessarily conscious and do not involve the regulation of emotion or emotional expression in accordance with social norms (Elfenbein & Ambady, 2003b). In fact, display rules regulate the expression of emotion, including the dialect, and do not constitute the dialect itself. Thus, from this account, the ingroup advantage in the recognition of facial expression occurs because members of a given culture are used to perceiving a particular manifestation (the dialect) of a universal facial expression of emotion, and therefore are more accurate in identifying it.

Neither the existence of a cultural ingroup advantage nor the dialect account of it has gone without criticism, however. Matsumoto (2005), for instance, has pointed out that while a statistical interaction between the culture that is expressing the emotion and the culture that is identifying the emotion is generally found in such research, the interaction does not indicate that culture A recognizes expressions displayed by members of its own culture better than those of culture B, and that culture B recognizes expressions displayed by members of its own culture better than those of culture A. Rather, the results actually mean that there is a difference such that there is an advantage in the recognition of the within-culture expressions, but that one of the cultures, say culture A, recognizes all facial expressions with greater accuracy than culture B. Put statistically, this means that there is a main effect for culture indicating that one culture is doing better than the other overall. Matsumoto (2005) questions whether such interactions really mean that there is an ingroup advantage. He suggests that such findings show a relative, but not an absolute ingroup advantage. The dialect theory is an account of an absolute advantage.

Matsumoto (2005) also points out that the implication of the dialect theory is that members of different cultures express emotions on the face in slightly different ways, perhaps by the use of different muscle contractions or configurations of contractions. He suggests therefore that the strongest demonstration of a cultural ingroup advantage would involve, first, a demonstration that the patterns of muscles that are used to express an emotion in different cultures are actually different, even to a slight degree. Second, it would be necessary to show that any face expressing the emotion in a way specific to a culture is more accurately recognized by members of that culture. The use of "any" face might be important because thus far "culture" has very often been confounded with race in the actual stimuli used to represent facial expressions and cultural groups. Since members of different races have slightly different facial morphology, morphological differences have therefore also been confounded with culture. Future research is likely to address just these issues.

Expressing Emotions

Expressiveness of Northerners and Southerners

Charles de Secondat Montesquieu published an important treatise on human behavior in 1748 entitled *The Spirit of the Law*. In that book, drawing on 18th-century beliefs about physiology, he argued that the warmer climate found in more southern countries (of the northern hemisphere) tends to cause the skin to become more relaxed and the nerve endings more sensitive, while colder climates make the nerves of the skin less sensitive to all forms of stimulation. Because of these differences in the effect of weather on physiology, individuals in northern countries, he argued, were generally stolid and reserved in character, while those in southern countries were more social and emotional. Part of this view is communicated in the stereotype of Scandinavians that we offered at the beginning of the chapter.

Pennebaker, Rimé and Blankenship (1996) set out to examine this stereotype by investigating individuals' beliefs about the expressiveness of people who lived in the north and the south of their own countries. They also examined the possible validity of the stereotype by asking the participants about their own expressiveness. To do this, Pennebaker and colleagues solicited participants from 26 countries and asked them whether individuals in the northern and southern regions of their country were emotionally expressive, and whether they themselves were emotionally expressive. The results supported Montesquieu's hypothesis, particularly in Europe and Asia where the populations have been stable, without strong migration and immigration influences, for thousands of years. That is, participants in European and in Asian countries thought that individuals who lived in the southern regions of their country were more expressive than those in the northern regions. Moreover, participants from southern regions also described themselves as more expressive than did the participants in the northern regions. Interestingly, further analysis also showed that the north–south differences were not entirely accounted for by average temperature differences. So, perhaps variations that originated with temperature and climatic differences have developed into cultural practices that solidify the routine display versus control of emotional expression.

A related question about expressiveness was addressed in a more recent laboratory study (Tsai & Chentsova-Dutton, 2003). The cultures of Irish Americans and Scandinavian Americans, due in part to the immigration patterns, reflect the content of the southern and northern stereotypes just discussed. Specifically, the culture of the Irish is oriented toward dramatic expressions of tragedy and the use of laughter and humor in the social sharing of the experiences of life (Greeley, 1979, 1981). Scandinavians, contrariwise, have been characterized as a people who promote the moderation of emotional expression and a certain stoicism in the service of maintaining social order.

The research by Tsai and Chentsova-Dutton (2003) was designed to test these presumed differences in a laboratory study. Participants, Americans with the relevant cultural backgrounds, performed the relived emotions task, which is an effective elicitor of emotions (e.g., Levenson, Carstensen, Friesen, & Ekman, 1991; Oliveau & Willmuth, 1979). In the task, participants were provided with a label for a target emotion, such as "happiness," and also a description of a situation in which the target emotion occurred, such as "a time when you did something or something happened that you wanted very much, so that you felt very good." Participants had to recall a time when they had experienced the target emotion, focus on it, and relive it. When they were able to feel the emotion, they pressed a button to signal their success at the task. In all, the participants were exposed to five target emotions. As the participants relived the target emotions, their facial expressions were recorded by a hidden video camera. Facial expressions were then later coded with the use of the Facial Action Coding System (FACS; Ekman & Friesen, 1978). As can be seen in Figure 9.3, Irish Americans were more facially expressive than were Scandinavian Americans for all five emotions, except pride, and particularly for the emotions of happiness and love.

Display Rules

The research on expressiveness within cultures focusses on the general tendency to be free versus constrained in one's outward emotionality. Display rules, as discussed in Chapter 4, were originally proposed within Ekman's (1972) and Friesen's (1972) neurocultural theory of emotion. The

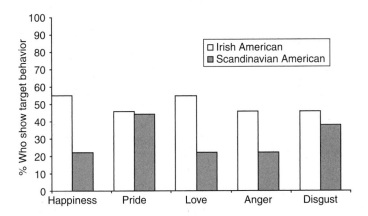

FIGURE 9.3. Percentage of Irish-American and Scandinavian-American participants who show target emotional behavior during each relived emotion. Differences for love and happiness are statistically significant. From Tsai, J. L., & Chentsova-Dutton, Y. (2003). Variation among European Americans in emotional facial expression. *Journal of Cross-Cultural Psychology, 34,* 650–657.

theory holds that there exist innate facial affect programs that are biologically evolved templates for expression that produce universal facial expressions, and also display rules, which are responsible for cultural variation in the norms for situational and interpersonal expression of emotion. Display rules are thus more specific than the general cultural imperative to express or inhibit in general, and involve imperatives about when to display which emotions to whom. And more precisely, they are "what people learn, probably quite early in their lives, about the need to manage the appearance of particular emotions in particular situations" (Ekman & Friesen, 1975, p. 137). Research on emotional development and the understanding of rules for managing emotional expression has demonstrated that American mothers tend to imitate positive emotions such as interest and happiness when their infants are as young as 2 to 7 months old. They very rarely, however, imitate the infant's negative emotions such as anger or sadness (Malatesta, Grigoryev, Lamb, Albin, & Culver, 1986; Malatesta & Haviland, 1982). This suggests the American desire to express – and experience – positive emotions is taught at a very young age! By the time American children are 3 years old, their mothers have begun to teach display rules quite explicitly (e.g., Miller & Sperry, 1987).

Probably the first study to demonstrate the existence of cultural differences in display rules involved the participation of Japanese and American individuals who were exposed to a stressful film (Ekman, 1973; Friesen, 1972). When the participants watched the film alone, they all showed evidence of facial disgust, fear, and distress, and differences were not detected. When the participants then watched the films in the presence of a higher status experimenter, American participants continued to express the negative emotions of disgust, fear, and distress, while the Japanese tended to mask their negative feelings with smiles. Although the presence of others can inhibit the expression of negative emotions even among Americans (e.g., Kleck, Vaughan, Cartwright-Smith, Vaughan, Colby, & Lanzetta, 1976), the desire not to negatively influence social harmony through the expression of negative emotions and the dialectic between negative and positive emotions demonstrated by smiling when confronted by negative stimulation in the presence of others, are both consistent with the collectivist cultural model of emotion.

More specific cultural analyses of display rules have also been advanced (e.g., Matsumoto, 1990; Matsumoto, Takeuchi, Andayani, Kouznetsova, & Krupp, 1998). In a study of Americans and Japanese, for instance, Matsumoto (1990) tested a number of hypotheses regarding display rules of individuals from individualist versus collectivist cultures. Triandis, Botempo, Villareal, Asai, and Lucca (1988) have offered refined theorizing about ingroup/outgroup relationships in terms of the distinction between individualist and collective cultures. For example, they suggest that, in collectivist cultures, the values regarding ingroup harmony and the requirement for strong identification with the ingroup results in a sharp distinction between the ingroup and the outgroup, and boundaries between them are very salient. In contrast, in individualist cultures, in which individuals do not define themselves in terms of their group to the same degree, individuals are likely to be members of more groups, and lines between ingroups and outgroups are therefore less salient.

Drawing on this analysis, Matsumoto (1990) proposed that Japanese and Americans' display rules for ingroup and outgroup settings should differ. Specifically, he proposed that the Japanese should possess displays rules according to which the expression of negative emotions to the outgroup is permissible because it emphasizes the ingroup–outgroup boundary and enhances ingroup identity and solidarity. At the same time, the Japanese should not condone expression of negative emotions to the ingroup, because this would disrupt group harmony. The Americans, he proposed should condone just the opposite set of rules. Specifically, for Americans it should be fine to express negative emotions to the ingroup because in that context one can demonstrate one's individuality and "let it all hang out." By the same token, displaying negative emotions to the outgroup would not be condoned because the oppositional role of the outgroup is much less clear, and one might just become a member of that group in the future, since group membership is more fluid.

In the study, Japanese and American participants were exposed to pictures of faces expressing anger, disgust, fear, happiness, sadness, and surprise. They rated the extent to which it was "appropriate" to display these expressions to different groups, some of which were ingroups, and others which were outgroups. Some support for the hypotheses was observed. Specifically, Americans thought that it was more appropriate to express disgust and sadness to the ingroup, and rated happiness as more appropriate to express in public than did the Japanese. At the same time, the Japanese thought that it was more appropriate to express anger to the outgroup than did the Americans.

A study by Fischer et al. (1999) investigated normative beliefs about the expression of anger, pride and shame in Spain, which, as we have seen, is an honor culture, and the Netherlands, a country in which honor is not a fundamental value and in which individualistic values are more dominant. Major differences with respect to the normative beliefs concerning the expression of the self-conscious emotions of pride and shame were found. Dutch participants more often reported social approval of expressions of pride, and sharing their pride with others, and they also referred more to the positive effects on themselves. The Spanish participants more often mentioned the negative effects of pride on social relations and referred more to the control and suppression of pride. Concerning the emotion of shame, Spanish participants mentioned more positive beliefs about expressing shame as showing one's vulnerability that makes others think positively about oneself compared to members of the more individualistic Dutch culture.

To summarize the research on the expression of emotion, particularly on the face, we have seen quite predictable and extensive cultural differences. Individuals from collectivist cultures perceive facial expressions through a lens that implicates other individuals and the meaning of the situation for other individuals. In addition, they tend to endorse display rules that relate sensibly to their concerns with identity development and maintenance by reference to their ingroup. Individuals from individualist cultures tend to see emotions as something intrinsic to the person having the emotion. Emotional expressions are linked largely to the person expressing. And display rules emphasize one's individuality and distinctness from larger groups.

Do Emotions Feel the Same?

Physiology

What are the bodily states underlying the psychological states that individuals from different cultures label with specific emotion words? Despite the fact that researchers have not been able to link a specific pattern of physiology to specific emotions, the fact that some physiological changes seem to characterize some emotions has motivated researchers to explore emotion physiology across cultures.

For instance, Chapter 2 introduced research by Levenson, Ekman, and Friesen (1990), which was conducted with the participation of American university students. That study revealed findings suggestive of some differentiation of emotion in the autonomic nervous system, apparently elicited by the guided contraction of facial muscles that produced the expressions of the basic emotions. Of interest to this chapter, the same study was conducted some years later in Indonesia, using Minangkabau men from West Sumatra as participants (Levenson, Ekman, Heider, & Friesen, 1992). The experimenter-guided muscle contraction procedure was again used to produce recognizable facial expressions of emotion, and heart rate, finger temperature, skin conductance, finger pulse, transmission time, finger pulse amplitude, respiratory period, and respiratory depth were measured. The physiological responses of the Minangkabau and the (previously studied) Americans were quite similar; differences in only two of the physiological measures were observed. This might be taken as some indication of cross-cultural similarity in the physiology of emotion.

However, Boiten (1996) subsequently argued that the physiological changes were likely due more to metabolic demands of the muscle contraction task than to any presumably resulting emotion, and thus that the cultural comparison offers little in the way of evidence about physiological differences or similarities of emotions (Zajonc & McIntosh, 1997). Consistent with this conclusion, as Markus and Kitayama (1994) have highlighted, many Minangkabau men reported experiencing little or no emotion. This might be predicted from our consideration of cultural models of emotions, according to which emotions are more intense among members of collectivist cultures when themes of social engagement characterize the potentially emotion-provoking situation (Kitayama et al., 2004). That is, without a social context – in fact, with only changes in facial musculature – the Minangkabau men did not really experience, subjectively, a change in emotional state at all. Many American participants, in contrast, did experience subjective changes. Therefore, it is difficult to draw strong conclusions from the observed similarity in physiology.

In a more recent study, Tsai and Levenson (1997) examined the question of cultural differences in emotion physiology further. These researchers acknowledged that, consistent with the critiques of the work of Levenson and colleagues that we have just summarized, most of the few existing studies of this issue had not looked at emotion physiology in the context of social interaction, and therefore were limited in their assessment of cultural difference in emotion physiology to situations in which the individual is alone (e.g., Lazarus, Tomita, Opton, & Kodama, 1966; Tsai, Levenson, & Carstensen, 2000). We should note that previous research generally also lacked a guiding theory of cultural differences, so usually no specific hypotheses were tested. Instead, prior studies of cultural differences in physiology simply asked the question: are there any cultural differences in physiology that are significant from a whole host of different physiological measures?

Tsai and Levenson (1997) were specifically interested in whether the emotional moderation intrinsic to the Asian model of emotion was observed on the level of physiology. They thus posed a specific hypothesis that stated that they would observe less physiological reactivity during emotional states in Asians than in European Americans in the laboratory. The researchers accordingly brought Chinese dating couples and American dating couples (all living in the United States) into the laboratory. The two groups of couples were demonstrated, on questionnaire measures of assimilation to Chinese versus American culture, to be oriented toward their culture of ethnicity, that is, Chinese and American cultures, respectively. The couples were directed to engage, first, in a discussion of the events that had occurred to them prior to coming to the laboratory (a baseline discussion), and then in a discussion of strongest area of conflict in their couple (emotional discussion). This latter type of discussion typically leads members of the couple to become quite emotional. Both self-report and physiological indicators of emotions were assessed. Results showed that while discussion of a conflict compared to the baseline discussion did indeed elicit emotions, as shown by the two types of indicator, physiological changes did not differ by culture. In fact, self-reports of emotion did not differ very much either. Similar studies conducted in different countries representative of the different cultures, rather than involving participation of culturally identified individuals from the same country, are now needed in order to accept the conclusion that emotion physiology varies very little across culture.

Self-reported Bodily Sensations and "Social Schemata"

A number of researchers have also asked individuals to verbally describe the kinds of physiological changes that occur during emotional states. The question here is whether individuals perceive different physiological changes during different emotions. Initial studies, mostly conducted within a single culture, showed that emotions are reported to be associated with very specific bodily sensations, and that these reported sensations are consensual across individuals (Neuwenhuyse, Offenberg, & Frijda, 1987; Pennebaker, 1982; Shaver et al., 1987). What is interesting is that in fact individuals are actually not accurate at perceiving the specific bodily changes associated with emotions, such as heart rate changes (e.g., Koenigsberg, Katkin, & Blascovich, 1981; Pennebaker, 1982) or gastric activity (e.g., Whitehead & Drescher, 1980). So how can they report differentiated and consensual bodily changes in emotion?

In a series of important studies, Rimé, Philippot, and Cisamolo (1990) showed that people seem to rely on socially shared schemata – or stereotypes – when reporting bodily sensations of emotion. For instance, Rimé and colleagues found that when their research participants had to report their stereotypes about such sensations, those stereotypes were almost identical to other participants' reports of bodily sensations during actual recalled emotional experiences. These researchers asked participants about the extent to which the following sensations characterized joy, anger, fear, and sadness: lump in throat, breathing problems, stomach sensations, feeling cold, feeling warm, feeling hot, heartbeat acceleration, muscle tension, muscle relaxation, and perspiration. The large similarities between people's beliefs, or stereotypes, and the bodily sensations recalled from actual emotion experiences can be seen in Figure 9.4. As can also be seen from the figure, the four emotions studied were thought to be associated with quite distinct peripheral bodily changes, and this result was replicated many times by the authors themselves. Subsequent research by Philippot (1991) showed that these perceived sensations are not correlated with physiological changes during actual emotions experienced by the very people who report the sensations. So, when people describe the bodily sensations associated with specific emotions, they are relying on their stereotypes and not their internal states.

Given the lack of or loose relationship between underlying physiology and perceived bodily sensations during emotions, Philippot and Rimé (1997) reasoned that important cultural differences could likely be observed in the reports of bodily sensations of emotion. A number of prior studies had reported findings suggesting that there were very few differences in reported bodily sensations across culture. For instance, in an analysis of the data collected in the context of the very large cross-cultural study by Scherer, Wallbott and Summerfield (1986), described above, Rimé and Giovannini (1986) found that the bodily sensations held to be associated with different emotions showed high similarity across a number of countries. Other studies, as well as Scherer and Wallbott's own analysis (1994), had reached the same conclusion (e.g., Hupka, Zaleski, Otto, Riedl, & Tanabrina, 1996).

Philippot and Rimé (1997) suggested a number of possible limits to the prior work, including that in some studies participants had been instructed to freely list the sensations that came to mind when thinking of

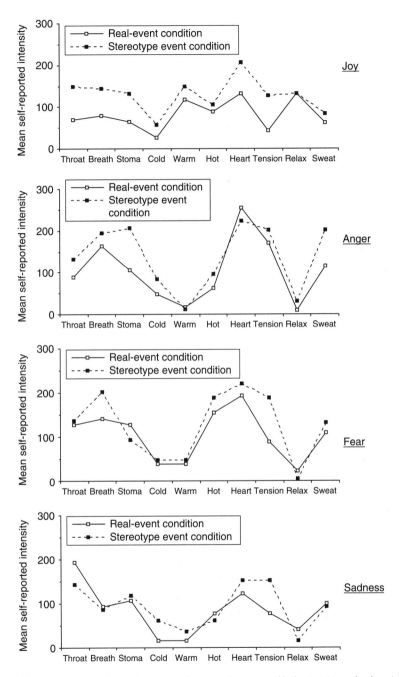

FIGURE 9.4. Patterns of peripheral changes for joy, anger, fear, and sadness reported in the stereotype and real event conditions (stoma = stomach). From Rimé, B. et al. (1990). Social schemata of peripheral changes in emotion. *Journal of Personality and Social Psychology, 59*, 38–49.

a given emotion, which may be a very difficult task for individuals to perform. They also pointed out that in some of the existing studies the participants were presented with a list of possible sensations that they could endorse or rate as characteristic of each emotion. However, often the number of proposed sensations was very limited or unspecific. Thus, in two studies in which a much larger number of possible specific sensations were proposed to participants from different countries, Philippot, Rimé and colleagues examined the reported bodily sensations of emotions from individuals from Belgium, Bolivia, Indonesia, Italy, and the United States (reported in Philippot & Rimé, 1997). Despite the intended improvements in their methodology, these authors reached the same conclusion as those of previous such studies, namely that reports of bodily sensations during emotions vary very little across culture.

One might still ask how, within and across culture, consensus in the stereotypes of bodily sensations of emotion come about, given that individuals are such poor perceivers of specific physiological events. Philippot and Rimé (1997) suggest, among other things, that very intense prototypic states may actually share greater similarity to the stereotypes. Thus, if we could relate the stereotypes to intense prototypic emotions perhaps there would be greater correspondence in perceived and reported physiology. For now, however, it is not clear just where these consensual beliefs come from.

Underlying Structure of Feelings

Another way to ask about the way emotions feel is to ask whether the same pairs of emotions are judged to be similar or different across different cultures and languages. We saw in Chapter 2 that one way to describe the underlying structure of the experience of emotion is in terms of two dimensions, which we called pleasant versus unpleasant and activated versus deactivated. Russell, Lewicka, and Niit (1989) asked whether these dimensions describe the experience of feelings of individuals in a number of different countries. And they did so in two ways. In a first study, they asked Estonian, Greek, and Polish participants to rate the similarity of all possible pairs of emotions words that, in the English language, had been shown to produce a circumplex described by the pleasantness and activation dimensions when Americans rated the similarities between all possible pairs (see Chapter 2 for illustration and discussion of these findings). Results showed that Estonian, Greek, and Polish participants described their feelings in ways that look strongly like the ways in which Americans characterize their feelings. That is, there is evidence both of the two dimensions of pleasantness and activation, and there is also some evidence of a circumplex structure.

In a second study, Chinese (some living in Canada, others in Hong Kong) and Greek participants rated the similarity between all possible pairs of a set of 10 facial expressions of emotion including six expressions called expressions of basic emotions – happiness, surprise fear, anger, disgust, and sadness – and four more expressions that represented excitement, calm, sleepiness, and boredom. Russell and Bullock (1985) had shown that when the similarity between all possible pairs of these faces, as rated by American students, was subjected to multidimensional scaling analyses, the two dimensions of pleasantness and activation were again revealed, along with the circumplex structure. The same structures were revealed in the analysis of ratings of Chinese and Greek participants.

In the study of emotion appraisals, described earlier in the chapter, Mauro and his colleagues (Mauro et al., 1992) also asked participants in the United States, Japan, Hong Kong, and the People's Republic of China to rate the extent to which they had experienced a number of feelings during a set of emotional situations that had been recalled by the participant. Analyses of these feelings provided a more fine-grained account of the major dimensions of feelings, but also supported the centrality of the pleasantness and activation dimensions. More importantly, the findings also demonstrated large cross-cultural similarity in the structure of emotional experience.

In sum, a number of analyses relying on very different measurement and statistical techniques suggest that the underlying physiology and perception of bodily sensations and feelings are quite similar across cultures. Of course, all such work, and there is not very much of it, is limited by the facts that:

1. no cultural model or construct was used in designing the study or generating or testing hypotheses
2. we are not yet certain whether specific bodily changes are related to specific feelings in the first place.

Thus, given that there exist large cultural variations in the meaning of antecedent events for emotion, and also in the ways in which emotions are expressed and recognized, it is somewhat difficult to interpret the observed similarities in the ways in which emotions appear to "feel" across cultures.

Summary

To return now to the example of the Navajos' emotional reactions to dead bodies, we might ask again if the Navajo actually experience disgust or fear when confronted with a dead body. Based on the findings reviewed in this chapter, it seems that if the body were that of an unknown person, confronted in the laboratory, then the Navajo might well respond with feelings and behavior that look like disgust to a western researcher. Contrariwise, if the body were that of a family member and the confrontation with it occurred in their own village, then the cultural meanings and practices around dead bodies would probably constitute a context in which fear was experienced. That is, the appraisals of the situations and the actions taken, perhaps even underlying physiology, would indicate that the person was experiencing fear. And when asked to nominate situations in which they experienced fear very often, the Navajo would likely nominate experiences with dead bodies. In order to compare the experiences of the Navajo with other cultures, as we emphasized in the first part of this chapter, cultures must be conceptualized in terms of fundamental meanings and values. These can be applied to the development of specific cultural models of emotional experience and emotional practices.

In reviewing the existing literature on the experience of emotion across cultures, we saw that events that cause emotions are not universal. And while some of the fundamental appraisal dimensions indeed serve to differentiate specific emotions in the same ways across cultures, the social meaning of potentially emotional situations differs importantly. Similarly, although a subset of facial expressions of emotion are also recognized well above chance across cultures, suggesting a universal language of emotional expression, there are also some interesting cultural differences particularly in the extent to which intensity is perceived, and perhaps even in the accuracy of recognition depending upon whether the expresser is a cultural ingroup member or not. Finally, the research on the physiology and bodily sensations associated with discrete emotions that we reviewed in this chapter suggests that there is quite strong similarity across cultures, but what those findings mean is still open to interpretation.

In the end, the study of cultural similarities and differences in emotional lives is a new and uncharted domain. What we do know is that despite their common physiology, because cultures impute such vastly different meanings and practices to daily emotional experience, people's psychological experience of emotion does vary fundamentally across cultures.

References

Abele, A., Gendolla, G. H. E., & Petzold, P. (1998). Positive mood and in-group–out-group differentiation in a minimal group setting. *Personality and Social Psychology Bulletin*, 24, 1343–1357.

Abele, A., & Petzold, P. (1994). How does mood operate in an impression formation task? An information integration approach. *European Journal of Social Psychology*, 24, 173–184.

Adelmann, P. K., & Zajonc, R. B. (1989). Facial efference and the experience of emotion. *Annual Review of Psychology*, 40, 249–280.

Adler, P., Kless, S., & Adler, P. (1992). Socialization to gender roles: Popularity among elementary school boys and girls. *Sociology of Education*, 65, 169–187.

Albarracín, D., & Kumkale, G. T. (2003). Affect as information in persuasion: A model of affect identification and discounting. *Journal of Personality and Social Psychology*, 84, 453–469.

Albas, D. C., McCluskey, K. W., & Albas, C. A. (1976). Perception of the emotional content of speech: A comparison of two Canadian groups. *Journal of Cross-Cultural Psychology*, 7, 481–490.

Algoe, S., Buswell, B., & DeLamater, J. (2000). Gender and job status as contextual cues for the interpretation of facial expression of emotion. *Sex Roles*, 42, 183–208.

Allport, G. W. (1954). *The nature of prejudice*. Cambridge, MA: Addison-Wesley.

Amir, Y. (1969). Contact hypothesis in ethnic relations. *Psychological Bulletin*, 71, 319–342.

Anderson, J. R., & Bower, G. H. (1973). *Human associative memory*. Washington, DC: Winston.

Armon-Jones, C. (1986a). The social function of emotion. In R. Harré (Ed.), *The social construction of emotions* (pp. 57–82). Oxford: Blackwell.

Armon-Jones, C. (1986b). The thesis of constructionism. In R. Harré (Ed.), *The social construction of emotions* (pp. 32–56). Oxford: Blackwell.

Arnold, M. B. (1960). *Emotions and personality* (2 Vols.). New York: Columbia University Press.

Ausubel, D. P. (1955). Relationships between shame and guilt in the socializing process. *Psychological Review*, 62(5), 378–390.

Averill, J. R. (1980a). A constructivist view of emotion. In R. Plutchik, & H. Kellerman (Eds.), *Emotion: Theory, research, experience* (Vol. 1, pp. 305–339). New York: Academy Press.

Averill, J. R. (1980b). The emotions. In E. Staub (Ed.), *Personality: Basic aspects and current research* (pp. 134–199). Englewood Cliffs, NJ: Prentice-Hall.

Averill, J. R. (1982). *Anger and aggression: An essay on emotion*. New York: Springer-Verlag.

Ax, A. F. (1953). Physiological differentiation between fear and anger in humans. *Psychosomatic Medicine, 15,* 433–442.

Bacon, F. (1890). *The essays of counsels, civils and morals.* Oxford: Clarendon. (Original work published 1597)

Bagozzi, R. P., Gopinath, M., & Nyer, P. (1999a). The role of emotions in marketing. *Academy of Marketing Science, 27*(2), 184–206.

Bagozzi, R. P., Wong, K. S., & Yi, Y. (1999b). The role of culture and gender in the relationship between positive and negative affect. *Cognition and Emotion, 13*(6), 641–672.

Balota, D. A., & Chumbley, J. I. (1985). The locus of word-frequency effects in the pronunciation task: Lexical access and/or production? *Journal of Memory and Language, 24,* 89–106.

Bandura, A. (1976). *Social learning theory.* Englewood Cliffs, NJ: Prentice-Hall.

Banse, R., & Scherer, K. R. (1996). Acoustic profiles in vocal emotion expression. *Journal of Personality and Social Psychology, 70,* 614–636.

Bargh, J. A. (1997). The automaticity of everyday life. In S. R. Wyer (Ed.), *Advances in social cognition* (Vol. 10, pp. 1–61). Mahwah, NJ: Lawrence Erlbaum Associates, Inc.

Baron, R. S., Inman, M. L., Kao, C. F., & Logan, H. (1992). Negative emotion and superficial social processing. *Motivation and Emotion, 16,* 323–346.

Baron, R. S., Logan, H., Lilly, J., Inman, M. L., & Brennan, M. (1994). Negative emotion and message processing. *Journal of Experimental Social Psychology, 30,* 181–201.

Barrett, K. C. (1995). A functionalist approach to shame and guilt. In J. P. Tangney, & K. W. Fischer (Eds.), *Self conscious emotions* (pp. 25–63). New York: Guilford Press.

Barrett, K. C., & Campos, J. J. (1987). Perspectives on emotional development II: A functionalist approach to emotions. In J. D. Osofsky (Ed.), *Handbook of infant development* (2nd ed.) (pp. 555–578). New York: John Wiley & Sons.

Barrett, L. B. (in press-a). Are emotions natural kinds? *Perspectives on Psychological Science.*

Barrett, L. B. (in press-b). The experience of emotion: A social psychological model. *Personality and Social Psychology Bulletin.*

Barrett, L. F. (2004). Feelings or words? Understanding the content in self-report ratings of emotional experience. *Journal of Personality and Social Psychology, 87,* 266–281.

Barrett, L. F. (2006). Solving the emotion paradox: Categorization and the experience of emotion. *Personality and Social Psychology Review, 10,* 20–46.

Barrett, L. F., & Russell, J. A. (1999). Structure of current affect. *Current Directions in Psychological Science, 8,* 10–14.

Barsalou, L. W. (1999). Perceptual symbol systems. *Behavioral and Brain Sciences, 22,* 577–609.

Bartlett, J. C., Burleson, G., & Santrock, J. W. (1982). Emotional mood and memory in young children. *Journal of Experimental Child Psychology, 34,* 59–76.

Baumeister, R., Bratslavsky, E., Muraven, M., & Tice, D. (1998). Ego depletion: Is the active self a limited resource? *Journal of Personality and Social Psychology, 74,* 1252–1265.

Baumeister, R. F., Smart, L., & Boden, J. M. (1996). Relation of threatened egotism to violence and aggression: The dark side of high self-esteem. *Psychological Review, 103,* 5–33.

Bavelas, J. B., Black, A., Lemery, C. R., & Mullett, J. (1986). "I know how you feel": Motor mimicry as a communicative act. *Journal of Personality and Social Psychology, 50,* 322–329.

Bellah, R. N., Madsen, R., Sullivan, W., Swidler, A., & Tiption, S. M. (1985). *Habits of hearts.* Berkeley, CA: University of California Press.

Bem, D. (1972). Self-perception theory. In L. Berkowitz (Ed.), *Advances in experimental social psychology* (Vol. 6, pp. 1–62). New York: Academic Press.

Bem, S. L. (1979). Theory and measurement of androgyny: A reply to the Pedhazur–Tetenbaum and Locksley–Colten critiques. *Journal of Personality and Social Psychology, 37,* 1047–1054.

Berbdsebn, M., van der Plig, J., Doosje, B., & Manstead, A. S. R. (2004). Guilt and regret: The determining role of interpersonal and intrapersonal harm. *Cognition and Emotion, 18,* 55–70.

Bertram, B. C. R. (1975). Social factors influencing reproduction in wild lions. *Journal of Zoology, 177,* 463–482.

Biehl, M., Matsumoto, D., Ekman, P., Hearn, V., Heider, K., Kudoh, T., et al. (1997). Matsumoto and Ekman's Japanese and Caucasian facial expressions of emotion (JACFEE): Reliability data and cross-national differences. *Journal of Nonverbal Behavior, 21,* 3–21.

Birdwhistell, R. (1970). *Kinesics and context.* Philadelphia, PA: University of Pennsylvania Press.

Birnbaum, D. (1983). Preschoolers' stereotypes about sex differences in emotionality: A reaffirmation. *Journal of Genetic Psychology, 143,* 139–140.

Birnbaum, D., & Croll, W. (1984). The ethiology of children's stereotypes about sex differences in emotionality. *Sex Roles, 10,* 677–691.

Birnbaum, D., Nosanchuk, T., & Croll, W. (1980). Children's stereotypes about sex differences in emotionality. *Sex Roles, 6,* 435–443.

Bizman, A., Yinon, Y., & Krotman, S. (2001). Group-based emotional distress: An extension of self-discrepancy theory. *Personality and Social Psychology Bulletin, 27,* 1291–1300.

Blaney, P. H. (1986). Affect and memory: A review. *Psychological Bulletin, 99,* 229–246.

Blascovich, J., & Mendes, B. (2000). Challenge and threat appraisals: The role of affective cues. In J. Forgas (Ed.), *Feeling and thinking: The role of affect in social cognition* (pp. 59–82). Paris: Cambridge University Press.

Blascovich, J., & Tomaka, J. (1996). The biopsychosocial model of arousal regulation. *Advances in Experimental Social Psychology, 28,* 1–51.

Bless, H. (2001). Mood and the use of general knowledge structures. In L. L. Martin, & G. L. Clore (Eds.), *Theories of mood and cognition: A user's guidebook* (pp. 9–26). Mahwah, NJ: Lawrence Erlbaum Associates, Inc.

Bless, H., Bohner, G., Schwarz, N., & Strack, F. (1990). Mood and persuasion: A cognitive response analysis. *Personality and Social Psychology Bulletin, 16,* 331–345.

Bless, H., Clore, G. L., Schwarz, N., Golisano, V., Rabe, C., & Wölk, M. (1996b). Mood and the use of scripts: Does a happy mood really lead to mindlessness? *Journal of Personality and Social Psychology, 71,* 665–679.

Bless, H., & Fiedler, K. (1995). Affective states and the influence of activated general knowledge. *Personality and Social Psychology Bulletin, 21,* 766–778.

Bless, H., Mackie, D.M., & Schwarz, N. (1992). Mood effects on attitude judgments: Independent effects of mood before and after message elaboration. *Journal of Personality and Social Psychology, 63,* 585–595.

Bless, H., Schwarz, N., & Wieland, R. (1996a). Mood and the impact of category membership and individuating information. *European Journal of Social Psychology, 26,* 935–959.

Bochner, S., & Hesketh, B. (1994). Power distance, individualism/collectivism, and job-related attitudes in a culturally diverse work group. *Journal of Cross-Cultural Perspectives, 25,* 233–257.

Boden, J. M., & Baumeister, R. F. (1997). Repressive coping: Distraction using pleasant thoughts and memories. *Journal of Personality and Social Psychology, 73,* 45–62.

Bodenhausen, G. V., Kramer, G. P., & Süsser, K. (1994a). Happiness and stereotypic thinking in social judgment. *Journal of Personality and Social Psychology, 66,* 621–632.

Bodenhausen, G. V., Sheppard, L. A., & Kramer, G. P. (1994b). Negative affect and social judgment: The differential impact of anger and sadness. *European Journal of Social Psychology, 24,* 45–62.

Bohner, G., Crow, K., Erb, H. P., & Schwarz, N. (1992). Affect and persuasion: Mood effects on the processing of message content and context cues and on subsequent behaviour. *European Journal of Social Psychology, 22,* 511–530.

Boiten, F. (1996). Autonomic response patterns during voluntary facial action. *Psychophysiology, 33,* 123–131.

Borgatta, E. F. (1961). Mood, personality, and interaction. *Journal of General Psychology, 64,* 105–137.

Boucher, J., & Carlson, G. (1980). Recognition of facial expression in three cultures. *Journal of Cross-Cultural Psychology, 11,* 263–280.

Boulton, M. J., & Smith, P. K. (1992). The social nature of play fighting and play chasing: Mechanisms and strategies underlying cooperation and compromise. In J. H. Barkow, & L. Cosmides (Eds.), *Adapted mind: Evolutionary psychology and the generation of culture* (pp. 429–444). London: Oxford University Press.

Bower, G. H. (1981). Mood and memory. *American Psychologist, 36,* 129–148.

Bower, G. H. (1987). Commentary on mood and memory. *Behavior Research and Therapy, 25,* 443–455.

Bower, G. H. (1991). Mood congruity in social judgments. In J. P. Forgas (Ed.), *Emotion and social judgments* (pp. 31–53). Oxford: Pergamon Press.

Bower, G. H., Gilligan, S. G., & Monteiro, K. P. (1981). Selectivity of learning caused by affective states. *Journal of Experimental Psychology: General, 110,* 451–473.

Bower, G. H., & Mayer, J. D. (1985). Failure to replicate mood-dependent retrieval. *Bulletin of the Psychonomic Society, 23,* 39–42.

Bower, G. H., Monteiro, K. P., & Gilligan, S. G. (1978). Emotional mood as a context of learning and recall. *Journal of Verbal Learning and Verbal Behavior, 17,* 573–585.

Boyle, G. J. (1984). Reliability and validity of Izard's Differential Emotions Scale. *Personality and Individual Differences, 5,* 747–750.

Bozzi, P. (1985). Semantica dei bicordi. In G. Stefani, & F. Ferrari (Eds.), *La psicologia della musica del Europa e in Italia.* Bologna: CLUEB.

Bradley, M. M., Codispoti, M., Sabatinelli, D., & Lang, P. J. (2001). Emotion and motivation: Sex differences in picture processing. *Emotion, 1,* 300–319.

Bradley, M. M., & Lang, P. J. (1994). Measuring emotion: The self-assessment manikin and the semantic differential. *Journal of Behavior Therapy and Experimental Psychiatry, 25,* 49–59.

Bradley, M. M., & Lang, P. J. (2000). Affective reactions to acoustic stimuli. *Psychophysiology, 37,* 204–215.

Brandstätter, H. (1981). Time sampling of subjective well-being. In H. Hartmann, W. Molt, & P. Stringer (Eds.), *Advances in economic psychology.* Heidelberg: Meyn.

Brandstätter, H. (1983). Emotional responses to other persons in everyday life situations. *Journal of Personality and Social Psychology, 45,* 871–883.

Branscombe, N. R., Doosje, B., & McGarty, C. (2002). Antecedents and consequences of collective guilt. In D. M. Mackie, & E. R. Smith (Eds.), *From prejudice to intergroup emotions: Differentiated reactions to social groups* (pp. 49–66). Philadelphia, PA: Psychology Press.

Brebner, J. (2003). Gender and emotions. *Personality and Individual Differences, 34,* 387–394.

Bretherton, I., & Beeghly, M. (1982). Talking about internal states: The acquisition of an explicit theory of mind. *Developmental Psychology, 18,* 906–912.

Brigham, J. C. (1971). Ethnic stereotypes. *Psychological Bulletin, 76,* 15–38.

Bringle, R. G. (1991). Psychosocial aspects of jealousy: A transactional model. In P. Salovey (Ed.), *The psychology of envy and jealousy* (pp. 103–131). New York: Guilford Press.

Briton, N., & Hall, J. (1995). Beliefs about female and male nonverbal communication. *Sex Roles, 32,* 79–90.

Britt, T. W., Boniecki, K. A., Vescio, T. K., Biernat, M., & Brown, L. M. (1996). Intergroup anxiety: A person x situation approach. *Personality and Social Psychology Bulletin, 22,* 1177–1188.

Brody, L. (1985). Gender differences in emotional development: A review of theories and research. *Journal of Personality, 53,* 102–149.

Brody, L. (1997). Beyond stereotypes: Gender and emotion. *Journal of Social Issues, 53,* 369–393.

Brody, L. (1999). *Gender, emotion, and the family.* Cambridge, MA: Harvard University Press.

Brody, L. (2000). The socialization of gender differences in emotional expression: Display rules, infant temperament, and differentiation. In A. Fischer (Ed.), *Gender and emotion: Social psychological perspectives* (pp. 24–47). London: Cambridge University Press.

Brody, L. R., & Hall, J. A. (1993). Gender and emotion. In M. Lewis & J. M. Haviland (Eds.), *Handbook of emotions* (pp. 447–460). New York: Guilford Press.

Brody, L. R., & Hall, J. A. (2000). Gender, emotion, and expression. In M. Lewis & J. M. Haviland-Jones (Eds.), *Handbook of emotions* (2nd ed.) (pp. 338–349). New York: Guilford Press.

Brody, L., Lovas, G., & Hay, D. (1995). Gender differences in anger and fear as a function of situational context. *Sex Roles, 32,* 47–78.

Bucci, W. (1995). The power of the narrative: A multiple code account. In J. Pennebaker (Ed.), *Emotion, disclosure, & health* (pp. 93–122). Washington, DC: American Psychological Association.

Buck, R. (1977). Nonverbal communication of affect in preschool children: Relationships with personality and skin conductance. *Journal of Personality and Social Psychology, 35,* 225–236.

Buck, R. (1978). The slide-viewing technique for measuring nonverbal sending accuracy: A guide for replication. *Catalog of Selected Documents in Psychology, 8,* 63.

Buck, R. (1979). Individual differences in nonverbal sending accuracy and electrodermal responding: The externaling–internalizing dimension. In R. Rosenthal (Ed.), *Skills in nonverbal communication.* Cambridge, MA: Oelgeschlager, Gunn & Hain.

Buck, R. (1980). Nonverbal behavior and the theory of emotions: The facial feedback hypothesis. *Journal of Personality and Social Psychology, 38,* 811–824.

Buck, R. (1983). Emotional development and emotional education. In R. Plutchik, & H. Kellerman (Eds.), *Emotion in early development.* New York: Academic Press.

Buck, R. (1984). *The communication of emotion.* New York: Guilford Press.

Buck, R. (1988). The perception of facial expression: Individual regulation and social coordination. In: T. R. Alley (Ed.), *Social and applied aspects of perceiving faces* (pp. 141–165). Hillsdale, NJ: Lawrence Erlbaum Associates, Inc.

Buck, R. (1994). Social and emotional functions in facial expression and communication: The readout hypothesis. *Biological Psychology, 38,* 95–115.

Buck, R., Loslow, J., Murphy, M., & Costanzo, P. (1992). Social factors in facial display and communication. *Journal of Personality and Social Psychology, 63,* 962–968.

Buck, R., Miller, R., & Caul, W. (1974). Sex, personality, and physiological variables in the communication of affect via facial expression. *Journal of Personality and Social Psychology, 30,* 587–596.

Buck, R., Savin, V. J., Miller, R., & Caul, W. (1972). Communication of affect through facial expressions in humans. *Journal of Personality and Social Psychology, 23,* 362–371.

Bull, N. (1945). Towards a clarification of the concept of emotion. *Psychosomatic Medicine, 7,* 210–214.

Bush, L., Barr, C., McHugo, G., & Lanzetta, J. (1989). The effects of facial control and facial mimicry on subjective reactions to comedy routines. *Motivation and Emotion, 13,* 31–52.

Bushman, B. J., & Baumeister, R. F. (1998). Threatened egotism, narcissism, self-esteem, and direct and displaced aggression: Does self-love or self-hate lead to violence? *Journal of Personality and Social Psychology, 75*, 219–229.

Buss, A. (1980). *Self-consciousness and social anxiety*. San Francisco: W.H. Freeman.

Buss, D. M. (1989). Sex differences in human mate preferences: Evolutionary hypotheses tested in 37 countries. *Behavioral and Brain Sciences, 12*, 1–49.

Buss, D. M. (1995). Evolutionary psychology: A new paradigim for psychological science. *Psychological Inquiry, 6*, 1–49.

Buss, D. M., & Barnes, M.F. (1986). Preferences in human mate selection. *Journal of Personality and Social Psychology, 50*, 559–570.

Buss, D. M., Larsen, R. J., Westen, D., & Semmelroth, J. (1992). Sex differences in jealousy: Evolution, physiology, and psychology. *Psychological Science, 7*, 251–255.

Buss, D. M., Shackelford, T. K., Choe, J., Buunk, B. P., & Dijkstra, P. (2000). Distress about mating rivals. *Personal Relationships, 7*, 235–243.

Buss, D. M., Shackelford, T. K., Kirkpatrick, L. A., Choe, J., Lim, H. K., Hasegawa, M. et al. (1999). Jealousy and the nature of beliefs about infidelity: Tests of competing hypotheses about sex differences in the United States, Korea, and Japan. *Personal Relationships, 6*, 125–150.

Butler, E., Egloff, B., Wilhelm, F., Smith, N., Erickson, E., & Gross, J. (2003). The social consequences of expressive suppression. *Emotion, 3*, 48–67.

Buunk, B. P. (1983). Het rol van attributies en afhankelijkheid bij jaloezie [The role of dependency and attribution in jealousy]. *Nederlands Tijdschrift voor de Psychologie, 38*, 301–311.

Buunk, B. P. (1988). The anticipated sexual jealousy scale. In C. M. Davis, W. L. Yarber, & S. L. Davis (Eds.), *Sexuality related measures: A compendium* (pp. 192–194). Lake Millis, IA: Graphic.

Buunk, B. P. (1991). Jealousy in close relationships: An exchange-theoretical perspective. In P. Salovey (Ed.), *The psychology of jealousy and envy* (pp. 148–177). New York: Guilford Press.

Cacioppo, J. T., Bush, L. K., & Tassinary, L. G. (1992). Micro expressive facial actions as a function of affective stimuli: Replication and extension. *Personality and Social Psychology Bulletin, 63*, 962–968.

Cacioppo, J. T., Gardner, W. L., & Berntson, G. G. (1999). The affect system has parallel and integrative processing components: Form follows function. *Journal of Personality and Social Psychology, 76*, 839–855.

Cacioppo, J. T., Klein, D. J., Berntson, G. C., & Hatfield, E. (1993). The psychophysiology of emotion. In M. Lewis, & J. M. Haviland (Eds.), *Handbook of emotions* (pp. 119–142). New York: Guilford Press.

Cacioppo, J. T., Petty, R. E., Losch, M. E., & Kim, H. S. (1986). Electromyographic activity over facial muscle regions can differentiate the valence and intensity of affective reactions. *Journal of Personality and Social Psychology, 50*, 260–268.

Cacioppo, J. T., Tassinary, L. G., & Fridlund, A. F. (1990). The skeletomotor system. In J. Cacioppo, & L. Tassinary (Eds.), *Principles of physiology: Physical, social and inferential elements* (pp. 325–384). Cambridge and New York: Cambridge University Press.

Calder, A. J., Young, A. W., Perrett, D. I., Etcoff, N. L., & Rowland, D. (1996). Categorical perception of morphed facial expressions. *Visual Cognition, 3*, 81–117.

Campos, J. J., & Barrett, K. C. (1984). Toward a new understanding of emotions and their development. In C. E. Izard, J. Kagan, & R. B. Zajonc (Eds.), *Emotions, cognition, and behavior* (pp. 229–263). Cambridge: Cambridge University Press.

Campos, J. J., & Stenberg, C. R. (1981). Perception, appraisal, and emotion: The onset of social referencing. In M. Lamb, & L. Sherrod (Eds.), *Infant social perception* (pp. 273–314). Hillsdale, NJ: Lawrence Erlbaum Associates, Inc.

Camras, L., Holland, E., & Patterson, M. (1993). Facial expression. In M. Lewis, & J. M. Haviland (Eds.), *Handbook of emotions* (pp. 199–206). New York: Guilford Press.

Camras, L. A., Oster, H., Campos, J. J., Miyake, K., & Bradshaw, A. J. (1997). Japanese and American infants' responses to arm restraint. In P. Ekman, & E. L. Rosenberg (Eds.), *What the face reveals: Basic and applied studies of spontaneous expression using the Facial Action Coding System (FACS)* (pp. 289–301). New York: Oxford University Press.

Cantor, N., Norem, J. K., Niedenthal, P. M., Langston, C., & Brower, A. (1987). Social intelligence in a life transition. *Journal of Personality and Social Psychology, 53*, 1178–1191.

Carlson, M., Charlin, V., & Miller, N. (1988). Positive mood and helping behavior: A test of six hypotheses. *Journal of Personality and Social Psychology, 55*, 211–229.

Carrera-Levillain, P., & Fernandez-Dols, J.-M. (1994). Neutral faces in context: Their emotional meaning and their function. *Journal of Nonverbal Behavior, 18*(4), 281–299.

Carroll, J., & Russell, J. (1996). Do facial expressions signal specific emotions? Judging emotion from the face in context. *Journal of Personality and Social Psychology, 70*, 205–218.

Carroll, J. M., & Russell, J. A. (1997). Facial expressions in Hollywood's portrayal of emotions. *Journal of Personality and Social Psychology, 72*, 164–176.

Carstensen, L. L., Gottman, J. M., & Levenson, R. W. (1995). Emotional behavior in long-term marriage. *Psychology and Aging, 10*, 140–149.

Catanzaro, S. J., & Mearns, J. (1990). Measuring general expectancies for negative mood regulation: Initial scale development and implications. *Journal of Personality Assessment, 54*, 546–563.

Chaiken, S., Liberman, A., & Eagly, A. H. (1989). Heuristic and systematic information processing within and beyond the persuasion context. In J. S. Uleman, & J. A. Bargh (Eds.), *Unintended thought* (pp. 212–252). New York: Guilford Press.

Chailley, J. (1985). *Element de philologie musicale*. Paris: Leduc.

Challis, B. H., & Krane, R. V. (1988). Mood induction and the priming of semantic memory in a lexical decision task: Asymmetrical effects of elation and depression. *Bulletin of the Psychonomic Society, 26*, 309–312.

Chovil, N. (1991). Social determinants of facial display. *Journal of Nonverbal Behavior, 15*, 141–154.

Christensen, T. C., Feldman Barrett, L., Bliss-Moreau, E., Lebo, K., & Kashub, C. (2003). A practical guide to experience-sampling procedures. *Journal of Happiness Studies, 4*, 53–78.

Cialdini, R. B., Borden, R. J., Thorne, A., Walker, R. M. R., Freeman, S., & Sloan, L. R. (1976). Basking in reflected glory: Three (football) field studies. *Journal of Personality and Social Psychology, 34*, 366–375.

Clark, D. M., & Teasdale, J. D. (1985). Constraints on the effects of mood on memory. *Journal of Personality and Social Psychology, 48*, 1595–1608.

Clark, D. M., Teasdale, J. D., Broadbent, D. E., & Martin, M. (1983). Effect of mood on lexical decisions. *Bulletin of the Psychonomic Society, 21*, 175–178.

Cline, M. (1956). The influence of social context on the perception of faces. *Journal of Personality, 2*, 142–158.

Clore, G. L., & Ortony, A. (2000). Cognitive neuroscience of emotion. In R. D. Lane, & L. Nadel (Eds.), *Cognitive neuroscience of emotion* (pp. 24–61). New York: Oxford University Press.

Clore, G. L., Schwarz, N., & Conway, M. (1994). Affective causes and consequences of social information processing. In R. S. Wyer, & T. K. Srull (Eds.), *Handbook of social cognition* (2nd ed.) (pp. 323–418). Hillsdale, NJ: Lawrence Erlbaum Associates, Inc.

Clore, G. L., Wyer, R. S., Dienes, B., Gasper, K., Gohm, C., & Isbell, L. (2001). Affective feelings as feedback: Some cognitive consequences. In L. L. Martin, & G. L. Clore (Eds.),

Theories of mood and cognition. A user's guidebook (pp. 27–62). Mahwah, NJ: Lawrence Erlbaum Associates, Inc.

Coats, E., & Feldman, R. (1996). Gender differences in nonverbal correlates of social status. *Personality and Social Psychology Bulletin, 22*, 1014–1022.

Cohen, D. (1998). Culture, social organization, and patterns of violence. *Journal of Personality and Social Psychology, 75*, 408–419.

Cohen D., & Gunz, A. (2002). As seen by the other ...: Perspectives on the self in the memories and emotional perceptions of easterners and westerners. *Psychological Science, 13*, 55–59.

Cohen, D., & Nisbett, R. E. (1994). Self-protection and the culture of honor: Explaining southern violence. *Personality and Social Psychology Bulletin, 20*(5), 551–567.

Cohen, D., Nisbett, R. E., Bowdle, B. F., & Schwarz, N. (1996). Insult, aggression, and the southern culture of honor: An "experimental ethnography". *Journal of Personality and Social Psychology, 70*, 945–960.

Cole, P. M., Bruschi, C. J., & Tamang, B. L. (2002). Cultural differences in children's emotional reactions to different situations. *Child Development, 73*, 983–996.

Collins, A. M., & Loftus, E. F. (1975). A spreading-activation theory of semantic processing. *Psychological Review, 82*, 407–428.

Collins, N., & Miller, L. (1994). Self-disclosure and liking: A meta-analytic review. *Psychological Bulletin, 116*, 457–475.

Condry, J., & Condry, S. (1976). Sex differences: A study in the eye of the beholder. *Child Development, 47*, 819–821.

Conway, M. A., & Bekerian, D. A. (1987). Situational knowledge and emotions. *Cognition and Emotion, 1*, 145–191.

Copeland, A., Hwang, H., & Brody, L. (1996). *Asian–American Adolescents: Caught between cultures?* Poster presented at the Society for Research in Adolescence, Boston, MA.

Corenblum, B., & Stephan, W. G. (2001). White fears and native apprehensions: An integrated threat theory approach to intergroup attitude. *Canadian Journal of Behavioral Science, 33*, 251–268.

Cornelius, A. R. (1996). *The science of emotion: Research and tradition in the psychology of emotion*. Englewood Cliffs, NJ: Prentice-Hall.

Cosmides, L., & Tooby, J. (1987). From evolution to behavior: Evolutionary psychology as missing link. In J. Dupre (Ed.), *The latest on the best: Essays on evolution and optimality*. Cambridge, MA: MIT Press.

Cosmides, L., & Tooby, J. (2000). Evolutionary psychology and the emotions. In M. Lewis, & J. M. Haviland-Jones (Eds.), *Handbook of Emotions* (2nd ed.) (pp. 91–115). New York: Guilford Press.

Costa, M., Fine, P., & Ricci Bitti, P. E. (2004). Interval distributions, mode, and tonal strength of melodies as predictors of perceived emotion. *Music Perception, 22*(1), 1–14.

Costa, M., Ricci Bitti, P. E., & Bonfiglioli, L. (2000). Psychological connotations of harmonic musical intervals. *Psychology of Music, 28*, 4–22.

Cottrell, C. A., & Neuberg, S. L. (2005). Different emotional reactions to different groups: A sociofunctional threat-based approach to "prejudice". *Journal of Personality and Social Psychology, 88*, 770–789.

Crocker, J., Cornwell, B., & Major, B. (1993). The stigma of overweight: Affective consequences of attributional ambiguity. *Journal of Personality and Social Psychology, 64*, 60–70.

Cupchik, G., & Leventhal, H. (1974). Consistency between expressive behavior and the evaluation of humorous stimuli: The role of sex and self-observation. *Journal of Personality and Social Psychology, 30*, 429–442.

Dabbs, J. M., & Janis, I. L. (1965). Why does eating while reading facilitate opinion change? An experimental inquiry. *Journal of Experimental Social Psychology, 1,* 133–144.

Dalle, N., & Niedenthal, P. M. (2001). Le mariage de mon meilleur ami: Emotional response categorization and naturally induced emotions. *European Journal of Social Psychology, 31,* 737–742.

Dalle, N., & Niedenthal, P. M. (2003). Emotion et cohérence conceptuelle. *L'Année Psychologique, 104,* 585–616.

Daly, M., & Wilson, M. (1983). *Sex, evolution and behavior.* Belmont, CA: Wadsworth.

Daly, M., Wilson, M., & Weghorst, S. J. (1982). Male sexual jealousy. *Ethology and Sociobiology, 3,* 11–27.

Damasio, A. R. (1989). Time-locked multiregional retroactivation: A systems-level proposal for the neural substrates of recall and recognition. *Cognition, 33,* 25–62.

Damasio, A. R. (1994). *Descartes' error: Emotion, reason, and the human brain.* New York: Putnam.

D'Andrade, R. G. (1984). Culture meaning systems. In R. A. Shweder, & R. A. Levine (Eds.), *Culture theory: Essays on mind, self, and emotion* (pp. 88–119). Cambridge: Cambridge University Press.

Darwin, C. (1872/1998). *The expression of the emotions in man and animals.* New York/Oxford: Oxford University Press.

Davidson, R. J. (1992). Emotion and affective style: Hemispheric substrates. *Psychological Science, 3,* 39–43.

Davidson, R., Scherer, K. R., & Goldsmith, H. H. (2003). *Handbook of affective sciences.* New York: Oxford University Press.

Davis, M. H. (2004). Empathy: Negotiating the border between self and other. In L. Z. Tiedens, & C. W. Leach (Eds.), *The social life of emotions* (pp. 19–42). Cambridge: Cambridge University Press.

Davis, M., LaRosa, P., & Foshee, D. (1992). Emotion work in supervisor–subordinate relations: Gender differences in the perception of angry displays. *Sex Roles, 26,* 513–531.

de Gelder, B., Teunisse, J. P., & Benson, P. J. (1997). Categorical perception of facial expressions: Categories and their internal structure. *Cognition and Emotion, 11*(1), 1–23.

de Jong, P. J. (1999). Communicative and remedial effects of social blushing. *Journal of Nonverbal Behavior, 23,* 197–217.

de Rivera, J. (1977). *A structural theory of the emotions.* New York: International Universities Press.

Deaux, K. (1993). Commentary: Sorry, wrong number – A reply to Gentile's call. *Psychological Science, 4,* 125–126.

Deaux, K., & Major, B. (1987). Putting gender into context: An interactive model of gender-related behavior. *Psychological Review, 94,* 369–389.

DePaulo, B. (1992). Nonverbal behavior and self-presentation. *Psychological Bulletin, 111,* 203–243.

Derryberry, D., & Tucker, D. M. (1994). Motivating the focus of attention. In P. Niedenthal, & S. Kitayama (Eds.), *The heart's eye: Emotional influences in perception and attention* (pp. 167–196). San Diego, CA: Academic Press.

DeSteno, D. A., Bartlett, M. Y., Braverman, J., & Salovey, P. (2002). Sex differences in jealousy: Evolutionary mechanism or artifact of measurement? *Journal of Personality and Social Psychology, 83,* 1103–1116.

DeSteno, D., Dasgupta, N., Bartlett, M. Y., & Cajdric, A. (2004). Prejudice from thin air: The effect of emotion on intergroup attitudes. *Psychological Science, 15,* 319–324.

DeSteno, D., Petty, R. E., Wegener, D. T., & Rucker, D. D. (2000). Beyond valence in the perception of likelihood: The role of emotion specificity. *Journal of Personality and Social Psychology, 78,* 397–416.

DeSteno, D. A., & Salovey, P. (1995). Jealousy and envy. In A. S. R. Manstead, M. Hewstone, S. T. Fiske, M. A. Hogg, H. T. Reis, & G. R. Semin (Eds.), *Blackwell Encyclopedia of Social Psychology* (pp. 342–343). Oxford: Blackwell.

DeSteno, D. A., & Salovey, P. (1996). Evolutionary origins of sex differences jealousy: Questioning the "fitness" of the model. *Psychological Science, 7*, 367–372.

Deutsch, D., LeBaron, D., & Fryer, M. M. (1987). What is in a smile? *Psychology of Women Quarterly, 11*, 314–352.

Devine, P. G. (1989). Stereotypes and prejudice: Their automatic and controlled components. *Journal of Personality and Social Psychology, 56*, 5–18.

Devos, T., Mackie, D. M., Silver, L. A., & Smith, E. R. (2002). Experiencing intergroup emotions. In D. M. Mackie, & E. R. Smith (Eds.), *From prejudice to intergroup emotions: Differentiated reactions to social groups* (pp. 111–134). New York: Psychology Press.

Diamond, L., & Aspinwall, L. (2003). Emotion regulation across the life span: An integrative perspective emphasizing self-regulation, positive affect, and dyadic processes. *Motivation and Emotion, 27*, 125–156.

Dienstbier, R. A. (1984). The role of emotion in moral socialization. In C. E. Izard, J. Kagan, & R. B. Zajonc (Eds.), *Emotions, cognition, and behavior* (pp. 484–514). New York: Cambridge University Press.

Dijker, A. J. M. (1987). Emotional reactions to ethnic groups. *European Journal of Social Psychology, 17*, 305–325.

Dijker, A. J. M., Koomen, W., van den Heuvel, H., & Frijda, N. H. (1996). Perceived antecedents of emotional reactions in inter-ethnic relations. *British Journal of Social Psychology, 35*, 313–329.

Dijkstra, P., & Buunk, B. P. (2001). Gender differences in the jealousy-evoking nature of a rival's body build. *Evolution and Human Behavior, 22*, 335–341.

Dijkstra, P., & Buunk, B. P. (2002). Sex difference in the jealousy evoking effect of rival characteristics. *European Journal of Social Psychology, 32*, 829–852.

Dimberg, U. (1982). Facial reactions to facial expressions. *Psychophysiology, 19*, 643–647.

Dimberg, U. (1988). Facial electromyography and the experience of emotion. *Journal of Psychophysiology, 2*, 277–282.

Dimberg, U., & Lundqvist, L. (1990). Gender differences in facial reactions to facial expressions. *Biological Psychology, 30*, 151–159.

Dion, K. K., & Dion, K. L. (1975). Self-esteem and romantic love. *Journal of Personality, 43*, 39–57.

Doherty, R. (1997). The emotional contagion scale: A measure of individual differences. *Journal of Nonverbal Behavior, 21*, 131–154.

Dollar, J., Miller, N. E., Doob, L. W., Mowrer, O. H., & Sears, R. R. (1939). *Frustration and aggression.* New Haven, CT: Yale University Press.

Doosje, B., Branscombe, N. R., Spears, R., & Manstead, A. S. R. (1998). Guilty by association: When one's group has a negative history. *Journal of Personality and Social Psychology, 75*, 872–886.

Dovidio, J. F., Gaertner, S. L., Isen, A., & Lowrance, R. (1995). Group representations and intergroup bias: Positive affect, similarity, and group size. *Personality and Social Psychology Bulletin, 21*, 856–865.

Dovidio, J. F., Gaertner, S. L., & Loux, S. (2000). Subjective experiences and intergroup relations: The role of positive affect. In H. Bless, & J. P. Forgas (Eds.), *The message within: The role of subjective experience in social cognition and behavior* (pp. 340–371). Philadelphia, PA: Psychology Press.

Drummond, P. D. (2001). The effect of true and false feedback on blushing in women. *Personality and Individual Differences, 29*, 1123–1132.

Duchenne de Boulogne, G.-B. (1862/1990). *Mécanisme de la physionomie humaine* [The mechanism of human facial expression]. Cambridge/New York: Cambridge University Press.

Duclos, S., & Laird, J. (2001). The deliberate control of emotional experience through control of expressions. *Cognition and Emotion, 15*, 27–56.

Duclos, S., Laird, J., Schneider, E., Sexter, M., Stern, L., & Van Lighten, O. (1989). Emotion-specific effects of facial expressions and postures on emotional experience. *Journal of Personality and Social Psychology, 57*, 100–108.

Duffy, W. (1941). An explanation of "emotional" phenomena without the use of the concept "emotion." *Journal of General Psychology, 25*, 283–293.

Dumont, M., Yzerbyt, V., Wigboldus, D., & Gordijn, E. H. (2003). Social categorization and fear reactions to the September 11th terrorist attacks. *Personality and Social Psychology Bulletin, 29*, 1509–1520.

Duncan, J., & Laird, J. (1977). Cross-modality consistencies in individual differences in self-attribution. *Journal of Personality, 45*, 191–206.

Duncan, J., & Laird, J. (1980). Positive and reverse placebo effects as a function of differences in cues used in self-perception. *Journal of Personality and Social Psychology, 39*, 1024–1036.

Eagly, A. (1987). *Sex differences in social behavior: A social-role interpretation.* Hillsdale, NJ: Lawrence Erlbaum Associates, Inc.

Eagly, A. H., & Mladinic, A. (1989). Gender stereotypes and attitudes towards women and men. *Personality and Social Psychology Bulletin, 15*, 543–558.

Eagly, A., & Steffen, V. (1984). Gender stereotypes stem from the distribution of women and men into social roles. *Journal of Personality and Social Psychology, 46*, 735–754.

Eagly, A., & Steffen, V. (1986). Gender and aggressive behavior: A meta-analytic review of the social psychological literature. *Psychological Bulletin, 100*, 3–22.

Eagly, A., & Wood, W. (1991). Explaining sex differences in social behavior: A meta-analytic perspective. *Personality and Social Psychology Bulletin, 17*, 306–315.

Edelmann, R. J. (1981). Embarrassment: The state of research. *Current Psychological Reviews, 34*, 125–138.

Edwards, P. (1996). Honour, shame, humiliation, and modern Japan. In O. Leaman (Ed.), *Friendship east and west: Philosophical perspectives* (pp. 32–155). Richmond, VA: Curzon.

Ehrlichman, H., & Halpern J. N. (1988). Affect and memory: Effects of pleasant and unpleasant odors on retrieval of happy and unhappy memories. *Journal of Personality and Social Psychology, 55*, 769–779.

Eibl-Eibesfeldt, I. (1973). The expressive behavior of the deaf- and blind-born. In M. von Cranach, & I. Vine (Eds.), *Social communication and movement* (pp. 162–194). London: Academic Press.

Eibl-Eibesfeldt, I. (1989). *Human ethology.* Hawthorne, NY: Aldine de Gruyter.

Eich, E. (1995). Searching for mood dependent memory. *Psychological Science, 6*, 67–75.

Eich, E., Macaulay, D., & Ryan, L. (1994). Mood dependent memory for events of the personal past. *Journal of Experimental Psychology: General, 123*, 201–215.

Eich, E., & Metcalfe, J. (1989). Mood dependent memory for internal versus external events. *Journal of Experimental Psychology: Learning, Memory, & Cognition, 15*, 443–455.

Eisenberg, N. (1986). Teasing: Verbal play in two Mexico homes. In B. B. Schieffelin, & E. Ochs (Eds.), *Language socialisation across cultures. Studies in the social and cultural foundation of language, No. 3* (pp. 182–198). New York: Cambridge University Press.

Eisenberg, N. (2000). Emotion, regulation, and moral development. *Annual Review of Psychology, 51*, 665–697.

Eisenberg, N., & Miller, P. (1987). The relation of empathy to prosocial and related behaviors. *Psychological Bulletin, 101*, 91–119.

Ekman, P. (1972). Universals and cultural differences in facial expression of emotion. In J. R. Cole (Ed.), *Nebraska symposium on motivation* (pp. 207–283). Lincoln, NE: University of Nebraska Press.

Ekman, P. (1973). Cross-cultural studies of facial expression. In P. Ekman (Ed.), *Darwin and facial expression*. New York: Academic Press.

Ekman, P. (1982). *Emotion in the human face* (2nd ed.). Cambridge: Cambridge University Press.

Ekman, P. (1984). Expression and the nature of emotion. In P. Ekman, & K. Scherer (Eds.), *Approaches to emotion* (pp. 319–343). Hillsdale, NJ: Lawrence Erlbaum Associates, Inc.

Ekman, P. (1992). Argument for basic emotions. *Cognition and Emotion, 6*, 169–200.

Ekman, P. (1994). Strong evidence for universals in facial expression: A reply to Russell's mistaken critique. *Psychological Bulletin, 115*, 268–287.

Ekman, P., & Davidson, R. J. (1994). *The nature of emotion*. New York: Oxford University Press.

Ekman, P., Davidson, R., & Friesen, W. (1990). The Duchenne Smile: Emotional expression and brain physiology II. *Journal of Personality and Social Psychology, 58*, 342–353.

Ekman, P., & Friesen, W. (1971). Constants across cultures in the face and emotion. *Journal of Personality and Social Psychology, 17*, 124–129.

Ekman, P., & Friesen, W. (1974). Detecting deception from the body or face. *Journal of Personality and Social Psychology, 29*, 288–298.

Ekman, P., & Friesen, W. (1975). *Unmasking the human face: A guide to recognizing emotions from facial expressions*. Englewood Cliffs, NJ: Prentice-Hall.

Ekman, P., & Friesen, W. (1978). *The Facial Action Coding System (FACS): A technique for the measurement of facial movement*. Palo Alto, CA: Consulting Psychologists' Press.

Ekman, P., & Friesen, W. (1982). Measuring facial movements with the Facial Action Coding System. In P. Ekman (Ed.), *Emotion in the human face* (2nd ed.) (pp. 178–211). Cambridge/New York: Cambridge University Press.

Ekman, P., Friesen, W., & Ancoli, S. (1980). Facial signs of emotional experience. *Journal of Personality and Social Psychology, 39*(6), 1125–1134.

Ekman, P., Friesen, W., & Ellsworth, P. (1982a). Methodological decisions. In P. Ekman (Ed.), *Emotion in the human face* (2nd ed.) (pp. 22–38). Cambridge/New York: Cambridge University Press.

Ekman, P., Friesen, W., & Ellsworth, P. (1982b). Does the face provide accurate information? In P. Ekman (Ed.), *Emotion in the human face* (2nd ed.) (pp. 56–97). Cambridge/New York: Cambridge University Press.

Ekman, P., Friesen, W., & Ellsworth, P. (1982c). What are the relative contributions of facial behavior and contextual information to the judgment of emotion? In P. Ekman (Ed.), *Emotion in the human face* (2nd ed.) (pp. 111–127). Cambridge/New York: Cambridge University Press.

Ekman, P., Friesen, W. V., O'Sullivan, M., Chan, A., Diacoyanni-Tarlatzis, I., Heider, K., et al. (1987). Universals and cultural differences in the judgements of facial expressions of emotion. *Journal of Personality and Social Psychology, 53*(4), 712–717.

Ekman, P., Friesen, W., & Tomkins, S. (1971). Facial affect scoring technique: A first validity study. *Semiotica, 3*, 37–38.

Ekman, P., Levenson, R. W., & Friesen, W. V. (1983). Autonomic nervous activity distinguishes among emotions. *Science, 21*, 1208–1210.

Ekman, P., & O'Sullivan, M. (1991). Facial expression: Methods, means, and moues. In R. Feldman, & B. Rimé (Eds.), *Fundamentals of nonverbal behavior* (pp. 163–199). Cambridge/New York: Cambridge University Press.

Ekman, P., Sorenson, E. R., & Friesen, W. V. (1969). Pan-cultural elements in the facial displays of emotions. *Science, 164*, 86–88.

Elfenbein, H. A., & Ambady, N. (2002a). Is there an ingroup advantage in emotion recognition? *Psychological Bulletin, 128*(2), 243–249.

Elfenbein, H. A., & Ambady, N. (2002b). On the universality and cultural specificity of emotion recognition: A meta-analysis. *Psychological Bulletin, 128*(2), 205–235.

Elfenbein, H. A., & Ambady, N. (2003a). Universals in cultural differences in recognizing emotions. *Current Directions in Psychological Science, 12,* 159–164.

Elfenbein, H. A., & Ambady, N. (2003b). When familiarity breeds accuracy: Cultural exposure and facial emotion recognition. *Journal of Personality and Social Psychology, 85,* 276–290.

Elfenbein, H. A., Mandal, M. K., Ambady, N., & Harizuka, S. (2002). Cross-cultural patterns in emotion recognition: Highlighting design and analytic techniques. *Emotion, 2*(1), 75–84.

Ellsworth, P. C., & Scherer, K. R. (2003). Appraisal processes in emotion. In R. Davidson, K. R. Scherer, & H. H. Goldsmith (Eds.), *Handbook of affective sciences* (pp. 572–595). Oxford: Oxford University Press.

Ellsworth, P. C., & Smith, C. A. (1988). From appraisal to emotion: Differences among unpleasant feelings. *Motivation and Emotion, 12,* 271–302.

Erber, R., & Erber, M. W. (1994). Beyond mood and social judgment: Mood incongruent recall and mood regulation. *European Journal of Social Psychology, 24,* 79–88.

Erber, R., Wegner, D. M., & Therriault, N. (1996). On being cool and collected: Mood regulation in anticipation of social interaction. *Journal of Personality and Social Psychology, 70,* 757–766.

Esses, V. M., & Dovidio, J. F. (2002). The role of emotions in determining willingness to engage in intergroup contact. *Personality and Social Psychology Bulletin, 28,* 1202–1214.

Esses, V. M., Haddock, G., & Zanna, M. P. (1993). Values, stereotypes, and emotions as determinants of intergroup attitudes. In D. M. Mackie, & D. L. Hamilton (Eds.), *Affect, cognition, and stereotyping: Interactive group processes in group perception* (pp. 137–166). San Diego, CA: Academic Press.

Esses, V. M., & Zanna, M. P. (1995). Mood and the expression of ethnic stereotypes. *Journal of Personality and Social Psychology, 69,* 1052–1068.

Esterling, B., Antoni, M., Fletcher, M., Margulies, S., & Schneiderman, N. (1994). Emotional disclosure through writing or speaking modulates latent Epstein–Barr virus antibody titers. *Journal of Consulting and Clinical Psychology, 62,* 130–140.

Etcoff, N. L., & Magee, J. J. (1992). Categorical perception of facial expressions. *Cognition, 44,* 227–240.

Fabes, R., & Martin, C. (1991). Gender and age stereotypes of emotionality. *Personality and Social Psychology Bulletin, 17,* 532–540.

Fehr, B., & Russell, J. A. (1984). Concept of emotion viewed from a prototype perspective. *Journal of Experimental Psychology: General, 113,* 464–486.

Feldman Barrett, L. (1995a). Valence focus and arousal focus: Individual differences in the structure of affective experience. *Journal of Personality and Social Psychology, 69,* 153–166.

Feldman Barrett, L. (1995b). Variation in the circumplex structure of emotion. *Personality and Social Psychology Bulletin, 21,* 806–817.

Feldman Barrett, L., & Barrett, D. J. (2001). Computerized experience-sampling: How technology facilitates the study of conscious experience. *Social Science Computer Review, 19,* 175–185.

Feldman Barrett, L., & Gross, J. J. (2001). Emotional intelligence: A process model of emotion representation and regulation. In T. Mayne, & G. Bonanno (Eds.), *Emotions: Current issues and future directions* (pp. 286–310). New York: Guilford Press.

Feldman Barrett, L., Gross, J., Christensen, T., & Benvenuto, M. (2001). Knowing what you're feeling and knowing what to do about it: Mapping the relation between emotion differentiation and emotion regulation. *Cognition and Emotion, 15,* 713–724.

Feldman Barrett, L., Lane, R., Sechrest, L., & Schwartz, G. (2000). Sex differences in emotional awareness. *Personality and Social Psychology Bulletin, 26,* 1027–1035.

Feldman Barrett, L., Robin, L., Pietromonaco, P., & Eyssell, K. (1998). Are women the more emotional sex? Evidence from emotional experiences in social context. *Cognition and Emotion, 12,* 555–578.

Feldman Barrett, L., & Russell, J. A. (1998). Independence and bipolarity in the structure of current affect. *Journal of Personality and Social Psychology, 74,* 967–984.

Ferguson, T., & Crowley, S. (1997). Gender differences in the organization of guilt and shame. *Sex Roles, 37,* 19–44.

Ferguson, T., & Eyre, H. (2000). Engendering gender differences in shame and guilt: Stereotypes, socialization, and situational pressures. In A. Fischer (Ed.), *Gender and emotion: Social psychological perspectives* (pp. 254–276). London: Cambridge University Press.

Ferguson, T. J., Stegge, H., & Damhuis, I. (1991). Children's understanding of guilt and shame. *Child Development, 62,* 827–839.

Fernandez-Dols, J.-M., & Carroll, J. (1997). Is the meaning perceived in facial expression independent of its context? In J. Russell, & J. Fernandez-Dols (Eds.), *The psychology of facial expression* (pp. 275–294). Cambridge: Cambridge University Press.

Fernandez-Dols, J.-M., & Ruiz-Belda, M.-A. (1995). Are smiles a sign of happiness? Gold medal winners at the Olympic Games. *Journal of Personality and Social Psychology, 69,* 1113–1119.

Fernandez-Dols, J.-M., Sierra, B., & Ruiz-Belda, M.-A. (1993). On the clarity of expressive and contextual information in the recognition of emotions: A methodological critique. *European Journal of Social Psychology, 23,* 195–202.

Fernandez-Dols, J.-M., Wallbott, H., & Sanchez, F. (1991). Emotion category accessibility and the decoding of emotion from facial expression and context. *Journal of Nonverbal Behavior, 15*(2), 107–123.

Festinger, L. (1954). A theory of social comparison processes. *Human Relations, 7,* 117–140.

Fiedler, K. (1990). Mood-dependent selectivity in social cognition. In W. Stroebe, & M. Hewstone (Eds.), *European Review of Social Psychology* (Vol. 1, pp. 1–32). New York: John Wiley & Sons.

Fiedler, K. (1991). On the task, the measures and the mood in research on affect and social cognition. In J. P. Forgas (Ed.), *Emotion and social judgments* (pp. 83–104). Elmsford: Pergamon Press.

Fiedler, K. (2001). Affective states trigger processes of assimilation and accommodation. In L. L. Martin, & G. L. Clore (Eds.), *Theories of mood and cognition. A user's guidebook* (pp. 85–98). Mahwah, NJ: Lawrence Erlbaum Associates, Inc.

Fiedler, K., Pampe, H., & Scherf, U. (1986). Mood and memory for tightly organized social information. *European Journal of Social Psychology, 16,* 149–164.

Fiedler, K., & Stroehm, W. (1986). What kind of mood influences what kind of memory. *Memory & Cognition, 14,* 181–188.

Field, T. (1982). Individual differences in the expressivity of neonates and young infants. In R. Feldman (Ed.), *Development of nonverbal behavior in children* (pp. 279–298). New York: Springer-Verlag.

Finkenauer, C., & Rimé, B. (1998a). Socially shared emotional experiences vs. emotional experiences kept secret: Differential characteristics and consequences. *Journal of Social and Clinical Psychology, 17,* 295–318.

Finkenauer, C., & Rimé, B. (1998b). Keeping emotional memories secret: Health and subjective well-being when emotions are not shared. *Journal of Health Psychology, 3,* 47–58.

Fischer, A. (1993a). Emotions and gender: A conceptual model of emotion in social interaction. In H. Stam, W. Thorngate, L. Mos, & B. Kaplan (Eds.), *Recent trends in theoretical psychology* (Vol. 3, pp. 325–332). New York: Springer-Verlag.

Fischer, A. H. (1993b). Sex differences in emotionality: Fact or stereotype? *Feminism and Psychology, 3,* 303–318.

Fischer, A. H., & Manstead, A. S. R. (2000). The relation between gender and emotion in different cultures. In A. Fischer (Ed.), *Gender and emotion: Social psychological perspectives* (pp. 71–94). London: Cambridge University Press.

Fischer, A. H., Manstead A. S. R., Evers, C., Timmers, M., & Valk, G. (2004). Motives and norms underlying emotion regulation. In R. Feldman, & P. Philippot (Eds.), *The regulation of emotion* (pp. 187–210). Mahwah, NJ: Lawrence Erlbaum Associates, Inc.

Fischer, A. H., Manstead, A. S. R., & Rodriguez Mosquera, P. (1999). The role of honor-based versus individualistic values in conceptualizing pride, shame, and anger: Spanish and Dutch cultural prototypes. *Cognition and Emotion, 13,* 149–179.

Fischer, K. W., & Tangney, J. P. (1995). Self-conscious emotions and the affect revolution: Framework and overview. In J. P. Tangney, & K. W. Fischer (Eds.), *Self-conscious emotions: Shame, guilt, embarrassment, and pride* (pp. 3–22). New York: Guilford Press.

Fisk, R. (1991). *Pity the nation: Lebanon at war.* Oxford: Oxford University Press.

Fiske, S. T., Cuddy, A. J. C., & Glick, P. (2002). Emotions up and down: Intergroup emotions result from perceived status and competition. In D. M. Mackie, & E. R. Smith (Eds.), *From prejudice to intergroup emotions: Differentiated reactions to social groups* (pp. 247–264). New York: Psychology Press.

Fiske, S. T., Cuddy, A. J. C., Glick, P., & Xu, J. (2002). A model of (often mixed) stereotype content: Competence and warmth respectively follow from perceived status and competition. *Journal of Personality and Social Psychology, 82,* 878–902.

Flack, W., Laird, J., & Cavallaro, L. (1999). Separate and combined effects of facial expressions and bodily postures on emotional feelings. *European Journal of Social Psychology, 29,* 203–217.

Folkman, S., & Lazarus, R. S. (1985). If it changes it must be a process: Study of emotion and coping during three stages of a college examination. *Journal of Personality and Social Psychology, 48,* 150–170.

Forgas, J. P. (1992a). On mood and peculiar people: Affect and person typicality in impression formation. *Journal of Personality and Social Psychology, 62,* 863–875.

Forgas, J. P. (1992b). Affect in social judgment and decisions: A multi-process model. In M. P. Zanna (Ed.), *Advances in experimental social psychology* (Vol. 25, pp. 227–275). New York: Academic Press.

Forgas, J. P. (1993). On making sense of odd couples: Mood effects on the perception of mismatched relationships. *Personality and Social Psychology Bulletin, 19,* 59–71.

Forgas, J. P. (1995a). Mood and judgment: The affect infusion model (AIM). *Psychological Review, 117,* 39–66.

Forgas, J. P. (1995b). Strange couples: Mood effects on judgments and memory about prototypical and atypical targets. *Personality and Social Psychology Bulletin, 21,* 747–765.

Forgas, J. P., & Bower, G. H. (1987). Mood effects on person perception judgments. *Journal of Personality and Social Psychology, 53,* 53–60.

Forgas, J. P., Bower, G. H., & Krantz, S. (1984). The influence of mood on perceptions and social interactions. *Journal of Experimental Social Psychology, 20,* 497–513.

Forgas, J. P., Burnham, D. K., & Trimboli, C. (1988). Mood, memory, and social judgments in children. *Journal of Personality and Social Psychology, 54,* 697–703.

Forgas, J. P., & Ciarrochi, J. V. (2002). On managing moods: Evidence for the role of homeostatic cognitive strategies in affect regulation. *Personality and Social Psychology Bulletin, 28,* 336–345.

Forgas, J. P., & Fiedler, K. (1996). Us and them: Mood effects on discrimination. *Journal of Personality and Social Psychology, 70,* 28–40.

Forgas, J. P., & Moylan, S. J. (1987). After the movies: The effects of transient mood states on social judgments. *Personality and Social Psychology Bulletin, 13,* 478–489.

Frank, M., & Stennett, J. (2001). The forced-choice paradigm and the perception of facial expression of emotion. *Journal of Personality and Social Psychology, 80,* 75–85.

Fredrickson, B. L. (1998). What good are positive emotions? *Review of General Psychology, 2,* 300–319.

Fredrickson, B. L. (2001). The role of positive emotions in positive psychology: The broaden-and-build theory of positive emotions. *American Psychologist, 56,* 218–226.

Fredrickson, B. L., & Levenson, W. R. (1998). Positive emotions speed recovery from the cardiovascular sequelae of negative emotions. *Cognition and Emotion, 12,* 191–220.

Freud, S. (1920/2005). *A general introduction to psychoanalysis.* New York: Horace Liveright.

Freud, S. (1930/1961). *Civilization and its discontents.* (J. Strachey, Trans.) New York: Norton (Original work published 1930).

Frick, R. W. (1985). Communicating emotion: The role of prosodic features. *Psychological Bulletin, 97,* 412–429.

Fridlund, A. (1991). Sociality and solitary smiling: Potentiation by an implicit audience. *Journal of Personality and Social Psychology, 60,* 229–240.

Fridlund, A. (1992). The behavioral ecology and sociality of human faces. In M. S. Clark (Ed.), Emotion and social behavior. *Review of Personality and Social Psychology, 13,* 90–121.

Fridlund, A. (1994). *Human facial expression: An evolutionary view.* San Diego, CA: Academic Press.

Fridlund, A. (1997). The new ethology of human facial expressions. In J. Russell, & J. Fernandez-Dols (Eds.), *The psychology of facial expression* (pp. 103–129). Cambridge: Cambridge University Press.

Friedman, H., & Miller-Herringer, T. (1991). Nonverbal display of emotion in public and in private: Self-monitoring, personality, and expressive cues. *Journal of Personality and Social Psychology, 61,* 766–775.

Friesen, W. V. (1972). *Cultural difference in facial expressions in a social situation: An experimental test of the concept of display rules.* Unpublished doctoral dissertation, University of California, San Francisco.

Frijda, N. H. (1969). The recognition of emotion. In L. Berkowitz (Ed.), *Advances in experimental social psychology: Vol. 4.* New York: Academic Press.

Frijda, N. H. (1986). *The emotions.* Cambridge: Cambridge University Press.

Frijda, N. H. (1987). Emotion, cognitive structure, and action tendency. *Cognition and Emotion, 1,* 115–143.

Frijda, N. H. (1988). The laws of emotion. *American Psychologist, 43,* 349–358.

Frijda, N. H. (1995). Expression, emotion, neither, or both? *Cognition and Emotion, 9,* 617–635.

Frijda, N. H., Kuipers, P., & ter Schure, E. (1989). Relations among emotion, appraisal, and emotional action readiness. *Journal of Personality and Social Psychology, 57,* 212–228.

Frijda, N. H., Markam, S., Sato, K., & Wiers, R. (1995). Emotion and emotion words. In J. A. Russell (Ed.), *Everyday conceptions of emotion* (pp. 121–143). Dordrecht, The Netherlands: Kluwer Academic Publishers.

Frijda, N. H., & Mesquita, B. (1994). The social roles and functions of emotions. In S. Kitamay, & H. R. Markus (Eds.), *Emotion and culture: Empirical studies of mutual influence* (pp. 51–87). Washington, DC: American Psychological Association.

Frijda, N., & Tscherkassof, A. (1997). Facial expressions as modes of action readiness. In J. Russell, & J. Fernandez-Dols (Eds.), *The psychology of facial expression* (pp. 78–102). Cambridge: Cambridge University Press.

Frost, W., & Averill, J. (1982). Differences between men and women in the everyday experience of anger. In J. Averill, *Anger and aggression: An essay on emotion* (pp. 281–316). New York: Springer-Verlag.

Fujita, F., Diener, E., & Sandvik, E. (1991). Gender differences in negative affect and well-being: The case for emotional intensity. *Journal of Personality and Social Psychology, 61*, 427–434.

Gagnon, L., & Peretz, I. (2003). Mode and tempo relative contributions to "happy–sad" judgements in equitone melodies. *Cognition and Emotion, 17*, 25–40.

Garnefski, N., Kraaij, V., & Spinhoven, P. (2001). Negative life events, cognitive emotion regulation and emotional problems. *Personality and Individual Differences, 30*, 1311–1327.

Garnefski, N., van den Kommer, T., Kraaij, V., Teerds, J., Legerstee, J., & Onstein, E. (2002). The relationship between cognitive emotion regulation strategies and emotional problems: Comparison between a clinical and a non-clinical sample. *European Journal of Personality, 16*, 403–420.

Gates, G. S. (1926). An observational study of anger. *Journal of Experimental Psychology, 9*, 325–331.

Geertz, C. (1984). From the nature point of view. In R. A. Shweder, & R. L. Levine (Eds.), *Culture theory: Essays on mind, self, and emotion* (pp. 123–136). Cambridge: Cambridge University Press.

Gehm, T. L., & Scherer, K. R. (1988). Relating situation evaluation to emotion differentiation: Nonmetric analysis of cross-cultural questionnaire data. In K. R. Scherer (Ed.), *Facets of emotion: Recent research* (pp. 61–78). Hillsdale, NJ: Lawrence Erlbaum Associates, Inc.

George, J. (1990). Personality, affect, and behavior in groups. *Journal of Applied Psychology, 75*, 107–116.

Gergen, K. J. (1985). The social constructionist movement in modern psychology. *American Psychologist, 40*, 266–275.

Gergen, K. J., & Davis, K. E. (1985). *The social constructionist movement in modern psychology*. New York: Springer-Verlag.

Gerrig, R. J., & Bower, G. H. (1982). Emotional influences on word recognition. *Bulletin of the Psychonomic Society, 19*, 197–200.

Gilbert, D. T. (1989). Thinking lightly about others: Automatic components of the social inference process. In J. S. Uleman, & J. A. Bargh (Eds.), *Unintended thought* (pp. 189–211). New York: Guilford Press.

Gilbert, D. T., & Hixon, J. G. (1991). The trouble of thinking: Activation and application of stereotypic belief. *Journal of Personality and Social Psychology, 54*, 193–202.

Gilbert, D., Krull, D., & Pelham, B. (1988). Of thoughts unspoken: Social inference and the self-regulation of behavior. *Journal of Personality and Social Psychology, 55*, 685–694.

Goffman, E. (1967). *Interaction ritual: Essay on face-to-face behavior*. Garden City, NY: Anchor.

Goldberg, H. (1951). The role of "cutting" in the perception of motor pictures. *Journal of Applied Psychology, 35*, 70–71.

Goldsmith, H. H. (1993). Temperament: Variability in developing emotion systems. In M. Lewis, & J. M. Haviland (Eds.), *Handbook of emotions* (pp. 353–364). New York: Guilford Press.

Gonzaga, G. C., Keltner, D., Londahl, E. A., & Smith, M. D. (2001). Love and the commitment problem in romantic relationships and friendship. *Journal of Personality and Social Psychology, 81*, 247–262.

Goodenough, F. L., & Tinker, M. A. (1931). The relative potency of facial expression and verbal description of stimulus on the judgment of emotion. *Comparative Psychology, 12,* 365–370.

Goos, L., & Silverman, I. (2002). Sex-related factors in the perception of threatening facial expressions. *Journal of Nonverbal Behavior, 26,* 27–41.

Gordijn, E. H., Wigboldus, D., & Yzerbyt, V. (2001). Emotional consequences of categorizing victims of negative outgroup behavior as ingroup or outgroup. *Group Processes & Intergroup Relations, 4,* 317–326.

Gottman, J., & Levenson, R. (1986). Assessing the role of emotion in marriage. *Behavioral Assessment, 8,* 31–48.

Gouaux, C. (1971). Induced affective states and interpersonal attraction. *Journal of Personality and Social Psychology, 20,* 37–43.

Gouaux, C., & Summers, K. (1973). Interpersonal attraction as a function of affective state and affective change. *Journal of Research in Personality, 7,* 254–260.

Graham, J., Gentry, K., & Green, J. (1981). The self-presentational nature of emotional expression: Some evidence. *Personality and Social Psychology Bulletin, 7,* 467–474.

Greeley, A. M. (1979). The American Irish: A report from Great Ireland. *International Journal of Comparative Sociology, 20,* 67–82.

Greeley, A. M. (1981). *The Irish–Americans.* New York: Harper & Row.

Green, D. P., Goldman, S. L., & Salovey, P. (1993). Measurement error masks bipolarity in affect ratings. *Journal of Personality and Social Psychology, 64,* 1029–1041.

Greenland, K., & Brown, R. (1999). Categorization and intergroup anxiety in contact between British and Japanese nationals. *European Journal of Social Psychology, 29,* 503–521.

Greenland, K., Masser, B., & Prentice, T. (2001). "They're scared of it": Intergroup determinants of attitudes toward children with HIV. *Journal of Applied Social Psychology, 31,* 2127–2148.

Griffitt, W. B. (1970). Environmental effects on interpersonal affective behavior: Ambient effective temperature and attraction. *Journal of Personality and Social Psychology, 15,* 240–244.

Gross, E., & Stone, G. P. (1964). Embarrassment and the analysis of role requirements. *American Journal of Sociology, 70,* 1–15.

Gross, J. (1989). Emotional expression in cancer onset and progression. *Social Science and Medicine, 28,* 1239–1248.

Gross, J. (1998a). The emerging field of emotion regulation: An integrative view. *Review of General Psychology, 2,* 1–29.

Gross, J. (1998b). Antecedent- and response-focused emotion regulation: Divergent consequences for experience, expression, and physiology. *Journal of Personality and Social Psychology, 74,* 224–237.

Gross, J. (1999). Emotion regulation: Past, present, future. *Cognition and Emotion, 13,* 551–573.

Gross, J., & John, O. (1995). Facets of emotional expressivity: Three self-report factors and their correlates. *Personality and Individual Differences, 19,* 555–568.

Gross, J., & John, O. (1997). Revealing feelings: Facets of emotional expressivity in self-reports, peer ratings, and behavior. *Journal of Personality and Social Psychology, 72,* 435–448.

Gross, J., & John, O. (2003). Individual differences in two emotion regulation processes: Implication for affect, relationship, and well-being. *Journal of Personality and Social Psychology, 85,* 348–362.

Gross, J., & Levenson, R. (1993). Emotional suppression: Physiology, self-reports, and expressive behavior. *Journal of Personality and Social Psychology, 64,* 970–986.

Gross, J., & Levenson, R. W. (1995). Emotion elicitation using film. *Cognition and Emotion, 9,* 87–108.

Gross, J., & Levenson, R. (1997). Hiding feelings: The acute effects of inhibiting negative and positive emotions. *Journal of Abnormal Psychology, 106,* 95–103.

Gross, J., & Munoz, R. (1995). Emotion regulation and mental health. *Clinical Psychology: Science and Practice, 2,* 151–164.

Grossman, M., & Wood, W. (1993). Sex differences in intensity of emotional experience: A social role interpretation. *Journal of Personality and Social Psychology, 65,* 1010–1022.

Gudykunst, W. B., & Shapiro, R. B. (1996). Communication in everyday interpersonal and intergroup encounters. *International Journal of Intercultural Relations, 20,* 19–45.

Hager, J., & Ekman, P. (1981). Methodological problems in Tourangeau and Ellsworth's study of facial expression and experience of emotion. *Journal of Personality and Social Psychology, 40,* 358–362.

Haidt, J. (2003). The moral emotions. In R. J. Davidson, K. S. Scherer, & H. H. Goldsmith (Eds.), *Handbook of affective sciences* (pp. 852–870). Oxford: Oxford University Press.

Haidt, J., & Keltner, D. (1999). Culture and facial expression: Open-ended methods find more expressions and a gradient of recognition. *Cognition and Emotion, 13,* 225–266.

Haidt, J., Koller, S. H., and Dias, M. G. (1993). Affect, culture and morality, or is it wrong to eat your dog? *Journal of Personality and Social Psychology, 65,* 613–628.

Haidt, J., Rozin, P., McCauley, C., & Imada, S. (1997). Body, psyche, and culture: The relationships between disgust and morality. *Psychology and Developing Societies, 9,* 107–131.

Halberstadt, J. B., Niedenthal, P. M., Kushner, J. (1995). Resolution of lexical ambiguity by emotional state. *Psychological Science, 6,* 278–282.

Hall, J. (1978). Gender effects in decoding nonverbal cues. *Psychological Bulletin, 85,* 845–857.

Hall, J. (1984). *Nonverbal sex differences: Communication accuracy and expressive style.* Baltimore, MD: Johns Hopkins University Press.

Hall, J., Carter, J., & Horgan, T. (2000). Gender differences in nonverbal communication of emotion. In A. Fischer (Ed.), *Gender and emotion: Social psychological perspectives* (pp. 97–117). London: Cambridge University Press.

Hall, J., & Friedman, G. (1999). Status, gender, and nonverbal behavior: A study of structured interactions between employees of a company. *Personality and Social Psychology Bulletin, 25,* 1082–1091.

Hall, J., & Matsumoto, D. (2004). Gender differences in judgments of multiple emotions from facial expressions. *Emotion, 4,* 201–206.

Hamilton, D. L. (1981). *Cognitive processes in stereotyping and intergroup behavior.* Hillsdale, NJ: Lawrence Erlbaum Associates, Inc.

Hamilton, D. L., & Gifford, R. K. (1976). Illusory correlation in interpersonal perception: A cognitive basis of stereotypic judgments. *Journal of Experimental Social Psychology, 12,* 392–407.

Harder, D. W. (1995). Shame and guilt assessment, and relationships of shame- and guilt-proneness to psychopathology. In J. P. Tangney, & K. W. Fischer (Eds.), *Self-conscious emotions: The psychology of shame, guilt, embarrassment and pride* (pp. 368–392). New York: Guilford Press.

Harder, D. W., & Lewis, S. J. (1987). The assessment of shame and guilt. In J. N. Butcher, & C. D. Spielberger (Eds.), *Advances in personality assessment* (Vol. 6, pp. 89–114). Hillsdale, NJ: Lawrence Erlbaum Associates, Inc.

Harnad, S. (1987). *Categorical perception: The groundwork of cognition.* New York: Cambridge University Press.

Harré, R. (1980). *Social being: A theory for social psychology.* Totowa, NJ: Littlefield, Adams.

Harré, R. (1986). *The social construction of emotion.* Oxford: Blackwell.

Harré, R., & Parrott, G. (1996). *The emotions: Social, cultural and biological dimensions*. London: Sage.

Harris, C. R., & Christenfeld, N. (1996). Gender, jealousy, and reason. *Psychological Science, 7*, 364–366.

Harris, P. (1989). *Children and emotion: The development of psychological understanding*. Oxford: Blackwell.

Harris, P. L. (1993). Understanding emotion. In M. Lewis, & J. M. Haviland (Eds.), *Handbook of emotions* (pp. 563–573). New York: Guilford Press.

Hart, D., & Karmel, M. P. (1996). Self-awareness and self-knowledge in humans, apes, and monkeys. In A. E. Russon, K. A. Bard, & S. T. Parker (Eds.), *Reaching into thought: The minds of the great apes* (pp. 325–347). Cambridge: Cambridge University Press.

Harter, S. (1999). *The construction of the self*. New York: Guilford Press.

Harter, S., & Whitesell, N. (1989). Developmental changes in children's understanding of simple, multiple, and blended emotion concepts. In C. Saarni, & P. Harris (Eds.), *Children's understanding of emotion* (pp. 81–116). Cambridge: Cambridge University Press.

Hatfield, E., Cacioppo, J. T., & Rapson, R. L. (1992). Primitive emotional contagion. In M. S. Clark (Ed.), Emotion and social behavior. *Review of Personality and Social Psychology, 14*, 151–177.

Hatfield, E., Cacioppo, J. T., & Rapson, R. L. (1993). Emotional contagion. *Current Directions in Psychological Science, 3*, 96–99.

Hatfield, E., Cacioppo, J. T., & Rapson, R. (1994). *Emotional contagion*. New York: Cambridge University Press.

Hatfield, E., Hsee, C., Costello, J., Weisman, M., & Denney, C. (1995). The impact of vocal feedback on emotional experience and expression. *Journal of Social Behavior and Personality, 10*, 293–312.

Heider, F. (1958). *The psychology of interpersonal relations*. New York: John Wiley & Sons.

Heine, S. J., Lehman, D. R., Markus, H. R., & Kitayama, S. (1999). Is there a universal need for positive self-regard? *Psychological Review, 106*, 766–794.

Heise, D. R., & O'Brien, J. (1993). Emotion expression in groups. In M. Lewis, & J. M. Haviland (Eds.), *Handbook of emotions* (pp. 489–497). New York: Guilford Press.

Heller, W. (1990). The neuropsychology of emotion: Developmental patterns and implications for psychopathology. In N. Stein, B. L. Leventhal, & T. Trabasso (Eds.), *Psychological and biological approaches to emotion* (pp. 167–211). Hillsdale, NJ: Lawrence Erlbaum Associates, Inc.

Heller, W. (1993). Neuropsychological mechanisms of individual differences in emotion, personality, and arousal. *Neuropsychology, 7*, 476–489.

Herrald, M. M., & Tomaka, J. (2002). Patterns of emotion-specific appraisal, coping, and cardiovascular reactivity during an ongoing emotional episode. *Journal of Personality and Social Psychology, 83*, 434–450.

Hess, U. (2001). The experience of emotion: Situational influences on the elicitation and experience of emotions. In A. Kaszniak (Ed.), *Emotions, Qualia, and Consciousness* (pp. 386–396). Singapore: World Scientific Publishing.

Hess, U., Adams, R., & Kleck, R. (2004). Facial appearance, gender, and emotion expression. *Emotion, 4*, 378–388.

Hess, U., Adams, R., & Kleck, R. (2005). Who may frown and who should smile? Dominance, affiliation, and the display of happiness and anger. *Cognition and Emotion, 19*, 515–536.

Hess, U., Adams, R., & Kleck, R. (in press). When two do the same it might not mean the same: The perception of emotional expressions shown by men and women. In

U. Hess, & P. Philippot (Eds.), *Group dynamics and emotional expression*. New York: Cambridge University Press.

Hess, U., Banse, R., & Kappas, A. (1995). The intensity of facial expression is determined by underlying affective state and social situation. *Journal of Personality and Social Psychology, 69*, 280–288.

Hess, U., Blairy, S., & Kleck, R. (1997). The intensity of emotional facial expressions and decoding accuracy. *Journal of Nonverbal Behavior, 21*, 241–257.

Hess, U., Blairy, S., & Kleck, R. (2000). The influence of facial emotion displays, gender, and ethnicity on judgment of dominance and affiliation. *Journal of Nonverbal Behavior, 24*, 265–283.

Hess, U., Sénecal, S., Kirouac, G., Herrera, P., Philippot, P., & Kleck, R. (2000). Emotional expressivity in men and women: Stereotypes and self-perceptions. *Cognition and Emotion, 14*, 609–642.

Higgins, E. T. (1987). Self-discrepancy. A theory relating self and affect. *Psychological Review, 94*, 319–340.

Higgins, E. T. (1989). Self-discrepancy theory: What patterns of self-beliefs cause people to suffer? In L. Berkowitz (Ed.), *Advances in experimental social psychology* (Vol. 22, pp. 93–136). San Diego, CA: Academic Press.

Hirt, E. R., Levine, G. M., McDonald, H. E., Melton, J., & Martin, L. L. (1997). The role of mood in quantitative and qualitative aspects of performance: Single or multiple mechanisms? *Journal of Experimental Social Psychology, 33*, 602–629.

Hirt, E. R., Melton, R. J., McDonald, H. E., & Harackiewicz, J. M. (1996). Processing goals, task interest, and the mood-performance relationship: A mediational analysis. *Journal of Personality and Social Psychology, 71*, 245–261.

Hirt, E. R., Zillman, D., Erickson, G. A., & Kennedy, C. (1992). Costs and benefits of allegiance: Changes in fans' self-ascribed competencies after team victory versus defeat. *Journal of Personality and Social Psychology, 63*, 724–738.

Hjörtsjö, C. (1969). *Man's face and mimic language*. Lund, Sweden: Student Literature.

Hochschild, A. R. (1983). *The managed heart: Commercialization of human feeling*. Berkeley, CA: University of California Press.

Hoffman, M. L. (1977). Personality and social development. *Annual Review of Psychology, 28*, 295–321.

Hoffman, M. L. (1983). Affective and cognitive processes in moral internalization. In E. T. Higgins, D. Ruble, & S. W. Hartup (Eds.), *Social cognition and social development: A sociocultural perspective* (pp. 236–274). Cambridge: Cambridge University Press.

Hoffman, M. L. (1984). Interaction of affect and cognition on empathy. In C. E. Izard, J. Kagan, & R. B. Zajonc (Eds.), *Emotion, cognition, and behavior* (pp. 103–131). Cambridge: Cambridge University Press.

Hofstede, G. H. (1980). *Culture's consequences: International differences in work-related values*. Beverly Hills, CA: Sage.

Hofstede, G. (1983). Dimensions of national cultures in fifty countries and three regions. In J. Deregowski, S. Dziurawiec, & R. Annis (Eds.), *Expectations in cross-cultural psychology*. Amsterdam, The Netherlands: Swets & Zeitlinger.

Hofstede, G. H. (2001). *Culture's consequences: Comparing values, behaviors, institutions and organizations across nations* (2nd ed.). Thousand Oaks, CA: Sage.

Horowitz, M. (1976/1992). *Stress response syndromes*. Northvale, NJ: Jason Aronson.

Hrdy, S. B. G. (1979). Infanticide among animals: A review, classification, and examination of the implications for reproductive strategies of females. *Ethology and Sociobiology, 1*, 14–40.

Hsee, C. K., Hatfield, E., Carlson, J. G., & Chemtob, C. (1990). The effect of power on susceptibility to emotional contagion. *Cognition and Emotion, 4*, 317–340.

Hubbert, K. N., Gudykunst, W. B., & Guerrero, S. L. (1999). Intergroup communication over time. *International Journal of Intercultural Relations, 23,* 13–46.

Hupka, R. B. (1984). Jealousy: Compound emotion or label for particular situation? *Motivation and Emotion, 8,* 141–155.

Hupka, R. B., Zaleski, Z., Otto, J., Reidl, L., & Tanabrina, N. V. (1996). Anger, envy, fear, and jealousy as felt in the body: A five-nation study. *Cross-Cultural Research, 30,* 243–264.

Hutson-Comeaux, S., & Kelly, J. (2002). Gender stereotypes of emotional reactions: How we judge an emotion as valid. *Sex Roles, 47,* 1–10.

Ingram, R. E. (1984). Toward an information processing analysis of depression. *Cognitive Therapy and Research, 8,* 443–478.

Innes-Ker, A., & Niedenthal, P. M. (2002). Emotion concepts and emotional states in social judgment and categorization. *Journal of Personality and Social Psychology, 83,* 804–816.

Isbell, L. M., & Wyer, R. S. (1999). Correcting for mood-induced bias in the evaluation of political candidates: The roles of intrinsic and extrinsic motivation. *Personality and Social Psychology Bulletin, 25,* 237–249.

Isen, A. M. (1984). Toward understanding the role of affect in cognition. In R. S. Wyer, & T. K. Srull (Eds.), *Handbook of social cognition* (Vol. 3, pp. 179–236). Hillsdale, NJ: Lawrence Erlbaum Associates, Inc.

Isen, A. M. (1987). Positive affect, cognitive processes, and social behaviour. In L. Berkowitz (Ed.), *Advances in experimental social psychology* (Vol. 20, pp. 203–253). New York: Academic Press.

Isen, A. M., & Daubman, K. A. (1984). The influence of affect on categorization. *Journal of Personality and Social Psychology, 47,* 1206–1217.

Isen, A. M., Daubman, K. A., & Nowicki, G. P. (1987). Positive affect facilitates creative problem solving. *Journal of Personality and Social Psychology, 52,* 1122–1131.

Isen, A. M., Johnson, M. M., Mertz, E., & Robinson, G. F. (1985). The influence of positive affect on the unusualness of word associations. *Journal of Personality and Social Psychology, 48,* 1413–1426.

Isen, A. M., & Means, B. (1983). The influence of positive affect in decision making strategy. *Social Cognition, 2,* 18–31.

Isen, A. M., Niedenthal, P. M., & Cantor, N. (1992). The influence of positive affect on social categorization. *Motivation and Emotion, 16,* 65–78.

Isen, A. M., Shalker, T. E., Clark, M., & Karp, L. (1978). Affect, accessibility of material in memory, and behavior: A cognitive loop? *Journal of Personality and Social Psychology, 36,* 1–12.

Islam, M. R., & Hewstone, M. (1993). Dimensions of contact as predictors of intergroup anxiety, perceived out-group variability, and out-group attitude: An integrative model. *Personality and Social Psychology Bulletin, 19,* 700–710.

Izard, C. E. (1971). *The face of emotion.* New York: Appleton-Century-Crofts.

Izard, C. E. (1972). *Patterns of emotions.* New York: Academic Press.

Izard, C. E. (1977). *Human emotions.* New York: Plenum Press.

Izard, C. E. (1979). *The maximally discriminative facial movement coding system (MAX).* Newark, DE: University of Delaware Office of Instructional Technology.

Izard, C. E. (1990). Facial expressions and the regulation of emotions. *Journal of Personality and Social Psychology, 58,* 487–498.

Izard, C. E. (1994). Innate and universal facial expressions: Evidence from developmental and cross-cultural research. *Psychological Bulletin, 115,* 288–299.

Izard, C. E., Ackerman, B. P., & Schultz, D. (1999). Independent emotions and consciousness: Self-consciousness and dependent emotions. In J. A. Singer, & P. Singer (Eds.), *At play in the fields of consciousness: Essays in honor of Jerome L. Singer* (pp. 83–102). Mahwah, NJ: Lawrence Erlbaum Associates, Inc.

Izard, C. E., & Dougherty, L. (1980). A system for identifying affect expressions by holistic judgments. Newark, DE: Instructional Resources Center.

Izard, C. E., Dougherty, F. E., Bloxom, B. M., & Kotsch, N. E. (1974). *The differential emotion scale: A method of measuring the meaning of subjective experience of discrete emotions.* Nashville, TN: Vanderbilt University, Department of Psychology.

Izard, C. E., & Malatesta, C. Z. (1987). Perspectives on emotional development I: Differential emotions, theory of early emotional development. In J. D. Osofsky (Ed.), *Handbook of infant development* (2nd ed.) (pp. 494–554). New York: John Wiley & Sons.

Jackson, L. A., Hodge, C. N., Gerard, D. A., Ingram, J. M., Ervin, K. S., & Sheppard, L. A. (1996). Cognition, affect, and behavior in the prediction of group attitudes. *Personality and Social Psychology Bulletin, 22,* 306–316.

Jakobs, E., Manstead, A., & Fischer, A. (1999). Social motives and emotional feelings as determinants of facial displays: The case of smiling. *Personality and Social Psychology Bulletin, 25,* 424–435.

Jakobs, E., Manstead, A., & Fischer, A. (2001). Social context effects on facial activity in a negative emotional setting. *Emotion, 1,* 51–69.

Jakupcak, M., Salters, K., Gratz, K., & Roemer, L. (2003). Masculinity and emotionality: An investigation of men's primary and secondary emotional responding. *Sex Roles, 49,* 111–119.

James, L. R., Demaree, R. G., & Wolf, G. (1984). Estimating within-group interrater reliability with and without response bias. *Journal of Applied Psychology, 69,* 85–98.

James, W. (1890). *The principles of psychology.* New York: Holt.

Jansz, J. (2000). Masculine identity and restrictive emotionality. In A. Fischer (Ed.), *Gender and emotion: Social psychological perspectives* (pp. 166–186). London: Cambridge University Press.

Ji, L., Nisbett, R. E., & Peng, K. (2001). Culture, change, and prediction. *Psychological Science, 12,* 450–456.

Johnson, E. J., & Tversky, A. (1983). Affect, generalization, and the perception of risk. *Journal of Personality and Social Psychology, 45,* 20–31.

Johnson, J., & Shulman, G. (1988). More alike than meets the eye: Perceived gender differences in subjective experience and its display. *Sex Roles, 19,* 67–79.

Johnson-Laird, P. N., & Oatley, K. (1989). The language of emotions: An analysis of a semantic field. *Cognition and Emotion, 3,* 81–123.

Johnson-Laird, P. N., & Oatley, K. (1992). Basic emotions, rationality, and folk theory. *Cognition and Emotion, 6,* 201–223.

Johnstone, T., & Scherer, K. R. (2000). Vocal communication of emotion. In M. Lewis, & J. M. Haviland-Jones (Eds.), *Handbook of emotions* (2nd ed.) (pp. 226–235). New York: Guilford Press.

Jones, E., & Davis, K. (1965). From acts to dispositions: The attribution process in person perception. In L. Berkowitz (Ed.), *Advances in experimental social psychology* (Vol. 2, pp. 219–266). New York: Academic Press.

Jones, H. E. (1935). The galvanic skin response as related to overt expression. *American Journal of Psychology, 47,* 241–251.

Jones, H. E. (1960). The longitudinal method in the study of personality. In I. Iscoe, & H. W. Stevenson (Eds.), *Personality development in children* (pp. 3–27). Austin, TX: University of Texas Press.

Josephson, B. R., Singer, J. A., & Salovey, P. (1996). Mood regulation and memory: Repairing sad moods with happy memories. *Cognition and Emotion, 10,* 437–444.

Jussim, L., Nelson, T. E., Manis, M., & Soffin, S. (1995). Prejudice, stereotypes, and labeling effects: Sources of bias in person perception. *Journal of Personality and Social Psychology, 68*, 228–246.

Kaiser, C. R., & Major, B. (2004). Judgments of deserving and the emotional consequences of stigmatization. In L. Z. Tiedens, & C. W. Leach (Eds.), *The social life of emotions* (pp. 270–291). Cambridge: Cambridge University Press.

Kappen, D. M., & Branscombe, N. R. (2001). The effects of reasons given for ineligibility on perceived gender discrimination and feelings of injustice. *British Journal of Social Psychology, 40*, 295–313.

Keating, C. F., Mazur, A., Segall, M. H., Cysneiros, P. G., Divale, W. T., Kilbride, J. E. et al. (1981). Culture and the perception of social dominance from facial expression. *Journal of Personality and Social Psychology, 40* (4), 615–626.

Kelley, H. H. (1979). *Personal relationships: Their structures and processes.* Hillsdale, NJ: Lawrence Erlbaum Associates, Inc.

Kelley, H. H. (1986). Personal relationships: Their nature and significance. In R. Gilmour, & S. Duck (Eds.), *The emerging field of personal relationships* (pp. 3–19). Hilldale, NJ: Lawrence Erlbaum Associates, Inc.

Kelly, A., & Kahn, J. (1994). Effects of suppression of personal intrusive thoughts. *Journal of Personality and Social Psychology, 66*, 998–1006.

Kelly, J. R., & Barsade, S. G. (2001). Mood and emotions in small groups and work teams. *Organizational Behavior and Human Decision Processes, 86*, 99–130.

Kelly, J., & Hutson-Comeaux, S. (1999). Gender-emotion stereotypes are context specific. *Sex Roles, 40*, 107–120.

Kelly, J., & Hutson-Comeaux, S. (2000). The appropriateness of emotional expression in women and men: The double-bind of emotion. *Journal of Social Behavior and Personality, 15*, 515–528.

Keltner, D. (1995). The signs of appeasement: Evidence for the distinct displays of embarrassment, amusement, and shame. *Journal of Personality and Social Psychology, 68*, 441–454.

Keltner, D., & Buswell, B. N. (1996). Evidence for the distinctness of embarrassment, shame, and guilt: A study of recalled antecedents and facial expressions of emotion. *Cognition and Emotion, 10*, 155–171.

Keltner, D., & Buswell, B. (1997). Embarrassment: Its distinct form and appeasement functions. *Psychological Bulletin, 122*, 250–270.

Keltner, D., & Gross, J. J. (1999). Functionalist accounts of emotions. *Cognition and Emotion, 13*, 467–480.

Keltner, D., & Haidt, J. (1999). Social function of emotions at four levels of analysis. *Cognition and Emotion, 13*, 505–521.

Keltner, D., & Haidt, J. (2001). Social functions of emotions. In T. Mayne, & G. A. Bonanno (Eds.), *Emotions: Current issues and future directions.* New York: Guilford Press.

Keltner, D., Young, R. C., Heerey, E. A., Oemig, C., & Monarch, N. D. (1998). Teasing in hierarchical and intimate relations. *Journal of Personality and Social Psychology, 75*, 1231–1247.

Kemper, T. (1978). *A social interactional theory of emotion.* New York: John Wiley & Sons.

King, L., & Emmons, R. (1990). Conflict over emotional expression: Psychological and physical correlates. *Journal of Personality and Social Psychology, 58*, 864–877.

Kitayama, S. (2002). Cultural and basic psychological processes – Toward a system view of culture: Comment on Oyserman et al. *Psychological Bulletin, 128*, 189–196.

Kitayama, S., & Markus, H. R. (1994). *Emotion and culture: Empirical studies of mutual influence.* Washington, DC: American Psychological Association.

Kitayama, S., & Markus, H. (1995). Culture and self: Implications for internal psychology. In N. R. Goldberger, & J. B. Veroff (Eds.), *The culture of psychology reader* (pp. 366–383). New York: State University of New York Press.

Kitayama, S., Markus, H. R., & Kurokawa, M. (2000). Culture, emotion, and well-being: Good feelings in Japan and the United States. *Cognition and Emotion, 14,* 93–124.

Kitayama, S., Markus, H. R., & Matsumoto, H. (1995). A cultural perspective on self-conscious emotions. In J. P. Tangney, & K. W. Fischer (Eds.), *Self-conscious emotions: The psychology of shame, guilt, embarrassment, and pride* (pp. 439–464). New York: Guilford Press.

Kitayama, S., Mesquita, B., & Karasawa, M. (2004). *Culture and emotional experience: Socially engaging and disengaging emotions in Japan and the United States.* Unpublished manuscript, University of Michigan, Ann Arbor, MI.

Klass, E. T. (1990). Guilt, shame, and embarrassment: Cognitive behavioral approaches. In H. Leitenberg (Ed.), *Handbook of social and evaluation anxiety* (pp. 385–414). New York: Plenum.

Kleck, R., Vaughan, R., Cartwright-Smith, J., Vaughan, K., Colby, C., & Lanzetta, J. (1976). Effects of being observed on expressive, subjective, and physiological responses to painful stimuli. *Journal of Personality and Social Psychology, 34,* 1211–1218.

Klineberg, O. (1938). Emotional expression in Chinese literature. *Journal of Abnormal and Social Psychology, 33,* 517–520.

Klinger, M. R., Burton, P. C., & Pitts, G. S. (2000). Mechanisms of unconscious priming: I. Response competition, not spreading activation. *Journal of Experimental Psychology: Learning, Memory, and Cognition, 26,* 441–455.

Klinnert, M. D. (1984). The regulation of infant behavior by maternal facial expression. *Infant Behavior and Development, 7,* 447–465.

Klinnert, M. D., Emde, R. N., Butterfield, P., & Campos, J. J. (1986). Social referencing: The infant's use of emotional signals from a friendly adult with mother present. *Developmental Psychology, 22,* 427–432.

Knudsen, H. R., & Muzekari, L. H. (1983). The effects of verbal statements of context on facial expressions of emotion. *Journal of Nonverbal Behavior, 7,* 202–212.

Knutson, B. (1996). Facial expressions of emotion influence interpersonal trait inferences. *Journal of Nonverbal Behavior, 20,* 165–182.

Koenigsberg, M. R., Katkin, E. S., & Blascovich, J. (1981). The effect of pretraining instructional set on the acquisition and maintenance of heart beat detection in males and females. *Psychophysiology, 18,* 196–197.

Kopel, S., & Arkowitz, H. (1974). Role playing as a source of self-observation and behavior change. *Journal of Personality and Social Psychology, 29,* 677–686.

Koriat, A., Melkman, R., Averill, J., & Lazarus, R. (1972). The self-control of emotional reactions to a stressful film. *Journal of Personality, 40,* 601–619.

Kramer, T., Buckhout, R., Fox, P., Widman, E., & Tusche, B. (1991). Effects of stress on recall. *Applied Cognitive Psychology, 5,* 483–488.

Kraut, R. (1982). Social presence, facial feedback, and emotion. *Journal of Personality and Social Psychology, 42,* 853–863.

Kraut, R. E., & Johnston, R. E. (1979). Social and emotional messages of smiling: An ethological approach. *Journal of Personality and Social Psychology, 37,* 1539–1553.

Krauth-Gruber, S., & Ric, F. (2000). Affect and stereotypic thinking: A test of the mood-and-general-knowledge model. *Personality and Social Psychology Bulletin, 26,* 1587–1597.

Kring, A. M. (2000). Gender and anger. In A. Fischer (Ed.), *Gender and emotion: Social psychological perspectives* (pp. 211–231). London: Cambridge University Press.

Kring, A. M., & Gordon, A. H. (1998). Sex differences in emotion: Expression, experience and physiology. *Journal of Personality and Social Psychology, 74,* 686–703.

Kring, A. M., Smith, D., & Neale, J. (1994). Individual differences in dispositional expressiveness: Development and validation of the emotional expressivity scale. *Journal of Personality and Social Psychology, 66*, 934–949.

Krosnick, J. A., Betz, A. L., Jussim, L. J., & Lynn, A. R. (1992). Subliminal conditioning of attitudes. *Personality and Social Psychology Bulletin, 18*, 152–162.

Kuebli, J., & Fivush, R. (1992). Sex differences in parent–child conversations about past emotions. *Sex Roles, 27*, 683–698.

Kune, G., Kune, S., Watson, L., & Bahnson, C. (1991). Personality as a risk factor in large bowel cancer: Data from the Melbourne Colorectal Cancer Study. *Psychological Medicine, 21*, 29–41.

LaBarre, W. (1947). The culture basis of emotions and gestures, *Journal of Personality, 16*, 49–68.

LaFrance, M., & Banaji, M. (1992). Towards a reconsideration of the gender–emotion relationship. In M. S. Clark (Ed.), Emotion and social behavior. *Review of Personality and Social Psychology, 14*, 178–201.

LaFrance, M., & Hecht, M. (2000). Gender and smiling: A meta-analysis. In A. Fischer (Ed.), *Gender and emotion: Social psychological perspectives* (pp. 118–142). London: Cambridge University Press.

LaFrance, M., Hecht, M., & Levy Paluck, E. (2003). The contingent smile: A meta-analysis of sex differences in smiling. *Psychological Bulletin, 129*, 305–334.

LaFrance, M., & Henley, N. (1994). On oppressing hypotheses: Or differences in nonverbal sensitivity revisited. In H. Radke, & H. Stam (Eds.), *Power/gender, social relations in theory and practice* (pp. 287–311). London: Sage.

Laird, J. D. (1974). Self-attribution of emotion: The effects of expressive behavior on the quality of emotional experience. *Journal of Personality and Social Psychology, 29*, 475–486.

Lambert, A. J., Khan, S. R., Lickel, B. A., & Fricke, K. (1997). Mood and the correction of positive versus negative stereotypes. *Journal of Personality and Social Psychology, 72*, 1002–1016.

Lane, R. D., & Nadel, L. (Eds.) (2000). *Cognitive neuroscience of emotion*. New York: Oxford University Press.

Lane, R., Reiman, E. M., Bradley, M. M., Lang, P. J., Ahern, G. L., Davidson, R. J. et al. (1997). Neuroanatomical correlates of pleasant and unpleasant emotion. *Neuropsychologia, 35*, 1437–1444.

Lang, P. J. (1977). Psychological assessment of anxiety and fear. In J. D. Cone, & R. P. Hawkins (Eds.), *Behavioral assessment: New directions in clinical psychology* (pp. 178–195). New York: Brunner/Mazel.

Lang, P. J. (1979). A bio-informational theory of emotional imagery. *Psychophysiology, 16*, 495–512.

Lang, P. J. (1984). Cognition in emotion: Cognition in action. In C. E. Izard, J. Kagan, & R. B. Zajonc (Eds.), *Emotions, cognition, and behavior* (pp. 192–226). New York: Cambridge University Press.

Lang, P. J., Bradley, M. M., & Cuthbert, B. N. (1990). Emotion, attention and the startle reflex. *Psychological Review, 97*, 377–395.

Lange, C. G. (1885/1922). The emotions: A psychophysiological study. In C. G. Lange, & W. James (Eds.), *The emotions* (pp. 33–90). Baltimore, MD: Williams & Wilkins.

Langlois, J. H., & Roggman, L. A. (1990). Attractive faces are only average. *Psychological Science, 1*, 115–121.

Lantermann, E. D., & Otto, J. H. (1996). Correction of effects of memory valence and emotionality on content and style of judgments. *Cognition and Emotion, 10*, 505–527.

Lanzetta, J., Biernat, J., & Kleck, R. (1982). Self-focused attention, facial behavior, autonomic arousal and the experience of emotion. *Motivation and Emotion, 6*, 49–63.

Lanzetta, J., Cartwright-Smith, J., & Kleck, R. (1976). Effects of nonverbal dissimulation on emotional experience and autonomic arousal. *Journal of Personality and Social Psychology, 33,* 354–370.

Lanzetta, J. T., & Kleck, R. E. (1970). Encoding and decoding of nonverbal affect in humans. *Journal of Personality and Social Psychology, 1,* 12–19.

LaPiere, R. T. (1934). Attitudes versus actions. *Social Forces, 13,* 230–237.

Larsen, R. J., & Diener, E. (1992). Promises and problems with the circumplex model of emotion. In M. S. Clark (Ed.), Emotion and social behavior. *Review of Personality and Social Psychology, 13,* 25–59.

Larsen, R. J., Diener, E., & Cropanzano, R. (1987). Cognitive operations associated with individual differences in affect intensity. *Journal of Personality and Social Psychology, 53,* 767–774.

Larsen, R. J., Kasimatis, M., & Frey, K. (1992). Facilitating the furrowed brow: An unobtrusive test of the facial feedback hypothesis applied to unpleasant affect. *Cognition and Emotion, 6,* 321–338.

Lazarus, R. S. (1991). *Emotion and adaptation.* New York: Oxford University Press.

Lazarus, R. S., & Alfert, E. (1964). Short-circuiting of threat by experimentally altering cognitive appraisal. *Journal of Abnormal and Social Psychology, 69,* 195–205.

Lazarus, R. S., Averill, J., & Option, E. M. (1970). Towards a cognitive theory of emotion. In M. B. Arnold (Ed.), *Feelings and emotions: The Loyola symposium* (pp. 207–232). New York: Academic Press.

Lazarus, R. S., Tomita, M., Opton, E. Jr., & Kodama, M. (1966). A cross-cultural study of stress-reaction patterns in Japan. *Journal of Personality and Social Psychology, 4,* 622–633.

Le Bon, G. (1895/1963). *Psychologie des foules.* Paris: Presses Universitaires de France.

Leach, C. W., Spears, R., Branscombe, N. R., & Doosje, B. (2003). Malicious pleasure: Schadenfreude at the suffering of another group. *Journal of Personality and Social Psychology, 84,* 932–943.

Leach, E. (1972). The influence of cultural context on non-verbal communication in man. In R. Hinde (Ed.), *Nonverbal communication* (pp. 315–344). London: Cambridge University Press.

Leary, M. R., Britt, T. W., Cutlip, W. D., & Templeton, J. L. (1992). Social blushing. *Psychological Bulletin, 111,* 446–460.

Leary, M. R., Landel, J. L., & Patton, K. M. (1996). The motivated expression of embarrassment following a self-presentational predicament. *Journal of Personality, 64,* 619–636.

Lee, V., & Wagner, H. (2002). The effect of social presence on the facial and verbal expression of emotion and the interrelationship among emotion components. *Journal of Nonverbal Behavior, 26*(1), 3–25.

Leppänen, J., & Hietanen, J. (2003). Affect and face perception: Odors modulate the recognition advantage of happy faces. *Emotion, 3,* 315–326.

Lerner, J. S., Goldberg, J. H., & Tetlock, P. E. (1998). Sober second thought: The effects of accountability, anger, and authoritarianism on attribution of responsibility. *Personality and Social Psychology Bulletin, 24,* 563–574.

Lerner, J. S., & Keltner, D. (2000). Beyond valence: Toward a model of emotion specific influences on judgment and choice. *Cognition and Emotion, 14,* 473–493.

Lerner, J. S., & Keltner, D. (2001). Fear, anger, and risk. *Journal of Personality and Social Psychology, 81,* 146–159.

Leu, J., Mesquita, B., & Ellsworth, P. C. (2005). Culture and emotional valence: Dialecticism in East Asian contexts and a positivity bias in European American contexts. Manuscript submitted for publication.

Levenson, R. W. (1992). Autonomic nervous system differences among emotions. *Psychological Science, 3*, 23–27.

Levenson, R. W. (1996). Biological substrates of empathy and facial modulation of emotion: Two facets of the scientific legacy of John Lanzetta. *Motivation and Emotion, 20*, 185–204.

Levenson, R. W., Carstensen, L. L., Friesen, W. V., & Ekman, P. (1991). Emotion, physiology and expression in old age. *Psychology and Aging, 6*, 28–35.

Levenson, R. W., Carstensen, L., & Gottman, J. (1994). Influence of age and gender on affect, physiology, and their interrelations: A study of long-term marriages. *Journal of Personality and Social Psychology, 67*, 56–68.

Levenson, R. W., Ekman, P., & Friesen, W. V. (1990). Voluntary facial action generates emotion-specific autonomic nervous system activity. *Psychophysiology, 27*(4), 363–384.

Levenson, R. W., Ekman, P., Heider, K., & Friesen, W. V. (1992). Emotion and autonomic nervous system activity in the Minangkabau of West Sumatra. *Journal of Personality and Social Psychology, 62*, 972–988.

Leventhal, H., & Cupchik, G. (1975). The informational and facilitative effects of an audience upon expression and the evaluation of humorous stimuli. *Journal of Experimental Social Psychology, 11*, 363–380.

Leventhal, H., & Mace, W. (1970). The effect of laughter on evaluation of a slapstick movie. *Journal of Personality, 38*, 16–30.

Leventhal, H., & Scherer, K. R. (1987). The relationship of emotion to cognition: A functional approach to semantic controversy. *Cognition and Emotion, 1*, 3–28.

Lewis, H. B. (1971). *Shame and guilt in neurosis.* New York: International Universities Press.

Lewis, M. (1992). *Shame: The exposed self.* New York: Free Press.

Lewis, M. (1993). The emergence of human emotions. In M. Lewis, & J. M. Haviland (Eds.), *Handbook of emotions* (pp. 563–573). New York: Guilford Press.

Lewis, M. (2000). Self-conscious emotions: Embarrassment, pride, shame, and guilt. In M. Lewis, & J. M. Haviland-Jones (Eds.), *Handbook of emotions* (2nd ed.) (pp. 623–636). New York: Guilford Press.

Lewis, M., Alessandri, S. M., & Sullivan, M. W. (1992). Differences in shame and pride as a function of children's gender and task difficulty. *Child Development, 63*, 630–638.

Lewis, M., & Brooks-Gunn, J. (1979). *Social cognition and acquisition of the self.* New York: Plenum.

Lewis, M., Sullivan, M. W., Stanger, C., & Weiss, M. (1989). Self-development and self-conscious emotions. *Child Development, 60*, 146–156.

Leyens, J. P., Demoulin, S., Désert, M., Vaes, J., & Philippot, P. (2002). Expressing emotions and decoding them: In-groups and out-groups do not share the same advantages. In D. M. Mackie, & E. R. Smith (Eds.), *From prejudice to intergroup emotions: Differentiated reactions to social groups* (pp. 135–151). New York: Psychology Press.

Lindsay-Hartz, J. (1984). Contrasting experiences of shame and guilt. *American Behavioral Scientist, 27*, 689–704.

Lindsay-Hartz, J., de Rivera, J., & Mascolo, M. F. (1995). Differentiating guilt and shame and their effects on motivation. In J. Tangney, & K. Fischer (Eds.), *Self-conscious emotions: Shame guilt, embarrassment, and pride* (pp. 274–299). New York: Guilford Press.

Lu, L. (2001). Understanding happiness: A look into Chinese folk psychology. *Journal of Happiness Studies, 2*, 407–432.

Lukes, S. (1973). *Individualism.* New York: Harper & Row.

Luminet, O., Bouts, P., Delie, F., Manstead, A., & Rimé, B. (2000). Social sharing of emotion following exposure to a negatively valenced situation. *Cognition and Emotion, 14*, 661–688.

Luminet, O., Zech, E., Rimé, B., & Wagner, H. (2000). Predicting cognitive and social consequences of emotional episodes: The contribution of emotional intensity, the five-factor model, and alexithymia. *Journal of Research in Personality, 34*, 471–497.

Lundqvist, D., & Öhman, A. (2005). Emotion regulates attention: The relation between facial configurations, facial emotion, and visual attention. *Visual Cognition, 12*(1), 51–84.

Lutz, C. (1987). Goals, events and understanding in Ifaluk emotion theory. In N. Quinn, & D. Holland (Eds.), *Cultural models in language and thought* (pp. 290–312). Cambridge: Cambridge University Press.

Lutz, C. (1988). *Unnatural emotions: Everyday sentiments on a Micronesian atoll and their challenge to western theory*. Chicago, IL: University of Chicago Press.

Mackie, D. M., Devos, T., & Smith, E. R. (2000). Intergroup emotions: Explaining offensive action tendencies in an intergroup context. *Journal of Personality and Social Psychology, 79*, 602–616.

Mackie, D. M., Queller, S., Stroessner, S. J., & Hamilton, D. L. (1996). Making stereotypes better or worse: Multiple roles for positive affect in group impressions. In R. M. Sorrentino, & E. T. Higgins (Eds.), *Handbook of motivation and cognition* (Vol. 3, pp. 371–396). New York: Guilford Press.

Mackie, D. M., & Worth, L. T. (1989). Processing deficit and the mediation of positive affect in persuasion. *Journal of Personality and Social Psychology, 57*, 27–40.

MacLean, P. D. (1993). Cerebral evolution of emotion. In M. Lewis, & J. M. Haviland (Eds.), *Handbook of emotions* (pp. 67–87). New York: Guilford Press.

MacLeod, C., Tata, P., & Mathews, A. (1987). Perception of emotionally valenced information in depression. *British Journal of Clinical Psychology, 26*, 67–68.

Macrae, C., Bodenhausen, G., Milne, A., & Jetten, J. (1994). Out of mind but back in sight: Stereotypes on the rebound. *Journal of Personality and Social Psychology, 67*, 808–817.

Major, B., Kaiser, C. R., & McCoy S. K. (2003). It's not my fault: When and why attributions to prejudice protect self-esteem. *Personality and Social Psychology Bulletin, 29*, 772–781.

Major, B., Quinton, W. J., & McCoy, S. K. (2002). Antecedents and consequences of attributions to discrimination: Theoretical and empirical advances. In M. P. Zanna (Ed.), *Advances in experimental social psychology* (Vol. 34, pp. 251–330). San Diego, CA: Academic Press.

Malatesta, C. Z., Grigoryev, P., Lamb, C., Albin, M., & Culver, C. (1986). Emotion socialization and expressive development in preterm and full-term infants. *Child Development, 57*, 316–330.

Malatesta, C. Z., & Haviland, J. M. (1982). Learning display rules: The socialization of emotion expression in infancy. *Child Development, 53*(4), 991–1003.

Mandler, G. (1975). *Mind and emotion*. New York: John Wiley & Sons.

Manstead, A. S. R. (1991). Expressiveness as an individual difference. In R. S. Feldman, & B. Rimé (Eds.), *Fundamentals of nonverbal behavior* (pp. 285–328). Cambridge/New York: Cambridge University Press.

Manstead, A. S. R., & Fischer, A. H. (2000). Emotion regulation in full. *Psychological Inquiries, 11*, 188–191.

Manstead, A. S. R., Fischer, A., & Jakobs, E. (1999). The social and emotional functions of facial displays. In P. Philippot, R. Feldman, & E. Coats (Eds.), *The social context of nonverbal behaviour* (pp. 287–313). Cambridge: Cambridge University Press.

Manstead, A. S. R., & Semin, G. R. (1981). Social transgression, social perspectives, and social emotionality. *Motivation and Emotion, 5*, 249–261.

Manstead, A. S. R., & Tetlock, P. E. (1989). Cognitive appraisal and emotional experience: Further evidence. *Cognition and Emotion, 3*, 225–240.

Marcus, D. K., & Miller, R. S. (1999). The perception of "live" embarrassment: A social relations analysis of class presentations. *Cognition and Emotion, 13*, 105–117.

Marcus, D. K., Wilson, J. R., and Miller, R. S. (1996). Are perceptions of emotion in the eye of the beholder? A social relations analysis of embarrassment. *Personality and Social Psychology Bulletin, 22,* 1220–1228.

Markus, H. R., & Kitayama, S. (1991). Culture and the self: Implications for cognition, emotion, and motivation. *Psychological Review, 98*(2), 224–253.

Markus, H. R., & Kitayama, S. (1994). The cultural construction of self and emotion: Implications for social behavior. In S. Kitayama, & H. R. Markus (Eds.), *Emotion and culture: Empirical studies of mutual influence* (pp. 89–130). Washington, DC: American Psychological Association.

Markus, H. R., & Kitayama, S. (2004). Models of agency: Sociocultural diversity in the construction of action. In V. Murphy-Berman, & J. J. Berman (Eds), *Cross-cultural differences in perspectives on the self: Nebraska symposium on motivation* (Vol. 49, pp. 1–57). Lincoln, NE: University of Nebraska Press.

Markus, H. R., Kitayama, S., & Heinman, R. (1996). Culture and "basic" psychological principles. In E. T. Higgins, & A. W. Kruglanski (Eds.), *Social psychology: Handbook of basic principles.* New York: Guilford Press.

Martin, B. (1964). Expression and inhibition of sex motive arousal in the college male. *Journal of Abnormal and Social Psychology, 68,* 307–312.

Martin, L. L., Ward, D. W., Achee, J. W., & Wyer, R. S. (1993). Mood as input: People have to interpret the motivational implications of their moods. *Journal of Personality and Social Psychology, 64,* 317–326.

Masuda, T., Ellsworth, P. C., Mesquita, B., Leu, J., & Veerdonk, E. (2005). *Putting the face in context: Cultural differences in the perception of emotions from facial behavior.* Unpublished manuscript, University of Michigan, Ann Arbor, MI.

Mathews, A., & MacLeod, C. (1994). Cognitive approaches to emotion and emotional disorders. *Annual Review of Psychology, 45,* 25–50.

Matsumoto, D. (1987). The role of facial response in the experience of emotion: More methodological problems and a meta-analysis. *Journal of Personality and Social Psychology, 52,* 769–774.

Matsumoto, D. (1989). Cultural influences on the perception of emotion. *Journal of Cross-Cultural Psychology, 20*(1), 92–105.

Matsumoto, D. (1990). Cultural similarities and differences in display rules. *Motivation and Emotion, 14,* 195–214.

Matsumoto, D. (1992). American–Japanese cultural differences in the recognition of universal facial expressions. *Journal of Cross-Cultural Psychology, 23*(1), 72–84.

Matsumoto, D. (2003). Cross-cultural research. In S. Davis (Ed.), *The handbook of research methods in experimental psychology* (pp. 189–208). Oxford: Blackwell.

Matsumoto, D. (2005). Apples and oranges: Methodological requirements for testing a possible ingroup advantage in emotion judgments from facial expressions. In U. Hess, & P. Philippot (Eds.), *Group dynamics and emotional expression.* New York: Cambridge University Press.

Matsumoto, D., Consolacion, T., Yamada, H., Suzuki, R., Franklin, B., Paul, S., Ray, & Uchida (2002). American–Japanese cultural differences in judgments of emotional expressions of different intensities. *Cognition and Emotion, 16,* 721–747.

Matsumoto, D., Kudoh, T., Scherer, K., & Wallbott, H. (1988). Antecedents and reactions to emotions in the United States and Japan. *Journal of Cross-Cultural Psychology, 19,* 267–286.

Matsumoto, D., Kudoh, T., & Takeuchi, S. (1996). Changing patterns of individualism and collectivism in the United States and Japan. *Culture and Psychology, 2,* 77–107.

Matsumoto, D., Takeuchi, S., Andayani, S., Kouznetsova, N., & Krupp, D. (1998). The contribution of individualism vs. collectivism to cross-national differences in display rules. *Asian Journal of Social Psychology, 1*, 147–165.

Matsumoto, D., Weissman, M., Preston, K., Brown, B., & Kupperbusch, C. (1997). Context-specific measurement of individualism–collectivism on the individual level: The ic interpersonal assessment inventory (iciai). *Journal of Cross-Cultural Psychology, 28*, 743–767.

Mauro, R., Sato, K., & Tucker, J. (1992). The role of appraisal in human emotions: A cross-cultural study. *Journal of Personality and Social Psychology, 62*, 301–317.

Mayer, J. D., & Gaschke, Y. N. (1988). The experience and meta-experience of mood. *Journal of Personality and Social Psychology, 55*, 102–111.

Mayer, J. D., Gayle, M., Meehan, M. E., & Haarman, A. K. (1990). Toward better specification of the mood-congruency effect in recall. *Journal of Experimental Social Psychology, 26*, 465–480.

Mayer, J. D., McCormick, L. J., & Strong, S. E. (1995). Mood-congruent memory and natural mood: New evidence. *Personality and Social Psychology Bulletin, 21*, 736–746.

Mayer, J. D., & Salovey, P. (1988). Personality moderates the interaction of mood and cognition. In K. Fiedler, & J. P. Forgas (Eds.), *Affect, cognition, and social behavior* (pp. 87–99). Toronto: Hogrefe.

Mayer, J. D., Salovey, P., & Caruso , D. (2000). Competing models of emotional intelligence. In R. Sternberg (Ed.), *Handbook of human intelligence* (2nd ed.) (pp. 396–420). New York: Cambridge University Press.

McCanne, T., & Anderson, J. (1987). Emotional responding following experimental manipulation of facial electromyographic activity. *Journal of Personality and Social Psychology, 52*, 759–768.

McClure, E. (2000). A meta-analytic review of sex differences in facial expression processing and their development in infants, children and adolescents. *Psychological Bulletin*, 424–453.

McCrae, R. R., & Costa, P. T. Jr. (1991). Adding Liebe und Arbeit: The full five-factor model and well-being. *Personality and Social Psychology Bulletin, 17*, 227–232.

McHugo, G., Lanzetta, J., & Bush, L. (1991). The effect of attitudes on emotional reactions to expressive display of political leaders. *Journal of Nonverbal Behavior, 15*, 19–41.

McIntosh, D. (1996). Facial feedback hypotheses: Evidence, implications, and directions. *Motivation and Emotion, 20*, 121–147.

McIntosh, D., Zajonc, R., Vig, P., & Emerick, S. (1997). Facial movement, breathing, temperature, and affect: Implications of the vascular theory of emotional efference. *Cognition and Emotion, 11*, 171–195.

Mead, M. (1967). *Cooperation and competition among primitive people.* Boston, MA: Beacon Press.

Mead, M. (1975). Review of Darwin and facial expression. *Journal of Communication, 25*, 209–213.

Mendes, B., Reis, H., Seery, M., & Blascovich, J. (2003). Cardiovascular correlates of emotional expression and suppression: Do content and gender context matter? *Journal of Personality and Social Psychology, 84*, 771–792.

Mendolia, M., & Kleck, R. (1993). Effects of talking about a stressful event on arousal: Does what we talk about make the difference? *Journal of Personality and Social Psychology, 64*, 283–292.

Merten, J. (1997). Facial-affective behavior, mutual gaze, and emotional experience in dyadic interactions. *Journal of Nonverbal Behavior, 21*, 179–201.

Mervis, C. B., & Crisafi, M. A (1982). Order of acquisition of subordinate-, basic-, and superordinate-level categories. *Child Development, 53*, 258–266.

Mesquita, B. (2001a). Culture and emotions: Different approaches to the question. In T. Mayne, & G. Bonanno (Eds.), *Emotion: Current issues and future directions* (pp. 214–250). New York: Guilford Press.

Mesquita, B. (2001b). Emotions in collectivist and individualist contexts. *Journal of Personality and Social Psychology, 80*, 68–74.

Mesquita, B. (2003). Emotions as dynamic cultural phenomena. In R. Davidson, H. Goldsmith, & K. R. Scherer (Eds.), *The handbook of the affective sciences* (pp. 871–890). New York: Oxford University Press.

Mesquita, B., & Frijda, N. H. (1992). Cultural variations in emotions: A review. *Psychological Bulletin, 112*, 179–204.

Mesquita, B., Frijda, N. H., & Scherer, K. R. (1997). Culture and emotion. In P. Dasen, & T. S. Saraswathi (Eds.), *Handbook of cross-cultural psychology* (Vol. 2, pp. 255–297). Boston, MA: Allyn & Bacon.

Mesquita, B., & Haire, A. (2004). Culture and emotion. In C. D. Spielberger (Ed.), *Encyclopedia of applied psychology* (Vol. 1, pp. 731–737). San Diego, CA: Academic Press.

Mesquita, B., & Karasawa, M. (2002). Different emotional lives. *Cognition and Emotion, 16*, 127–141.

Mesquita, B., & Markus, H. R. (2004). Culture and emotion: Models of agency as sources of cultural variation in emotion. In N. H. Frijda, A. S. R. Manstead, & A. H. Fischer (Eds.), *Feelings and emotions: The Amsterdam symposium* (pp. 341–358). Cambridge, MA: Cambridge University Press.

Mignault, A., & Chaudhuri, A. (2003). The many faces of a neutral face: Head tilt and perception of dominance and emotion. *Journal of Nonverbal Behavior, 27*, 11–132.

Miller, D. A., Smith, E. R., & Mackie, D. M. (2004). Effects of intergroup contact and political predispositions on prejudice: Role of intergroup emotions. *Group Processes and Intergroup Relations, 7*, 221–237.

Miller, P., & Sperry, L. (1987). Young children's verbal resources for communicating anger. *Merrill-Palmer Quarterly, 33*, 1–31.

Miller, R. S. (1992). The nature and severity of self-reported embarrassing circumstances. *Personality and Social Psychology Bulletin, 18*, 190–198.

Miller, R. S. (1995). Embarrassment and social behavior. In J. P. Tangney, & K. W. Fischer (Eds.), *Self-conscious emotions: The psychology of shame, guilt, embarrassment, and pride* (pp. 322–339). New York: Guilford Press.

Miller, R. S. (1996). *Embarrassment: Poise and peril in everyday life.* New York: Guilford Press.

Miller, R. S. (2004). Emotion as adaptive interpersonal communication: The case of embarrassment. In L. Z. Tiedens, & C. W. Leach (Eds.), *The social life of emotions* (pp. 87–104). Cambridge: Cambridge University Press.

Miller, R. S., & Leary, M. R. (1992). Social sources and interactive functions of emotion: The case of embarrassment. In M. S. Clark (Ed.), Emotion and social behavior. *Review of Personality and Social Psychology, 13*, 202–221.

Miller, R. S., & Tangney, J. P. (1994). Differentiating embarrassment and shame. *Journal of Social and Clinic Psychology, 13*, 273–287.

Miller, W. I. (1993). *Humiliation and other essays on honors, social discomfort and violence.* Ithaca, NY: Cornell University Press.

Miller, W. I. (1997). *The anatomy of disgust.* Cambridge, MA: Harvard University Press.

Mineka, S., & Cook, M. (1993). Mechanisms involved in the observational conditioning of fear. *Journal of Experimental Psychology: General, 122*, 23–38.

Modigliani, A. (1968). Embarrassment and embarrassibility. *Sociometry, 31*, 313–326.

Modigliani, A. (1971). Embarrassment, facework, and eye contact: Testing a theory of embarrassment. *Journal of Personality and Social Psychology, 17*, 15–24.

Mondillon, L., Niedenthal, P. M., Brauer, M., Rohmann, A., Dalle, N., & Uchida, Y. (2005). "Cultures" of power and beliefs about power and emotional experience. *Personality and Social Psychology Bulletin, 31,* 1112–1122.

Montesquieu, C. de S. (1989). *The spirit of the law.* Cambridge: Cambridge University Press. [Original work published in 1748]

Morf, C. C., & Rhodewalt, F. (2001). Unraveling the paradoxes of narcissism: A dynamic self-regulatory processing model. *Psychological Inquiry, 12,* 177–196.

Morris, W. N. (1989). *Mood: The frame of mind.* New York: Springer-Verlag.

Mueser, K. T., Grau, B. W., Sussman, S., & Rosen, I. (1984). You're only as pretty as you feel: Facial expression as a determinant of physical attractiveness. *Journal of Personality and Social Psychology, 46,* 469–478.

Munn, N. (1940). The effect of knowledge of the situation upon judgment of emotion from facial expressions. *Journal of Abnormal and Social Psychology, 35,* 324–338.

Muraven, M., Tice, D., & Baumeister, R. (1998). Self-control as a limited resource: Regulatory depletion pattern. *Journal of Personality and Social Psychology, 74,* 774–789.

Muris, P., Merkelbach, H., van den Hout, M., & de Jong P. (1992). Suppression of emotional and neutral material. *Behavior Research Therapy, 30,* 639–642.

Murphy, S. T., Monahan, J. L., & Zajonc, R. B. (1995). Additivity of nonconscious affect: Combined effects of priming and exposure. *Journal of Personality and Social Psychology, 69,* 589–602.

Murphy, S. T., & Zajonc, R. B. (1993). Affect, cognition, and awareness: Affective priming with suboptimal and optimal stimulus. *Journal of Personality and Social Psychology, 64,* 723–739.

Murray, N., Sujan, H., Hirt, E. R., & Sujan, M. (1990). The influence of mood on categorization: A cognitive flexibility interpretation. *Journal of Personality and Social Psychology, 59,* 411–425.

Nadelman, L., & Begun, A. (1982). The effect of the newborn on the older sibling: Mothers' questionnaires. In M. Lamb, & B. Sutton-Smith (Eds.), *Sibling relationships: Their nature and significance across the lifespan* (pp. 13–38). Hillsdale, NJ: Lawrence Erlbaum Associates, Inc.

Nakamura, M., Buck, R., & Kenny, D.A. (1990). Relative contributions of expressive behavior and contextual information to the judgment of the emotional state of another. *Journal of Personality and Social Psychology, 59,* 1032–1039.

Nasby, W., & Yando, R. (1982). Selective encoding and retrieval of affectively valent information: Two cognitive consequences of children's mood states. *Journal of Personality and Social Psychology, 43,* 1244–1253.

Natale, M., & Hantas, M. (1982). Effect of temporary mood states on selective memory about the self. *Journal of Personality and Social Psychology, 49,* 927–934.

Nesse, R. (1990). Evolutionary explanations of emotions. *Human Nature, 1,* 261–289.

Neu, J. (1980). Jealous thoughts. In A. O. Rorty (Ed.), *Explaining emotions* (pp. 425–463). Berkeley, CA: University of California Press.

Neuberg, S. L., & Cottrell, C. A. (2002). Intergroup emotions: A biocultural approach. In D. M. Mackie, & E. R. Smith (Eds.), *From prejudice to intergroup emotions: Differentiated reactions to social groups* (pp. 265–283). New York: Psychology Press.

Neumann, R., Seibt, B., & Strack, F. (2001). The influence of mood on the intensity of emotional responses: Disentangling feeling and knowing. *Cognition and Emotion, 15,* 735–747.

Neumann, R., & Strack, F. (2000). "Mood contagion": The automatic transfer of mood between persons. *Journal of Personality and Social Psychology, 79,* 211–223.

Neuwenhuyse, B., Offenberg, L., & Frijda, N. H. (1987). Subjective emotion and reported body experience. *Motivaton and Emotion, 11,* 169–182.

Niedenthal, P. M. (1990). Implicit perception of affective information. *Journal of Experimental Social Psychology, 26,* 505–527.

Niedenthal, P. M., Auxiette, C., Nugier, A., Dalle, N., Bonin, P., & Fayol, M. (2004). A prototype analysis of the French category "émotion". *Cognition and Emotion, 18*, 289–312.

Niedenthal, P. M., Barsalou, L. W., Ric, F., & Krauth-Gruber, S. (2005a). Embodiment in the acquisition and use of emotion knowledge. In L. Barrett, P. M. Niedenthal, & P. Winkielman (Eds.), *Emotion and consciousness*. New York: Guilford Press.

Niedenthal, P. M., Barsalou, L. W., Winkielman, P., Krauth-Gruber, S., & Ric, F. (2005b). Embodiment in attitudes, social perception, and emotion. *Personality and Social Psychology Review, 9*, 184–211.

Niedenthal, P., Brauer, M., Halberstadt, J., & Innes-Ker, A. (2001). When did her smile drop? Facial mimicry and the influence of emotional state on the detection of change in emotional expression. *Cognition and Emotion, 15*, 853–864.

Niedenthal, P. M., & Cantor, N. (1984). Making use of social prototypes: From fuzzy concepts to firm decisions. *Fuzzy Sets and Systems, 14*, 5–27.

Niedenthal, P. M., & Dalle, N. (2001). Le mariage de mon meilleur ami: Emotional response categorization during naturally-induced emotional states. *European Journal of Social Psychology, 31*, 737–742.

Niedenthal, P. M., Halberstadt, J. B., & Innes-Ker, A. H. (1999). Emotional response categorization. *Psychological Review, 106*, 337–361.

Niedenthal, P., Halberstadt, J., Margolin, J., & Innes-Ker, A. (2000). Emotional state and the detection of change in facial expression of emotion. *European Journal of Social Psychology, 30*, 211–222.

Niedenthal, P. M., Halberstadt, J. B., & Setterlund, M. B. (1997). Being happy and seeing "happy": Emotional state mediates visual word recognition. *Cognition and Emotion, 11*, 403–432.

Niedenthal, P. M., & Setterlund, M. B. (1994). Emotion congruence in perception. *Personality and Social Psychology Bulletin, 20*, 401–411.

Niedenthal, P. M., Setterlund, M. B., & Jones, D. E. (1994a). Emotional organization of perceptual memory. In P. M. Niedenthal, & S. Kitayama (Eds.), *The heart's eye: Emotional influences in perception and attention* (pp. 87–113). New York: Academic Press.

Niedenthal, P. M., Tangney, J. P., & Gavanski, I. (1994b). "If only I weren't" versus "If only I hadn't": Distinguishing shame and guilt in counterfactual thinking. *Journal of Personality and Social Psychology, 67*, 585–595.

Nisbett, R. E. (1993). *Rules for reasoning*. Hillsdale, NJ: Lawrence Erlbaum Associates, Inc.

Nisbett, R. E., & Cohen, D. (1995). *The culture of honor: The psychology of violence in the south*. Boulder, CO: Westview Press.

Nolen-Hoeksema, S. (1987). Sex differences in unipolar depression: Evidence and theory. *Psychological Bulletin, 101*, 259–282.

Nolen-Hoeksema, S., McBride, A., & Larsen, J. (1997). Rumination and physiological distress among bereaved partners. *Journal of Personality and Social Psychology, 72*, 855–862.

Nolen-Hoeksema, S., & Morrow, J. (1993). Effects of rumination and distraction on naturally occurring depressed mood. *Cognition and Emotion, 7*, 561–570.

Nowlis, W. (1965). Research with the mood adjective check list. In S. S. Tomkins, & E. Izard (Eds.), *Affect, cognition, and personality* (pp. 352–389). New York: Springer-Verlag.

Oatley, K., & Duncan, E. (1992). Episode of emotion in daily life. In K. T. Strongman (Ed.), *International review of studies on emotion* (Vol. 2, pp. 249–293). Chichester: John Wiley & Sons.

Oatley, K., & Duncan, E. (1994). The experience of emotions in everyday life. *Cognition and Emotion, 8*, 369–381.

Oatley, K., & Johnson-Laird, P. N. (1987). Towards a cognitive theory of emotions. *Cognition and Emotion, 1*, 29–50.

Oatley, K., & Johnson-Laird, P. N. (1996). The communicative theory of emotions: Empirical tests, mental models, and implications for social interaction. In L. L. Martin, & A. Tesser (Eds.), *Striving and feeling: Interaction among goal, affect, and self-regulation* (pp. 363–393). Mahwah, NJ: Lawrence Erlbaum Associates, Inc.

Ochsner, K., & Barrett, L. F. (2001). The neuroscience of emotion. In T. Mayne, & G. Bonnano (Eds.), *Emotion: Current issues and future directions* (pp. 38–81). New York: Guilford Press.

Öhman, A. (1986). Face the beast and fear the face. Animal and social fears as prototypes for evolutionary analyses of emotion. *Psychophysiology, 23,* 123–145.

Oliveau, D., & Willmuth, R. (1979). Facial muscle electromyography in depressed and non-depressed hospitalized subjects: A partial replication. *American Journal of Psychiatry, 136,* 548–550.

Olson, J. M. (1992). Self-perception of humor: Evidence for discounting and augmentation effects. *Journal of Personality and Social Psychology, 62,* 369–377.

Oltmanns, T. F., & Emery, R. E. (1995). *Abnormal psychology.* Englewood Cliffs, NJ: Prentice-Hall.

Ortega, J. E., Iglesias, J., Fernandez, J. M., & Corraliza, J. A. (1983). La expression facial en los ciegos congenitos [Facial expression in the congenitally blind]. *Infancia y Aprendizaje, 21,* 83–96.

Ortony, A., & Turner, T. J. (1990). What's basic about basic emotions? *Psychological Review, 97,* 315–331.

Osgood, C. E., & Suci, G. J. (1955). Factor analysis of meaning. *Journal of Experimental Psychology, 50,* 25–338.

Ottati, V. C., & Isbell, L. M. (1996). Effects of mood during exposure to target information on subsequently reported judgments: An on-line model of misattribution and correction. *Journal of Personality and Social Psychology, 71,* 39–53.

Padgett, C., & Cottrell, C. W. (1998). A simple neural network models categorical perception of facial expression. In *Proceedings of the Twentieth Annual Cognitive Science Conference*, Madison, WI. Mahwah, NJ: Lawrence Erlbaum Associates, Inc.

Paez, D., Velasco, C., & Gonzalez, J. (1999). Expressive writing and the role of alexithymia as a dispositional deficit in self-disclosure and psychological health. *Journal of Personality and Social Psychology, 77,* 630–641.

Page, A., Locke, V., & Trio, M. (2005). An online measure of thought suppression. *Journal of Personality and Social Psychology, 88,* 421–431.

Panksepp, J. (1998). *Affective neuroscience: The foundations of human and animal emotions.* New York: Oxford University Press.

Park, J., & Banaji, M. R. (2000). Mood and heuristics: The influence of happy and sad states on sensitivity and bias in stereotyping. *Journal of Personality and Social Psychology, 78,* 1005–1023.

Parkinson, B. (1996). Emotions are social. *British Journal of Psychology, 87,* 663–683.

Parkinson, B., Fischer, A. H., & Manstead, A. S. R. (2004). *Emotion in social relations: Cultural, group, and interpersonal processes.* New York: Psychology Press.

Parkinson, B., & Manstead, A. S. R. (1992). Appraisal as a cause of emotion. In M. S. Clark (Ed.), Emotion and social behavior. *Review of Personality and Social Psychology, 13,* 122–149.

Parkinson, B., Totterdell, P., Briner, R., & Reynolds, S. (1996). *Changing moods: The psychology of mood and mood regulation.* Harlow: Addison-Wesley Longman.

Parrott, W. G. (1991). The emotional experience of envy and jealousy. In P. Salovey (Ed.), *The psychology of envy and jealousy* (pp. 3–30). New York: Guilford Press.

Parrott, W. G., & Sabini, J. (1990). Mood and memory under natural conditions: Evidence for mood incongruent recall. *Journal of Personality and Social Psychology, 59,* 321–336.

Parrott, W. G., Sabini, J., & Silver, M. (1988). The roles of self-esteem and social interaction in embarrassment. *Personality and Social Psychology Bulletin, 14*, 191–202.

Parrott, W. G, & Smith, R. H. (1993). Distinguishing the experience of envy and jealousy. *Journal of Personality and Social Psychology, 64*, 906–920.

Pasupathi, M. (2003). Emotion regulation during social remembering: Differences between emotion elicited during an event and emotions elicited when talking about it. *Memory, 11*, 151–163.

Pasupathi, M., Carstensen, L., Levenson, R., & Gottman, J. (1999). Responsive listening in long-married couples: A psycholinguistic perspective. *Journal of Nonverbal Behavior, 23*, 173–193.

Peng, K., & Nisbett, R. E. (1999). Culture, dialectics, and reasoning about contradiction. *American Psychologist, 54*(9), 741–754.

Peng, K., & Nisbett, R. E. (2000). Dialectical responses to questions about dialectical thinking. *American Psychologist, 55*(9), 1067–1068.

Pennebaker, J. W. (1982). *The psychology of physical symptoms.* New York: Springer-Verlag.

Pennebaker, J. W. (1989). Confession, inhibition and disease. In L. Berkowitz (Ed.), *Advances in experimental social psychology* (Vol. 22, pp. 211–244). San Diego, CA: Academic Press.

Pennebaker, J. W., & Beall, S. (1986). Confronting a traumatic event: Towards an understanding of inhibition and disease. *Journal of Abnormal Psychology, 95*, 274–281.

Pennebaker, J. W., Hughes, C., & O'Heeron, R. (1987). The psychophysiology of confession: Linking inhibitory and psychosomatic processes. *Journal of Personality and Social Psychology, 52*, 781–793.

Pennebaker, J. W., Kiecolt-Glaser, J., & Glaser, R. (1988). Disclosure of traumas and immune function: Health implications for psychotherapy. *Journal of Consulting and Clinical Psychology, 58*, 239–245.

Pennebaker, J. W., Rimé, B., & Blankenship, V. E. (1996). Stereotypes of emotional expressiveness of northerners and southerners: A cross-cultural test of Montesquieu's hypotheses. *Journal of Personality and Social Psychology, 70*(2), 372–380.

Pennebaker, J., Zech, E., & Rimé, B. (2001). Disclosing and sharing emotion: Psychological, social, and health consequences. In M. Stroebe, R. Hansson, W. Stroebe, & H. Schut (Eds.), *Handbook of bereavement research* (pp. 517–543). Washington, DC: American Psychological Association.

Petrie, K., Booth, R., & Davidson, K. (1995). Repression, disclosure, and immune function: Recent findings and methodological issues. In J. Pennebaker (Ed.), *Emotion, disclosure, and health* (pp. 223–237). Washington, DC: American Psychological Association.

Petrie, K., Booth, R., & Pennebaker, J. (1998). The immunological effects of thought suppression. *Journal of Personality and Social Psychology, 75*, 1264–1272.

Petty, R. E., Schumann, D. W., Richman, S. A., & Strathman, A. J. (1993). Positive mood and persuasion: Different roles for affect under high- and low-elaboration conditions. *Journal of Personality and Social Psychology, 64*, 5–20.

Philippot, P. (1991). Reported and actual physiological changes in emotion. In A. J. W. Boelhouwer, & C. H. M. Brunia (Eds.), *Proceedings of the First European Physiological Conference* (p. 132). Tilburg, The Netherlands: Tilburg Press.

Philippot, P. (1993). Inducing and assessing differentiated emotion-feeling states in the laboratory. *Cognition and Emotion, 7*, 171–193.

Philippot, P., & Rimé, B. (1997). The perception of bodily sensations during emotion: A cross-cultural perspective. *Polish Psychological Bulletin, 28*(2), 175–188.

Pitt-Rivers, J. (1965). Honor and social status. In J. G. Peristiany (Ed.), *Honor and shame: The value of Mediterranean society* (pp. 18–77). London: Weidenfeld & Nicolson.

Plant, E. A., Kling, K., & Smith, G. (2004). The influence of gender and social role on the interpretation of facial expression. *Sex Roles, 51*, 187–196.

Plant, E. A., Hyde, J., Keltner, D., & Devine, P. (2000). The gender stereotyping of emotions. *Psychology of Women Quarterly, 24*, 81–92.

Plutchik, R. (1980). Emotion: A psychoevolutionary synthesis. In K. R. Blankstein, P. Pliner, & J. Polivy (Eds.), *Assessment and modification of emotional behavior* (pp. 3–33). New York: Harper & Row.

Plutchik, R. (1984). Emotions: A general psychoevolutionary theory. In K. R. Scherer, & P. Ekman (Eds.), *Approaches to emotion* (pp. 197–219). Hillsdale, NJ: Lawrence Erlbaum Associates, Inc.

Queller, S., Mackie, D. M., & Stroessner, S. J. (1996). Ameliorating some negative effects of positive mood: Encouraging happy people to perceive intragroup variability. *Journal of Experimental Social Psychology, 32*, 361–386.

Quigley, B. M., & Tedeschi, J. T. (1996). Mediating effects of blame attributions on feeling of anger. *Personality and Social Psychology Bulletin, 22*, 1280–1288.

Rahman, Q., Wilson, G., & Abrahams, S. (2004). Sex, sexual orientation, and identification of positive and negative facial affect. *Brain and Cognition, 54*, 179–185.

Rawls, J. (1971). *A theory of justice.* Cambridge, MA: Harvard University Press.

Razran, G. H. S. (1940). Conditioned response changes in rating and appraising sociopolitical slogans. *Psychological Bulletin, 37*, 481.

Reisenzein, R. (1994). Pleasure-arousal theory and the intensity of emotions. *Journal of Personality and Social Psychology, 67*, 525–539.

Reisenzein, R., & Hofmann, T. (1990). An investigation of dimensions of cognitive appraisal in emotion using a repertory grid technique. *Motivation and Emotion, 14*, 19–38.

Renniger, K. A., Hidi, S., & Knapp, A. (Eds.). (1992). *The role of interest in learning and development.* Hillsdale, NJ: Lawrence Erlbaum Associates, Inc.

Rhodewalt, F., Madrian, J., & Cheney, S. (1997). Narcissism, self-knowledge organization, and emotional reactivity: The effect of daily experiences on self-esteem and affect. *Personality and Social Psychology Bulletin, 24*, 75–87.

Richards, J., Butler, E., & Gross, J. (2003). Emotion regulation in romantic relationships: The cognitive consequences of concealing feelings. *Journal of Social and Personal Relationships, 20*, 599–620.

Richards, J., & Gross, J. (1999). Composure at any cost? The cognitive consequences of emotion suppression. *Personality and Social Psychology Bulletin, 25*, 1033–1044.

Richards, J., & Gross, J. (2000). Emotion regulation and memory: The cognitive costs of keeping one's cool. *Journal of Personality and Social Psychology, 79*, 410–424.

Rimé, B., Finkenauer, C., Luminet, O., Zech, E., & Philippot, P. (1998). Social sharing of emotion: New evidence and new questions. In W. Stroebe, & M. Hewstone (Eds.), *European review of social psychology* (Vol. 9, pp. 145–189). Chichester: John Wiley & Sons.

Rimé, B., & Giovannini, D. (1986). The physiological patterning of emotional states. In K. R. Scherer, H. G. Wallbott, & A. B. Summerfield (Eds.), *Experiencing emotion: A cross-cultural study* (pp. 84–97). Cambridge: Cambridge University Press.

Rimé, B., Mesquita, B., Philippot, P., & Boca, S. (1991a). Beyond the emotional event: Six studies on the social sharing of emotion. *Cognition and Emotion, 5*, 435–465.

Rimé, B., Noël, P., & Philippot, P. (1991b). Episode émotionnel, réminiscences mentales et réminiscences sociales [Emotional episode, mental reminiscences, and social reminiscences]. *Les Cahiers Internationaux de Psychologie Sociale, 11*, 93–104.

Rimé, B., Philippot, P., Boca, S., & Mesquita (1992). Long-lasting cognitive and social consequences of emotion: Social sharing and rumination. In W. Stroebe, & M. Hewstone (Eds.), *European review of social psychology* (Vol. 3, pp. 225–258). Chichester: John Wiley & Sons.

Rimé, B., Philippot, P., & Cisamolo, D. (1990). Social schemata of peripheral changes in emotion. *Journal of Personality and Social Psychology, 59*, 38–49.

Rinn, W. (1984). The neuropsychology of facial expression: A review of the neurological and psychological mechanisms for producing facial expressions. *Psychological Bulletin, 95*, 52–77.

Rinn, W. (1991). Neuropsychology of facial expression. In R. Feldman, & B. Rimé (Eds.), *Fundamentals of nonverbal behavior* (pp. 3–30). Cambridge/New York: Cambridge University Press.

Riskind, J. (1984). They stoop to conquer: Guiding and self-regulatory functions of physical posture after success and failure. *Journal of Personality and Social Psychology, 47*, 479–493.

Riskind, J., & Gotay, C. (1982). Physical posture: Could it have regulatory or feedback effects on motivation and emotion? *Motivation and Emotion, 6*, 273–298.

Robinson, M. D., & Clore, G. L. (2002). Belief and feeling: Evidence for an accessibility model of emotional self-report. *Psychological Bulletin, 128*(6), 934–960.

Robinson, M. D., Johnson, J., & Shields, S. (1998). The gender heuristic and the database: Factors affecting the perception of gender-related differences in the experience and display of emotions. *Basic and Applied Social Psychology, 20*, 206–219.

Rodriguez Mosquera, P. M., Manstead, A. S. R., & Fischer, A. H. (2002). The role of honour concerns in emotional reactions to offences. *Cognition and Emotion, 16*, 143–163.

Roese, N. J., & Olson, J. M. (1995). Counterfactual thinking: A critical overview. In N. J. Roese, & J. M. Olson (Eds.), *What might have been: The social psychology of counterfactual thinking* (pp. 1–55). Mahwah, NJ: Lawrence Erlbaum Associates, Inc.

Rokeach, M. (1973). *The nature of human values.* New York: Free Press.

Rosch, E. H. (1973). Natural categories. *Cognitive Psychology, 4*, 328–350.

Rosch, E. H. (1975). Cognitive representations of semantic categories. *Journal of Experimental Psychology: General, 104*, 192–233.

Rosch, E. H., & Mervis, C. B. (1975). Family resemblance: Studies in the internal structure of categories. *Cognitive Psychology, 7*, 573–605.

Rosch, E. H., Mervis, C. B., Gray, W., Johnson, D., & Boyes-Braem, P. (1976). Basic objects in natural categories. *Cognitive Psychology, 8*, 382–439.

Roseman, I. J. (1984). Cognitive determinant of emotion: A structural theory. In P. Shaver (Ed.), *Review of personality and social psychology* (Vol. 5, pp. 11–36). Beverley Hills, CA: Sage.

Roseman, I. J. (1991). Appraisal determinant of discrete emotions. *Cognition and Emotion, 5*, 161–200.

Roseman, I. J., Dhawan, N., Rettek, S. I., Naidu, R. K., & Thapa, K. (1995). Cultural differences and cross-cultural similarities in appraisals and emotional responses. *Journal of Cross-Cultural Psychology, 26*, 23–48.

Rosenberg, E., & Ekman, P. (1994). Coherence between expressive and experiential systems in emotion. *Cognition and Emotion, 8*, 201–229.

Ross, C., & Mirowsky, J. (1984). Men who cry. *Social Psychological Quarterly, 47*, 146–159.

Rotter, N., & Rotter, G. (1988). Sex differences in the encoding and decoding of negative facial emotions. *Journal of Nonverbal Behavior, 12*, 139–148.

Rozin, P., Haidt, J., & McCauley, C. R. (2000). Disgust. In M. Lewis, & J. M. Haviland-Jones (Eds.), *Handbook of emotions* (2nd ed.) (pp. 637–653). New York: Guilford Press.

Ruby, P., & Decety, J. (2004). How would she feel versus how do you think she would feel? A neuroimaging study of perspective-taking with social emotions. *Journal of Cognitive Neuroscience, 16*, 988–999.

Ruiz-Belda, M.-A., Fernandez-Dols, J.-M., Carrera, P., & Barchard, K. (2003). Spontaneous facial expressions of happy bowlers and soccer fans. *Cognition and Emotion, 17*(2), 315–326.

Russell, B. (1930). *The conquest of happiness.* New York: Horace Liveright.

Russell, J. A. (1980). A circumplex model of affect. *Journal of Personality and Social Psychology, 39*, 1161–1178.

Russell, J. A. (1989). Measure of emotion. In R. Plutchik, & H. Kellerman (Eds.), *Emotion: Theory, research and experience* (Vol. 4, pp. 83–111). New York: Academic Press.

Russell, J. A. (1994). Is there universal recognition of emotion from facial expression? A review of cross-cultural studies. *Psychological Bulletin, 115*, 102–141.

Russell, J. A. (1995). Facial expressions of emotion: What lies beyond minimal universality? *Psychological Bulletin, 118*, 379–391.

Russell, J. A., & Bullock, M. (1985). Multidimensional scaling of emotional facial expressions: Similarity from preschoolers to adults. *Journal of Personality and Social Psychology, 48*, 1290–1298.

Russell, J. A., & Fehr, B. (1987). Relativity in the perception of facial expression. *Journal of Experimental Psychology: General, 116*(3), 223–237.

Russell, J. A., & Feldman Barrett, L. (1999). Core affect, prototypical emotional episodes, and other things called emotion: Dissecting the elephant. *Journal of Personality and Social Psychology, 76*, 805–819.

Russell, J. A., Lewicka, M., & Niit, T. (1989). A cross-cultural study of a circumplex model of affect. *Journal of Personality and Social Psychology, 57*, 848–856.

Russon, A. E., & Galdikas, B. M. (1993). Imitation in free-ranging rehabilitant orangutans (Pongo pygmaeus). *Journal of Comparative Psychology, 107*, 147–161.

Rusting, C. L., & DeHart, T. (2000). Retrieving positive memories to regulate negative mood: Consequences for mood-congruent memory. *Journal of Personality and Social Psychology, 78*, 737–752.

Rutledge, L., & Hupka, R. (1985). The facial feedback hypothesis: Methodological concerns and new supporting evidence. *Motivation and Emotion, 9*, 219–240.

Saarni, C. (1993). Socialization of emotion. In M. Lewis, & J. M. Haviland (Eds.), *Handbook of emotions* (pp. 435–447). New York: Guilford Press.

Sabini, J., Siepmann, M., Stein, J., & Meyerowitz, M. (2000). Who is embarrassed by what? *Cognition and Emotion, 14*, 213–240.

Sabini, J., & Silver, M. (1982). *Moralities of everyday life.* New York: Oxford University Press.

Sabini, J., & Silver, M. (1997). Volcan redux. *Journal for the Theory of Social Behaviour, 27*, 499–502.

Sabini, J., & Silver, M. (1998). The not altogether social construction of emotions: A critique of Harré and Gillett. *Journal for the Theory of Social Behaviour, 28*, 223–235.

Salovey, P. (1991). Social comparison processes in envy and jealousy. In J. Suls, & T. A. Wills (Eds.), *Social comparison: Contemporary theory and research* (pp. 261–285). Hillsdale, NJ: Lawrence Erlbaum Associates, Inc.

Salovey, P., Bedell, B., Detweiler, J., & Mayer, J. (2000). Current directions in emotional intelligence research. In M. Lewis, & J. M. Haviland-Jones (Eds.), *Handbook of emotions* (2nd ed.) (pp. 504–520). New York: Guilford Press.

Salovey, P., Hsee, C. K., & Mayer, D. (1993). Emotional intelligence and the self-regulation of affect. In D. M. Wegner, & J. W. Pennebaker (Eds.), *Handbook of mental control* (pp. 258–277).

Salovey, P., & Rodin, J. (1984). Some antecedents and consequences of social-comparison jealousy. *Journal of Personality and Social Psychology, 47*, 780–792.

Salovey, P., & Rodin, J. (1986). The differentiation of social-comparison jealousy and romantic jealousy. *Journal of Personality and Social Psychology, 50,* 1100–1112.

Salovey, P., & Rodin, J. (1988). Coping with envy and jealousy. *Journal of Social and Clinical Psychology, 7,* 15–33.

Salovey, P., & Rothman, A. J. (1991). Envy and jealousy. In P. Salovey (Ed.). *The psychology of envy and jealousy* (pp. 271–286). New York: Guilford Press.

Sander, D., & Koenig, O. (2002). No inferiority complex in the study of emotion complexity: A cognitive neuroscience computational architecture of emotion. *Cognitive Science Quarterly, 2,* Special issue: *Desires, goals, intention, and values: Computational architectures,* 249–272.

Schachter, S. (1959). *The psychology of affiliation.* Stanford, NY: Stanford University Press.

Schachter, S., & Singer, J. E. (1962). Cognitive, social, and physiological determinants of emotional state. *Psychological Review, 69,* 379–399.

Scheff, T. J. (1987). The shame–rage spiral: A case study of an interminable quarrel. In H. B. Lewis (Ed.), *The role of shame in symptom formation* (pp. 109–149). Hillsdale, NJ: Lawrence Erlbaum Associates, Inc.

Scheff, T. J. (1988). Shame and conformity: The deference–emotion system. *American Sociological Review, 53,* 395–406.

Scheff, T. J. (1990). Socialization of emotions: Pride and shame as causal agent. In T. D. Kemper (Ed.), *Research agendas in the sociology of emotions. SUNY series in sociology of emotions* (pp. 281–304). New York: State University of New York Press.

Scheff, T. J. (1995). Editor's introduction: "Shame and related emotions: An overview". *American Behavioral Scientist, 38,* 1053–1059.

Scherer, K. R. (1984a). Emotion as a multicomponent process: A model and some cross-cultural data. In P. R. Shaver (Ed.), *Review of personality and social psychology* (Vol. 5, pp. 37–63). Beverley Hills, CA: Sage.

Scherer, K. R. (1984b). On the nature and function of emotion: A component process approach. In K. R. Scherer, & P. Ekman (Eds.), *Approaches to emotion* (pp. 293–317). Hillsdale, NJ: Lawrence Erlbaum Associates, Inc.

Scherer, K. R. (1985). Emotions can be rational. *Social Science Information, 24,* 331–335.

Scherer, K. R. (1988). Criteria for emotion-antecedent appraisal: A review. In V. Hamilton, G. H. Bower, & N. H. Frijda (Eds.), *Cognitive perspectives on emotion and motivation* (pp. 89–126). Dordrecht, The Netherlands: Nijhoff.

Scherer, K. R. (1997). Profiles of emotion-antecedent appraisal: testing theoretical predictions across cultures. *Cognition and Emotion, 11,* 113–150.

Scherer, K. R. (1999). Appraisal theory. In T. Dalgleish, & M. Power (Eds.), *Handbook of cognition and emotion.* New York: John Wiley & Sons.

Scherer, K. R. (2000). Emotion. In M. Hewstone, & W. Stroebe (Eds.), *Introduction to social psychology: A European perspective* (3rd ed.) (pp. 151–191). Oxford: Blackwell.

Scherer, K. R. (2001). The future of emotion. *Social Science Information, 40,* 125–151.

Scherer, K. R., Banse, R., & Wallbott, H. G. (2001). Emotion inferences from vocal expression correlate across languages and cultures. *Journal of Cross-Cultural Psychology, 32,* 76–92.

Scherer, K. R., Banse, R., Wallbott, H. G., & Goldbeck, T. (1991). Vocal cues in emotion encoding and decoding. *Motivation and Emotion, 15,* 123–148.

Scherer, K. R., & Ceschi, G. (1997). Lost luggage: A field study of emotion-antecedent appraisal. *Motivation and Emotion, 21,* 211–235.

Scherer, K. R., & Wallbott, H. G. (1994). Evidence for universality and cultural variation of differential emotion response patterning. *Journal of Personality and Social Psychology, 66*(2), 310–328.

Scherer, K. R., Wallbott, H. G., Matsumoto, D., & Kudoh, T. (1988). Emotional experience in cultural context: A comparison between Europe, Japan, and the United States. In K. R. Scherer (Ed.), *Facets of emotions* (pp. 5–30). Hillsdale, NJ: Lawrence Erlbaum Associates, Inc.

Scherer, K. R., Wallbott, H. G., & Summerfield, A. B. (Eds.). (1986). *Experiencing emotion: A cross-cultural study.* Cambridge: Cambridge University Press.

Schiffbauer, A. (1974). Effect of observer's emotional state on judgments of the emotional state of others. *Journal of Personality and Social Psychology, 30,* 31–35.

Schimmack, U., Oishi, S., & Diener, E. (2002). Cultural influences on the relation between pleasant emotions and unpleasant emotions: Asian dialectic philosophies or individualism–collectivism? *Cognition and Emotion, 16*(6), 705–719.

Schlenker, B. R., & Leary, M. R. (1982). Social anxiety and self-presentation: A conceptualization model. *Psychological Bulletin, 92,* 641–669.

Schlosberg, H. (1941). A scale for judgment of facial expressions. *Journal of Experimental Psychology, 29,* 497–510.

Schlosberg, H. (1952). A description of facial expressions in terms of two dimensions. *Journal of Experimental Psychology, 44,* 229–237.

Schmitt, M. T., & Branscombe, N. R. (2002). The meaning and consequences of perceived discrimination in disadvantaged and privileged social groups. In W. Stroebe, & M. Hewstone (Eds.), *European review of social psychology* (Vol. 12, pp. 167–199). Chichester: John Wiley & Sons.

Schmitt, M. T., Branscombe, N. R., & Postmes, T. (2003). Women's emotional responses to pervasiveness of gender discrimination. *European Journal of Social Psychology, 33,* 297–312.

Schoeck, H. (1969). *Envy: A theory of social behavior* (M. Glenny, & B. Ross, Trans.). Indianapolis, IN: Liberty Press. (Original work published 1966)

Schupp, H. T., Cuthbert, B. N., Bradley, M. M., Hillman, C. H., Hamm, A. O., & Lang, P. (2004). Brain processes in emotional perception: Motivated attention. *Cognition and Emotion, 18,* 593–611.

Schwartz, G., Brown, S., & Ahern, G. (1980). Facial muscle patterning and subjective experience during affective imagery: Sex differences. *Psychophysiology, 17,* 75–82.

Schwartz, S. H. (1992). Universals in the content and structure of values: Theoretical advances and empirical tests in 20 countries. In M. Zanna (Ed.), *Advances in experimental social psychology* (Vol. 25, pp. 1–65). New York: Academic Press.

Schwartz, S. H. (1994a). Are there universals in the content and structure of values? *Journal of Social Issues, 50,* 19–45.

Schwartz, S. H. (1994b). Beyond individualism/collectivism: New cultural dimensions of values. In U. E. Kim, H. C. Triandis, C. Kagitcibasi, S. Choi, & G. Yoon (Eds.), *Individualism and collectivism: Theory, method, and applications* (Vol. 18, pp. 85–119). Newbury Park, CA: Sage.

Schwarz, M. T. (2001). *Navajo lifeways.* Norman, OK: University of Oklahoma Press.

Schwarz, N. (1990). Feelings as information: Informational and motivational functions of affective states. In R. M. Sorrentino, & E. T. Higgins (Eds.), *Handbook of motivation and cognition: Foundation of social behavior* (Vol. 2, pp. 527–561). New York: Guilford Press.

Schwarz, N. (2001). Feeling as information: Implications for affective influences on information processing. In L. L. Martin, & G. L. Clore (Eds.), *Theories of mood and cognition. A user's guidebook* (pp. 159–176). Mahwah, NJ: Lawrence Erlbaum Associates, Inc.

Schwarz, N., Bless, H., & Bohner, G. (1991). Mood and persuasion: Affective states influence the processing of persuasive communications. In L. Berkowitz (Ed.), *Advances in experimental social psychology* (Vol. 24, pp. 161–199). New York: Academic Press.

Schwarz, N., & Clore, G. L. (1983). Mood, misattribution, and judgements of well-being: Informative and directive functions of affective states. *Journal of Personality and Social Psychology, 45*, 513–523.

Schwarz, N., & Clore, G. L. (1988). How do I feel about it? The informative function of affective states. In K. Fiedler, & J. P. Forgas (Eds.), *Affect, cognition, and social behavior* (pp. 44–62). Toronto: Hogrefe.

Schwarz, N., Strack, F., Kommer, D., & Wagner, D. (1987). Soccer, rooms and the quality of your life: Mood effects on judgments of satisfaction with life in general and with specific life-domains. *European Journal of Social Psychology, 17*, 69–79.

Scott, J. P. (1958). *Animal behavior*. Chicago, IL: University of Chicago Press.

Sedikides, C. (1995). Central and peripheral self-conceptions are differently influenced by mood: Tests of the differential sensitivity hypothesis. *Journal of Personality and Social Psychology, 69*, 759–777.

Seidlitz, L., & Diener, E. (1998). Sex differences in the recall of affective experiences. *Journal of Personality and Social Psychology, 74*, 262–271.

Semin, G. R., & Manstead, A. S. R. (1982). The social implications of embarrassment displays and restitution behavior. *European Journal of Social Psychology, 12*, 367–377.

Semin, G. R., & Papadopoulou, K. (1990). The acquisition of reflexive social emotions: The transmission and reproduction of social control through joint action. In G. Duveen, & B. Lyod (Eds.), *Social representations and the development of knowledge* (pp. 107–125). Cambridge: Cambridge University Press.

Senior, C., Phillips, M. L., Barnes, J., & David, A. S. (1999). An investigation into the perception of dominance from schematic faces: A study using the World Wide Web. *Behavior Research Methods, Instruments and Computers, 31*, 341–346.

Shaver, P., Schwartz, J., Kirson, D., & O'Connor, C. (1987). Emotion knowledge: Further exploration of a prototype approach. *Journal of Personality and Social Psychology, 52*, 1061–1086.

Shields, S. A. (2000). Thinking about gender, thinking about theory: Gender and emotional experience. In A. Fischer (Ed.), *Gender and emotion: Social psychological perspectives* (pp. 3–23). London: Cambridge University Press.

Shields, S. A. (2002). *Speaking from the heart: Gender and the social meaning of emotion*. Cambridge: Cambridge University Press.

Shields, S. A. (1987). Women, men, and the dilemma of emotion. In P. Shaver, & C. Hendrick (Eds.), *Sex and gender*. Newbury Park, CA: Sage.

Shields, S. A., Steinke, P., & Koster, B. (1995). The double bind of caregiving: Representation of gendered emotion in American advice literature. *Sex Roles, 33*, 467–488.

Shiota, M. N., Campos, B., Keltner, D., & Hertenstein, M. J. (2004). Positive emotion and the regulation of interpersonal relationships. In P. Philippot, & R. S. Feldman (Eds.), *The regulation of emotion* (pp. 127–155). Mahwah, NJ: Lawrence Erlbaum Associates, Inc.

Shulman, M., & Meckler, E. (1985). *Bringing up a moral child*. New York: Addison-Wesley.

Shweder, R. A. (1993). The cultural psychology of the emotions. In M. Lewis, & J. M. Haviland (Eds.), *Handbook of emotions* (pp. 417–433). New York: Guilford Press.

Shweder, R. A. (1994). "You're not sick, you're just in love". Emotion as interpretative system. In P. Ekman, & R. Davidson (Eds.), *The nature of emotions: Fundamental questions* (pp. 32–44). New York: Oxford University Press.

Shweder, R. A. (2002). "What about female genital mutilation?" and why understanding culture matters in the first place. In R. Shweder, M. Minow, & H. Markus (Eds.), *Engaging cultural differences: The multicultural challenge in liberal democracies*. New York: Russell Sage Foundation Press.

Shweder, R. A., & Haidt, J. (2000). The cultural psychology of emotions: Ancient and new. In M. Lewis, & J. M. Haviland-Jones (Eds.), *Handbook of Emotions* (2nd ed.) (pp. 397–414). New York: Guilford Press.

Siegman, A., Anderson, R., & Berger, T. (1990). The angry voice: Its effects on the experience of anger and cardiovascular reactivity. *Psychosomatic Medicine, 52,* 631–643.

Silver, M., & Sabini, J. (1978). The social construction of envy. *Journal for the Theory of Social Behaviour, 8,* 313–332.

Silver, M., Sabini, J., & Parrott, W. G. (1987). Embarrassment: A dramaturgic account. *Journal for the Theory of Social Behavior, 17,* 47–61.

Simon, H. A. (1967). Motivational and emotional controls of cognition. *Psychological Review, 74,* 29–39.

Sinclair, R. C., Mark, M. M., & Clore, G. L. (1994). Mood-related persuasion depends on (mis)attributions. *Social Cognition, 12,* 309–326.

Skinner, B. F. (1948). *Walden two.* Englewood Cliffs, NJ: Prentice-Hall.

Smith, C. A., & Ellsworth, P. C. (1985). Patterns of cognitive appraisal in emotion. *Journal of Personality and Social Psychology, 48,* 813–838.

Smith, C. A., & Ellsworth, P. C. (1987). Patterns of appraisal and emotions related to taking an exam. *Journal of Personality and Social Psychology, 52,* 475–488.

Smith, E. R. (1993). Social identity and social emotions: Toward new conceptualizations of prejudice. In D. M. Mackie, & D. L. Hamilton (Eds.), *Affect, cognition, and stereotyping: Interactive group processes in group perception* (pp. 297–315). San Diego, CA: Academic Press.

Smith, P. B., & Schwartz, S. H. (1999). Values. In M. H. Segall, & C. Kagitcibasi (Eds.), *Handbook of cross-cultural psychology* (Vol. 3, pp. 77–118). Boston, MA: Allyn & Bacon.

Smith, R. H., Kim, S. H., & Parrott, W. G. (1988). Envy and jealousy: Semantic problems and experiential distinctions. *Personality and Social Psychology Bulletin, 14,* 401–409.

Smith, R. H., Parrott, W. G., Ozer, D., & Moniz, A. (1994). Subjective injustice and inferiority as predictors of hostile and depressive feelings in envy. *Personality and Social Psychology Bulletin, 20,* 705–711.

Smith, S. M., & Petty, R. E. (1995). Personality moderators of mood congruency effects on cognition: The role of self-esteem and negative mood regulation. *Journal of Personality and Social Psychology, 68,* 1092–1107.

Smith, T. (1992). Hostility and health: Current status of a psychosomatic hypothesis. *Health Psychology, 11,* 139–150.

Snyder, M., & White, P. (1982). Moods and memories: Elation, depression and the remembering of the events of one's life. *Journal of Personality, 50,* 149–167.

Solomon, R. C. (1976). *The passions: The myth and nature of human emotions.* Notre Dame, IN: University of Notre Dame Press.

Solomon, R. C. (1993). The philosophy of emotions. In M. Lewis, & J. M. Haviland (Eds.), *Handbook of emotions* (pp. 3–15). New York: Guilford Press.

Solomon, R. C. (1995). *A passion for justice: Emotions and the origins of the social contract.* Lanham, MD: Rowman & Littlefeld.

Soussignan, R. (2002). Duchenne smile, emotional experience, and autonomic reactivity: A test of the facial feedback hypothesis. *Emotion, 2,* 52–74.

Spackman, M. P., & Parrott, W. G. (2001). Emotionality in prose: A study of descriptions of emotions from three literary periods. *Cognition and Emotion, 15,* 553–575.

Spears, R., & Leach, C. W. (2004). Intergroup Schadenfreude: Conditions and consequences. In L. Z Tiedens, & C. W. Leach (Eds.), *The social life of emotions* (pp. 336–355). Cambridge: Cambridge University Press.

Sperber, D. (1996). *Explaining culture: A naturalistic approach.* Cambridge, MA: Blackwell.

Spignesi, A. W., & Shor, R. (1981). The judgment of emotion from facial expressions, context, and their combination. *Journal of General Psychology, 104*, 41–58.

Staats, A. W., & Staats, C. K. (1958). Attitudes established by classical conditioning. *Journal of Abnormal and Social Psychology, 57*, 37–40.

Stangor, C., Sullivan, L. A., & Ford, T. E. (1991). Affective and cognitive determinants of prejudice. *Social Cognition, 9*, 359–380.

Stapel, D. A., & Koomen, W. (2000). How far do we go beyond the information given? The impact of knowledge activation on interpretation and inference. *Journal of Personality and Social Psychology, 78*, 19–37.

Stapel, D. A., Koomen, W., & Ruys K. I. (2002). The effects of diffuse and distinct affect? *Journal of Personality and Social Psychology, 83*, 60–74.

Stapley, J., & Haviland, J. M. (1989). Beyond depression: Gender differences in normal adolescents' emotional experience. *Sex Roles, 20*, 295–309.

Stemmler, G. (1997). Selective activation of traits: Boundary conditions for the activation of anger. *Personality and Individual Differences, 22*, 213–233.

Stemmler, G., Heldmann, M., Pauls, C., & Scherer, T. (2001). Constraints for emotion specificity in fear and anger: The context counts. *Psychophysiology, 38*, 275–291.

Stephan, W. G., Boniecki, K. A., Ybarra, O., Bettencourt, A., Ervin, K. S., Jackson, L. A. et al. (2002). The role of threat in the racial attitudes of blacks and whites. *Personality and Social Psychology Bulletin, 28*, 1242–1254.

Stephan, W. G., & Stephan, C. (1985). Intergroup anxiety. *Journal of Social Issues, 41*, 157–176.

Stephan, W. G., Stephan, C. W., & Gudykunst, W. B. (1999). Anxiety in intergroup relations: A comparison of anxiety/uncertainty management theory and integrated threat theory. *International Journal of Intercultural Relations, 23*, 613–628.

Stepper, S., & Strack, F. (1993). Proprioceptive determinants of emotional and nonemotional feelings. *Journal of Personality and Social Psychology, 64*, 211–220.

Stern, D. N. (1985). *Interpersonal world of the infant*. New York: Basic Books.

Stoppard, J., & Gunn Grunchy, C. (1993). Gender, context, and expression of positive emotions. *Personality and Social Psychology Bulletin, 19*, 143–150.

Strack, F., Martin, L., & Stepper, S. (1988). Inhibiting and facilitating conditions of the human smile: A nonobtrusive test of the facial feedback hypothesis. *Journal of Personality and Social Psychology, 54*, 768–777.

Strack, F., Schwarz, N., & Geschneidinger, E. (1985). Happiness and reminiscing: The role of time perspective, mood and mode of thinking. *Journal of Personality and Social Psychology, 49*, 1460–1469.

Stroebe, W., Insko, C. A., Thompson, V. D., & Layton, B. D. (1971). Effects of physical attractiveness, attitude similarity, and sex on various aspects of interpersonal attractive. *Journal of Personality and Social Psychology, 18*, 79–91.

Stroessner, S. J., Hamilton, D. L., & Mackie, D. M. (1992). Affect and stereotyping: The effect of induced mood on distinctiveness-based illusory correlations. *Journal of Personality and Social Psychology, 62*, 564–576.

Stroessner, S. J., & Mackie, D. M. (1992). The impact of induced affect on the perception of variability in social group. *Personality and Social Psychology Bulletin, 18*, 546–554.

Strongman, K. T. (1996). *The psychology of emotion: Theories of emotion in perspective*. Chichester: John Wiley & Sons.

Sullins, E. (1991). Emotional contagion revisited: Effects of social comparison and expressive style on mood convergence. *Personality and Social Psychology Bulletin, 17*, 166–174.

Symons, D. (1979). *The evolution of human sexuality*. New York: Oxford University Press.

Tajfel, H. (1982). Social identity and intergroup relations. Cambridge: Cambridge University Press.

Tangney, J. P. (1990). Assessing individual differences in proneness to shame and guilt: Development of the self-conscious affect and attribution inventory. *Journal of Personality and Social Psychology*, 59, 102–111.

Tangney, J. P. (1991). Moral affect: The good, the bad, and the ugly. *Journal of Personality and Social Psychology*, *61*, 598–607.

Tangney, J. P. (1992). Situational determinants of shame and guilt in young adulthood. *Personality and Social Psychology Bulletin*, *18*, 199–206.

Tangney, J. P. (1994). The mixed legacy of the super-ego: Adaptive and maladaptive aspects of shame and guilt. In J. M. Masling, & R. F. Bornstein (Eds.), *Empirical perspectives on object relations theory* (pp. 1–28). Washington, DC: American Psychological Association.

Tangney, J. P. (1995). Recent advances in the empirical study of shame and guilt. *American Behavioral Scientist*, *38*, 1132–1145.

Tangney, J. P. (1999). The self-conscious emotions: Shame, guilt, embarrassment and pride. In T. Dalgleish, & M. Power (Eds.), *Handbook of cognition and emotion* (pp. 541–567). New York: John Wiley & Sons.

Tangney, J. P. (2002a). Humility. In C. R. Snyder, & S. J. Lopez (Eds), *The handbook of positive psychology* (pp. 411–419). Oxford: Oxford University Press.

Tangney, J. P. (2002b). Self-conscious emotions: The self as a moral guide. In A. Tesser, D. A. Stapel, & J. V. Wood (Eds.), *Self and motivation: Emerging psychological perspectives* (pp. 97–117). Washington, DC: American Psychological Association.

Tangney, J. P., & Dearing, R. L. (2002). *Shame and guilt*. New York: Guilford Press.

Tangney, J. P., & Fischer, K. W. (Eds.). (1995). *Self-conscious emotions*. New York: Guilford Press.

Tangney, J. P., Marschall, D. E., Rosenberg, K., Barlow, D. H., & Wagner, P. E. (1994). *Children and adults' autobiographical accounts of shame, guilt and pride experiences: An analysis of situational determinants and interpersonal concerns*. Manuscript submitted for publication.

Tangney, J. P., Miller, R. S., Flicker, L., & Barlow, D. H. (1996). Are shame, guilt, and embarrassment distinct emotions? *Journal of Personality and Social Psychology*, *70*, 1256–1269.

Taylor, G. (1985). *Pride, shame, and guilt: Emotions of self-assessment*. Oxford: Clarendon Press.

Taylor, G. (1988). Envy and jealousy: Emotions and vices. *Midwest Studies of Philosophy*, *13*, 233–249.

Teasdale, J. D. (1983). Negative thinking in depression: Cause, effect or reciprocal thinking? *Advances in Behavioral Research and Therapy*, *5*, 3–25.

Teasdale, J. D., & Fogarty, S. J. (1979). Differential effects of induced mood on retrieval of pleasant and unpleasant events from episodic memory. *Journal of Abnormal Psychology*, *88*, 248–257.

Teasdale, J. D., Taylor, R., & Fogarty, S. J. (1980). Effects of induced elation–depression on the accessibility of memories of happy and unhappy experiences. *Behavior Research and Therapy*, *18*, 339–346.

Tesser, A. (1988). Toward a self-evaluation maintenance model of social behavior. In L. Berkowitz, *Advances in experimental social psychology* (pp. 181–227). San Diego, CA: Academic Press.

Tesser, A., & Campbell, J. (1982). Self-evaluation maintenance and the perception of friends and strangers. *Journal of Personality*, *50*, 261–279.

Tesser, A., Campbell, J. D., & Smith, M. (1984). Friendship choice and performance: Self-evaluation maintenance in children. *Journal of Personality and Social Psychology*, *46*, 561–574.

Tesser, A., & Smith, J. (1980). Some effects of task relevance and friendship on helping: You don't always help the one you like. *Journal of Experimental Social Psychology*, *44*, 482–590.

Thayer, J., & Jonsen, B. (2000). Sex differences in judgment of facial affect: A multivariate analysis of recognition errors. *Scandinavian Journal of Psychology, 41*, 243–246.

Thayer, R., Newman, R., & McClain, T. (1994). Self-regulation of mood: Strategies for changing bad mood, raising energy, and reducing tension. *Journal of Personality and Social Psychology, 67*, 910–925.

Thayer, S. (1980a). The effect of facial expression sequence upon judgments of emotion. *Journal of Social Psychology, 111*, 305–306.

Thayer, S. (1980b). The effect of expression sequence and expressor identity on judgments of the intensity of facial expression. *Journal of Nonverbal Behavior, 5*(2), 71–79.

Thibaut, J. W., & Kelley, H. H. (1959). *The social psychology of groups*. New York: John Wiley & Sons.

Thoits, P. (1984). Coping, social support, and psychological outcomes. In P. Shaver (Ed.), *Review of personality and social psychology* (Vol. 5, pp. 219–238). Beverley Hills, CA: Sage.

Thompson, J. (1941). Development of facial expression of emotion in blind and seeing children. *Archives of Psychology, 37*, 1–47.

Timmers, M., Fischer, A. H., & Manstead, A. S. R. (1998). Gender differences in motives for regulating emotions. *Personality and Social Psychology Bulletin, 24*, 974–985.

Timmers, M., Fischer, A. H., & Manstead, A. S. R. (2003). Ability versus vulnerability: Beliefs about men and women's emotional behavior. *Cognition and Emotion, 17*, 41–63.

Tomaka, J., Blascovich, J., Kibler, J., & Ernst, J. (1997). Cognitive and physiological antecedents of threat and challenge appraisal. *Journal of Personality and Social Psychology, 73*, 63–72.

Tomkins, S. S. (1962). *Affect, imagery, and consciousness: Vol. 1: The positive effects*. New York: Springer-Verlag.

Tomkins, S. S. (1963). *Affect, imagery, and consciousness: Vol. 2: The negative effects*. New York: Springer-Verlag.

Tooby, J., & Cosmides, L. (1990). The past explains the present. Emotional adaptations and the structure of ancestral environments. *Ethology and Sociobiology, 11*, 375–424.

Totterdell, P. (2000). Catching moods and hitting runs: Mood linkage and subjective performance in professional sport team. *Journal of Applied Psychology, 85*, 848–859.

Totterdell, P., Kellett, S., Teuchmann, K., & Briner, R. B. (1998). Evidence of mood linkage in work groups. *Journal of Personality and Social Psychology, 74*, 1504–1515.

Tracy, J. L., & Robins, R. W. (2004a). Putting the self into self-conscious emotions: A theoretical model. *Psychological Inquiry, 15*, 103–125.

Tracy, J. L., & Robins, R. W. (2004b). Show your pride: Evidence for a discrete emotion expression. *Psychological Science, 15*, 194–197.

Triandis, H. C. (1972). *The analysis of subjective culture*. New York: John Wiley & Sons.

Triandis, H. C. (1994). *Culture and social behavior*. New York: McGraw-Hill.

Triandis, H. C. (1995). *Individualism and collectivism*. Boulder, CO: Westview Press.

Triandis, H. C., Botempo, R., Villareal, M. J., Asai, M., & Lucca, N. (1988). Individualism and collectivism: Cross-cultural perspectives in self-ingroup relationships. *Journal of Personality and Social Psychology, 52*(2), 323–338.

Trivers, R. L. (1971). The evolution of reciprocal altruism. *Quarterly Review of Biology, 46*, 35–57.

Tropp, L. R., & Pettigrew, T. F. (2004). Intergroup contact and the central role of affect in intergroup prejudice. In L. Z Tiedens, & C. W. Leach (Eds.), *The social life of emotions* (pp. 247–269). Cambridge: Cambridge University Press.

Tsai, J. L., & Chentsova-Dutton, Y. (2003). Variation among European Americans in emotional facial expression. *Journal of Cross-Cultural Psychology, 34*, 650–657.

Tsai, J. L., & Levenson, R. W. (1997). Cultural influences on emotional responding: Chinese American and European American dating couples during the interpersonal conflict. *Journal of Cross-Cultural Psychology, 28*, 600–625.

Tsai, J. L., Levenson, R. W., & Carstensen, L. L. (2000). Autonomic, subjective, and expressive responses to emotional films in older and younger Chinese Americans and European Americans. *Psychology and Aging, 15*(4), 684–693.

Turner, J. C., Hogg, M. A., Oakes, P. J., Reicher, S. D., & Wetherell, M. (1987). *Rediscovering the social group: A self-categorization theory.* Oxford: Blackwell.

Van Bezooijen, R. (1984). *The characteristics and recognizability of vocal expression of emotions.* Dordrecht, The Netherlands: Foris.

Van Bezooijen, R., Otto, S. A., & Heenan, T. A. (1983). Recognition of vocal expressions of emotion: A three-nation study to identify universal characteristics. *Journal of Cross-Cultural Psychology, 14*, 387–406.

Van Zomeren, M., Spears, R., Fisher, A. H., & Leach, C. W. (2004). Put your money where your mouth is! Explaining collective action tendencies through group-based anger and group efficacy. *Journal of Personality and Social Psychology, 87*, 649–664.

Vanman, E. J., Paul, B. Y., Ito, T. A., & Miller, N. M. (1997). The modern face of prejudice and structural features that moderate the effects of cooperation on affect. *Journal of Personality and Social Psychology, 73*, 941–959.

Vaughan, K. B., & Lanzetta, J. T. (1981). The effect of modification of expressive displays on vicarious emotional arousal. *Journal of Experimental Social Psychology, 17*, 16–30.

Verbeke, W., Belschak, F., & Bagozzi R. P. (2004). The adaptive consequences of pride in personal selling. *Journal of the Academy of Marketing Science, 32*, 386–402.

Vingerhoets, A., & Becht, M. (1996). *The ISAR study: Some preliminary findings.* Paper presented at the International Study on Adult Crying Symposium, Tilburg, The Netherlands: Tilburg Press.

Vingerhoets, A., & Scheirs, J. (2000). Sex differences in crying: Empirical findings and possible explanations. In A. Fischer (Ed.), *Gender and emotion: Social psychological perspectives* (pp. 143–165). London: Cambridge University Press.

Wagner, H. (1993). On measuring performance in category judgment studies of nonverbal behavior. *Journal of Nonverbal Behavior, 17*, 3–28.

Wagner, H. (1997). Methods of the study of facial behavior. In J. Russell, & J. Fernandez-Dols (Eds.), *The psychology of facial expression* (pp. 31–54). Cambridge: Cambridge University Press.

Wagner, H., Buck, R., & Winterbotham, M. (1993). Communication of specific emotions: Gender differences in sending accuracy and communication measures. *Journal of Nonverbal Behavior, 17*, 29–52.

Wagner, H., & Smith, J. (1991). Social influence and expressiveness. *Journal of Nonverbal Behavior, 15*, 201–214.

Wallbott, H. (1988a). Faces in context: The relative importance of facial expression and context information in determining emotion attributions. In K. Scherer (Ed.), *Facets of emotion* (pp. 139–160). Hillsdale, NJ: Lawrence Erlbaum Associates, Inc.

Wallbott, H. (1988b). In and out of context: Influences of facial expression and context information on emotion attributions. *British Journal of Social Psychology, 27*, 357–396.

Wallbott, H. (1991). Recognition of emotion from facial expression via imitation? Some indirect evidence for an old theory. *British Journal of Social Psychology, 30*, 207–219.

Wallbott, H., & Scherer, K. R. (1988). How universal and specific is emotional experience? Evidence from 27 countries on five continents. In K. R. Scherer (Ed.), *Facets of emotions* (pp. 31–56). Hillsdale, NJ: Lawrence Erlbaum Associates, Inc.

Wallbott, H. G., & Scherer, K. R. (1995). Cultural determinants in experiencing shame and guilt. In J. P. Tangney, & K. W. Fischer (Eds.), *Self-conscious emotions: The psychology of shame, guilt, embarrassment, and pride* (pp. 465–487). New York: Guilford Press.

Watson, D., Clark, L. A., & Tellegen, A. (1988). Development and validation of brief measures of positive and negative affect: The PANAS scales. *Journal of Personality and Social Psychology, 54*, 1063–1070.

Watson, D., & Tellegen, A. (1985). Toward a consensual structure of mood. *Psychological Bulletin, 98*, 219–235.

Watson, D., Wiese, D., Vaidya, J., & Tellegen, A. (1999). The two general activation systems of affect: Structural findings, evolutionary considerations, and psychobiological evidence. *Journal of Personality and Social Psychology, 76*, 820–838.

Watson, S. G. (1972). Judgment of emotion from facial and contextual cue combinations. *Journal of Personality and Social Psychology, 24*, 334–342.

Wegener, D. T., & Petty, R. E. (1994). Mood-management across affective states: The hedonic contingency hypothesis. *Journal of Personality and Social Psychology, 66*, 1034–1048.

Wegener, D. T., & Petty, R. E. (1995). Flexible correction processes in social judgment: The role of naïve theories in correction for perceived bias. *Journal of Personality and Social Psychology, 68*, 36–51.

Wegener, D. T., Petty, R. E., & Smith, S. M. (1995). Positive mood can increase or decrease message scrutiny: The hedonic contingency view of mood and message processing. *Journal of Personality and Social Psychology, 69*, 5–15.

Wegner, D. M. (1989) *White bears and other unwanted thoughts: Suppression, obsessions, and the psychology of mental control*. New York: Penguin Books.

Wegner, D. M. (1994). Ironic processes of mental control. *Psychological Review, 101*, 34–52.

Wegner, D. M., Erber, R., & Zanakos, S. (1993). Ironic processes in the mental control of mood and mood-related thoughts. *Journal of Personality and Social Psychology, 65*, 1093–1104.

Wegner, D. M., & Gold, D. (1995). Fanning old flames: Emotional and cognitive effects of suppressing thoughts of a past relationship. *Journal of Personality and Social Psychology, 68*, 782–792.

Wegner, D. M., Lane, J., & Dimitri, S. (1994). The allure of secret relationships. *Journal of Personality and Social Psychology, 66*, 287–300.

Wegner, D. M., Schneider, D., Carter, S. III, & White, T. (1987). Paradoxical effects of thought suppression. *Journal of Personality and Social Psychology, 53*, 5–13.

Wegner, D. M., Schneider, D., Knutson, B., & McMahon, S. (1991). Polluting the stream of consciousness: The influence of thought suppression on the mind's environment. *Cognitive Therapy and Research, 15*, 141–152.

Wegner, D. M., Shortt, J., Blake, A., & Page, M. (1990). The suppression of exciting thoughts. *Journal of Personality and Social Psychology, 58*, 409–418.

Weinberger, D. A., Schwartz, G. E., & Davidson, R. J. (1979). Low-anxious, high-anxious, and repressive coping styles: Psychometric patterns and behavioral and physiological responses to stress. *Journal of Abnormal Psychology, 88*, 369–380.

Weiner, B. (1985). An attributional theory of achievement motivation and emotion. *Psychological Review, 92*, 548–573.

Wells, G. L., & Gavanski, I. (1989). Mental simulation of causality. *Journal of Personality and Social Psychology, 56*, 161–169.

Wenzlaff, R., & Wegner, D. (2000). Thought suppression. *Annual Review of Psychology, 51*, 59–91.

Wenzlaff, R., Wegner, D., & Klein, S. (1991). The role of thought suppression in the bonding of thought and mood. *Journal of Personality and Social Psychology, 60,* 500–508.

Wetzler, S. (1985). Mood-state-dependent retrieval: A failure to replicate. *Psychological Reports, 56,* 759–765.

Whitehead , W. E., & Drescher, V. M. (1980). Perception of gastric concentrations and self-control of gastric motility. *Psychophysiology, 17,* 552–558.

Wicker, F. W., Payne, G. C., & Morgan, R. D. (1983). Participant descriptions of guilt and shame. *Motivation and Emotion, 7,* 25–39.

Wierzbicka, A. (1986). Human emotions: Universal or culture-specific? *American Anthropologist, 88,* 584–594.

Wierzbicka, A. (1992). Talking about emotions: Semantics, culture, and cognition. *Cognition and Emotion, 6,* 285–319.

Wilder, D. A., & Shapiro, P. (1989a). Effects of anxiety on impression formation in a group context: An anxiety-assimilation hypothesis. *Journal of Experimental Social Psychology, 25,* 481–499.

Wilder, D. A., & Shapiro, P. N. (1989b). Role of competition-induced anxiety in limiting the beneficial impact of positive behavior by an out-group member. *Journal of Personality and Social Psychology, 56,* 60–69.

Winkielman, P., Zajonc, R. B., & Schwarz, N. (1997). Subliminal affective priming resists attributional intervention. *Cognition and Emotion, 11,* 433–465.

Winton, W. (1986). The role of facial response in self-reports of emotion, A critique of Laird. *Journal of Personality and Social Psychology, 50,* 808–812.

Worchel, S. (1986). The role of cooperation in reducing intergroup conflict. In S. Worchel, & W. G. Austin (Eds.), *Psychology of intergroup relations* (pp. 288–304). Chicago, IL: Nelson-Hall.

Worth, L. T., & Mackie, D. M. (1987). Cognitive mediation of positive affect in persuasion. *Social Cognition, 5,* 76–94.

Wright, J., & Mischel, W. (1982). Influence of affect on cognitive social learning person variables. *Journal of Personality and Social Psychology, 43,* 901–914.

Wrightsman, L. S. (1960). Effects of waiting with others on changes in level of felt anxiety. *Journal of Abnormal and Social Psychology, 61,* 216–222.

Wyer, R. S., & Carlston, D. (1979). *Social cognition, inference, and attribution.* Hillsdale, NJ: Lawrence Erlbaum Associates, Inc.

Wyer, R. S., Clore, G. L., & Isbell, L. (1999). Affect and information processing. In M. P. Zanna (Ed.), *Advances in experimental social psychology* (Vol. 31, pp. 3–78). New York: Academic Press.

Young, A. W., Rowland, D., Calder, A. J., Etcoff, N., Seth, A., & Perrett, D. I. (1997). Facial expression megamix: Tests of dimensional and category accounts of emotion recognition. *Cognition, 63,* 271–313.

Yzerbyt, V., Dumont, M., Gordijn, E., & Wigboldus, D. (2002). Intergroup emotions and self-categorization: The impact of perspective-taking on reactions to victims of harmful behavior. In D. M. Mackie, & E. R. Smith (Eds.), *From prejudice to intergroup emotions: Differentiated reactions to social groups* (pp. 67–88). New York: Psychology Press.

Yzerbyt, V., Dumont, M., Wigboldus, D., & Gordijn, E. (2003). I feel for us: The impact of categorization and identification on emotions and action tendencies. *British Journal of Social Psychology, 42,* 533–549.

Zajonc, R. B. (1985). Emotion and facial efference: A theory reclaimed. *Science, 228,* 15–21.

Zajonc, R. B., Adelmann, P. K., Murphy, S. T., & Niedenthal, P. M. (1987). Convergence in the physical appearance of spouses. *Motivation and Emotion, 11,* 335–346.

Zajonc, R. B., & McIntosh, D. N. (1997). Emotion research: Some promising questions, some questionable promises. *Psychological Science, 3,* 70–74.

Zajonc, R. B., & Markus, H. (1984). Affect and cognition: The hard interface. In C. Izard, J. Kagan, & R. B. Zajonc (Eds.), *Emotions, cognition and behavior* (pp. 73–102). Cambridge: Cambridge University Press.

Zajonc, R. B., Murphy, S. T., & Inglehart, M. (1989). Feeling and facial efference: Implications of the vascular theory of emotion. *Psychological Review, 96*, 395–416.

Zammuner, V. L. (1996). Felt emotions, and verbally communicated emotions: The case of pride. *European Journal of Social Psychology, 26*, 233–245.

Zammuner, V. L. (1998). Concepts of emotion: "Emotionness" and dimensional ratings of Italian motion words. *Cognition and Emotion, 12*, 243–272.

Zammuner, V. L. (2000). Men and women's lay theory of emotion. In A. Fischer (Ed.), *Gender and emotion: Social psychological perspectives* (pp. 48–70). London: Cambridge University Press.

Zammuner, V. L., & Fischer, A. H. (1995). The social regulation of emotions in jealousy situations. *Journal of Cross-Cultural Psychology, 26*, 189–208.

Zanna, M. P., & Rempel, J. K. (1988). Attitudes: A new look at an old concept. In D. Bar-Tal, & A. W. Kruglanski (Eds.), *The social psychology of knowledge* (pp. 315–334). Cambridge: Cambridge University Press.

Zech, E. (1999). Is it really helpful to verbalize one's emotions? *Gedrag & Gezondheid, 27*, 42–47.

Zech, E., & Rimé, B. (1996). *Does talking about an emotional experience affect emotional recovery?* Poster presented at the conference on the (Non)Expression of Emotion in Health and Disease, Tilburg, The Netherlands: Tilburg Press.

Zevon, M. A., & Tellegen, A. (1982). The structure of mood change: An idiographic/nomothetic analysis. *Journal of Personality and Social Psychology, 43*, 111–122.

Zuckerman, B., & Lubin, B. (1985). *Manual of multiple affect adjective check list revised*. San Diego, CA: EDITS.

Zuckerman, M., Klorman, R., Larrance, D., & Spiegel, N. (1981). Facial, autonomic, and subjective components of emotion: The facial feedback hypothesis versus the externalizer–internalizer distinction. *Journal of Personality and Social Psychology, 41*, 929–944.

Author Index

Subject Index